LOUIS IX
AND THE CHALLENGE
OF THE CRUSADE

LOUIS IX
AND THE CHALLENGE
OF THE CRUSADE

A Study in Rulership

WILLIAM CHESTER JORDAN

PRINCETON UNIVERSITY PRESS
PRINCETON, N. J.

Copyright © 1979 by Princeton University Press

Published by Princeton University Press, Princeton, New Jersey
In the United Kingdom: Princeton University Press, Guildford, Surrey

Library of Congress Cataloging in Publication Data will be
found on the last printed page of this book

Publication of this book has been aided by a grant from
The Andrew W. Mellon Foundation

This book has been composed in VIP Baskerville

Clothbound editions of Princeton University Press books
are printed on acid-free paper, and binding materials are
chosen for strength and durability

Printed in the United States of America by Princeton
University Press, Princeton, New Jersey

TO THE MEMORY OF
My Grandmother

CONTENTS

LIST OF TABLES AND FIGURE

TABLES

FIGURE

LIST OF MAPS

LIST OF ILLUSTRATIONS

PREFACE

For serious students of French social and administrative history the reign of Louis IX remains *"le plus malconnu"* of all the major kings of medieval France.[1] Partly, this problem is one of sources—not too few, but too many. There are so many excellent sources concerning Louis IX's reign and such a great number of them are unpublished that it will probably be a very long time before a comprehensive inventory of even the king's own acts can be prepared. The heroic individual efforts over the past several generations (one thinks immediately of Delisle, Delaborde, Strayer, and Carolus-Barré) to publish as many useful records as possible have paid off in literally hundreds, perhaps thousands, of specialized studies of aspects of the saint-king's reign. But, unfortunately, the results of this research have not been fully integrated into contemporary discussions of French medieval history.

The problem is that the best scholarly treatment of the king's rule remains the massive six-volume study by the seventeenth century monastic savant, Le Nain de Tillemont. It has been justly praised, among other reasons, for its accumulation of data in a recent article by Neveu. Nonetheless, it has fundamental weaknesses, at least from a modern point of view: its style is not suited to contemporary sensibilities; it has no fundamental theme other than an absorbing interest in the details of the king's life; it has a profoundly clerical tone which leaves one dubious about its objectivity; and it, of course, predates the explosion of scholarly literature of the last century.

The largest of modern biographies is Wallon's two-volume, *Saint Louis et son temps*, which went through several editions in the last quarter of the nineteenth century. While admirable in its own right and bearing the stamp of most of what was best in nineteenth century French historiography, it too was written before the major part of the serious collection and publication of sources was completed. To cite but one example, Wallon did not have access to Delisle's monumental survey of Louis's provincial administration in volume twenty-four of the *Recueil des historiens* (1904).

Since 1900 many biographies of the king have been published. They fall largely into two classes. There are those which are scholarly, but which tend to be very short, more like interpretative essays than sustained analyses of Louis's reign. Many of these have been carefully done and their authors have added important and suggestive conclu-

[1] As Professor Georges Duby remarked in comments before the Shelby Cullom Davis Center Seminar, Princeton University, 2 May 1975.

sions to the body of Saint Louis scholarship, but no one in this century has undertaken to write a synthetic treatment of the reign based on the range of existing scholarship. The other large class of studies has been popular biographies. Although, of course, they vary widely in intrinsic value, at their best, like Labarge's recent work, they blend an easy and compelling style with some of the salient results of recent research.

Where is Saint Louis scholarship now? A staggering number of studies have mined the published documents, and many of the records which still remain in manuscript have also been the subject of careful analyses. On the basis of these and similar studies (many comparative in scope), it should be possible to write a satisfying synthetic history of Louis's reign. Indeed, this book has been undertaken with that possibility in mind. Its scope, however, has been limited by my decision to concentrate only on those aspects of the reign that owe their fundamental form and content to the king's personal attention: for this is a study of a man and his efforts to rule well, not of the political and social history of his reign in general.

Even limited in the way I have described, the task has been formidable. The relative unevenness of specialized studies of the saint-king's impact in the south has necessitated a great deal of archival research in that region. The contradictions among various scholarly authorities have often led me to reappraise existing documentation. Some discussion of the difficult and elusive subject of the king's psychology has also seemed valuable, although no attempt has been made to write a complete psycho-biography. Finally, daily—or so it seems—new manuscripts are edited and new articles appear which bear on the general theme of Louis's rulership. Undoubtedly, therefore, this study is tentative: a time will certainly come when, by one of those great collective efforts the French are famous for, the surviving acts of the king will be known and critically edited; problems which now seem unsolvable will melt away under close scholarly scrutiny; and someone will be able to write as comprehensive a study of Louis's role in government as medievalists have a right to expect. But until that time comes, I hope this interim portrait of the king can meet our most pressing needs.

I have imposed one further fundamental limitation on my work. Above all, this study is *thematic*. It draws its organizing principle from the central concern of Louis's life, the crusade. It was the crusade—appearing as a distant possibility—that helped Louis take the decisive steps on the road to personal rule of his kingdom. It was to assure the success of the crusade of 1248-1254 that he dealt imaginatively and firmly with the problems that vexed the administration of his kingdom. And finally, it was the failure of the crusade that produced a profound crisis in his life, one whose outcome, the creation of the "ideal" medieval monarchy, was to leave a lasting impression in French government and politics. My close attention to the theme of the crusade should explain the particular aspects of Louis's rulership I have chosen to stress in this book.

Consequently, the study has fallen quite naturally into three parts. The first (chapters one through four) is a detailed account of Louis's preparations for the crusade. The second part (chapter five) examines the period of the crusade itself—the regency at home and the effect of the failure of the crusade on the personal development of the saint-king. The remaining chapters explore the continuing influence of the Holy War, both as a memory and as a new goal culminating in the crusade of 1270.

Several technical matters merit a few words. (1) With regard to currency I have used pounds and l. (the abbreviation for *livres*) interchangeably. I have always had French royal pounds (either *livres tournois* or *livres parisis*) in mind, not English sterling which was worth about four times more in the thirteenth century. The internal rate of exchange between *livres tournois* and *livres parisis* was five to four. Unfortunately, from time to time prices or wages have had to be quoted in local French currencies for which our knowledge of the exchange rates is less certain. (2) With regard to nomenclature, established conventions have been followed: a few famous names appear in English; the majority, however, are given in French or Latin depending on traditional scholarly preference. (3) Editorially I have usually preferred the Hague translation of Joinville to the Penguin version (edited by Shaw) not because it is better overall but because it preserves the short chapter notation of Natalis de Wailly's critical text which, unfortunately, Shaw's does not and because it is a more literal rendering of the original. (4) In general the notes refer first to primary materials, when appropriate, and then to secondary sources in which there are discussions of the issue addressed in the text. Some attempt has also been made to direct the reader to discussions of comparative interest. (5) The map at the beginning of the book should serve for all major references in the text and appendixes; a few specialized maps have been placed directly in the text.

The author and publishers are grateful to the following institutions for permission to reproduce copyright material: the Trustees of the Pierpont Morgan Library for illustration two, MS 240, fol. 4, Moralized Bible, ca. 1250; the Trustees of the British Library for illustration three, MS Cotton Titus A XVII, fol. 43 verso, sixteenth century; the Abbey of Saint-Maurice d'Agaune, Valais, Switzerland, for illustrations four and five, reliquaries from the *trésor*; the Cabinet des Médailles of the Bibliothèque Nationale for illustration six, the *écu d'or* of Louis IX; and the Department of Manuscripts of the Bibliothèque Nationale for the document published in Appendix Four, Languedoc-Doat volume 151 fols. 237-241 verso.

The maps for this book were drawn by Trudy Glucksberg.

I would like to take this opportunity to thank those people who at one time or another have stimulated me to think about the problems discussed in this book. Chief among them are the students I have taught and the colleagues I have worked with at Princeton University, especially my own teachers, Professors Gaines Post and Joseph Strayer. A substantial debt of gratitude is owed also to Professors Charles Wood and John Baldwin, whose vigorous criticisms helped light my way. Mention should also be made of the special libraries and archives which opened their facilities to me, and of the Ford Foundation, the Department of History of Princeton, and the University Committee on Research of Princeton which, at different times, helped support the research which went into this book. The list would not be complete, however, without the name of Miriam Brokaw of Princeton University Press, who gave me needed help and encouragement at every stage in the preparation of the manuscript for publication. There is no doubt in my mind that whatever is good in this study derives much more from the assistance I received from these scholars, students, and friends than from my own efforts. I can claim only the errors as uniquely my own.

ABBREVIATIONS AND SHORT TITLES

AC: Archives communales

AD: Archives départementales

AM: Archives municipales

ASHGâtinais: *Annales de la Société historique du Gâtinais*

BEC: *Bibliothèque de l'École des Chartes*

BN: Bibliothèque nationale

CUP: Denifle, *Chartularium universitatis parisiensis*

Exceptiones: *Exceptiones carcassonensium queremoniis objectae 1258, HF,* XXIV, 541-614

GC: *Gallia christiana*

HF: Bouquet, *Recueil des historiens des Gaules et de la France*

HGL: Vaissète, *Histoire générale du Languedoc*

Inq. in rem.: *Inquisitio in remensi et laudunensi dioecesibus 1248, HF,* XXIV, 269-96

MHP: *Mémoires de la Société de l'histoire de Paris et de l'île de France*

MP: Matthew Paris

PL: Migne, *Patrilogiae*

QBit: *Queremoniae biterrensium 1247, HF,* XXIV, 319-84

QCar: *Queremoniae carcassonensium 1247, HF,* XXIV, 296-319

QCen: *Queremoniae cenomannorum et andegavorum 1247, HF,* XXIV, 73-93

Q . . . exceptae: *Queremoniae in ambianensi, silvanectensi et viromandensi balliviis exceptae 1247/8, HF,* XXIV, 731-44

QNor: *Queremoniae normannorum 1247, HF,* XXIV, 1-72

QTur: *Queremoniae turonum, santonum, et pictavorum 1247, HF,* XXIV, 94-252

SA: *Société académique de*

Sententiae: *Sententiae a regiis nunciis in carcassonensi senescalia 1262, HF,* XXIV, 618-95

SL: Saint Louis (in article titles)

SL: *Saint Louis* (in book titles)

LOUIS IX
AND THE CHALLENGE
OF THE CRUSADE

MAP 1: Administrative Map of France under Louis IX. Most of the towns on the map were the seats of royal *bailliages* and *sénéchaussées* or of major dependent fiefs (including appanages) at some time during the reign of Louis IX. A few other frequently mentioned places are also included on the map.

• 1 •

SWEARING THE VOW

Louis IX first swore the crusader's vow at the *abbaye royale* of Maubisson in Pontoise in December 1244. Most chroniclers misrepresent the event by concentrating their attention on the happy juxtaposition of the *sacramentum* and the king's recovery from a grave illness. They give little hint that there might have been opposition to the vow or that the magic of this moment found less than a welcome response throughout the kingdom.[1] In fact, most Frenchmen—most of those whose opinion counted—probably disapproved of the decision. To the learned the vow was an aberration, a brief slipping into depression caused by the sickness. To others the idea of the crusade was discouraging in itself: there had been too many defeats and too many misguided efforts in the recent past. For some no doubt there was less uneasiness about the crusade than about the regency it would mean at home: social and political confusion was characteristic of regency governments.[2]

Louis's enthusiasm in the face of such opposition is not easy to explain. Of course, there is always something heroic in standing up to opposition, and this very likely played a part in his pertinacity in fulfilling the vow. But there was much more involved, for he was remarkably steady in his appeal for support; and gradually he found resonances in the desire of many of his people to relive the ancient heroisms. Under the force of his personality, recollection of the problems and failures of the past gave way to nostalgia and an intoxicating affirmation of traditional values.

Only sustained effort could have produced this change, and it was the personal commitment of the king that underlay that effort. His capacity to restore confidence in the idea of the crusade, however, was part of a broader "commitment" to the integrity of his own selfhood, for at the time of his vow in 1244 Louis IX was not yet an autonomous

---

[1] The early fourteenth century rhymed chronicle of Guillaume Guiart, to cite one example, makes it seem as if there was almost a mad rush to take the cross after Louis's vow; *HF*, XXII, 185. People closer to the immediate royal circle (such as Matthew Paris, the Minstrel of Reims, and Joinville), as we shall see, give a somewhat different impression.

[2] MP, v, 3-4; Minstrel of Reims, pp. 334-35 (cf. *HF*, XXII, 331-32). For general remarks on feelings about the crusade, see Labarge, *SL*, pp. 99-100, and Lecoy de La Marche, *France sous SL*, p. 149. Southern, *Making of the Middle Ages*, pp. 55-56, also has some cogent words on mid-thirteenth century cynicism about the crusades.

adult. He was thirty; he was married; he was a father; but he had not liberated himself—politically or personally—from the domination of his mother, Blanche of Castile.

In the peculiar conditions of the early thirteenth century, the Queen Dowager, a strong-willed and resolute woman, had become the focal point of central political authority in France.[3] Although she had not openly sought out this role, the untimely death of her husband, Louis VIII (1223-1226) and the youth of Louis IX, then only twelve, had thrust the regency and its powers upon her.[4] That Blanche regarded the regency as a trust and intended to carry out her husband's and the dynasty's traditional policies vigorously has never been questioned, either by her contemporaries many of whom she overcame in diplomacy and war or by historians who have evaluated her rule.[5]

But the first of the three regencies of Louis IX's long reign, successfully weathered though it was, raises some important and difficult questions. The foremost concerns the date of its termination, for although a picture of Blanche as a power-hungry despot bent on barring her son from his rightful kingship would be ridiculously overdrawn, the habit of power was apparently a comfortable life-style. Thus—or so it might seem—the chroniclers never mention Louis IX coming of age.[6] In the absence of explicit evidence historians have looked to circumstantial factors.

Many have regarded Louis's marriage to Margaret of Provence in 1234 and its neat coincidence with his twenty-first year as twin symbols of the end of the regency, but neither symbol is really persuasive. With the matter of age we seem to be encountering a modern juridical prejudice,[7] for there is little contemporary evidence that people believed royal minorities should end at twenty-one. When we do have evidence on the subject, the age is lower. Philip IV the Fair acceded without a regent at age seventeen in 1285, and a fourteenth century law on the subject laid down fourteen as the preferred age.[8]

[3] The best general evaluation of her character and her life remains Berger, *Blanche de Castille*. See also the brief remarks in Larcena, *SL*, p. 40; and Guth, *SL*, p. 42. Cf. Pernoud, *Chef d'état*, pp. 13-20, as well as her more recent biography, *Reine Blanche*.

[4] Pernoud, *Reine Blanche*, pp. 136-37.

[5] Berger, *Blanche de Castille*; the unanimity of opinions is striking: see also Labal, *Siècle de SL*, pp. 41-45; Larcena, *SL*, pp. 39-40; Wallon, *SL*, 1, 6-50; Boulenger, *Vie de SL*, pp. 9-28; Levron, *SL*, pp. 33-54; and Bailly, *SL*, pp. 19-33.

[6] Labarge, *SL*, p. 55; Berger, *Blanche de Castille*, pp. 244-45; Perry, *SL*, pp. 62-63; Guth, *SL*, p. 42.

[7] For the assertion that age twenty-one was the culmination of the regency, see Labal, *Siècle de SL*, p. 45; Boulenger, *Vie de SL*, pp. 28-29; Bailly, *SL*, p. 53; Wallon, *SL*, 1, 41, 50; Lévis Mirepoix, *SL*, p. 78. The assertion is correct only insofar as contracts with other seigneurs are concerned; cf. Arbois de Jubainville, *Histoire . . . de Champagne*, v, 250.

[8] On problems of the laws and customs governing royal majority, see Olivier-Martin,

The question of the marriage itself is more complicated. The marriage partner had been selected by Blanche for political reasons, but what commentators mean when they suggest that the marriage symbolized the end of the regency is that it should have been difficult for Louis to reconcile his new role as a husband to the tutelage of his mother.[9] There is some truth in this. Certainly, the opposition baronial party levied the charge up until about 1234 that Blanche was deliberately keeping Louis unwed,[10] from which it seems reasonable to conclude that contemporaries expected Louis's new role to free him to make his own policies.

But this expectation was not fulfilled. Policies did not change, and the barons were or should have been sadly disappointed in the king's deference to his mother even on the most intimate of subjects regarding his new married life. According to Jean de Joinville, the king's close friend and biographer, Blanche restricted her son's visits to his young wife (she was only fourteen at the time of marriage) and interfered in other ways.[11] Moreover, although the stories that Joinville tells about how they got around her interference (the secret visits, for example)[12] suggest that Margaret and Louis had a tender and happy marriage in the beginning,[13] it is evident from a wide variety of sources that a gradual stiffening developed in their personal relationship.[14] If anything, this temporarily strengthened the king's bond with and emotional dependence on his mother.

The platitude is that Margaret found it difficult to live with a saint, as any normal woman would.[15] This is true as far as it goes, but it does not go far enough. The fact is Louis soon discovered he could not trust Margaret. Edgar Boutaric, the author of the only substantial

---

Régences, pp. 77-81, 85-86 (he includes an analysis of the fourteenth century order of Charles V but doubts that it represented traditional practice).

[9] Lehmann, *Rôle de la femme*, pp. 341-42 (cf. 343); Levron, *SL*, p. 105.

[10] The baronial position is summarized by Painter, *Scourge of the Clergy*, p. 61.

[11] Joinville, chap. cxix. Cf. the rather refreshing pre-Freudian categorization of Blanche by Chaillou des Barres, "SL à Sens," p. 199: "une belle-mère tyrannique." Cf. Pernoud, *Reine Blanche*, p. 216. An anonymous chronicler (*HF*, xxi, 81) emphasizes the long period of time in the early part of their marriage during which Margaret had no children (the first was born in 1240). This too may have annoyed some contemporaries who perhaps expected early fatherhood to spur Louis on in overcoming his subservience to his mother.

[12] Joinville, chap. cxix.

[13] See also the general remark of the contemporary Senonais chronicler, Geoffroy de Courlon, who might be reflecting the prevailing views of the upper class soon after the marriage when he wrote: "Et rex se cum duxit uxorem dictam, filiam comitis Prouintie, Margaretam nomine, quam multum diligebat" (Julliot, *Chronique*, p. 524).

[14] On Margaret's personality, see Boutaric, "Marguerite de Provence," and Pernoud, *Reine Blanche*, pp. 345-47.

[15] Mauger, *SL*, pp. 125-26; Lévis Mirepoix, *SL*, p. 78; Guth, *SL*, pp. 41, 190-91; Bailly, *SL*, p. 58; Guillain de Bénouville, *SL*, pp. 73-74.

monograph on Louis's queen, has argued that the king and his mother found it necessary to limit Margaret's field of political action as early as 1241 and 1242. During this period, that of the last rebellion of the reign against the crown, she was compelled to swear to abide by royal policy whatever her own personal interests might be.[16] Nor was this bridling of his wife an isolated incident. Whether in important matters or the most trivial Louis consistently restricted her freedom of action, a situation Margaret bore with difficulty. She was not permitted to accept presents and loans of any importance, to appoint or give orders to the crown's officials, or to appoint her own without the prior consent of her husband and the royal curia. Her control over her children was also limited in mundane matters: without the consent of king and council, she was not allowed to accept presents on their behalf or to employ servants for them.[17]

Much more evidence could be furnished, especially from the later period of their life together, on the coldness of Louis's treatment of Margaret,[18] but Boutaric's argument strongly suggests that the roots of their tensions went back to Louis's long tutelage by Blanche. Substance is further given to this assertion by the fact that Margaret herself eventually tried to duplicate in her authority over her own son, the future Philip III, the type of ascendancy which Blanche had had over Louis. But when Louis discovered that his wife had persuaded the young Philip to take an oath to obey her, in the event of the king's death, until the age of thirty, he intervened and had the pope quash the oath. He then prohibited his son from encumbering himself again.[19]

[16] Boutaric, "Marguerite de Provence," p. 420.

[17] According to Joinville (chap. CXXIV), Margaret regarded the king as "*divers*" on the issue of her freedom of action. This is a hard word to translate. It has been rendered "difficult," "bizarre." The point is Margaret resented the king's restraints on her. See also Labarge, *SL*, p. 162.

[18] Joinville laments that Louis never talked of Margaret (or of his children) during the more than five years he spent as a crusader even though she was present in his entourage; Joinville, chap. CXVI; cf. chap. LXVII. Lehmann, *Rôle de la femme*, p. 349, while offering no alternative explanation, resists interpreting this as a sign of indifference. Even though most historians have no such qualms, indifference cannot be the explanation. Louis's close ties to his children suggest that he did not talk about his family on the crusade for other reasons. Margaret's antagonism toward his life style later in life is much more persuasive evidence of the coldness of their relationship. This antagonism as well as Louis's failure to talk about Margaret are discussed by Eydoux, *SL*, pp. 34-35; Labarge, *SL*, p. 57; and Guth, *SL*, p. 41. Judgments—in the main, favorable—on Louis's attitude toward his children are offered by Perry, *SL*, p. 281; and Wallon, *SL*, II, 468-70.

[19] For the events narrated here and their interpretation, see the "Notes" in the Hague translation of Joinville, p. 290; Olivier-Martin, *Régences*, pp. 95-96; Pernoud, *Reine Blanche*, pp. 352-53; and Lehmann, *Rôle de la femme*, p. 351. Most biographers have been struck by the echo of the king's own life in the incident (see Mauger, *SL*, pp. 126-27; Boulenger, *Vie de SL*, p. 79; Bailly, *SL*, p. 160; and Wallon, *SL*, II, 428).

If marriage was not the singular event that should be taken to symbolize Louis's passage from tutelage to full authority as a ruler, what should? This is not an easy question. It would be more appropriate, or so I shall argue, to regard the silence of the chroniclers on Louis's coming of age as evidence that a gradual and quite natural shift from the rulership of the aging Blanche to that of her youthful son occurred almost imperceptibly. Blanche may have clung to her powers as regent slightly longer and more tenaciously than another mother would have; this might account for the appearance which persisted that she dominated government. It could also account for the fact that the transmission of authority to her son was punctuated by many difficult moments of which the marriage, or more properly the presence in the household of Margaret, was one of the most important.

One senses this gradual translation of the focus of rulership to Louis in his assumption of his mother's former role as a military leader against hostile barons. He grew in stature as he progressively took over military authority. Some historians see the decisive moment in 1230; others in 1235.[20] Joinville implicitly seems to favor a later date, the early 1240s, when Louis led the victorious troops who crushed the last rebellions. Writers of fiction tend to follow Joinville's sketch.[21]

Of all the events which mark the phases in the gradual transmission of rulership to Louis, the one which created the most public tension between the king and his mother and played the most important symbolic role was his vow to go on crusade. The circumstances are well known. Soon after reducing the last vestiges of rebellion, the king fell desperately ill, so ill, as Joinville reports, that an attendant wished to cover his face with a sheet because she believed he had already passed on. Barely able, Louis vowed to fight another war, a Holy War, if God would permit him to live.[22] Regarding his recovery as God's gift in return for the vow, the young king set about almost immediately to make preparations for the crusade.

Blanche, fundamentally opposed to his projected course of action

---

[20] Cf. Labarge, *SL*, pp. 39-40; Lehmann, *Rôle de la femme*, pp. 333, 336, 338-39; and Painter, *Scourge of the Clergy*, pp. 94-97. Painter placed his emergence as a military leader in 1235; Lehmann put it closer to 1230.

[21] The events in Joinville are reported in chaps. XXII, XXIII. For an example of a fictional work which follows Joinville's picture, see Delaporte, *SL 1242, drame historique*; cf. also Gastine, *Roi des rois*—a sort of historical romance. On the legends which grew up around Louis's victories over the last rebels, such as the story of the sprouting lances at the battle of Saintes (borrowed from the pseudo-Turpin, *Roland*), see Smyser, *Pseudo-Turpin*, p. 26 n. 1.

[22] Joinville, chap. XXIV. The apparent nearness of death also encouraged him to do right over disputes in which he was involved; cf. Bloch, "Blanche de Castille," p. 235, and Vidier, "Marguilliers," pp. 213-14.

("when she heard he had taken the Cross . . . she was as miserable as if she had seen him dead"), was the first and in some ways the most significant obstacle in his path.[23] She started by objecting to the quality of her son's vow. With the aid of the bishop of Paris she persuaded Louis to renounce the vow because a vow sworn during an illness was not binding. According to Matthew Paris, who was soon to be a familiar in the royal household and would have access to such information, Louis's renunciation of the original vow was followed immediately by a new promise given in perfect health.[24] Yet Blanche would not be deterred. She had lost her husband on crusade; she could not help but be apprehensive over the safety of Louis and her three other sons who intended to accompany him. She pleaded with tears in her eyes, it is related by the gossipy Minstrel of Reims, and tried at the last to keep her son from leaving her with her own physical strength, but to no avail.[25]

For Louis the crusade (or the idea of it) quickly became the fundamental vehicle for his profound piety.[26] Because the crusade was service for God, his defiance of his mother could be justified or rationalized in his own mind. This is not to say that his struggle with Blanche was without pain to himself. He sincerely loved his mother, but if her piety, which was as deep and genuine as his, did not express itself in enthusiasm for the crusades (a trait she shared with many of her generation), in a certain way this was a positive factor for the young king. It allowed him to assume the sole leadership of a major policy for perhaps the first time in his life. Indeed, in the years immediately preceding the crusade one detects in him a creative vigor so ebullient at times and so full of bravado that one is tempted to associate it less with his religious zeal per se than with an outpouring of energy triggered by his successful liberation from parental domina-

[23] The quotation is from Joinville, chap. XXIV. Cf. Pernoud, *Reine Blanche*, pp. 277-83.

[24] MP, v, 3-4. For the canon law on vows, see *Dictionnaire du droit canonique*, VII, s.v. "Voeu."

[25] Minstrel of Reims, pp. 334-35. Cf. Joinville, chap. LXXXII; and MP, v, 312, 354 (on problems confronting France during the king's absence, problems foreseen by Blanche). The Minstrel's testimony has been fully accepted on the points in the text by Pernoud, *Reine Blanche*, pp. 300-303, 351; Boulenger, *Vie de SL*, pp. 93-94; Levron, *SL*, p. 161; and Guth, *SL*, pp. 43-44. Cf. Perry, *SL*, p. 63. On the general reliability of the Minstrel (which I affirm), opinions vary widely. Negative: Lecoy de La Marche, *Société*, pp. 126-27 (following Natalis de Wailly). Positive: Bémont, "Campagne de Poitou," pp. 290-91; Franchet, *SL*, p. 40.

[26] He perhaps regarded it also as the fulfillment of his destiny (cf. Richard's effort to set Louis's crusade in a broader context of Frankish politics; "Politique orientale de SL," pp. 197-207). In any case, Louis's three immediate predecessors had been crusaders, his father, of course, dying on the Albigensian Crusade. The death of Louis VIII, which might have been a bitter memory to Blanche, could have strengthened her son's determination to go through with his enterprise, that is, to live up to the memory of his father.

tion.[27] By invoking God against his mother he had, as it were, assured his own personal emancipation.

Louis, as it has been pointed out, was thirty years old in 1244. Nonetheless, emotionally he was still an adolescent when he swore the crusader's vow. The transition from adolescence to maturity commenced in earnest at the moment he decided that nothing and no one would be allowed to stand in his way in fulfilling the vow. The pattern, suggested here, is a familiar one, for although adolescence is the final phase of biological childhood, the adolescent process, it has been shown, reaches its appropriate culmination only when a "new kind of identification" or, rather, commitment "for life" replaces the hitherto undifferentiated and constantly shifting identifications of childhood. There is no precise year or series of years in the life cycle when this transformation must take place: as cultures and families vary, so do the fundamental life experiences of those who must confront the demands of culture and family in order to take their proper place in society.[28]

We must, therefore, always keep in mind that the French royal court in the thirteenth century possessed, as it were, a special ambiance, that it was endowed with its own rules and unique behavior. Louis's search for autonomy within this setting was indeed disruptive, but only up to a point, for his environment was the sort in which fervent religious devotion was constantly stressed. There was tension only because people in the royal circle differed about the proper form it should take, although by modern standards the range of these differences was extremely narrow. In this respect what Louis did in finding his own proper place in the structure of relationships in the royal household—the swearing of the crusader's vow during an illness; the defiance of his mother in the name of the vow—paralleled the actions of his sister, Isabella, in finding hers.

In the summer of 1243 Isabella had rejected the offer of marriage of the heir presumptive of the emperor. The union, proposed by Frederick II and at the time supported both by Blanche of Castile and Pope Innocent IV, was declined by Isabella after her recovery from a dangerous illness. Anticipating Louis, she successfully opposed the plans for her future with the vow that if she recovered from her illness she would be forever virgin and dedicate her life to God.[29] As the

[27] Cf. Spieg, "A Review of Contributions to a Psychoanalytic Theory of Adolescence," p. 5.
[28] Erikson, *Identity*, pp. 155, 258.
[29] The information on Isabella is drawn largely from the thirteenth century *Vita* of Isabella by her confidante, Abbess Agnès de Harcourt, who governed the nunnery founded by Isabella (see below n. 41). The best modern biography of Isabella is Garreau, *Bienheureuse Isabelle de France* (for the events narrated in this paragraph, see pp. 26-27, 33-34).

crusade would dominate Louis's life, so too the commitment to virginity would be the unifying theme of Isabella's.

Besides the biographical evidence of Isabella's friend and biographer, Agnès de Harcourt, on this point,[30] we know that those around her came to regard her chastity as the fulfillment of her life. Thirty years later, the designers of her tomb felt it necessary and appropriate to draw the attention of pious pilgrims to the theme.[31] And those who accepted the deceased Isabella as an intercessor for their tribulations on earth saw in her chastity the mark and characteristic of her holiness. In one of the miracles attributed to her, she was to demonstrate, or so the recipient of her intercession believed, that she could be counted on to use her power to protect that precious gift: seeing a maiden tempted by worldly attractions and *in periculo perdendae virginitatis*, Isabella interceded to convince her to abandon the world, enter the convent which Isabella had founded, and remain forever chaste.[32]

The similarity of Isabella's affirmation of a commitment for life to her brother's decision to become a crusader becomes more important when it is recognized that in the royal household she and Louis were the closest of friends. Again, though Agnès's own evidence is the most direct,[33] various sources suggest the vigor of their friendship. She displayed in many ways an ideal religiosity which Louis consciously or unconsciously tried to imitate. She led the life of a nun without being a nun, much as Louis would someday lead the life of a friar without taking the vows.[34] She wore simple clothes as part of her humility, a motif which Louis would one day adopt for himself.[35] Love for the poor was as important a theme in her piety as in his.[36] Such ties were indissoluble by death: both brother and sister would be portrayed at

[30] Agnès de Harcourt, *Vita*, pp. 799, 802, and elsewhere.

[31] The epitaph no longer exists, but various descriptions remain: *Acta sanctorum*, VI August, 791; Van Langeraad and Vidier, "Description de Paris par Arnold Van Buchel," p. 91; and the so-called *Abrégé de la vie . . . de la bienheureuse Isabel*, p. 10.

[32] The miracles are reported in Agnès's *Vita* and in the *Abrégé de la vie* as supplements. On the convent, below n. 41.

[33] Agnès de Harcourt, *Vita*, p. 801.

[34] Even though Isabella wrote and later probably aided in revising a monastic rule for the convent she founded, she preferred to remain at home and follow the rule. She was buried in nun's habit (an occasion—or the subsequent commemoration of it—which deeply affected Louis IX). On these points, see Rouillard's *Life* of Isabella, p. 793; and the drawing in Montfaucon, *Monumens*, II, pl. XVII, no. 2. See also Garreau, *Bienheureuse Isabelle*, pp. 32, 47-48, 50; and especially on the authorship of the rule the summary views in "Isabella of France, Bl.," *New Catholic Encyclopedia*, VII, 655. On Louis IX's imitation of the friars, below chapter 5 n. 163.

[35] *Abrégé de la vie*, p. 9. See the illustration in Guth, *SL*, p. 206, of what purports to be one of Isabella's tunics. On Louis IX, below chapter 5 n. 158.

[36] The evidence on Isabella is summarized by Garreau, *Bienheureuse Isabelle*, pp. 24-27, 38, 55; on Louis IX, below chapter 5 n. 153.

her tomb.[37] The pious would see them working their wonders to-gether in Paradise.[38] Ultimately both would be recognized as saints.[39]

The relationship was not one-way. Indeed, it is hard always to know who was influencing whom; but if Louis did learn from and admire his sister, she too could understand and appreciate his longings, his need to act the king. Further, she recognized the tension which this need precipitated in her brother's relations with the other women in the household. At every opportunity she was deferential to the king. She would kneel before him in awe of the sanctity she recognized in him.[40] She abhorred the exercise of power: she refused to be prioress of the convent which she founded at Longchamp in Normandy and which Louis richly endowed, preferring to make the preparations for its foundation through her brother as an act of humility.[41] Louis's ideas on obedience, the obedience of a wife to her husband and of social inferiors to their superiors, which he considered a necessary part of "perfect" love, reflect the ideal which his sister manifested. He explicitly desired his daughters to imitate this ideal in their relations with the men with whom they would spend their lives, for he sum-marized his notions at the end of his life in a set of instructions ad-dressed to the daughter he named after his sister.[42]

The king's sister, it must be remembered, was a decidedly peculiar phenomenon in the king's circle—not in the intensity of her religious devotion but in her ascetic unworldliness.[43] For all their mutual dis-like, the other adult women constantly around Louis—his mother and

[37] For the references to the tomb, above n. 31.

[38] They appear jointly, for example, as intercessors in a miracle reported by Agnès de Harcourt, *Vita*, p. 806.

[39] Louis was canonized in 1297. Isabella was beatified in the sixteenth century, but, as her miracles attest, she was considered a saint in the thirteenth century; cf. "Isabella of France, Bl.," *New Catholic Encyclopedia*, VII, 664-65.

[40] Agnès de Harcourt, *Vita*, pp. 801-2; *Abrégé de la vie*, p. 5. See also Tillemont, *Vie de SL*, v, 379.

[41] On her foundation, the contemporary evidence is enormous; besides Agnès de Harcourt's information which pervades her *Vita*, see Joinville, chap. CXXXIX; *Layettes*, IV, no. 5253; Guillaume de Nangis, "Chronicon," *HF*, xx, 557. See also *Abrégé de la vie*, p. 5. For scholarly interpretations of this evidence, see Garreau, *Bienheureuse Isabelle*, pp. 49, 53; and "Isabella of France, Bl.," *New Catholic Encyclopedia*, VII, 664-65.

[42] On Louis's instructions to his daughter, see O'Connell, *Propos de SL*, pp. 191-94, for a modern French text (he dates the orginial 1267-1268). The OF text may be con-sulted in Wallon, *SL*, II, 470ff., but a better edition with some valuable commentary is in O'Connell's "Teachings and Instructions of SL," a Princeton dissertation. Drawing out the influence of Isabella on Louis's children, Garreau, *Bienheureuse Isabelle*, p. 36, has emphasized the fact that the king's sister was the daughter Isabella's godmother.

[43] I have not adduced all the available evidence of the bond that tied Louis to his sister. One additional indication, however, ought to throw some light on the depth of their admiration for each other. As Louis, in his humiliation over the failure of the crusade, would someday allow himself to be disciplined by a beating with chains; so, Isabella endured flagellation *ad sanguinem* for her imagined sins. Louis, evidently, sent her the chains for accomplishing this penance. His own chains he sent as a gift to his

his wife—were alike in their enjoyment of a life of activity. Isabella, throughout her life (she died in 1269, the year before Louis), was retiring and contemplative and, therefore, a perfect counterweight to the able and aggressive Blanche and the able but frustrated Margaret.[44] That Isabella had managed to be herself in such a world and to resist the role that had been mapped out for her as an empress and that she had done so in the name of God were remarkable achievements. Louis had watched her, and when the time came, perhaps without consciously intending to do so, he followed in her footsteps.

This joining or even confusion of personal autonomy with religious devotion was a fundamental element of Louis's personality. An episode directly relevant to this issue was to occur in the Holy Land in the 1250s. There Louis met the young prince of Antioch, Bohemond VI. The king could not resist putting his support behind Bohemond's desire to end the cautious regency of the prince's mother in order that he might assume leadership of his besieged crusader principality. It was not to the point that Bohemond's mother wanted to continue the regency as she knew best. How could she have known the best course? The enemies of Christ needed to be confronted and destroyed (or so the explicit argument ran). I am convinced, however, that in this instance piety again became the handmaiden in a struggle for personal selfhood.[45]

It is no surprise then that Louis's preparations for crusade, viewed as the culmination of his own search for autonomy, have about them a bouyancy and even overconfidence unparalleled in any other period of his life. It was as if nothing were too much for him (was not God on his side?). He foresaw his crusade as the biggest in history.[46] He was prepared to risk a great many resources and most of his prestige by undertaking to construct a completely new port in the south of France so that his crusaders would have the benefit of departing en masse and well organized to do battle with Christ's enemies. Here he actually accomplished what few men could have believed was possible.[47] He envisioned himself leading the troops; against the cautious wisdom of his associates he personally—almost recklessly—led the assault on the beaches of the Infidel.

---

daughter Isabella. Agnès de Harcourt, *Vita*, p. 800; *Abrégé de la vie*, p. 8; Guillaume de Saint-Pathus, *HF*, xx, 83. See also Garreau, *Bienheureuse Isabelle*, p. 56; Labarge, *SL*, p. 208.

[44] I call Margaret able because of the impressive way she handled herself and the garrison at Damietta when the king's crusade collapsed in 1250; Joinville, chap. LXXVIII.

[45] Joinville, chap. CI, and below chapter 5 nn. 177-80, for further discussion of this incident.

[46] In 1246 he was already thinking of spending six years on crusade; *Layettes*, II, no. 3537. The emphasis on "bigness" has been noticed by Labarge, *SL*, p. 98.

[47] Cf. Jordan, "Supplying Aigues-Mortes," and below chapter 4 nn. 53-80.

When the king heard that the ensign of St. Denis was ashore he strode across the galley, refusing even for the Legate who was with him to lag behind the standard, and leapt into the water, which came up to his armpits. His shield round his neck, his helmet on his head, lance in hand, he joined his men on the beach. . . . He couched his lance under his arm and put his shield before him, and would have flung himself upon . . . [the Saracens] had not his wiser companions held him back.[48]

All this was still ahead in 1244, but it did not take long for his adolescent exuberance over this new and dangerous adventure to strike his contemporaries. A story told by Matthew Paris is especially instructive. Around 1246, Louis surreptitiously instructed his tailors to sew crosses on the robes that he intended to present to his barons at the traditional gift-giving ceremonies. By voluntarily accepting the gifts (and who could refuse?), they too "took" the cross casting their lot with the king.[49]

The sense of joy and eagerness implicit in this story, this "whimsical piety" as it has been called, [50] is far removed from what we would expect of a thirty-year-old king. It challenges our notions that at every stage in the king's life he was dominated by the somewhat more somber piety of his mother, a piety whose essence historians find in her admonition to her son that death was eminently preferable to the commission of a mortal sin.[51] Whatever we wish to call the cluster of emotions that characterized Louis and explain the earnestness and zeal in his behavior between late 1244 when he took the vow for the first time and June 1248 when he departed Paris, it is fairly certain that in those years he became his own man. A spirit of personal freedom with an accompaniment of religious messianism penetrated his policies and gave them, one might say, an immoderate aspect which it is difficult to ignore. Perhaps some stupid or regrettable things were done in the colossal effort of preparing for the crusade, but no hindrance could dampen the king's overall enthusiasm and determination. The future, as he regarded it, was clear and straight. To put it another way, on the eve of the crusade, Louis was (or, at least, he felt himself to be) finally, firmly free.

[48] Joinville, chap. xxxv; "Letter of John Sarrasin," p. 244.

[49] MP, IV, 502-3; cf. IV, 490. See also Pernoud, *Reine Blanche*, p. 287.

[50] The phrase is Barker and Smail's, "Crusades," p. 789.

[51] The remark, often repeated by Louis, is reported by Guillaume de Saint-Pathus (Margaret's confessor) in his life of the king, *HF*, xx, 64, and by Joinville, chap. xvi. A fuller discussion of Louis's piety, with specific reference to its symbolic manifestations on the eve of the crusade, will be found below chapter 5 nn. 1-28.

· 2 ·

BARONS AND PRINCES:
THE SEARCH FOR PEACE AND ALLIES

A Christian world at peace was always an ideal, but the crusade gave the need for peace a critical immediacy.[1] Only in an atmosphere of domestic peace could Louis IX assure for himself the collection of needed revenues for the crusade. Only in an atmosphere of international cooperation could foreign princes join meaningfully into his preparations. A full explanation for his activity in this sphere, however, must also take into consideration the idyllic vision, to which the king certainly ascribed, of the eve of a crusade as a time of pulling together among conflicting social and political groups.[2]

The need to enunciate and put into practice special efforts for maintaining internal peace was far from imaginary: as recently as 1241-1243 baronial rebellions had disturbed France. Nor was this manifestation of aristocratic hostility to the monarchy an isolated instance of civil strife. For twenty years the royal government had had to contest with recalcitrant feudatories over the proper governance of the kingdom. Three fundamental issues had been at stake, or, rather, three waves of fighting can be distinguished.

The least important of these, at least in its immediate influence on the insurrectionary disturbances of the 1240s, was baronial antagonism to the regency of a woman, Blanche of Castile, in the early years of the minority of Louis IX.[3] Although genuinely concerned barons might have misgivings about the prospect of regency government during the coming crusade, it is hard to believe that their specific grievance would center around Louis's selection of his mother to head the government in his absence. By the 1240s Blanche was highly regarded as an effective ruler. More worrisome was the barons' feeling that it was their proper responsibility to govern in periods of crisis (such as they felt existed in the 1220s and 1230s), an ominous

[1] The original idea of the Jerusalem-oriented crusade, as it had been enunciated by Pope Urban II in 1095, was that civil wars within Christendom ought to be brought to an end in the interest of the war for God; Munro, "Speech of Pope Urban," p. 239.

[2] Canon 17 of the Canons of the Council of Lyon (1245) called for four years of peace in Europe; MP, IV, 461. Purcell, *Papal Crusading Policy*, discusses this and other provisions of the conciliar decrees and publishes the declaration of the crusade in appendix 1.

[3] For fuller narratives and discussions of the insurrections see the references below n. 9.

portent of their likely attitude in case of troubles during the second regency.[4]

More directly relevant to the events of the 1240s was the legacy of distrust inherited from the long rivalry between the Angevins and the Capetians that had reached its political zenith in 1204 when by force of arms Philip II Augustus successfully dispossessed King John of England of all his continental possessions except Aquitaine. Neither John nor his son and successor, Henry III, reconciled themselves easily to this loss: intermittently from 1214 to the 1250s there were abortive military attempts to recover the former possessions. The natural allies of the English in this effort were disgruntled local lords in the conquered territories so that what was ostensibly a dynastic confrontation between two kingdoms inevitably brought with it aspects of rebellion and civil war.[5]

A final and equally ominous precursor to the uprisings of 1241-1243 was the still unresolved situation in the deep south, Languedoc (or Occitania as scholars are beginning to prefer). For the southerners the issue was the wounds inflicted in the Albigensian Crusade, a papally authorized war or, rather, series of wars, which had not only brought about the conquest and confiscation of many great seigneuries in the south, including part of the county of Toulouse, but had eventually delivered the majority of the forfeited lands into the hands of the French crown. In geographical terms the Mediterranean littoral from Narbonne to the Rhône, with a generous hinterland of about one hundred kilometers, came under direct royal administration in the mid-1220s. Additionally, the Albigensian settlement promised that Capetian power would expand, for the designated successor to the remainder of the county of Toulouse was Alfonse of Poitiers, Louis IX's brother.[6]

The royal presence in the south coupled with the eventuality of Capetian succession in the heartland of Occitania heralded a fundamental transformation in meridional politics, a transformation that was deeply resented.[7] Periodically the resentment took military form. In 1240 the rebellion of the erstwhile viscount of Béziers, Raymond

[4] Baronial attitudes and actions during the second regency are discussed at some length below, chapter 5 nn. 95-119.

[5] The best book on Anglo-French rivalry in the late twelfth and early thirteenth centuries is Powicke, *Loss of Normandy*. For the role of the English in the rebellions in France, below nn. 9-12.

[6] This paragraph merely summarizes the essential points. Much more will have to be said about the details of southern politics. A clear discussion of the events narrated in this paragraph is Strayer's short book, *The Albigensian Crusades*.

[7] Persistent anti-French (that is, anti-north French) sentiments in Languedoc are analyzed in the perceptive article by Dossat, "Patriotisme méridional."

Trencavel, was thwarted by local representatives of the king.[8] But most important, in 1241 the southerners combined with the English in what was to be—as it turned out—the last major attempt, for almost one hundred years, to upset the settlements of the early thirteenth century.[9]

They did not succeed. Louis personally commanded in the decisive battles at Taillebourg and Saintes on 31 July 1242. Throughout 1243 and into 1244, pacts of submission and promises of obedience were exacted with meticulous care from the defeated rebels.[10] With England, Louis capped his victory with a five-year truce in 1243.[11]

For us what is significant is that under the impetus of preparing for the crusade, the pacts of submission and truce of 1243 became the partial basis of an ad hoc system designed to prolong the peace. A very few of the original agreements were renewed rather rapidly both with the former rebels and with Henry III.[12] The haste of these renewals is itself suggestive, and we know enough about the negotiations with Henry to tie the early renewal of the Anglo-French truce to Louis's concerns about the crusade. These negotiations will be dealt with in considerable detail somewhat later.[13]

[8] The rebellion and its major ramifications in Languedoc are discussed in Julia, *Béziers*, pp. 129-32; Sabatier, *Béziers*, pp. 260-61; and Poux, *Cité de Carcassonne*, I, 89-126; I discuss some aspects of its economic implications in "Problems of the Meat-Market of Béziers," p. 44.

[9] In general on the revolts of 1241-1243 and their relation to earlier patterns of insurrectionary disturbances, see Wallon, *SL*, I, 1-50, 76-90, 137-78; Tillemont, *Vie de SL*, I, 428-84, 518-39, and II, 1-21, 31-73, 81-94, 99-107, 210-20, 275-81, 372-77, 428-73; Berger, *Blanche de Castille*, pp. 46-253, 342-53; and Boutaric, *SL et Alfonse de Poitiers*, pp. 40-61.

[10] Pacts of submission, recorded in *Layettes* II, were forced on the Lusignans (nos. 2980-81), on Count Raymond of Toulouse (nos. 2995-96, 3013), on Almaric, the viscount of Narbonne (no. 3014), and on Roger, count of Foix (no. 3015). Other notables whose loyalty was suspect were also forced to make these written pledges: for example, Trencavel (*Layettes*, III, no. 3616; *HGL*, VIII, cc. 1212-14); Bernard, count of Comminges (*Layettes*, II, no. 3030); Bertrand, brother of Count Raymond of Toulouse (*Layettes*, II, no. 3057); Raoul, bishop of Angoulême, and Guillaume, abbot of Corona (*Layettes*, II, no. 3110); et al. As recorded again in *Layettes* II, the consuls, knights, and *bourgeois* of Villeneuve (no. 3112), of Mézin (no. 3171), of Agen (no. 3045), of Montauban (no. 3056), of Narbonne (no. 3162), and of Toulouse (no. 3029), among other towns, also were forced to swear to keep the peace.

[11] A letter representing the truce of 1243 is preserved in *Layettes*, II, no. 3075. Henry III was to pay Louis an indemnity of one thousand pounds sterling each year for the duration of the truce; MP, IV, 242.

[12] The Lusignans apparently renewed their pledge in 1246; *Layettes*, II, no. 3526. The oaths taken by Maurice de Craon in August 1245 and by Philippe, lord of Montbazon in the Touraine, in November 1245 may also be renewals of former pledges, but I have found no earlier distinct records of their pledges (see *Layettes*, II, no 3396; and "Scripta de feodis ad regem spectantibus," *HF*, XXIII, 677). The truce with England was renewed in 1246; MP, IV, 506.

[13] Below nn. 61-72.

With regard to the rebels we have less evidence. The reason for this is probably that Louis hit upon another, more trustworthy way to keep them in line: they could do very little to disrupt conditions in France during the king's absence if they accompanied him abroad. Among those who took the vow to go on crusade were the Lusignan counts of La Marche and Angoulême; Raymond, count of Toulouse; Olivier, lord of Termes; Lord Goceran de Pinos; and Lord Bernard de Caracelles.[14] Of the inducements offered them, we know little. Perhaps some took their defeat as a sign from heaven and came in order to atone for the still unforgiven sin of supporting the Albigensian heretics.[15] Others may have acted out of a genuine attempt to convey to Louis IX their acceptance of the new order in southern politics. The small size of many of their contingents and the loans that the royal government had to make to them in order to sustain their contingents do suggest, however, that most were pressured, although by what means is not always clear, into joining the king's enterprise.[16]

Consider, for example, the case of the count of Toulouse. Direct and explicit evidence is hard to come by, but it is likely that the king persuaded Count Raymond to join his crusade by offering to employ his good offices in working out a reconciliation between the count and the papacy over the lingering problems of the Albigensian Crusade. At least, from 1245 on one begins to notice the king playing a more active role in the delicate negotiations between Raymond and the pope.[17] Raymond had wanted an agreement of some sort for a long time.[18] There was no suspicion of the orthodoxy of Raymond VII, unlike that of his father, to compromise the French king's own piety; and an accommodation between the two old enemies would have had a truly beneficial effect on Occitania.

It was true that a reconciliation between Raymond VII and the church might once have been a two-edged sword, for it could have been argued that as a true son of the church the count no longer needed to be barred from passing on his county in the normal way. The Albigensian settlement had insisted that the county of Toulouse pass to Raymond's daughter, Jeanne, who had been constrained to marry Alfonse of Poitiers, Louis IX's brother. As long as she was both the designated heir and the natural heir, there was no problem. And

---

[14] On the Lusignans (the count and two of his sons) see MP, vi, 159, and v, 158, 204; also *Layettes*, v, no. 529. On Raymond of Toulouse see *HGL*, vi, 787. For Olivier de Termes, see *HGL*, vi, 786, and viii, c. 1222; for Goceran and Bernard, see *HGL*, viii, c. 1224.

[15] Below chapter 3 n. 30.   [16] Below chapter 4 nn. 16-17.

[17] *Layettes*, ii, nos. 3346, 3348, and iii, no. 3625. Cf. with the records of negotiations before 1245, in the following note.

[18] Ibid., ii, nos. 3144, 3156, 3163, 3184.

as long as the count, who was a widower, remained unmarried there was no possibility of a problem. But it is an indication of the unexpected difficulties constantly intruding themselves into the best of Louis's plans, that in 1245 Count Raymond set about to arrange a marriage for himself, one which presaged the most dangerous consequences for France and jeopardized the recent rapprochement between him and the king.[19]

The count of Provence-Forcalquier, Raymond Berenger, had had four daughters. He had arranged for one, Margaret, to marry Louis IX and for two others to marry the king of England, Henry III, and his brother, the future king of the Romans, Richard of Cornwall. He now wished, that is in 1245, to arrange the marriage of the fourth and youngest girl, Beatrice. The count had no sons.[20]

For the count of Toulouse to be interested in marrying Beatrice of Provence was annoying. As has already been suggested, the possible birth of a male child to the house of Toulouse coupled with Raymond's proposed reconciliation with the church had a very great likelihood of challenging the royal position in the south. That the marriage had reached the negotiating stage in 1245 was dangerous enough; that Raymond Berenger should die in the same year and provide in his will that the county of Provence pass to Beatrice betokened a far more dangerous possibility, the emergence of a too powerful principality in the south formed from the dynastic union of the houses of Toulouse and Provence.

These issues made an especially vexing problem: Louis IX wanted to see the church and Raymond of Toulouse reconciled. He would strive for that goal because it was right and also because it was probably the chief inducement for Raymond to join him on crusade. But Louis could not favor Raymond's marriage to Beatrice of Provence because of its implications for the future of royal hegemony in Occitania. Fortunately there was a way out of the tangle. With the consent of those instructed to carry out Raymond Berenger's testament, Louis proposed that Beatrice marry his own youngest brother, Charles of Anjou.[21] Her acceptance of this offer effectively thwarted Raymond of Toulouse as well as his plans—whatever they might have been. If Raymond was resentful, he did not show it: he continued

[19] Although not considering the effect of a reconciliation per se, the remarks of Strayer, *Albigensian Crusades*, p. 137, suggest some of the problems that would have arisen in any circumstances had Raymond VII had a male child after the Albigensian settlement.

[20] For the discussion in this and the succeeding paragraph, see *Layettes*, II, nos. 3367, 3371, 3382; the history of southern politics by the contemporary observer, Guillaume de Puylaurens, *HF*, xx, 768. In general, see also Labarge, *SL*, pp. 89-90.

[21] Guillaume de Puylaurens, "Historiae," *HF*, xx, 768. See also Labarge, *SL*, pp. 89-90.

preparations for his penance, that is, his participation in the king's crusade.[22] Only his death on the very eve of his departure prevented him from fulfilling his vow.[23] Beatrice and Charles were married in 1246.

How other recent rebels were induced to take the cross, I cannot say. But enough information is available to show that the king's plan was not limited to recent enemies. The Holy War also provided an opportunity for ridding the country of a few rebels whose crimes reached back to a more distant period. This is most easily explained by the fear that these men had never really reconciled themselves to their humiliation by the monarchy.

The apprehension, as an example drawn from Narbonne suggests, was not misplaced. After a brief rebellion and the murder of a royal sympathizer in 1237, several men of Narbonne (including a certain Guillaume Teularia) had, among other things, been condemned to go on crusade. The sentence was not carried out, the scholarly supposition being that this leniency was a token of beneficence to the city since the men were notables. The government surely expected these men to be loyal in the future; yet, despite the royal leniency and several intervening years of peace in the south, they joined the rebellion of 1241-1243. Thus, in 1246 the king decided that the crusading vow had to be reimposed as a penance.[24]

With perhaps the possibility of similar occurrences in the king's mind, we find that the unsuccessful rebel of 1240, Raymond Trencavel, the dispossessed viscount of Béziers, was "induced" to join Louis's crusade of 1248 even though he was beginning to get a reputation as a loyal baron and, in any case, was financially unable to sustain a revolt.[25] And it is not surprising that the archrebel, the consistently disagreeable Peter Mauclerc, the titular count of Brittany, who had been instrumental in the baronial opposition of the first decades of the reign, found himself on the king's first crusade and died on his return trip home.[26]

[22] The reconciliation of Raymond VII and the papacy followed rapidly (cf. *Layettes*, III, nos. 3662-65, 3667). However, the count never succeeded in persuading the church to permit his father to be buried in consecrated ground.

[23] On the contingent he raised, however, see below chapter 3 nn. 30-31.

[24] For the events and documents relevant to the discussion in this paragraph, see Emery, *Heresy and Inquisition*, pp. 87-88, 88 n. 30, and 174. That the fomentors of the outrage of 1237 supported the rebellion of 1241-1243 I infer from the subscription of Guillaume Teularia to the capitulation of Narbonne in early 1244; *Layettes*, II, no. 3162.

[25] *HGL*, VIII, c. 1223, and VI, 792.

[26] Mauclerc may have seen it in his best interest spiritually to go abroad. His career was over and he had passed on on the county to his son. He had been on crusade in 1239. His death is recounted with characteristic pathos by Joinville, chap. LXXIV. The best discussion of Peter's life is the biography by Painter, *Scourge of the Clergy*. See also below chapter 4 n. 15.

Many barons were to join the king's crusade for healthier reasons by the standards of the thirteenth century. It would be simplistic to think otherwise. Some came for adventure, some out of piety, some for hope of profit.[27] In time we shall try to evaluate their contributions to the war.[28] But the fundamental argument here is that a specific selection of barons, those who had violently opposed the political will of the crown, was prevented from disturbing the peace of the kingdom during Louis's absence by his apparent insistence that they join him on crusade.

Obvious and useful as it may have been, however, to decide to take unruly barons with him, this simple policy must not be allowed to obscure the complexity of Louis's relations with his baronage from 1245 through 1248. Hostile or traditionally hostile nobles rapidly discovered that they could pressure the king to defend certain of their interests by threatening to put obstacles in the way of his preparations for war. The single most important illustration of this fact was the king's interference in an argument between the papacy and a determined group of his barons in 1247.

In November of the year before, a league of nobles had been formed comprising at least nineteen barons, each of whom pledged one one-hundredth of his revenues to be used against the church.[29] Leagues of this nature had been formed before, in 1225 and in 1235, and the one in 1235 had played a brief part in the history of royal and baronial confrontations in Louis's reign. Like its successor, the league of 1235 proclaimed the difficulty of the nobility "to sustain with equanimity" certain "new customs" (*novas consuetudines*) of the church.[30]

The members of the league of 1246 selected four leaders, two of whom—the duke of Burgundy and the count of Brittany—had had a

---

[27] For the varied privileges of a crusader, see Brundage, *Medieval Canon Law and the Crusader*, p. 30 and chaps. v and vi; Lunt, *Papal Revenues*, I, 115-21. The royal archives kept on hand, according to an inventory of the 1280s, a form letter "pro querendis militibus et balistariis pro negocio Terre Sancte" (*Formulaires*, no. 6, item 10).

[28] Below chapter 4 nn. 8-33.

[29] The documentary constitution of the league (*la compaignie*) is printed in *Layettes*, II, no. 3569. Except for the leaders little is known about the barons who belonged to the league, but there are nineteen places for *cordons* (with seals of attestation) on the document. Unfortunately the seals have been lost (see note to *Layettes*, II, no. 3569). Campbell, "Protest of *SL*," p. 413 n. 30, talks as if there were more than one league at this time, but Berger, *SL et Innocent IV*, pp. 246-50, argues, as I shall, that the league represented baronial interests throughout the kingdom.

[30] For the slight evidence on the league of 1225, see Petit-Dutaillis, *Étude . . . Louis VIII*, App. vi, no. 302. On the purpose, quoted in the text, of the league of 1235, *Layettes*, II, no. 2024. The barons of 1246 expressed their purpose thus: "qui voudront estre de ceste compaignie" are obliged "a deffendre noz droiz . . . anvers le clergié"; *Layettes*, II, no. 3569.

role in the collective leadership of the league of 1235.[31] Besides continuity of leadership and purpose, the neat geographical spread of the territories of the four leaders in 1246 suggests that they were chosen on a regional principle as well.[32] For the east there was the duke of Burgundy; for the west the count of Brittany; for the southwest the count of Angoulême; and for the north the count of Saint-Pol.[33] The league was evidently welcomed ("received") and supported in other counties.[34]

Two of the leaders—the counts of Brittany and of Angoulême, Peter Mauclerc and Hugh le Brun respectively—had also led revolts against the king.[35] More important, by the time of their appointment, all of the four leaders had taken the crusader's vow.[36] The organization's elaborate rules, presuming that one or two of these people would always be in France, permit us to surmise that the members had agreed to forsake their vows or use the threat of forsaking them as leverage in maintaining their rights against the church.[37] Louis IX, it follows, was necessarily mindful of the league and, in a sense, was forced into doing something about it.

The French church was fully supported by the papacy in its opposition to the nobles. Pope Innocent IV, already involved in a life-and-death struggle with the empire,[38] was unwilling to compromise

[31] *Layettes*, II, nos. 2024, 3569. Berger, *SL et Innocent IV*, pp. 46, 246, and Fournier, "Conflits de juridiction," p. 442, identify three of the leaders of 1235 with those of 1246, but the count of La Marche and Angoulême in 1235, Hugh X, had assigned his son Hugh le Brun the county of Angoulême before the league of 1246 came into existence (*Layettes*, II, no. 3526; Labarge, *SL*, p. 91). However, they both represented the same interest. Continuity of leadership may even have stretched as far back as the league of 1225; cf. Petit-Dutaillis, *Étude . . . Louis VIII*, App. VI, no. 302.

[32] Cf. Berger, *SL et Innocent IV*, pp. 246-50.

[33] Only Aquitaine (a possession of the English) and the Mediterranean south were unrepresented in the leadership. Whether barons from these areas sealed the document has not been determined.

[34] Huillard-Bréholles (*Historia diplomatica*, VI, pt. 1, pp. 469-70 n. 1), who may have examined the constitutive document of the league before the editors of the *Layettes*, noted the nineteen places for *cordons* and three other seals: "Senescallus Campanie (Joinville?); G. . . . . . de Beollement; . . . . de Valeri." He surmised that these three seals were those of the receivers of the league in the county of Champagne. Fournier, "Conflits de juridiction," pp. 439-42, suggested that forty-one barons made up the league (citing Huillard-Bréholles). The nineteen places for *cordons*, that is, could represent places for thirty-eight seals, and then the three supplementary seals would mean that forty-one barons adhered to this particular example of the document. But this argument does not take into consideration that the league may have been received in other counties, in which case we would have to augment the number of adherents.

[35] Mauclerc, of course, in the 1230s; and Hugh le Brun, count of Angoulême, who had supported his father, Hugh of Lusignan, count of La Marche, in 1241-1243.

[36] This occurred at a colloquium or meeting of the royal court in Paris in October 1245; see Joinville, chap. XXIV; Guillaume de Nangis, "Vie de SL," *HF*, XX, 353; and MP, IV, 489-90.

[37] *Layettes*, II, no. 3569 (toward the bottom of p. 645).

[38] See below nn. 70-101.

on issues of ecclesiastical authority and jurisdiction. To destroy the movement he summarily ordered the excommunication of all adherents and supporters of the league including the nuncios who circulated the constitutive document of the organization, the scribes who wrote or copied it, and the barons, lords, nobles, powers, consuls, governors, and officers who allowed it to be published in regions under their control.[39] It is clear, from contemporary observation as well as from internal evidence of the papal bull, that Innocent IV suspected the emperor, Frederick II, of being behind developments in France.[40]

Louis decided to intervene in the dispute and invited representatives of the league to present their demands before him at a meeting in Paris during Lent 1247. Members of the clergy would also attend and offer counterarguments. At the assembly the central question concerned the limits of ecclesiastical jurisdiction,[41] and after a great deal of debate Louis agreed to send an emissary to the pope to work out a compromise on this basic issue. To Archbishop Boniface of Canterbury, then at the papal court, this agreement with excommunicates was tantamount, on the king's part, to supporting the league.[42]

In the summer of 1247 when the embassy arrived at Lyon, where the pope had taken refuge from the menace of Emperor Frederick II, Innocent readily agreed to prohibit further extensions of ecclesiastical jurisdiction. When pressed he also promised to correct some specific abuses such as appointing foreign clerks to French benefices. But he refused to give up ecclesiastical jurisdiction over secular mat-

---

[39] The order of January 1247 was directed to the legate, Eudes de Châteauroux, who was in France to preach the crusade, and it is published, among other places, in Huillard-Bréholles, *Historia diplomatica*, VI, pt. 1, pp. 483-86: ". . . facias excommunicatos omnes illos qui servari fecerint statuta predicta et consuetudines (i.e., of the league) vel potius abusiones introductas contra Ecclesie libertatem. Item excommunicatos nuncies et nunciari facias statutarios et scriptores statutorum ipsorum necnon barones et dominos terrarum ac alios nobiles, potestates, consules, rectores et consilarios locorum ubi hujusmodi statuta vel consuetudines edita fuerunt servata, necnon et illos qui secundum ea presumpserint judicare vel in publicam formam scribere judicata." The list of those to be excommunicated went on and on.

[40] See Berger's analysis, *SL et Innocent IV*, p. 251 (also Huillard-Bréholles, *Historia diplomatica*, VI, pt. 1, p. 485). Cf. also a letter of Archbishop Boniface of Canterbury (MP, VI, 131) indicating that he was convinced that imperial and French developments were connected in the eyes of the pope. It was Fournier, "Conflits de juridiction," pp. 439-40, who suggested that the constitutive document of the league bears some external resemblances to a letter of Frederick II.

[41] MP, VI, 132 (letter of Archbishop Boniface that the matters were discussed *in curia*); IV, 607 (on the great amount of discussion at the meeting in mid-Lent 1247 and on the presence of both nobles and churchmen).

[42] Archbishop Boniface was shocked by the "appositio sigilli regalis una cum sigillis baronum eorundem" on the document requesting a compromise settlement; ibid., VI, 132.

ters where this was sanctioned by custom.[43] Since the most important point the nobles argued was that an unjust extension of jurisdiction could not be justified *per consuetudinem*,[44] the embassy can be said to have failed.

At this juncture the involvement of the king took a new and decidedly more hostile turn against the church (although, of course, the monarchy's traditional *political* relations with the ecclesiastical hierarchy were far from idyllic).[45] In response to the pope's pronouncement, Louis, in the fall of 1247, sent another ambassador to Lyon who was instructed to express the king's displeasure over the failure of earlier negotiations.[46] The record of his embassy, called the "Protest of St. Louis," is worth examining in some detail.

The ambassador used a threatening tone;[47] his conception of the kingly power and estate was grandiose, even extreme.[48] Specifically, while granting the exceptional character of the priesthood, he stressed, through tortuous scriptural analogies, the traditional and unfair persecution of kings by priests.[49] He balanced these statements of royal humiliation with affirmations (and an implied threat) of righteous resistance: "we are not children of the bondwoman but of the free."[50] The ambassador also spoke admiringly of Charlemagne and his rights over (or, rather, in) the church.[51] He suggested that

[43] Archbishop Boniface wrote that the pope said, "de illis autem de quibus ecclesia extitit in possessione vel quasi, non intendit immutare"; ibid.

[44] This is inferred from ibid.; cf. the league of 1235, that the nobles could not sustain the new customs of the church (*Layettes*, ii, no. 2024). By 1246 the church surely regarded the "new" customs as true customs, and the pope did not intend to modify them.

[45] On this general point, see Campbell, "Protest of SL," pp. 412-13; Labarge, *SL*, pp. 92-93 (she relies heavily on Campbell); Berger, *SL et Innocent IV*, pp. 271, 296-97. The earlier league of nobles, 1235, had issued its demands in the name of the crown; *Layettes*, ii, no. 2024.

[46] This embassy has been preserved in the appendixes of MP, vi, 99-112. It has been the subject of a lively debate on how much the representations of the ambassador are his own and how much they reflect faithfully Louis's views. Generally speaking it is agreed that the essence of Louis's views has been preserved; see Campbell, "Protest of SL," pp. 416-18; Labarge, *SL*, pp. 92-93; Congar, "Église et l'état," pp. 266-68; Kienast, *Deutschland und Frankreich*, iii, pp. 635-36 n. 1830. Earlier views either saw the record of the embassy as a document independent of the league (Fournier, "Conflits de juridiction," p. 442) or refused to acknowledge its authenticity. See, for the latter opinion, the set of articles by Verdier, "SL et la monarchie chrétienne," "SL et l'église de France au XIIIe siècle," and "SL et les papes au XIIIe siècle" (two parts); cf. St.-M., Review of Gerin, *Pragmatique sanction*; and Meyer, *Ludwig IX. von Frankreich und Innozenz IV*, pp. 49-54, 61-64.

[47] MP, vi, 99.   [48] Ibid., 100-01, 104-07.

[49] The passages alleged include Luke 23:31; Genesis 47:19, 22; Matthew 10:23. Like many medieval interpreters the ambassador (or the clerk that prepared his dossier) twisted the meaning of passages as he saw fit.

[50] Galatians 4:31; cf. also Psalms 2:1; Acts 20:34; 1 Thessalonians 2:9.

[51] MP, vi, 110.

Louis's protest represented all interests, even those of the French church (which had its own grievances against the popes),[52] and that the papacy was ruining all the interests of the Frankish kingdom.[53] Perhaps, indeed, the church at its directional focus was unfit to administer its own treasury, for in necessity, he warned, the king could seize the treasury of the church.[54]

Recent scholars argue that the last statement is the ambassador's interpolation, for the king (it is said) never seized church property without consent.[55] This argument is only partly convincing, for unfortunately the ambassador's threat has been read out of context. In the "Protest," the statement on seizing the treasury of the church is immediately followed by remarks about the king having taken the cross, and in this necessity, the ambassador continued, the king would require the treasury of the church.[56] The threat may have been overstated. More likely, the ambassador tried to reproduce the intensity of Louis IX's own feelings on the matter of the crusade. Innocent IV, whatever he may have thought about this and similar threats,[57] recognized that the general impression the ambassador tried to impart was quite in line with Louis's state of mind. Although we know few of the details, the pope seems to have reached agreement quickly on the matters originally raised by the barons.[58]

By the vigorous nature of his protest to the pope (and the resulting settlement), Louis earned the respect of the baronage. Perhaps for the first time in his reign he effected something of an alliance between a true cross section of the nobility and the crown—at least insofar as their mutual relations with the church were concerned.[59] This was no doubt a useful development.

On the other hand, the king's role in the crisis of 1246-1247 disposed at least some churchmen to be suspicious of him. Louis had made a choice: the crusade came first. In making that choice during the crisis of the league, he felt it was worth the risk and perhaps right (or, at least, unavoidable) to antagonize these churchmen. As long as

[52] Campbell, "Protest of SL," p. 412.

[53] MP, vi, 99: "Dominus rex jam dudum moleste sustinuit gravamina quae inferuntur ecclesiae Gallicanae et per consequens sibi et regno."

[54] Ibid., 110. With regard to the papacy's incompetence in money matters, the ambassador criticized the misuse of Franciscans as papal revenue agents (p. 106).

[55] Campbell, "Protest of SL," pp. 417-18; Labarge, SL, p. 92.

[56] MP, vi, 111-12.

[57] Louis's claim to have inherited the right of Charlemagne to select the pope (ibid., 110-11) might have disturbed Innocent. The right to select implied the right to depose (or could be so construed). The implication may not have been intended, but it could not be ignored.

[58] Berger, SL et Innocent IV, pp. 296-98, has described the "amicable" outcome of this crisis.

[59] Cf. Campbell, SL's Ecclesiastical Policy in France, p. 60.

Frederick II continued to menace the papacy and the pope needed Louis as an active friend, ecclesiastical reactions were muted. But much could change. And not the least important of the paradoxes in this situation was that Louis himself, again in the interest of the crusade, would try to work out a reconciliation between emperor and pope, a reconciliation that might have given Innocent a freer hand in dealing with events in France if it had succeeded. The break, however, in the impasse between Innocent and Frederick did not come until two years after the king had departed from France, námely, with the emperor's death in 1250. When it did come, the papacy had not forgotten or forgiven its humbling at the hands of the French king in 1247.[60]

Problems of internal peace had a much wider context than French politics only. The papacy and England, as we have seen, as well as the empire had special interests in monitoring and sometimes trying to exacerbate domestic tensions in France. Louis IX could not fail to recognize that this was the case or that, behind it all, was the unsettled nature of international conditions. But the instability of international affairs also had a more direct bearing on the crusade, for in theory it was an international enterprise. As long as there was war or the threat of war among Christian states, there was not much chance that the crusade would attain its ideal international flavor.

Louis himself was at war with the English, but the truce that had closed hostilities in 1243 was renewed at Louis's request in 1246.[61] Although he continued to seek subsequent extensions (sending emissaries for this purpose even from the Holy Land),[62] he was far from satisfied with the ad hoc nature of these extensions. What was at stake, after all, was the security of France during his absence; and since the chief threat to that security, despite his personal weaknesses, was the king of England, Henry III, it behooved Louis to put his major effort into conciliating him.

At first glance it seems that this effort should have yielded immediately successful results. Both kings were already known for their extravagant manifestations of piety.[63] Both seemed genuinely religious. They were also brothers-in-law. But circumstances had thrust them

---

[60] Below chapter 5 nn. 82-89.

[61] For the truce, *Layettes*, II, no. 3075; and MP, IV, 242. On the renewal, *Layettes*, III, no. 3713; and MP, IV, 506.

[62] *Layettes*, III, no. 4052.

[63] On Henry's rather dangerous extravagance and its effect on his ability to govern, Sayles, *Medieval Foundations of England*, p. 418, and Harriss, *King, Parliament, and Public Finance*, p. 140. On Louis's generous expenditures on pious works before 1245, see below chapter 4 n. 180.

into confrontation from the beginning of their reigns, and they were to grow old before they extricated themselves from the scandal. In the 1240s neither was ready to trust the other; both were pawns in what appeared to be a permanent rivalry in Western European politics.[64]

Behind it all was the fact that courageous military leadership was an implicit virtue when demonstrated in a just war. And Henry III considered his attempts to win back the old Angevin lands, his *patria*, as just and as right as Louis IX thought the French annexation was.[65] The crusade, however, was a new factor. It gave the French that additional element of religiosity that tipped the balance in their favor. Thus, Louis IX could request the pope to emphasize to the pious Henry the dreadful sinfulness of attacking a crusader's territories.[66] It is perhaps significant of the "religious" or "righteous" flavor of Henry's passion to recover his continental dominions that he was not moved by this argument: he made aggressive militaristic displays at least twice during Louis's absence abroad, in 1248 and in 1254.[67] Even his own barons, however, were reluctant to follow his attack upon the French (more because of his own incompetence than because of their moral scruples),[68] and the remnants of the French feudal host evidently succeeded in protecting the country.[69]

Eventually the problem of Anglo-French rivalry was to be complicated by the titanic struggle between Emperor Frederick II and Pope Innocent IV. The pope, using Louis's concern about the possibility of an English invasion during his absence on crusade, attempted to keep the French army in France. The real reason for this effort, on the pope's part, was to have readily at hand a counterweight to the military power of the emperor.[70] The monastic chronicler, Matthew Paris, reports that at Cluny Innocent incited Louis against Henry III for just this purpose.[71] Whether the monk's accusation is perfectly accurate (in most things Innocent IV appears more subtle)[72] the atmosphere was not conducive to English participation in the crusade.

[64] MP, IV, 594. Harriss, *King, Parliament, and Public Finance*, pp. 34-35.

[65] Henry considered the French attitude a threat to his *patria* (see his remarks of 1254 cited by Harriss, *King, Parliament, and Public Finance*, p. 35). Cf. a typical medieval commentary on what constituted a just war in Russell, *Just War*, p. 128. The actual moral position of the warrior in a just war was moot among the theologians; Russell, p. 217.

[66] MP, V, 23, 51, 346.

[67] These instances are reported in ibid., 71, 434. Harriss, *King, Parliament, and Public Finance*, p. 34, has analyzed the fiscal evidence of the reign and shows that Henry's threatening overtures required financial demands of his barons in 1248, 1253, and 1254.

[68] Cf. Harriss, *King, Parliament, and Public Finance*, pp. 35-36, esp. p. 36 n. 1.

[69] "Submonitiones anno M. CC. LIII factae," *HF*, XXIII, 730-31.

[70] This is the considered opinion of Purcell, *Papal Crusading Policy*, p. 74. Cf. Russell, *Just War*, p. 201 n. 202.

[71] MP, IV, 504.   [72] Below n. 88.

Matthew Paris, despite his antipapal sentiments, is the best informant on the difficulties at this time in the four-way struggle among the two kings, the pope, and the emperor. But although he gives that edge to his information which brings contemporary bitterness and disappointment to life, he is far from the only source of information on this vital subject.[73] Especially as the focus shifts to the continent, many observers paint the same picture, if in less vivid colors. According to Alberic, a chronicler-monk of Troisfontaines, as early as 1239 the French crown had sent the bishop of Langres and Lord Adam, a knight, to find out if there were any way to restore peace between empire and papacy. In 1239 there was none.[74]

When Louis took the cross in 1244 his efforts at effecting a reconciliation increased in tempo. He again put himself forward as an arbiter, and in everything he did he tried to maintain the posture of a man not overly disposed politically toward one side or the other in the clash of papal and imperial interests.[75] Thus, in 1245 Louis deliberately let it be known that the pope, who was fleeing Frederick's imminent attack on Rome, could take up residence on the "borders" of France, in Lyon, but not quite in France proper.[76] The position allowed him to be able to come to the aid of the pope without appearing as his official protector. When Innocent later that year deposed the emperor,[77] Louis tilted just slightly to the other side. He did not recognize the validity of the deposition (he continued to address Frederick as emperor), but he did little else to compromise his relations with the pope.[78]

Frederick, for his part, courted what he considered the French king's slender support by offering equipment and provisions for his

[73] Purcell, *Papal Crusading Policy*, p. 77, has evaluated and collated the evidence given by Matthew Paris with the sources of theological opinion with which she is most familiar and has come up with virtually the same conclusion: "Allowing for Matthew Paris' prejudices there is still a good deal of evidence to suggest that public reaction to King Louis' defeat in 1250 was directed against the pope's diversion of crusading energies against the Hohenstaufen."

[74] *HF*, xxi, 623. Cf. MP, iii, 626-27.

[75] Kienast, *Deutschland und Frankreich*, iii, pp. 609-13.

[76] MP, iv, 392; the king would let the pope come to France if he could get the approval of the *consilium optimatum suorum*. Most scholars are united in the opinion that this proviso (the agreement of the council) was tantamount to a negative reply, making the pope's choice of Lyon necessary; see Montfaucon, *Monumens*, ii, 134; Eydoux, *SL*, p. 19; Labarge, *SL*, p. 86; Maret, "Concile général," p. 427; and Purcell, *Papal Crusading Policy*, p. 24. Cf., however, Meyer's view (*Ludwig IX*, pp. 9-10) that the pope's choice was the natural one from the beginning since he did not want to be too dependent on any secular ruler.

[77] On the events surrounding the deposition, see Guillaume de Nangis, *HF*, xx, 346-52; MP, iv, 445-55.

[78] See the titulus to the letter published by Huillard-Bréholles, *Historia diplomatica*, vi, pt. 1, pp. 500-502. See also Perry, *SL*, pp. 152-53; and Congar, "Église et l'état," p. 266.

planned crusade,[79] freedom of passage through the empire, and his son's or his own presence on the crusade.[80] He appealed to Louis's sense of justice and argued forcefully against the legality of the deposition.[81] Moreover, Frederick knew how vital the resources of the empire were to the crusade; and as his entreaties suggest, he knew how vital the crusade was to Louis. Above all it would have been useful to use Sicily, the emperor's territory, as a supply point in preparing for the crusade.[82] All this and more were offered to the French king if he could convince the pope to lift the deposition.[83]

Two royal visits to the Lyonnais to discuss the reconciliation of the two lords of the world accomplished nothing concrete in this direction.[84] Although recognizing the intensity of Louis's zeal for the crusade, the pope remained firm. And here one senses something of the precariousness of Louis's position. It was hard for him to know exactly who was right and who was wrong. The king's actions after the crusade—his acceptance in the 1260s of the necessity of putting aside Hohenstaufen claims to the empire—suggests that he finally came to believe that the papacy, though ridiculously uncompromising, was basically accurate in its evaluation of the imperial situation.[85] But years were to intervene before Louis could come to this conclusion

[79] Layettes, II, nos. 3562-63. In these documents of November 1246—also printed in Huillard-Bréholles, Historia diplomatica, VI, pt. 1, pp. 465-66—Frederick ordered his officials ("justitiariis, magistris camerariis, magistris procuratoribus, magistris fundicariis et universis per regnum Sicilie constitutis, fidelibus suis") to supply "equos, arma, victualia et necessaria quelibet"; to the merchants of the empire he ordered that they provide Louis cum victualibus et rebus aliis. Within a few months Louis acknowledged the emperor's promise; Hulliard-Bréholles, VI, pt. 1, pp. 500-502. As late as July 1249 Frederick was still promising supplies to Louis (Huillard-Bréholles, VI, pt. 2, pp. 710-13) and to Alfonse—one thousand pack horses and fifty war horses (Huillard-Bréholles, VI, pt. 2, pp. 748-50). Cf. also MP, V, 70.

[80] Huillard-Bréholles, Historia diplomatica, VI, pt. 2, p. 640: "Ipso anno (July 1248) Fridericus venit in Aste et nuntios mandavit ad illustrem regem Franciae, exponens se et terram et homines suos ad passagium suum contra paganos, sicut publice dicebatur. . . ." Cf. also Layettes, II, no. 3380 (22 September 1245): ". . . predicto rege (Ludovico) ad deffensionem Xpistianitatis et statum pacificum conservandum in cismarinis partibus remanente, vel una cum eo, si hoc melius viderit eligendum, ad transmarinas partes per nos aut Conradum karissimum filium nostrum, Romanorum in regem electum, et regni Jerosolimitani heredem, omine prospero transfetare. . . ."

[81] Layettes, II, no. 3380 (22 September 1245); Huillard-Bréholles, Historia diplomatica, VI, pt. 1, pp. 472-74 (November/December 1246). Frederick's appeal is considered briefly by Purcell, Papal Crusading Policy, pp. 73-74.

[82] Layettes, II, no. 3562.

[83] Huillard-Bréholles, Historia diplomatica, VI, pt. 2, p. 640: "ut ipse dominus rex (Ludovicus) cum domino papa sic faceret quod releveratur a sententia excommunicationis et depositionis . . . sed nihil facere potuit." Cf. also pp. 745-46.

[84] These are discussed in several sources: Salimbene, Cronica, I, 256; MP, IV, 484, 504, 523-24; Guillaume de Nangis's life of Saint Louis, HF, XX, 352-57; and the latter's abbreviated chronicle, HF, XX, 551-52. See also Maret, "Concile général," p. 450.

[85] Below chapter 7 nn. 126-29.

and allow the sort of military effort against the Hohenstaufen that the papacy had been urging since the 1240s.[86]

Whatever may be said of the political motives of the papacy in all this strife, there were moral interests at stake which probably obliged Louis to refrain from too much maneuvering for position. Since the pope spoke as the moral leader of Christendom, Louis could not oppose him (and even an appeal for arbitration could look like opposition) without considering the moral aspects of the papacy's case. The problem was that Louis IX, for all the bravado, was severely constrained by his morality. If he might threaten to seize the revenues of the church, if he might bluster about the rights of Charlemagne in the church,[87] he did so knowing that morally, as opposed to politically, his salvation lay with the church.

In the contest of empire and papacy, morality consistently *appeared* to be on the pope's side.[88] Although Louis did not recognize the emperor's deposition, it is hard to believe that he was unimpressed by prevailing opinions on Frederick II. He was no doubt acquainted with the stories of the emperor's atheism or, at the best, of his apostasy;[89] and it is almost certain that he believed in these to a considerable degree. Frederick was known as a man who killed or imprisoned bishops—among them French bishops as Louis was aware.[90] He was a man whose pride countenanced a physical attack—even assassination—of the pope himself.[91] At every juncture, Louis had found it necessary to oppose these extreme measures with force or the threat of force.[92]

This moral aspect of the papal-imperial struggle had direct relevance for the survival of the crusade. Like Henry III, the emperor does not seem to have been impressed by Louis's superior moral position as a crusader. All Europe was attentive to the rumor that Frederick had informed his friend, the sultan, of the most vital military details of Louis's expedition.[93] And immediately after Louis was released from captivity in Egypt in 1250, the crusaders in his circle learned of emissaries whom the emperor had sent ostensibly to secure

---

[86] Strayer, "Crusade against Aragon," p. 108.   [87] Above nn. 47-54.

[88] I underscore the word *appeared* because Purcell has shown that the papal legate sent to Germany publicly to preach Louis's crusade was secretly instructed by the pope to preach the crusade against Frederick II; *Papal Crusading Policy*, p. 75.

[89] Kantorowicz, *Kaiser Friedrich*, I, 550-632 (Frederick as Antichrist).

[90] The incidents, in the thirties, are reported, for example, by Nangis (*HF*, xx, 330-33). See also Huillard-Bréholles, *Historia diplomatica*, VI, pt. 1, pp. 1-3.

[91] MP, IV, 605-7. Cf. Berger, *SL et Innocent IV*, pp. 95, 262-63 (and the notes).

[92] Guillaume de Nangis, *HF*, xx, 330-33; MP, IV, 392; Huillard-Bréholles, *Historia diplomatica*, VI, pt. 1, pp. 1-3, 544-47. See also Berger, *SL et Innocent IV*, pp. 262-63.

[93] Purcell, *Papal Crusading Policy*, p. 76, by her way of phrasing her analysis, seems to throw some suspicion not on the existence but on the truth of the rumor.

the king's release. In their view the emissaries had actually come to persuade the Moslems to keep the king locked up.[94]

The late 1240s were thus for Louis years filled with dilemmas. Concern about the paranoia and obduracy of the papacy balanced itself neatly with his suspicions of the emperor.[95] What Louis himself would not compromise on, however, was the crusade. The Italian friar, Salimbene, like Matthew Paris, tells us that Innocent IV called upon the French king to delay his departure for the East in the interest of the papacy.[96] When Louis refused, Innocent looked elsewhere for support. He eventually turned to the Frenchman's rival, the English king.[97] Acting in Louis's absence, Blanche of Castile kept the pope in a public posture of urging the king of England to help the French crusade.[98] Despite this the pope would not allow English crusaders to leave their country in 1249.[99] Frederick II turned his attention to the English monarch as well and tried to bring him over to the imperial side, but without success.[100]

Perhaps Louis found some small comfort in the pope's solicitation of Henry III as his active ally in his struggle with the emperor. Perhaps he hoped that in spending time and money on imperial affairs, Henry III would have less time and less money to spend on dismembering the French kingdom. But on the face of it the tortuous path Louis followed in trying to play the role of arbiter between pope and emperor is all against this interpretation. He had wanted peace in Europe, and he did not get it. On the eve of his departure, the empire was still aflame. With England, at best he had a truce which would be threatened twice during his absence. It is no wonder that Germans and Englishmen contributed so little to the French king's expedition.[101]

Spaniards—Castilians and Aragonese—also contributed little. Although Blanche was a Castilian princess and Louis greatly admired the reigning king of Castile, the future Saint Ferdinand, the French could neither have expected nor desired the Castilians to suspend their own efforts at *reconquista* in the interest of the Eastern

[94] Joinville, chap. LXXXVIII. See also chaps. XLI, XLII, LXV, for further notices of Frederick's reputation in the East.

[95] It seems unnecessary to continue this dreary history through every failed attempt at negotiation. The following sources have additional relevant material: MP, v, 22, 171, 601; Huillard-Bréholles, *Historica diplomatica*, VI, pt. 1, pp. 463-64, and pt. 2, pp. 641, 643-46, 710-13, 745-48, 769-71. There is some helpful discussion in Berger, *SL et Innocent IV*, pp. 110, 232-33, 371; and Meyer, *Ludwig IX*, pp. 22-37, 45-48.

[96] Salimbene, *Cronica*, I, 303-4.

[97] MP, v, 135.

[98] Ibid., 274.

[99] Ibid., 135.

[100] Huillard-Bréholles, *Historia dipolmatica*, VI, pt. 2, pp. 644-46.

[101] Below chapter 4 nn. 35-36.

crusade.[102] It may be, however, that Spain—or, rather, Castile—was considered a timely symbol of Holy War. At least, Louis showed his appreciation of the historic role of the Castilians by donating to the see of Toledo, in 1248, a precious relic of the Passion of Christ, part of the huge cache of relics he had purchased some years before from the Latin emperor of Constantinople.[103]

With the other major Spanish kingdom, Aragon, things were quite different. Here, as in the case of England, war or the threat of war intruded itself into prospects for the crusade. Aragon had supported Raymond Trencavel, the rebel viscount of Béziers in 1240.[104] It had also given support to the rebellions of Count Raymond of Toulouse[105] and of Hugh de Lusignan, the count of La Marche.[106] After the final defeat of the rebels in 1243 and in line with policy toward the English, who had also supported the rebels, Louis attempted a rapprochement with Aragon. Though not defined by truce (Aragon had never directly attacked France)[107] the probability of such an effort is suggested by a royal letter to the sénéchal or chief royal officer of Carcassonne-Béziers in 1247.

In that letter the sénéchal was instructed to protect and defend the estates of Count Raymond of Toulouse although the count was to pay a visit to Spain (that is, Aragon). Going to Aragon—which had been the rebels' habit and the king's bane for a long time—appears no longer to be construed as a hostile gesture.[108]

We know too little about relations between France and Aragon to be more specific on measures either took to assure the peace. There must have been efforts, for there were surely problems. King James of Aragon had been as eager as the count of Toulouse to wed the last daughter of the count of Provence, a match which was thwarted, as we have seen, by the timely action of Louis IX in securing the young girl's hand for his own brother, Charles of Anjou.[109] In a sense James's ef-

[102] MP, v, 311. See also Purcell, *Papal Crusading Policy*, p. 67; cf. Labarge, *SL*, p. 74.

[103] Riant, *Exuviae*, II, 137-38. The expenses of two Spaniards (to carry the precious gift back?) are recorded in the Account for the Ascension term 1248 as eleven pounds two shillings; *HF*, XXI, 262. On the relics, see below chapter 7 nn. 71-81.

[104] *Layettes*, II, no. 2942; *HGL*, VIII, c. 1067; cf. Guillaume de Puylaurens, *HF*, XX, 767. See also Shneidman, *Rise of the Aragonese-Catalan Empire*, II, 311; and Hillgarth, *Problem of a Catalan Mediterranean Empire*, pp. 13-14.

[105] *Layettes*, II, nos. 2905-6; *HGL*, VIII, cc. 1055-58; cf. Guillaume de Puylaurens, *HF*, XX, 767-68.

[106] *Layettes*, II, no. 2941. [107] Cf. Labarge, *SL*, p. 89.

[108] *HGL*, VIII, c. 1222: "Ludovicus, &c. dilecto & fideli suo J. de Cranis, &c. Cum dilectus et fidelis noster consanguineus R., comes Tholose, debeat ad partes Hyspanie profisci, mandamus vobis, quatinus in terra ipsius vel in eis, que ad ipsum pertinent, nihil interim forefaciatis, sed terram ipsius interim, donec redierit, deffendatis et protegatis."

[109] Above nn. 20-23; and Labarge, *SL*, pp. 88-90.

fort in the marriage was merely the natural extension of his territorial desires as a Mediterranean prince, for he came from a family whose origins were in Montpellier, on the French littoral, and whose patrimonial interests were still extensive there. These interests themselves must have complicated Louis's relations with him. They will be dealt with at a later time since they were involved deeply in the arduous preparations that Louis made in building the port which he intended his crusaders to use when they departed France.[110]

Two facts, however, seem to show that despite the lack of direct information the king of France did manage to convey his feelings to the Aragonese and that the Aragonese king understood and reacted beneficently to them. The first is simply the absence of military confrontation between the two kingdoms from 1245 to 1254. After a long period of hostility and suspicion, the importance of this interlude cannot be ignored. The second is the fact that a treaty would reconcile most of the jurisdictional problems facing the kingdoms within a few years after Louis IX's return from the Holy Land.[111] We can only guess that some such promise of a final and mutual working out of problems was conveyed to James by an emissary of Louis in the crowded years of the eve of the crusade.

I have used the word *crowded* advisedly because the king of France seems to have had a real vision of a European crusade. That meant not only the traditional great *dominia* were to be involved, but lesser principalities as well. All had an interest in the treasury of salvation that lay open for those who risked their lives in the name of the Eternal Christ. Not just Frenchmen could earn "the respect and gratitude of God and of men."[112] The guiding principles were two: first, where Louis had influence, he should use it to bring concord to intra-Christian rivalries. Second, where it was possible he should turn the attention of other princes to the crusade.

There were, for example, rather extensive negotiations with King Haakon of Norway for aid in the crusade. Although he did not join Louis in 1248, he insisted that it was only because he was impatient to get started on his own venture.[113] The truth was somewhat different. It is the general consensus that Haakon never intended to go to the East and that he used the clerical levy raised in his lands for his own purposes.[114] On the other hand, it has been argued that Haakon's

---

[110] Below chapter 4 n. 66.　　　[111] Below chapter 7 nn. 93-94.
[112] "St. Louis' Letter Concerning His Expedition," p. 254. For a discussion of the technical theological side of the grace obtainable by the devoted crusader, see Purcell, *Papal Crusading Policy*, pp. 36-51 (cf. also pp. 62-63).
[113] MP, VI, 651.
[114] Tillemont, *Vie de SL*, III, 113; Beaurepaire, *Saint-Germain-en-Laye*, p. 46; Strayer, "Crusades of Louis IX," p. 163.

failure to live up to his promise was due to his statesmanlike concern for the protection of northern Europe from the Mongols.[115]

Whether Louis was gullible enough to believe that Haakon would carry through on his own is a reasonably important question, for an answer to it might throw some light on the French king's state of mind. It seems to me that Louis was unsure of the ability (or desire) of the Norwegian king to mount an expedition. This may explain why he went so far as to offer to provision any Norwegian ships that stopped in French ports on their way to the Holy War.[116] That some Norwegians actually did make it to the Holy Land even in this case, that is, where it is so clear that the prince was not keen on' helping Louis IX, indicates at least that the prospect of a new crusade was beginning to capture men's imaginations once again.[117] We only know of the details of Louis's negotiations with Haakon because a chronicler, Matthew Paris, was asked to carry them out for the French king.[118] It would not be wrong to believe that what the French king tried to accomplish in Norway he tried also elsewhere.

Unfortunately we have only scraps of information on these other efforts. It is assumed, for example, that Louis could not possibly have recruited troops from the princes of Eastern Europe because of the unsettled conditions created by the Tatar invasion.[119] Those conditions had motivated representatives of the Eastern princes to come to the West (for example, to the Council of Lyon) to seek aid for their own threatened principalities.[120] The king's reaction, or so it appears, was to try to go to the heart of the trouble—to appeal to the Tatars themselves. What befitted the role of a crusader prince more? The Tatars were popularly considered the scourge sent by an angered God to chastise His wayward people. Louis intended nothing less than to show God that His children had learned their lesson by turning the great military foe He had sent to punish them into an even greater ally against the Moslem power in the East.

Friars with the requisite linguistic ability were sent to carry out the sensitive negotiations. Lately, owing to renewed Western interest in China, the raft of popular and scholarly literature recounting over and over again this well-known episode has blown it out of all proportion: Louis was utterly unsuccessful in currying favor with the Tatars. Even though they were uncommitted at the time in formal religion, they showed little inclination toward Christianity; they did not mollify

[115] Gjerset, *History of the Norwegian People*, pp. 430-31.   [116] MP, IV, 652.
[117] Joinville, chap. XCVI.   [118] MP, IV, 651-52.
[119] Purcell, *Papal Crusading Policy*, p. 69.
[120] MP, IV, 387, 430-31; Guillaume de Nangis, *HF*, XX, 342-43. Joinville, too (chap. XXX), gives evidence that the Eastern Empire was unable to help Louis's crusade and, in fact, sought to have the king of France divert some of his resources to it.

their aggressive policy toward Christian Europe; and they viewed the Christian embassy with contempt. Those are the facts. As Joinville put it, "The king, you may be sure, repented of having sent . . . [the] ambassadors."[121]

Still, Louis continued to try to bring peace to the Christian world. Although he failed with the Tatars, he had considerable success among minor Christian potentates who held him in higher esteem than the khan. The Templars and the Hospitallers were at odds on Cyprus; the king felt it was his duty, in the words of Matthew Paris, to pacify them "by pure and holy counsel."[122] When there was discord between the princes of Armenia and Antioch, Louis intervened and brought them to an agreement on a two-year truce.[123] To accomplish this it appears that he had to allow many of his own men to go to the aid of the Armenian ruler against the Moslems.[124]

These successes—no matter how flattering they might have been—were too little to do much good. What was essential was that the king had been unable to persuade the three most important political leaders of the West besides himself—Innocent IV, Emperor Frederick II, King Henry III—to put aside their own grievances in order to aid him in his crusade. He failed because he was dealing with powers as assuredly convinced of their God-given destinies as he was of his. Many of their problems loomed larger to them than the dream of the conquest of Jerusalem. All this was an important setback, but perhaps—or so Louis must have still believed in 1248—not a fatal one.

[121] Joinville, chap. xcv. In addition, on the French side of the problem of the Mongols, see Guillaume de Nangis, *HF*, xx, 352-67; Joinville, chaps. xxix, xciii (cf. chaps. xciv, cxiv); MP, iv, 607, and v, 87; as well as the histories of crusader events by Johannes de Columna, *HF*, xxiii, 114-15, and by the continuator of Guillaume de Tyr's chronicle ("Continuatio de Guillaume de Tyr," p. 569). The vast majority of material on this subject has now been summarized and analyzed by Bezzola, *Die Mongolen in Abendländischer Sicht*.

[122] MP, v, 71: "Rex interim Francorum, sano et sancto fretus consilio, multos magnates tam in Cipro, quam in aliis Christianorum climatibus, discordes, et Templarios et Hospitalarios plenius pacificavit, ut securius, nullis post terga relictis offendiculis, iter arriperet inchoatum."

[123] Johannes de Columna, *HF*, xxiii, 118: "ut inter se treugam per duos annos facerent."

[124] Johannes de Columna (ibid.) suggests that six hundred crossbowmen were sent by Louis. If he is talking about the same incident, Joinville (chap. xxxi) says that the men went to Armenia on their own to make a little money as mercenaries or from booty, and none returned.

• 3 •

GOVERNMENTAL REFORM

If the preservation of domestic order and international peace were the first requirement in preparing for the crusade, reform of royal administration was surely the second. The early years of Louis's reign, taken up by such demanding matters as the suppression of rebellion and resisting the attempts of the English to reconquer their lost possessions, were hardly fitted to the thoroughgoing reconsideration of administrative principles and techniques which was so necessary to the successful operation of government in the long-run. That there were general ideas about what government ought to be and how it ought to operate goes without question; that these ideas had a tenuous relation to reality after twenty years of almost continuous domestic turmoil is equally clear. To examine the structure of royal administration on the eve of the crusade and to describe Louis's attempts at circumventing or reforming it in the interest of the crusade are the two goals of the present chapter.

At the center of French government throughout Louis's reign were three departments—each primitively organized—the financial service, the chancery, and the judicature or, as it would eventually be called, the *Parlement* of Paris. The duties of these departments were not distinct since all three were variant groupings of the royal council. The king was the real focus of government. Dependent on good arithmeticians to go over the financial accounts and on clerks (many of whom were beneficed clergy) to write his letters, he was still the chief and most active judge and policy maker. His curia was constituted by great churchmen and nobles (the *proceres*), by administrators of the departments, and by local royal agents whenever they came to Paris to make reports. The historic problem of medieval central administration, the existence of overmighty household officials, had been solved by Philip II Augustus, Louis's grandfather, before 1223. There was no longer a *grand sénéchal du royaume*; the powers of the *grand chambrier* had been attenuated; and the chancellorship was ordinarily kept vacant. Government, in other words, was personal and very much royal and unbureaucratic at the center; and to the extent that Louis could keep in his own hands all the disparate threads of royal policies, this situation would remain unchanged throughout his rule.[1]

[1] The remarks in this paragraph have been synthesized from the following sources:

The flow of information from this central administration to what might be called, for want of a more felicitous phrase, the field administration was tortuous at best. The king would formulate policy either alone or in council;[2] he would then direct the chancery clerks to "translate" the orders arising from his policy into writs, but the forms of these instruments were decidedly inferior in economy of language and standardization to English writs.[3] After preparing the document and occasionally registering it for the archives, the chancery clerk would have it sealed and sent by *cursor* or *nuncius* to the appropriate province.[4] There it would be announced[5] or received by a local clerk on behalf of the local officer or by the local officer himself.[6] It was the local administrator's duty to carry out the order or assign a subordinate for that task or, if it were more appropriate, to reformulate the order through editing for the person or institution that it affected.[7] The transmission of the message, from start to finish, might take six weeks.[8]

Under certain precise conditions, these procedures were abbreviated. When the central government was acting as a court, for example, the litigants were informed directly of the decision probably by the king himself since the personal role of the king as judge seems to

---

Lot and Fawtier, *Histoire*, II, 52, 54-55, 57-58; Tessier, *Diplomatique*, pp. 134-37; Declareuil, *Histoire générale du droit*, pp. 450-56; and Lecoy de La Marche, *France sous SL*, pp. 63, 71 ("les conseillers du roi et les autres officiers associés au gouvernement central n'avaient qu'une autorité assez effacée en face de personne du souverain"). Cf. Shennan, *Parlement*, pp. 16-17, and Griffiths, "New Men."

[2] Cf. Griffiths, "New Men," p. 268.

[3] The best brief discussion is still that of Giry, *Manuel de diplomatique*, pp. 757-60, but he may have exaggerated the quality (*une clarté elegante*) of the *lettres royales*. See also Lot and Fawtier, *Histoire*, II, 85-94.

[4] This remark is appropriate to the entirety of Louis's reign, as are most of the remarks in this paragraph. For the central staff's *cursores* circa 1256, see *HF*, XXI, 352; *clerici regis*, without further designation, might also carry messages; *HF*, XXIV, "Chronologie," p. 249, document quoted at note 14. See also Lot and Fawtier, *Histoire*, II, 85-94.

[5] For example (year 1255): "Voluit etiam dominus rex quod istud perceptum ac inhibitio sic facta per ipsum prenominatis civibus viva voce fieret publice apud Cathalanum per nuncios suos quos ad hoc faciendum et publicandum duxerit destinandos"; Pélicier, "Deux lettres," pp. 229-31.

[6] For two interesting in-depth explorations of the staffs of field administrators in different regions, see Strayer, *Royal Domain*, preface; and Michel, *Beaucaire*. On the administrative resources of local officials, cf. Rogozinski, "Counsellors."

[7] One can get a good glimpse of this procedure in action from a letter of 1262 in *HF*, XXIV, 692 no. 1.

[8] The travel, for example to the south, might require this much time; cf. Bisson, "A Propos d'un registre municipal," pp. 84-85, who estimates twenty-six days to the south. Alef has calculated the maximum rate Frenchmen were traveling in their own county in the late Middle Ages as about ninety kilometers per day which does not compare well with rates in contemporary Muscovy or England; "Origin . . . of the Muscovite Postal Service," pp. 1-2. See also Henneman, *Royal Taxation*, p. 116.

have been quite pronounced in France.[9] It was just as likely in nonjud-icial matters that a representative of the organization or person for whom an order was intended or an interested party might come to Paris to receive the king's will *ore proprio* and thus circumvent com-pletely the procedures described above.[10] In such cases, however, it is a reasonable hypothesis that field administrators would be apprised of the king's will in the normative fashion.

The difference between the transmission of information applicable to a specific person or institution and information of a more public character was not very great. "Legislation" and "propaganda," two of the most obvious and important types of public information, fitted in comfortably to the traditional scheme. With regard to the first, most *ordonnances* in France were offshoots of the judicial decisions of the curia. A single order arising out of a judgment and, then, transmitted to a single officer might be taken by other officers as a general expres-sion of the king's will. It became *mutatis mutandis* an *ordonnance* or *établissement*.[11]

With regard to propaganda, any large meeting of the council, for a trial, for example, might become the setting for an exhortatory speech from the king's own lips. At worst, the message would spread informally; at best (or at the traditional best) it would be transmitted and channeled through clergy, received at the other end by clergy, and announced to the *populus Gallicanus* by clergy.[12] Another reason-able alternative was for the king to take the message himself into the provinces. To the extent that medieval kingship was peripatetic by na-ture, this alternative was continually employed. As we shall have occa-

[9] The personal role of Louis IX at *parlement* has been noted by Shennan, *Parlement*, p. 17. His active role as a judge will be discussed at some length in chapter six. The direct assumption of giving judgments evidently contrasts with the situation in England where royal judges had the obligation or privilege of pronouncing judgments even in the presence of the king; however, in England too one finds that the specialization could be put aside: for example in January 1235 Henry III "ore proprio pronuntiavit judicium" (see Turner, *King and His Courts*, pp. 136, 245).

[10] Petit, "Jully-les-Nonnains," pp. 771, 781, quotes evidence of one such occasion (June 1248) in which Hugo, the bishop of Langres, wrote to the collectors of the clerical levy for the crusade informing them that Louis IX "dixit ore proprio" that the monks of Jully-les-Nonnains should be exempt from the levy forever.

[11] Griffiths, "New Men," pp. 256, 267, 271; see also Cazelles, "Guerre privée," pp. 539, 543. Cf. Bisson, "A Propos d'un registre municipal," p. 88.

[12] Judging from the formulary of Jean de Caux who inventoried the possessions of the royal archives in the 1280s, *prelati* as a matter of course publicized the king's orders; see *Formulaires*, no. 6, items 7-9. I will be citing this formulary in many places. In some cases it is possible to determine more or less precisely when the inventoried records were first composed; in other instances it is not. Nonetheless, by its date the formulary at least does not err on the side of modernity. On sensitive issues where precise dating is necessary I will make only qualified use of the information in the formulary. On the issue raised in the text, see also Du Cange, "On the Origin and Usage of Tournaments," in Johnes, *Memoirs*, II, 87, 90; and *Formulaires*, no. 6, items 3, 117-18.

sion in the future to note, from one point of view it reached a new degree of importance and sophistication on the eve of the crusade.[13]

This description of the flow of information between the central government and the provinces suggests the intrinsic difficulties which accompanied the transmission of the king's will and policies to the people. The description would apply both to *Francia*, the heart of the royal patrimony,[14] and to Picardy, Languedoc, and the Mâconnais, newer accretions to the domain in which the king was also the immediate lord. There were, however, potentially troublesome exceptions to this system, of which Normandy and the appanages are the two we need to consider.

When the French conquered Normandy in 1204, it is quite probable that the machinery of its government was in advance of royal techniques.[15] Realizing this, but also perhaps to assuage the Normans, they preserved native institutions.[16] To a limited degree, royal institutions were superimposed on them, and this must have made government slightly more inefficient; but in general, administration in Normandy retained its pre-conquest features. The Exchequer, an advanced judicial and financial institution, constituted the machinery of highest resort in the province—and appeal from it to the curia at Paris was always rare or deliberately obscured by fictions.[17] Norman law operated as it had since the reign of Henry II Plantagenet.[18] Even the dates for collection of royal income in Normandy (Easter and Michaelmas) were not altered to coincide with collection dates in other parts of the domain (Candlemas, Ascension, All Saints').[19] Perhaps, this leniency with their institutions was successful in induc-

[13] Below chapter 5 nn. 2-28 and chapter 6 passim, both on the royal itinerary before the crusade and on more general issues raised by peripatetic kingship. On the peripatetic habit of other French kings, see Petit-Dutaillis, *Feudal Monarchy*, p. 321. Cf. Guenée and Lehoux, *Entrées royales*; and Le Patourel, *Norman Empire*, pp. 121-32.

[14] On *Francia* as a geographical term (a small region with Paris at its center), see Mortet, "Constitucions," p. 10 n. 1; and Rigollot, "Étude sur . . . La Trinité," p. 129. Cf. Bloch, *Ile-de-France*, pp. 4-5, who would give a slightly wider definition to the term than the two preceding authors (his evidence, however, is from 1285), but he still excludes the great northern fiefs. Lugge, *"Gallia" und "Francia,"* pp. 169-80, discusses the emerging use of the term *Francia* as a synonym for the whole kingdom.

[15] Strayer, "Normandy and Languedoc," pp. 47-48. In general, on the French absorption of Normandy the works of Strayer are standard. The most important of these will be cited in subsequent notes.

[16] Ibid., p. 49, and idem, *Administration of Normandy*, passim.

[17] Strayer, *Administration of Normandy*, p. 14; idem, "Exchequer and Parlement," pp. 656-57.

[18] Of course, it continued to evolve and, in time, it was affected by royal practices, but Norman custom for a century constituted a distinct thread in French legal practice. Cf. Strayer, "Normandy and Languedoc," p. 54; and idem, "Novel Disseisin," p. 6. See also Appendix Three.

[19] Strayer, *Administration of Normandy*, pp. 39-40. However, Anglo-Norman coinage was the one feature of the fiscal system in Normandy that obviously had to be

ing the Normans to accept the conquest of their province with equanimity. It is a fact that Normandy showed the least residual hostility to the royal presence of all the provinces that were conquered in the early thirteenth century.

It should not be supposed, however, that the persistent anomalies of royal administration in Normandy were allowed to compromise in any way the reality of royal power in the province. The crown may have lost some efficiency, but it gained a great deal of loyalty by making sure that all the important functionaries of the institutions that were preserved were themselves non-Normans; indeed, in the earliest years after the conquest, the military commanders who had carried through the conquest were sometimes given the top administrative posts.[20] Moreover, the king as duke of Normandy was as much a personal governor there as in the old royal domain. He exercised the traditional extensive powers of the duke.[21] Both by the direct assimilation of the ducal properties and by confiscation, he had vast properties in the duchy, and he was keen to increase them.[22] Finally, the province was close to his capital; he could and did visit the duchy once or twice per year.[23]

The appanages, an exception of potentially more consequence, were the counties given over to Louis IX's younger brothers (and later other cadet princes) following, at least in outline, the principles and wishes of the late Louis VIII. Artois went to Robert in 1237; Poitou (part of the old Angevin lands), Auvergne, and adjacent properties in the southwest to Alfonse in 1241; and Anjou and Maine (also former English possessions) to Charles in 1246. In every case rights of government, with a few exceptions, were also turned over to the cadet princes. They ruled with something approaching palatine force—although it was possible to appeal from their comital courts to the royal curia when failure of justice had occurred.[24]

---

supplanted by the introduction of French royal coinage (*tournois*); Blancard, *Réforme monétaire*.

[20] Strayer, "Normandy and Languedoc," p. 49; idem, *Administration of Normandy*, p. 92; Petit-Dutaillis, *Feudal Monarchy*, p. 321. On the career of Cadoc, a mercenary given the post of royal representative after the conquest, see Strayer, *Royal Domain*, p. 18.

[21] Strayer, "Normandy and Languedoc," p. 48.

[22] Ibid., p. 45; idem, *Royal Domain*, pp. 17-18.

[23] The itinerary of Louis IX: *HF*, xxi, 408-23 (with additions, modifications, and corrections, l-li, 498-99, 971). Of some value are the indications of royal residences (397-403; xxii, xxxv-xxxvi); and the information in the *Register of Eudes of Rouen*, Franciscan archbishop of Rouen and friend of the king. See also Brühl, *Fodrum*, i, 242 n. 90; Poulain, *Séjours . . . en Normandie*; and Petit-Dutaillis, *Feudal Monarchy*, p. 321.

[24] The views in this paragraph have been synthesized from the following discussions of the appanage system: Wood, *French Apanages*; Lot and Fawtier, *Histoire*, ii, 105-6, 122-39; Henneman, *Royal Taxation*, pp. 8-9; and Wood, "*Regnum Francie.*" Specific exceptions to the general statements laid down in the text which are relevant to the pres-

Louis's influence in the appanages is uncertain. His brothers often imitated his policies; and just as often he found something worth imitating in theirs. General principles of government tended to be accepted by all of them.[25] There would be times, such as 1247 and 1248 in Anjou and Maine, when the evidence suggests that the king rather than his brothers was directing the administration of the appanages.[26] But basically internal government remained in the princes' hands, and Louis got the results he wanted by means of his brothers not despite them.[27]

In sum, to have his will transmitted to the provinces and to give his ideas publicity, there were traditional methods which Louis IX was more or less obliged to follow. Normandy presents only a minor exception to this conclusion—there was, indeed, a traditional method, but it was slightly different from historic Capetian methods. The appanages, with the cadet princes as mediators between the king and his subjects, constituted a major structural divergence from customary Capetian methods of governing, but even in the appanages Louis could feel confident, as far as it can be determined, that his brothers would put no obstacles deliberately between his legitimate wishes and their transmission to local officialdom and, thence, to his ordinary subjects.

He could not have said the same about his relations with the great independently administered fiefs, like Aquitaine, the county of Toulouse, Burgundy, Flanders, Brittany, and Champagne-Brie. The list itself encapsulizes half the problems that had plagued the early reign. The lord of Aquitaine was Henry III of England; Toulouse remained hostile and intermittently rebellious through the early 1240s; between them, Brittany and Champagne had been the seedbed of every major insurrection in the north. But politics aside, in juridical terms the influence of Louis in these fiefs was seriously compromised by the structure of the vassalic system.

---

ent study will be discussed separately. See, for example, below n. 76, and chapter 4 n. 167. There has been an attempt recently to reevaluate the question of the appanages, especially with regard to the law of succession; Lewis, "Capetian Apanages."

[25] The only serious thorough work that has been done on the appanage administration of one of Louis's brothers concerns the government of Alfonse of Poitiers (see the works of Bisson, Dossat, and Fournier and Guébin listed in the bibliography). The old book by Boutaric, *SL et Alfonse*, is still useful; but the discussion by Molinier in *HGL*, VII, is better, although he cautions (VII, 476) against simply equating the policies of the brothers. See also below n. 90.

[26] Below n. 89.

[27] This conclusion should not be allowed to disguise the fact that administrative and jurisdictional difficulties over reserved rights could intrude themselves into the relations of Louis and the cadet princes. On such problems in the case of Artois, below n. 76. Carolus-Barré, *Chronologie des baillis de Clermont-en-Beauvaisis*, pp. 4-5, 8, 9, describes some other problems with the appanage of one of Louis's sons, Robert, the ancestor of the Bourbon line.

Unless rebellion had led to temporary confiscation, royal authority in the great fiefs was limited to the vassalic obligations of the feudatories. Differing from fief to fief, such obligations, like providing troops for the feudal host and suit at court, were important as far as they went.[28] Nonetheless, any great feudatory, no matter what the specific juridical aspects of his subordination to the crown might be, could have made it quite difficult in normal times for the king's wishes to reach an audience in his seigneurie. Unless the king were to challenge the very nature of the feudal relationship, one would expect him to be dependent largely on the good will of the seigneur in making his policies known and in having them carried out.

With those seigneurs who showed good will and enthusiasm there was no problem. With the others—whether their obduracy was a product of latent hostility or of their preoccupation with other questions—the problem was serious. Preparations for the crusade threw the issue into high relief. We have already watched the king grapple with those barons who rebelled in 1241-1243, and have suggested that he used the simple expedient of taking them on crusade along with other barons whose loyalty was suspect.[29] But this, in one sense, ignores the broader and more fundamental issue of stimulating support for the crown—and for the crown's crusade in particular—from the subjects of these seigneurs.

Raymond of Toulouse, for example, raised a sizable force for the king's crusade largely composed of Albigensian heretics granted absolution by Innocent IV.[30] Raymond's death, before his scheduled date of departure, evidently led to the evaporation of this detachment and perhaps the substitution of mercenaries hired from other regions by the royal government.[31] This conclusion is based on the fragmentary data which I have collected on approximately 290 supporters of the rebellion of 1241-1243. These men—knights, consuls, castel-

---

[28] The essays brought together by Lot and Fawtier, *Histoire*, I, chaps. 5, 7, 9, 11, 14, treat the great fiefs in detail (see also on La Marche the remarks of Villard, *Justices seigneuriales*, p. 270). An extremely juridical treatment is to be found in Viollet, *Histoire des institutions*, II, 448-66 (there is an interesting criticism of this juridical approach by Gutnova, "Sintez v oblasti istorii prava"); a brief and valuable summing up is given in Henneman, *Royal Taxation*, pp. 8-9. The proper setting for understanding the importance of the administrative autonomy of the great fiefs is of course the political history of the kingdom of France. To my mind, the two clearest expositions of this history remain Fawtier, *Capetian Kings of France*, and Petit-Dutaillis, *Feudal Monarchy*.

[29] Above chapter 2 nn. 14-26.

[30] *Layettes*, III, nos. 3625, 3651; *HGL*, VI, 788.

[31] The codicil to Raymond's will provided that fifty knights be raised from his personal fortune and despatched to the Holy Land; *Layettes*, III, no. 3803. Since, in 1249, Blanche of Castile handled the translation of the county to its designated successor, Alfonse, who was on crusade, it is not unlikely that this provision was carried out. I do not know who made up the reconstituted contingent.

41

lans—had been the backbone of the rebellion.[32] In the end, almost none of these "second echelon rebels" accompanied the hated northerner on crusade.

Even if, after his defeat, Raymond VII had put his whole life and soul into trying to overcome popular hatred of the conquerors in the county of Toulouse (a premise I doubt), the evidence adduced in the preceding paragraph shows that he failed. And although his failure may not have been typical, the suggestion that any of the defeated barons became completely loyal and enthusiastic transmitters of the royal will in the 1240s would require powerful proofs. I know of none.

With two of the major fiefs, however, peculiar situations had beneficial implications for Louis's preparations for the crusade. Both situations had fortuitously put important power, *de facto* if not *de jure*, into the king's hands, and with this happy development (from his point of view) he could be more sanguine about his traditional dependence on the seigneurs. The first of these examples concerns the county of Champagne.

Champagne was a rich seigneurie in the mid-thirteenth century, but its count, Thibaut IV, was unable to rule it effectively. His activities in Champagne in the 1220s and 1230s, in which he played a substantial role in the rebellions against the crown, might have had repercussions when he inherited the kingdom of Navarre in 1234, but Thibaut was not only an ineffective lord, he was inconsistent. He had earned the distrust of the baronial opposition in the early years of the reign by changing sides at a decisive moment and the suspicion of a wide selection of people by his attempt to gain power in France by making love to the pious Blanche of Castile. Best known not as a statesman but as a troubador, he perhaps preferred the pursuits of aristocratic culture to politics.[33]

Unrequited in love and a failure in his last attempt at rebellion in 1236, he was banished from Champagne and took (or was forced to take) the crusader's vow which he fulfilled in 1239. That enterprise, described by a recent historian as "a strange expedition," "a maze of confusion and cross-purposes . . . viewed without enthusiasm, if not actually with distaste," was a disastrous failure. Certainly, memory of it had something to do with the opposition to Louis's vow a few years later.[34]

---

[32] I determined these men from the pacts of submission published in the second volume of the *Layettes*; cf. above chapter 2 n. 10.

[33] On Thibaut's character and the facts narrated in this paragraph, see Labarge, *SL*, pp. 34-44, 58-60; cf. Evergates, *Feudal Society in the Bailliage of Troyes*, pp. 3-4.

[34] Painter, "Crusade of Theobald," pp. 463-85 (the quotations are at p. 463 along with notices of additional bibliography on the expedition).

Upon Thibaut's return in 1241, he became extremely interested in the rather backward kingdom of Navarre—then only a shadow compared to the commercially vigorous and politically important county of Champagne. Indeed despite the fact that there were probably no restrictions on his movements, he made only two or three brief trips back to his native territories during the rest of his life.[35] Perhaps distance rekindled his loyalty to the crown: an argument from silence has been made to suggest that he personally helped Louis suppress the rebellion of 1241-1243.[36] But the genesis of Thibaut's new-found loyalty must also be related to the fact that from the time of his obsessive interest in Navarre he and Louis became natural allies in their hostility to the English. In 1244 Thibaut fought a war with Henry III over jurisdictional claims arising from the confused boundary of English Gascony and Navarre. The war ended by truce (subsequently renewed), but the two countries remained hostile.[37]

Given this story of royal relations with Champagne, it was inevitable that the crown should have influence and authority in the county. One effect of the hostility to the English which Louis and Thibaut shared was that the king's wishes in the matter of the crusade found easy access to the sort of second echelon people who had proved so recalcitrant in Languedoc.[38] The ultimate result was that a very large contingent of Champenois lords and knights went on the king's crusade, larger by far, as it turns out, than practically all the contingents except the ones mounted from the royal family itself.[39]

An equally peculiar situation gave Louis considerable influence over the leadership of the county of Flanders where the conflicting

[35] On these events, Arbois de Jubainville, *Histoire . . . de Champagne*, VI, pt. 1, pp. 198-306. See also Evergates, *Feudal Society in the Bailliage of Troyes*, p. 4.

[36] According to Arbois de Jubainville, *Histoire . . . de Champagne*, IV, pt. 1, pp. 328-29, since there are no documents in this period originating in Navarre and Champagne and sealed by the count, he was in neither of his domains. Hence (says Arbois) it is natural to suppose that he was fighting rebels with King Louis.

[37] MP, IV, 396; V, 277; Arbois de Jubainville, *Histoire . . . de Champagne*, IV, pt. 1, pp. 329-30; V, nos. 2684, 2695, 2903.

[38] It may be the case that Thibaut actively put his prestige behind the crusade. He may have attended, for example, a meeting of the royal council at mid-Lent 1247 during which time the league of nobles put forth their demands with the implied threat that some of those who had sworn to go on crusade would not go (above chapter 2 nn. 37, 41). The league was welcomed in Champagne (above chapter 2 n. 34). The idea that Thibaut attended the conference is based on Arbois de Jubainville's reconstruction of his movements at that time (*Histoire . . . de Champagne*, IV, pt. 1, p. 331 n. a, citing Tillemont, *Vie de SL*, III, 147). Cf. on this, despite some evident jumbling of names, the so-called *Continuatio de Guillaume de Tyr*, p. 567; and the chronicle of Baudoin d'Avesnes, *HF*, XXI, 165 and 165 n. 5.

[39] On the number of troops in this contingent, see the arguments below chapter 4 nn. 10-12. Prévost, "Champenois aux croisades," has done a remarkable job in listing the petty Champenois seigneurs who accompanied the king on both his first (pp. 163-65) and his second crusade (pp. 165-77).

claims of the Dampierres and the d'Avesnes to the seigneurie were cause for alarm.[40] The claim of the male Dampierres rested upon the illegitimacy of their elder stepbrothers, the d'Avesnes. Both sets of children had the same mother, Margaret of Flanders, who had inherited Flanders and the less important county of Hainaut through her sister in 1244. Margaret did not love her elder set of sons, the offspring of an illicit marriage to a clerk. She was frightened of the impact that their legitimization—a process which was almost commonplace for important medieval bastards—might have on the inheritance rights of her younger children. It appears as if Margaret was the first person to seek a definitive judgment of the succession in the latter's favor.[41]

She turned to the king of France and to the papal legate who was in France to preach the crusade. The decision they rendered in 1246 recognized the legitimacy of the d'Avesnes but assigned the succession of the county of Flanders to the Dampierre offspring notwithstanding. By way of compensation, the d'Avesnes were to succeed to the county of Hainaut.[42]

The arbitration raises some difficult questions. First of all, Hainaut was an imperial fief.[43] Was it legitimate to decide on the disposition of this fief, even with the mutual consent of the parties to the dispute, without the presence of imperial procurators? It may be true that, from the point of view of the church, there could be no procurators because there was no emperor (Frederick II having been deposed), but if Louis IX did not recognize the deposition (and the evidence is quite unmistakable that he did not),[44] why did he do nothing about the absence of imperial arbiters? Perhaps the answer to this question is that the papal legate could not have participated in proceedings in which the (excommunicated) representatives of Frederick II took part. But if this is so, why did Louis get involved at all? If he sought peace and harmony, that is, if he sought to defuse the latent discontent of the Dampierres, did he not realize that the d'Avesnes, too, might react unfavorably to what they regarded as the denial of their birthright? Or did he think that no one would presume to question the motives or intentions of the French king?

Historians *have* questioned Louis's motives, not only because of the

---

[40] For the salient points of this situation, see Labarge, *SL*, pp. 106, 151-54; Wallon, *SL*, II, 406-12; Kienast, *Deutschland und Frankreich*, III, pp. 624-31.

[41] *Layettes*, II, no. 3403; "Inventaire . . . archives . . . , à Lille," pt. 1, pp. 351-52 no. 860, 358 no. 880 (cf. 376 no. 919).

[42] The collection of documents relevant to the arbitration is published in the *Layettes*, II, nos. 3403, 3406-8, 3527, 3534-35, 3552-53; III, 3730, 3981.

[43] Wallon, *SL*, II, 406-12; Duvivier, *Querelle*, I, 154.

[44] Above chapter 2 n. 78.

dark questions that overlay the arbitration but also because of what appears to be a conflict of interest to his role as arbiter. At issue here is the association of the king with Guillaume Dampierre, the eldest of the Dampierre males and the designated successor to Flanders. The close association of the two as political friends dates from the time when the arguments of the parties to the disputed succession were being reviewed by the king. In 1245, indeed, Guillaume had accompanied Louis to Cluny for sensitive negotiations with the pope about the crusade, negotiations which to this day remain obscure since the participants decided to keep them secret.[45] In 1245 Guillaume had also taken the crusader's vow, a fact noted in the chronicle of Baudoin d'Avesnes, one of the elder set of Countess Margaret's sons; no d'A-vesnes, as far as I know, took the vow.[46] Eventually Guillaume promised a large contingent for the crusade, and Louis helped him finance it.[47] Although this circumstantial evidence proves nothing, it is so open to suspicion that the most thorough historian of the arbitration concluded his discussion of it with an implied accusation against the crown's *Interessenpolitik*: it was "not Saint Louis," he wrote, "who pronounced [the disposition of the fiefs] . . . but the King of France."[48]

Thus far, Louis emerges as a ruler in command of events and official personalities at the center of government. The picture becomes more obscure when one tries to define his capacity to transmit his statements of policy and his specific orders to the provinces. There were traditional or normative structures, cumbersome and inefficient to be sure, to accomplish this in most areas under direct royal administration. On the other hand, the structures applicable to certain of these areas and to provinces outside direct royal administration were considerably more cumbersome, for they depended on the full support of institutions or seigneurs who mediated royal relations with the native population. In Normandy, fortunately, the intrusive features of these mediating institutions were mollified by a number of circumstances. In the appanages, the seigneurs, being the king's brothers and normally in agreement about the goals and operation of government, did not use their position to thwart him. But in the great fiefs the king could have been blocked. Military power, or the threat of military power, gave him a lever in his relations with former rebel sei-

---

[45] Duvivier, *Querelle*, 1, 138-39, 158-60.

[46] *HF*, xxi, 165. For lists of seigneurs who took the cross, see the "Vie de SL" of Guillaume de Nangis, *HF*, xx, 407; and Joinville, chap. LV. I have not found a d'Avesnes on these or any other lists.

[47] Below chapter 4 n. 14 and figure nine.

[48] Duvivier, *Querelle*, 1, 160. For futher discussion on the problems with Flanders, see below chapter 6 nn. 37-38.

gneurs, but it was not the sort of weapon that enamored him of their subjects. Accidents—the situations in Champagne and Flanders—could sometimes open a great seigneurie to his influence. And to watch him use that influence is frequently revealing of his state of mind and his concern for the crusade. But beyond such anomalies, he was dependent in carrying out royal policies on the good will and efficiency (of which there was not much) of the great feudatories. This was proper; he never challenged the principle.

If one allows for the fact that much of the administration of France was simply beyond his ken, the question that remains is how efficacious the king's authority was even in those areas under his direct control. The answer to this question may be stated very simply: Louis had, even by medieval standards, a very inadequate field administration before the crusade. To appreciate fully, however, what he had to work with, the sorts of deficiencies he had to overcome, and finally how he overcame them will require a brief look at provincial administration on the eve of his personal rule.[49]

Provincial administration depended on three types of officers, salaried regional administrators known as (*grands*) *baillis* (or *sénéchaux* in Languedoc),[50] subordinate administrators known as *prévôts*, *bayles*, *viguiers*, or viscounts depending on the regional vocabulary,[51] and a mass of inferior agents—collectors of tolls, keepers of the peace (sergeants), foresters, etc.[52] The crown exercised very little control over ranks lower than the *bailli*. The viscounts of Normandy received salaries which gave the government some leverage there,[53] but the vast majority of *prévôts* and other agents of their rank and below were

[49] There are many accounts of the expansion and development of local administration in France, the best of which I shall be citing in subsequent notes. General discussions which have been helpful in formulating my own synthesis include the summary statements of Laurent, "Bailliage de Sens," pp. 319-21; and the juristic treatment by Viollet, *Histoire des institutions*, III, 247-62. Also interesting from a comparative perspective is Lyon and Verhulst, *Medieval Finance*, especially pp. 20-26, on the origins of the bailiffs of Flanders in the twelfth century and, pp. 41-52, on the parallel developments of local administration in Normandy, Flanders, and *Francia*.

[50] See Appendix One; cf. below n. 121 on salary ranges.

[51] The *prévôts* were subordinate (usually urban) agents in *Francia*; the *bayles* were similar officers in the southwest and south. The viscounts were regional subordinates in Normandy, the *viguiers* in Languedoc. Men called castellans frequently had similar duties although their specific tasks were often narrowly military in nature. For three regional illustrations of terminological variety: (1) with respect to Artois, see Loisne, "Chronologie des baillis . . . d'Artois," pp. 311, 314-25, and Gravier, "Prévôts," pp. 556-58; (2) in Mâcon, see Fournier, "Origines des baillis de Mâcon," pp. 473-76, esp. nos. 1-4; and (3) in Sens, see Laurent, "Bailliage de Sens," p. 322, and Lecoy de La Marche, "Coutumes et péages de Sens," pp. 275-77.

[52] Michel, *Beaucaire*, pp. 56, 79, 92-93, and elsewhere; Strayer, *Royal Domain*, pp. 11-12; Borrelli de Serres, *Recherches*, I, 552-53; Fesler, "French Field Administration," p. 81; Gravier, "Prévôts," pp. 547-51, 807; Dossat, "Tentative de réforme," p. 506.

[53] Gravier, "Prévôts," pp. 557-58; Strayer, *Royal Domain*, pp. 9-11; idem, "Normandy and Languedoc," pp. 52, 54. Cf. Goineau, *Gisors*, pp. 155, 193.

revenue farmers who made their bids to the *baillis* and who, if they won the positions, also made their reports to them.[54]

A few *prévôts* whose *prévôtés* were very near Paris did not strictly conform to this pattern since they rendered their reports and accounts directly to the central government.[55] It is also true that the *prévôté* of Paris was a special case to which generalities about *prévôtine* administration do not apply.[56] Furthermore, the insulation of provincial *prévôtés* from the king could always be overcome by personal inspection. If he had used them, his frequent visits to provinces in the north would have given him the opportunity carefully to observe local conditions free of the mediation of upper level functionaries.[57]

The exceptions and unfulfilled possibilities aside, however, it was the *baillis* and *sénéchaux* who constituted the fundamental administrative contact between the king and his subjects. There was a constant danger that the *baillis*, being resident administrators, would acquire property and a network of relations that would compromise the efficient and honest operation of local government. Moreover, oversight of these administrators' activities was limited to the periodic submission of their accounts to the central government (twice a year in Normandy; three times a year elsewhere)[58] and to the occasional ad hoc inquiries such as had occurred during the reign of Philip Augustus.[59]

The apparent flimsiness of controls over the topmost level of provincial functionaries was aggravated by political conditions in the first part of Louis IX's reign, but no blame need be assigned to the monarchy for this. If Blanche of Castile is not known as a great reformer, it is because she is known as a great savior. The perpetual need for a defensive posture vis-à-vis the baronage had given her little opportunity to evaluate systematically either the structural weaknesses of provincial administration or the capabilities of its personnel, as long as they seemed loyal. Consequently, by 1245 the *baillis* in the north were an entrenched and exclusive group of officials; the *sénéchaux* of the deep south, owing to the recurrent rebellions after the Albigensian Crusade, were little more than military governors.[60]

[54] Gravier, "Prévôts," pp. 547, 557-58, 562 n. 4; Dossat, "Tentative de réforme," p. 506. Toward the end of the reign the *viguiers* of Languedoc began to be paid salaries; Strayer, "Viscounts and Viguiers," pp. 214, 230. That Saint Louis may have attempted at some time to make all *prévôtés* or equivalent administrative offices salaried (the view, for example, of Coët, *Roye*, II, 139), see below chapter 6 nn. 171-74.

[55] See the discussion in Gravier, "Prévôts," pp. 558-59, 566-68.

[56] Below chapter 6 nn. 222-87.

[57] Below chapter 5 nn. 2-28 and chapter 6 passim.

[58] On the fiscal sources that have survived, below chapter 4 n. 120.

[59] On Philip's supervision, see the documents printed in *HF*, xxiv, "Preuves de la Préface," pp. 286 no. 62 and 290 no. 76.

[60] For overviews, see Lot and Fawtier, *Histoire*, II, 151-52; Petit-Dutaillis, "*Queremoniae normannorum*"; and Langlois, "Doléances."

Louis's rule effectively rested on this small group of regional, salaried *grands baillis* and *sénéchaux*, no more than about twenty men at any one time between 1226 and 1270. Technically they owed their appointment to him,[61] but the familial character of succession in some *bailliages* suggests that the government had begun to compromise on this prerogative in order not to antagonize important provincial families during the strife-torn early years of the king's reign.[62] This apparent readiness to accept familial succession in the *bailliages* went against a fundamental axiom of government, namely, that high provincial officials should be selected from men born in the oldest parts of the royal domain, roughly the area from Paris to Bourges and from Chartres to Sens.[63] The idea was that these administrators should not have vested interests in the provinces they administered.

The implied limitation on vested interests was not restricted to familial connections. The majority of *baillis*, excluding their counterparts in the south, came from knightly and bourgeois backgrounds rather than from the higher nobility.[64] They therefore did not have, in the first instance, a natural community of class interests with the leaders of local society, the native aristocracies. Luckily, the early- and mid-thirteenth century was not a time for ennoblements.[65] Nonetheless, given enough time there was a certain inevitability that proprietary entanglements in their *bailliages* would impel the *baillis* to become spokesmen for and defenders of local, perhaps even aristocratic causes instead of royal interests.[66]

The effective authority of the king in the localities was apparently so tenuous in 1245 and the possible effect of this on the crusade so great that innovations in royal appointments to the dignity of *bailli* seemed necessary. An intensified scrutiny of candidates is suggested, for example, by the considerable intervals, beginning around 1245, between the death or retirement of old *baillis* and the appointment of new ones in the Norman *bailliages*. This anomaly, limited as it is to

[61] Griffiths, "New Men," p. 247. For the most up-to-date lists of *baillis* for the period under examination, see below Appendix One.

[62] See Appendix One, list of *baillis* in Caux (the de La Chapelle family), Sens (the Hautvillers), and also Beaucaire-Nîmes (the Latiniers).

[63] Stein, "Recherches"; *HF*, XXIV, "Chronologie." Also, Porée, "Note sur Pèlerin Latinier," pp. 62-63; Stein, "Un Sénéchal . . . Guillaume de Combreux," p. 332.

[64] See the lists in *HF*, XXIV, "Chronologie"; see also Fesler, "French Field Administration," p. 91; Griffiths, "New Men," p. 243; Carolus-Barré, note in *Bulletin de la Société nationale des antiquaires*, 1963, p. 160; Griffiths, "Pierre de Fontaines," p. 548. Cf. Strayer, "Development of Feudal Institutions," p. 87.

[65] Rogozinski, "Ennoblement," p. 273. But cf. Griffiths, "New Men," p. 243, and Borelli de Serres, *Recherches*, I, 548, 563. See also the seals of the thirteenth century royal *bailli* in Artois, Simon de Villers: his earliest seal did not carry the word *miles*, his later seals did; *HF*, XXIV, "Chronologie," p. 88.

[66] Cf. Lot and Fawtier, *Histoire*, II, 151-52. See also below chapter 6 nn. 140-51.

Normandy, might obscure the fact that there was a systematic scrutiny throughout the provinces of the people put forward for the office of *bailli* after 1245. It could take the particular form it did in Normandy because its *grands bailliages* were divided into a very small number of subdistricts whose ongoing separate supervision would not constitute too great a demand on the resources of the central administration.[67]

In particular circumstances, also notably in Normandy, the jurisdictional boundaries of individual *bailliages* were altered, presumably to improve the efficiency of administration. Such modifications as were undertaken in the short period from 1245 to 1248 were not only confined to the north where Louis and his advisers had readier access to information but the changes they made were all based on precedents.[68] Pont Audemer had ranked as a separate *bailliage* from 1204 to 1246, but from at least 1226, that is for twenty years, the *bailli* of Rouen oversaw its administration. With the suspension or death of the old *bailli* of Rouen in 1246, Pont Audemer briefly received its own chief officer.[69] Bayeux, the center of a separate *grand bailliage* in Normandy until 1226, had been united to the Cotentin after that date. The central government recreated it with separate status in 1248.[70] Finally, the *bailliage* of Étampes, which up through 1248 had been administered separately, was grafted onto Orléans in the next fiscal year.[71]

Certain *bailliages* and other units of local administration received special troubleshooters in the same space of years. The men who served the king in this way took with them the administrative status of *bailli* although they were normally restricted to dealing with affairs incident to the crusade. They moved into areas to help those regular *baillis* or other officials who had already proved themselves unable to

---

[67] This seems to be the case if the lacunae after 1245 or 1246 for Caux, Verneuil, and the Cotentin (Appendix One) are not the fault of poor documentation. On the small number of viscounties per *grand bailliage* in Normandy, compare the figures of Fesler, "French Field Administration," p. 88 nn. 19-20. Each *bailliage* in Normandy contained two to four viscounties; each elsewhere in the north, four to seventeen *prévôtés*. A *sénéchaussée* contained roughly thirty subdistricts, mostly served by revenue farming *bayles* than by *viguiers*. On the superior ability of the viscounts vis-à-vis other local subaltern agents, see Strayer, "Viscounts and Viguiers," pp. 218-19; and Delisle's comments, *HF*, xxiv, "Chronologie," pp. 97-98.

[68] Cf. Fesler, "French Field Administration," p. 88; he suggests that the individuality of *bailliages* was never lost even when two were administered by the same official simultaneously. The statement in the text should not be taken to mean that the readjustments in *bailliagère* geography settled boundaries forever. Some were of only temporary importance. See below chapter 5 n. 94 and chapter 6 nn. 79-80. See also the article by Dupont-Ferrier, "Ignorances et distractions administratives," which carries the story of tampering with the territorial limits of *bailliagère* jurisdictions into the later Middle Ages.

[69] *HF*, xxiv, "Chronologie," p. 133.

[70] Ibid., pp. 133, 146.

[71] Ibid., p. 53.

carry out one or more specific duties required by the king's crusading policy.

The examples are rather simple and straightforward. In the *bailliage* of Sens it is possible that the age of the regular *bailli*, Nicolas de Hautvillers, motivated Louis to appoint Thibaud Clairambaut as his associate. Nicolas had governed the *bailliage* of Sens for far more than twenty years; he was destined to retire from royal service in 1249.[72] In Mâcon and Artois, Louis's motivations were different. Guillaume Le Desréé was deputed to collect revenues for the crusade in the county of Mâcon in 1248,[73] and in the same year Simon de Villers, a former royal *bailli*, was employed to collect money for the crusade in the city of Tournai in the appanage of the count of Artois, Louis's brother Robert.[74] In both these instances the "frontier" character of the *bailliages* in question worked in favor of the special appointments: Mâcon, only acquired by purchase in 1239 and still badly organized, was a kind of administrative no man's land,[75] while Artois, technically the appanage of Count Robert, was the scene—as d'Hérbomez long ago pointed out—of the most complex jurisdictional disputes of the appanage system.[76]

Three other illustrations of Louis's appointments of troubleshooters concern the collection of clerical levies assigned for the crusade. In the first case, Thibaud Clairambaut was sent in 1247 as a *nuncius specialis*, probably no more than an observer for the king, during the collection of the levy in the diocese of Nevers.[77] Soon after he would be assigned expanded duties as the associate of the *bailli* of Sens.[78] In possibly another case, Dreu de Montigni, the *bailli* of Gisors, took a very special interest in the collection of the clerical levy in the diocese of Chartres in 1248[79] because the vacancy of the see had *de jure* obliged the king to supervise the public administration of the diocese.[80] In such cases it was usual for local royal authorities and episcopal officials to differ on how this should be accomplished. Dreu, only recently appointed *bailli* of Gisors, was probably instructed to make sure that

---

[72] References in Appendix One, s.v. "Sens."

[73] Appendix One, s.v. "Mâcon."

[74] *HF*, xxiv, "Chronologie," p. 88; d'Hérbomez, "A Propos des baillis d'Arras," p. 456.

[75] Fournier, "Origines des baillis de Mâcon," pp. 473-78.

[76] The reason for the disputes and confusion was probably the fact that Artois was the first appanage, for with any new system there are always unexpected problems. Cf. d'Hérbomez, "A Propos des baillis d'Arras," p. 456; Loisne, "Chronologie des baillis . . . d'Artois," pp. 311, 314-25; Gravier, "Prévôts," pp. 556-58.

[77] See the record of the levy published in *HF*, xxi, 539.   [78] Above n. 72.

[79] Appendix One, s.v. "Gisors"; cf. *HF*, xxiv, "Chronologie," p. 120.

[80] For the vacancy, see *HF*, xxi, 282 (record of royal expenses in administering the diocese). In general the long list of arrears appended to the accounts of the collection of the clerical levy indicates the magnitude of the problem of getting the church to pay for

these disagreements did not hinder the prompt and efficient collection of the levy for the crusade.

One wonders whether Guillaume de Pian was also instructed to oversee closely the collection of the clerical levy in the diocese of Châlons in 1247,[81] for there too a vacancy in the see had probably slowed down collection of revenues.[82] Guillaume's ability to handle difficult situations was already known. Since 1245 he had been *bailli* in Mâcon, where, as we have seen, the recency of the royal annexation had required a man who could be depended upon to make the transition to new administration as smooth as possible.[83] From Mâcon he was sent as chief officer to the really troublesome administrative district, the *sénéchaussée* of Carcassonne-Béziers, the old center of the Albigensian heresy and the seedbed of numerous rebellions.[84]

Taken together, Louis's efforts to deal with the problems of local government—the increased screening of replacements for natural vacancies in the *bailliages*, the territorial redefinition of a limited group of northern *bailliagère* jurisdictions, and the appointment of a handful of troubleshooters—were significant but rather unsystematic. The king could have stopped with these, but he did not. Motivated perhaps as much by piety (that part of the crusader's vow committing him to redress the grievances of his subjects)[85] as by a keen sense of what a properly operating administration might accomplish, the first months of 1247 saw the king commission investigators (*enquêteurs*) who were empowered to collect and adjudicate complaints about the activities of royal officials. Specifically they were instructed to hear and collect in writing and, in a prescribed manner, to inquire into any reasonable complaints against the king or his predecessors or against his *baillis*, *prévôts*, foresters, sergeants, or their families, making restitutions for any proven injuries to the injured party or his heirs.[86]

Records of payments to the *enquêteurs* for the fiscal term ending at Ascension 1248[87] as well as case summaries of their work for 1247 and 1248 establish that they covered the whole of the royal

---

the crusade. There may have been more troubleshooters employed by the king than the scanty documentary evidence suggests. For the accounts, ibid., 532-40. Also below chapter 4 nn. 106-15.

[81] Cf. ibid., xxiv, "Chronologie," p. 173.   [82] Ibid., xxi, 282.

[83] Appendix One, s.v. "Mâcon"; and above nn. 73, 75.

[84] Appendix One, s.v. "Carcassonne-Béziers."

[85] Labarge, *SL*, p. 106; for a full discussion of the crusader's vow, see Brundage, *Medieval Canon Law and the Crusader*, chaps. II-III.

[86] Writ of commission, *Layettes*, v, no. 490; cf. *Formulaires*, no. 6, items 7-9, 189, and *HF*, xxiv, "Préface," p. 4. On his motivation, cf. Sivery, "Enquête," p. 8.

[87] *HF*, xxi, 262, 264, 268-69, 273-74, 276, 280-81. Haskins, "Robert le Bougre," p. 243, inadvertently assigned these payments to the ecclesiastical Inquisition; cf. Wallon, *SL*, I, 254; *HF*, xxiv, "Préface," p. 5; also Bruel, "Notes de Vyon d'Hérouval," p. 618.

domain—Normandy, Vermandois, the *île de France*, the Mâconnais, and Languedoc.[88] In the appanages the king also took responsibility for earlier misdeeds of officials and, therefore, sent *enquêteurs* to inquire into the complaints of the population.[89] Nonetheless, Alfonse commissioned additional investigators slightly later; they did not begin their comital commissions in south-central France until after his departure for crusade in 1249.[90]

In the royal domain itself there was only a partial exception to the geographical completeness of the investigation. Less comprehensively covered than other regions was the viscounty or *prévôté* of Paris, one of the most populous districts in the country. This is clear from the fact that payments to the Paris investigators for their expenses were extremely small compared to those for *enquêteurs* outside the viscounty.[91] Since all or most of these payments, as can be demonstrated,[92] represented only the administrative expenses of the panels of investigators, the discrepancy suggests that a *limited* commission was empaneled. I can only explain this by reference to a curious correlation. While the royal *enquêteurs* worked in the north in 1247 (and most of their activity in the north seems to have been completed by the end of the year),[93] Louis IX confined his travel to the narrow orbit of the modern *département* of the Seine-et-Oise[94] in order to avoid the

[88] Most of the case summaries for the entire length of the reign may be found in the body of *HF*, XXIV; part of a long additional *enquête* is published in the "Preuves" of that volume, no. 152 (also Jordan, "Jews on Top," n. 34). A few remnants and associated documents have been published or summarized in Delisle, "Fragment d'un registre"; Strayer, "Conscience du roi"; Carolus-Barré, "Richart Laban"; and Verlaguet, *Cartulaire . . . de Silvanès*, pp. 442-45. (The record summarized by Verlaguet is provided *in extenso* in Appendix Four; I discuss it below chapter 6 nn. 175-86.)

[89] Cf. Fournier and Guébin, *Enquêtes administratives*, p. xv. Since the extent of royal jurisdiction was disputed in Artois, it would be difficult to say precisely what the territorial commission of the *enquêteurs* in the county entailed (in "Jews on Top," n. 8, I have taken a conservative view of their jurisdiction). The investigation of Anjou and Maine appears to have been completely under the king's aegis (*HF*, XXIV, 73-93).

[90] On the commission, see Fournier and Guébin, *pièce* 1. All the surviving registers of comital *enquêtes* (1251-1271) of Alfonse are published in this volume.

[91] Payments to the *enquêteurs* in the viscounty of Paris for approximately four months ending Ascension 1248 were thirty shillings (one and one-half pounds); *HF*, XXI, 262. In each of the four *prévôtés* of Amiens, Issoudun, Sens, and Moret-sur-Loing, these payments were ten pounds; pp. 264, 268-69. In the *bailliage* of Orléans for the same term, expenses were twenty-four pounds (twenty-three pounds at one time, twenty shillings at another); p. 273. In the *bailliage* of Mâcon they exceeded thirteen pounds; p. 280. And for the *bailliages* of Sens, Vermandois, and Tours, expenses varied from nine pounds to over thirty pounds; pp. 274, 276, 281.

[92] Below nn. 99 and 117.

[93] This may be inferred from the dates of the case summaries which have survived; *HF*, XXIV. As n. 91 shows, however, there was still some work going on in early 1248.

[94] There was one exception, a trip in June to the abbey of Pontigny, in a region outside the royal domain and rarely visited before 1247. See Carolus-Barré. "SL et la translation des corps saints," pp. 1089-91; Chardon, *Auxerre*, I, 192; Massé, *Vie de saint Edme*, pp. 356-57. Pontigny is, however, in the diocese of Auxerre, and Auxerre was visited by

bizarre possibility, or so I believe, of his presence in the provinces undermining the *enquêteurs'* commissions. Indeed, wherever it was traditional for the king to go, such as Normandy, he did not go in 1247.[95] Thus, the redress of grievances, as far as this was accomplished, proceeded through normal channels in Paris.

The *enquêteurs* come into the records in 1247, but surely a great deal of thought preceded their introduction. It is not enough to say, as at least some historians have, that they were similar to the Carolingian *missi dominici* as if that explains their place in French administrative history.[96] I do not know how much Louis IX or his advisers knew about Charlemagne's *missi*. What they did know might well have been inspirational,[97] but it cannot have obviated the need for "deep speech" before the *enquêteurs* got the king's approval. It is a pity we know so little about the details.

We can, however, argue backward from the evidence on the personnel of the *enquêteurs* to get some idea of the nature of discussions before their commission. Franciscan and Dominican friars formed the bulk of the appointees to the dignity before the crusade. There are only two proved exceptions among royal commissioners, and they were secular clerks.[98] In law the mendicants were spiritually dead, that is, they were supposedly deprived of the capacity to fulfill public functions.[99] Later evidence shows that there was opposition to the use of

enquêteurs receiving clerical complaints in January 1247 (above n. 86). I use the comparison of the *département* of the Seine-et-Oise even though recent changes in the administrative map of France have suppressed it. Since it was one of the revolutionary divisions of the country, however, there will always be maps, easy of access, indicating its boundaries. The districts that have taken its place are likely to be ephemeral.

[95] I base this conclusion on the itinerary of Louis IX (above n. 23). The itinerary is reliable (Brühl, *Fodrum*, 1, 242 n. 90) and especially thorough for Normandy since its preparation was largely the work of the great Norman scholar Léopold Delisle. But being based on charters and other official material (*HF*, xxi, 406-8) it is also incomplete. Nonetheless, exhaustive supplementary studies by Thoison (aided by Henri Stein, the Delisle of the Gâtinais) have double-checked the sources for the north-center of the country (Thoison, *Séjours*), and I have consulted the majority of published chronicles and local histories for the north, particularly Picardy, as a final check (under the rubric L.k7 at the BN). See also Sivery, "Enquête," p. 9.

[96] Julia, *Béziers*, p. 303 (one of the best of nineteenth century authorities); and Bruel, "Notes de Vyon d'Hérouval," p. 618.

[97] See the discussion of the *missi* in Ganshof, *Carolingians and the Frankish Monarchy*, pp. 148-49, 206.

[98] Information on the personnel (only twelve have been identified definitely before the crusade) may be found in Guillaume de Saint-Pathus, "Vie de SL," *HF*, xx, 119; MP, iv, 638; *Layettes*, v, nos. 492, 494. Discussions and analysis of this and additional evidence are in *HF*, xxiv, "Préface," pp. 8-9; Wyse, "*Enquêteurs*," pp. 52-54; Petit-Dutaillis, *Feudal Monarchy*, p. 298; Little, *Frater Ludovicus*, pp. 173-74. On the comital *enquêteurs* of Alfonse and the heavy dependence on friars, see Fournier and Guébin, pp. xiii-xlviii.

[99] For a good brief discussion of the problem, see Brissaud, *French Private Law*, pp. 880-88. There is nothing of value in E. Durtelle de Saint-Sauveur, *Recherches sur l'histoire de la théorie de la mort civile*. As a consequence of their spiritual death and vow of poverty,

friars as *enquêteurs* in Capetian government.[100] The difficulty of interpreting this evidence is immense. Since it is from the period after the crusade, when for many reasons *enquêteurs* were admitted as a permanent element in administration,[101] it may be that the opposition was concerned about the mendicants becoming "bureaucratized" and thus losing or compromising their religious vows. The king himself, in the "Protest of St. Louis," had objected to the use of Franciscans by the papacy as ordinary functionaries, collectors of papal revenues.[102] Nonetheless, the help the friars gave Louis in carrying out his crusader's vow, that is, by investigating the kingdom for him in 1247 and 1248 (much like their operation of the Inquisition) might originally have been considered a pious work fully accordable with their own profession of the religious life.[103]

Louis's preference for mendicants is easy to understand. They represented in the early thirteenth century the cutting edge of Christian piety.[104] The French monarchy had already begun to associate itself with the European expansion of the movement in the 1230s.[105] Blanche is usually given credit for this; and if the assertion is true (with the quality of early mendicant documentation there is really no way to verify it absolutely),[106] it is reasonable to believe that she influenced her son to admire and support the friars' work.[107] It is also asserted that Louis was educated by friars. This is more dubious since

the mendicants would not have been remunerated beyond administrative expenses; cf. also *HF*, xxiv, "Preface," pp. 4-5.

[100] Dossat, "Inquisiteurs ou enquêteurs," pp. 106-7. See also *HF*, xxiv, "Préface," p. 7, on the Dominican order's dislike for the almost inevitable use of horses by the itinerant *enquêteurs* in the year 1258.

[101] Below chapter 6 nn. 105-11.

[102] Above chapter 2 n. 54.

[103] Even associating with the king was considered a violation of vows by some (cf. Joinville's report, chap. CXXXII). The remarks in the first chapter of Thomson, *Friars in the Cathedral*, pp. 9-20, are quite helpful. He discusses the arguments used to justify the employment of friars as legates, as inquisitors, and as bishops. The title of the chapter sums up the whole issue nicely: "Perspectives on a Dilemma." Cf. also Sivery, "Enquête," p. 10.

[104] See Moliner, *Espiritualidad medieval*, pp. 31-37. See also Bougerol, "Théologie et spiritualité franciscaine au temps de SL." A work on this subject by Le Goff, presented to the Colloquy of Royaumont, 1970, has unfortunately not been published (*Septième centenaire de la mort de SL*, p. viii).

[105] This was particularly true with regard to the activities of the friars in the Inquisition in the south. Most historians have seen them as agents, consciously or unconsciously, of the centralizing tendencies of the monarchy. See, for example, Lacger, "Albigeois," pp. 35-41; and Le Goff's summation, "France du Nord et France du Midi," p. 137. Lépinois and Merlet, *Cartulaire . . . Chartres*, II, no. cclxxii, n. 1, give evidence of royal support for northern mendicants in the period 1229-1231.

[106] For a brief discussion of the quality of early mendicant records and ways to improve the dating of royal foundations of mendicant convents, see Jordan, "Contrats d'acquisition royaux."

[107] Wyse, "*Enquêteurs*," p. 47; cf. Little, *Frater Ludovicus*, pp. 38-39.

most of his youth was over before the friars penetrated French culture.[108] But it is certainly true that from young manhood on Louis drew friars to him.[109] Finally, he endowed a number of mendicant houses before the crusade and apparently was influential in the founding of several others.[110]

Still, he would not have succeeded in having the friars as his *enquêteurs* had it not been for strenuous efforts on his part. Did he discuss the project at Cluny during his secret meeting with the pope in 1245? Did he consult the heads of the two great mendicant orders? There is no explicit proof, but it is obvious that something of this sort must have taken place.[111]

As to the actual work of the friar-*enquêteurs*, there were marked regional differences both in the status of the petitioners who came before them and in the sorts of issues the petitioners raised. In the south and southwestern parts of the kingdom, those who were not afraid of possible reprisals[112] complained of the vicious royal officers who had

[108] The expansion of the mendicants into France, the first great spurt, occurred during the 1230s. In establishing this point, I have analyzed the data collected in the now standard catalogue, Emery, *Friars in Medieval France*, and have organized it into tables in Appendix Two. See also the maps in Ribaucourt, "Mendiants du Midi," pp. 30-31. It seems misleading, therefore, to talk about the education by friars of Louis IX as a young child; the evidence is summarized by Wyse, "*Enquêteurs*," p. 47. But friars penetrated the household early in the first regency and thus could have had an influence on Louis's adolescence (below n. 109). The only manuscript which is purported to have been used by Louis as a child (it is claimed that he learned to read from this psalter) does not seem to have any characteristics which can be called specifically Franciscan or Dominican. Photographs of the manuscript, MS BPL 76A, were graciously provided me by the Library of the University of Leiden, the Netherlands (see also Delisle, "Testament . . . Blanche de Navarre," pp. 2, 29-30 no. 200; cf. Branner, "SL et l'enluminure," p. 80 n. 4).
[109] Little, "SL's Involvement with the Friars"; Congar, "Église et l'état," pp. 262-63. Much more evidence will be adduced on this point, below chapter 7 nn. 19-32, 46-63.
[110] He endowed the Dominican house in Béziers in 1247; see *GC*, VI, "Instrumenta," c. 156 no. XXVI, and Soucaille, *État monastique*, p. 11. He approved the foundation of another at Carcassonne and endowed it in the same year; see Dossat, *Crise de l'Inquisition*, p. 190; idem, "Opposition des anciens ordres," pp. 264, 273; and Poux, *Carcassonne*, I, 139-40. He instituted annual alms for the Franciscans of Nîmes in 1248; Ménard, *Nismes*, I, "Preuves," p. 79 no. LVI. Martin, *Ordres mendiants en Bretagne*, p. 18, associates the foundation by Breton barons of three houses in Brittany, 1246-1248, with mounting enthusiasm for Louis IX's crusade. Cf. also above n. 105, and Appendix Two on the secular pattern of mendicant foundations in France.
[111] There is no doubt Louis had the formal approval of the orders (cf. *HF*, XXIV, "Préface," p. 4), but it is hard to imagine how he got it.
[112] In 1247, for example, a petitioner informed the *enquêteurs* that the *bailli* of Tours, Josse de Bonnes, had fined him (he said "extorted") one hundred shillings for an offense despite the fact that he had obtained a judgment from the royal court to the contrary. Josse had used the ominous words, "Et si tu se liberatus ab illo, tamen non es liberatus a me"; *HF*, XXIV, 76-77 no. 41. (For a summary and justifiably negative view of Josse's career, see Stein, "Recherches," *ASHGâtinais*, XXXII, 196-97; he was removed from office in 1248 [Appendix One].) Mr. Robert Bartlett has brought to my attention another example in which royal sergeants seem to have disregarded the presence of the

abused their powers while putting down rebellions against the king, a theme more fully treated in Appendix Three. The implicit message was that if the king wanted a more effective administration on the eve of the crusade or wanted to depart from his kingdom with a clear conscience, he should get rid of or chastise these officials. Especially moving were the complaints of widows of noblemen who had lost their property in the often ruthless and unjust confiscations carried out by the king's men.[113] Louis was so taken aback by these revelations that he later authorized a specific investigation into the problems of the "helpless"—widows, the sick, and orphans—who had suffered at the hands of his officials.[114]

In other parts of the realm there was less talk of the effects of war.[115] The complainants in the north and in Auvergne, for example, were more modest people who simply detailed the petty corruption of the king's men: how they stole wheat, wine, and meat; how they took possession of kitchen utensils (frying pans, pots, and cups) for their or their wives' comfort; and especially how they loved to deprive honest subjects of their heavy coats and good blankets. We need not accept all the complaints as true, but there are so many and they are so rarely contested[116] that it is hard to draw an entirely favorable picture of local officialdom.

---

king's *enquêteurs* evidently believing that nothing would happen to them for their misdeeds; *HF*, xxiv, 278-79 no. 44.

[113] The confiscations during and following the Albigensian Crusade had not respected the dower rights of the wives of heretics or wives of supporters of heretics; Wakefield, *Heresy*, p. 182. See, in general, Appendix Three.

[114] The remarkable evidence on widows and other vulnerable groups in the late southern royal *enquêtes* has already been the subject of a scholarly essay; Strayer, "Conscience du roi." For a supplementary discussion of the data, see Appendix Three. Louis's attitude is discussed by Strayer and in Appendix Three; other evidence relevant to his policies toward women is considered in chapter 6 n. 105 and chapter 7 nn. 46-54.

[115] For the detailed analysis supporting the conclusions with regard to status and the nature of cases in this paragraph, see Appendix Three. In general, see also Langlois, "Doléances," p. 24, and Petit-Dutaillis, "*Queremoniae normannorum*," p. 112. I do not want to suggest that in certain northern provinces, like Normandy, problems arising from the original conquest were not brought forward by petitioners. They certainly were (*HF*, xxiv, 23 nos. 166, 170; cf. Sivery, "Enquête"; and Petit-Dutaillis, p. 108), and widows seem to have had a difficult time. But owing to the lack of rebellions since the conquest, petitions arising from war did not constitute a fundamental theme in the *enquêtes* of the north.

[116] In one summary of cases published by Carolus-Barré, "Richart Laban, sergent du roi," pp. 260-63, the defendant, a forester, answered the complaints against him with "c'est mençonge." In the absence of other evidence the denial sufficed. His frequent failure to respond seems to have been regarded as a legal equivalent to the modern *nolo contendere*. For a good series of illustrations of the frequency of compromises before the *enquêteurs*, with the defendant usually giving about one-half the plaintiff's demand for compensation, see *QTur*. (Certainly the ease with which these compromises were reached suggests both the partial guilt of the officers accused and perhaps the tendency of plaintiffs to exaggerate.) Unfortunately most of the other pre-crusade *enquêtes* lack

Louis certainly did not. To fulfill the demands of his conscience and to improve the efficiency of the local administration the king punished many of these officials. Part of this was automatic, built in, as it were, to the *enquêteurs'* system of investigation. If an officer was guilty of an abuse of power which could be atoned for by a monetary payment to the petitioner, then he paid the petitioner directly. However, if the officer had carried out an order of the king or of his predecessors, whose effects turned out to be harmful to the petitioner without cause, then the king was adjudged responsible for the act and the compensation to the petitioner was drawn from the *de compoto* funds of the chief local officer.[117]

Modestly well-off subaltern royal officers (*prévôts* of royal towns other than Paris, *viguiers*, viscounts, *bayles*, sergeants, and foresters) who were found guilty of abuses of power very likely found the accumulated punishment of several small fines hard to bear. The immediate impact on them may have been compounded since most of these functionaries drew their income from revenue farming. In cases where the illegal activity of such an official was not sufficient in itself to result in his permanent dismissal and where his farm was not hereditary,[118] paying a heavy volume of small fines may well have reduced the possibility of a successful bid for the next annual (biennial, or triennial) farm.[119]

The *baillis*, although by the nature of their office, capable of many more and graver infractions of the law, may have been injured less than their subalterns by the fines the *enquêteurs* imposed. Not all their graft or with it their reserves of wealth could possibly be uncovered: for example, the protection they afforded local moneylenders in return for which they were handsomely paid off was so extensive that the *enquêteurs* devoted special sessions to investigating it.[120] Their fam-

---

decisions so it is impossible to be precise on rates of favorable decisions for the plaintiffs. (Strayer, *Royal Domain*, p. 19, has summarized the cases that he has been able to collate with later administrative documents in Normandy. Of the 15 decisions he recovered from the over 550 surviving cases in Normandy, 11 denied the petitioner's claim.)

[117] *HF*, XXIV, "Préface," pp. 4-6. The best general introduction to the *enquêtes* remains Langlois, "Doléances." Very stimulating is Petit-Dutaillis's study of the Norman records, "*Queremoniae normannorum*." See also François, "Initiatives de SL," and Froger, "Enquêtes à La Flèche."

[118] For fee farms that were heritable, see *HF*, XXIV, 14, 21, 34-35 nos. 87, 141, 267. See also Goineau, *Gisors*, pp. 208-9; Decq, "Administration des eaux et forêts," pp. 100-102; and Lecoy de La Marche, "Coutumes et péages de Sens," pp. 267-70.

[119] On the length of farms, see Gravier, "Prévôts," pp. 547-51. Cf. Lyon and Verhulst, *Medieval Finance*, p. 31. On bidding (a still obscure point), see Fesler, "French Field Administration," p. 100; Strayer, *Royal Domain*, p. 21 nn. 7-8; Fournier and Guébin, *pièce* 4 no. 79. Cf. *HF*, XXIV, "Chronologie," p. 23.

[120] Jordan, "Jews on Top," p. 42; Chazan, *Medieval Jewry*, pp. 119-20.

ily connections and their healthy salaries (three hundred to seven hundred pounds per year),[121] much of which, one supposes, they had invested in ostentatious *objets*, like silver goblets, that could be reconverted readily to cash,[122] probably cushioned them against the impact of the *enquêteurs'* fines. Moreover, like lower-level functionaries, they probably thought that this investigation was a one-time affair. They expected to be able to recoup their losses and perhaps teach a few of the petitioners a lesson.

They were in error. The work of the *enquêteurs* heralded an extraordinary reevaluation of upper-level field administrators. To see this, all one need do is examine the so-called *mouvements des baillis*, data on the frequency of annual appointments to (or, what amounts to the same thing, terminations from) the dignity of *bailli*, during the reign of Saint Louis.[123] I have assembled these data in table one and have schematized them in the figure. Some care has been taken to make the information as revealing of true trends as possible. Therefore, the figures do not include data on the *prévôté* of Paris or on the southern *sénéchaussées* (Carcassonne-Béziers, Beaucaire-Nîmes, the Limousin, Périgord-Quercy). The exclusion of the first from the aggregate schematization is due to its special *prévôté* form of administration: to include the data on the multiplicity of officials who administered the *prévôté* as revenue farmers would mask significant trends in the provincial administration. The exclusion of the *sénéchaussées* is due to the unsettled conditions of the first twenty years of royal administration in the south, a time when officials were changed frequently owing to the endemic rebellions.[124] Data on the precise chronology of such changes are often lacking. However, in specific instances, both for Paris and the *sénéchaussées*, I have taken care to indicate where I think the data conform to the more general trends described in table one and the accompanying figure.

[121] Borrelli de Serres, *Recherches*, 1, 566-67; Fesler, "French Field Administration," pp. 91, 94-95 (esp. n. 40); Carolus-Barré, "Baillis de Philippe le Hardi," p. 132.

[122] This picture emerges from a vignette in an *enquête* in which it is reported that a group of *baillis*, standing and talking in the royal garden, were bragging about their possessions. Though dating from after the crusade, there is no reason to think that this story is not representative of attitudes before. *HF*, xxiv, "Preuves de la Préface," no. 152 (deposition 198).

[123] The references in Appendix One provide a full bibliography of the research on the terms of office of the *baillis*. There is a good series of articles by Mailliard employing this method of analysis for various reigns; "Mouvements administratifs des baillis." Fiétier, "Choix des baillis," analyzes administration in the reign of Saint Louis from this perspective but he specifically excludes the period before 1250. His ideas on later reform will be taken up in a subsequent chapter. Cf. also Delisle, "Chronologie des baillis," *HF*, xxiv, 88, who seems to have noticed the major reevaluation of *bailliagère* officialdom in the late 1240s.

[124] On the administration of the *prévôté* of Paris, there is a full discussion below chapter 6 nn. 222-83. The list of *prévôts* and terms of office may be found in Appendix One,

TABLE 1 ● Appointments of *Baillis* Year by Year

Year	Appointments	Year	Appointments
1227	5	1244	0
1228	4	1245	3
1229	1	1246	1
1230	4	1247	5
1231	3	1248	6
1232	0	1249	9
1233	0	1250	0
1234	4	1251	1
1235	3	1252	4
1236	5	1253	7
1237	4	1254	8
1238	1	1255	2
1239	4	1256	9
1240	0	1257	0
1241	1	1258	4
1242	1	1259	0
1243	1	1260	–

The data in the table do not include the *sénéchaussées* of the south or the *prévôté* of Paris.

Around the mid-1240s a remarkable picture takes shape. In 1247, in the then seventeen *bailliages* under consideration, there were, or at least the best evidence suggests that there were, five new appointments at the *bailli* rank;[125] in 1248 (for eighteen *bailliages*) there were probably six more appointments;[126] and in 1249 in sixteen *bailliages*, there were nine new appointments.[127] These twenty appointments included two of the troubleshooters who commanded the status of *bailli* in their special work for the crusade in *bailliages* where the existing *bailli* continued to function.[128] The other eighteen appointments were regular, that is there were no special restrictions and the previous *baillis* had been removed by decision or by death by the time the appointments were made.

s.v. "Paris." The lists of *sénéchaux* are included there as well, under the appropriate headings.
[125] In Rouen, Caen, Gisors, Amiens, Bourges; see Appendix One under relevant headings. In the *prévôté* of Paris there were also two appointments in 1247.
[126] The appointments occurred in Caux, Verneuil, Bayeux, Sens, Orléans, Mâcon (?); Appendix One. The *sénéchaussée* of Carcassonne-Béziers also received a new officer in 1248.
[127] The appointments occurred in Verneuil (bis), the Cotentin, Amiens, Touraine (bis), Sens, Mâcon, Bourges; Appendix One.
[128] Included are Guillaume Le Desréé in Mâcon and Thibaud Clairambaut in Sens.

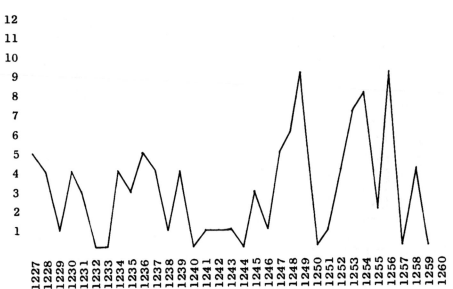

LEGEND: Appointments to the Dignity of *Bailli*.

What the figures taken alone mask is both the variety and the conservativeness of the king's actions. Certain *bailliagère* jurisdictions, as we have seen, were being reconsidered contemporary with the review of personnel, a fact which explains the changing number of *bailliages* over the short space of three years. A few officers, who came out of the *enquêteurs'* investigations unstained, were simply shifted from one *bailliage* to another. This was true, for example, of the *bailli* of Gisors who was transferred to the Cotentin (and of the *bailli* of Mâcon who became *sénéchal* of Carcassonne). One or two of the new appointees replaced men who decided to follow Louis on crusade. Such was the case of Luc de Villers who succeeded Jean de Maisons.[129] Several others among the new appointees were already part of the administration at lower levels, had performed similar functions earlier, or had some familiarity with local administration. Thus, Jean Le Jeune, who was appointed *bailli* of Caen in 1247 and of Verneuil in 1248, had been an active functionary in the finance wing of *bailliagère* administration in Caen in 1234; and Étienne de La Porte, appointed *bailli* of Rouen in 1247, had probably served with his bureaucratic relatives in some capacity before this date.[130]

It was difficult to find men of ability on short notice. Consequently one finds men being used in rapid succession in one *bailliage* after another. So, in Touraine, an obviously corrupt *bailli* was replaced in

[129] Appendix One, s.v. "Cotentin," and chapter 6 nn. 64-67.
[130] On Jean, *HF*, xxiv, "Chronologie," pp. 128, 137; Brussel, *Usage général des fiefs*, 1, 490. On Étienne, *HF*, xxiv, "Chronologie," p. 102.

1248 by what looks to be a temporary appointment. Later in the next year a more permanent replacement was found.[131] The rapid series of appointments for Jean Le Jeune, described in the previous paragraph, is also suggestive of the restricted number of people the king could call upon to fill these difficult administrative posts.

In other words, Louis was modifying the personnel of the administration with agents whose loyalty and integrity and ability he had reason already to trust. They were new appointees but they were not "new men." It goes almost without saying that the wholesale reshuffling of the top level of field administrators would work to forestall reprisals after the *enquêteurs'* departure.

One would like to say more about the criteria governing Louis's selection of the new *baillis*, for what has been said so far does no more than hint at the scale of his administrative reform. Unfortunately we know little about the other men who were appointed in this period (and we know nothing about possible attempts to reshuffle men at lower levels). Nonetheless, the delightful story told in the fourteenth century French political tract, "L'estat et le gouvernement," suggests the sort of forethought people began to associate with Louis's appointment of his officials.

And here upon it is cronykled of the holy kinge Lowes, sometyme of Fraunce, how he was accustomed and used to bere at his girdyll a peire of tables, in whiche he did be writen the names of suche persoones as he herd aboute in his lande well famed by good relacion and by good name, how thei were good, true and wise, covenable and convenient for suche offices. And whanne it felle that any suche office was voide or vacaunt, there was oft tymes made unto him greet meenye and prayere for preferrement of the seid office; to whiche it was the seide kinges maner and guyse to answere and say he wolde doo in the matere like as his table yave him counseill. And for so muche as he putt in office suche as were write and remembred in his tables aftir the good testimonye that he had herd of theire good conversacion, by that meene he was in his dayes purveide of good officers, by whos trouthe and wysdome the reaume was well governed in his tyme. Wherfore he is now in the reaume of paradise, that nevyr shall faile.[132]

As to the popular effect of the reform of administration or, rather, of the introduction of the friar-*enquêteurs*, much can be surmised. The *exemplum* just quoted would suggest that people came to believe that

---

[131] Appendix One, s.v. "Touraine."
[132] I quote from the fifteenth-century English translation edited by Genet, *Four English Political Tracts*, pp. 203-4 (on the date and provenance of the original and versions, see pp. 174-79).

the king was not concerned simply to get effective control of his administrators but to see that they did their work with propriety and honesty.[133] But the effect went deeper than this. The *enquêteurs* had "propagandized" for the monarchy. The phrases they used to describe the king who had sent them—phrases that exalted the royal majesty—were picked up by those who heard them.[134] The ways in which they sought out the helpless, allowed testimony from juveniles, and listened to the lamentations of widows, mothers, and orphans, all helped make the king appear to be a saint.[135] The informality of the courts permitted ordinary people to use them with ease:[136] sessions were held in convenient places;[137] petitioners could plead in the vernacular;[138] and decisions were final.[139] Everywhere they worked the *enquêteurs* became known for "equitable" justice.[140]

[133] Favorable contemporary evaluations of the *enquêteurs'* work are given by Matthew Paris, IV, 638-39, and Guillaume de Saint-Pathus, *HF*, XX, 119. Neither of these informants was unbiased but Matthew Paris, at least, could certainly criticize as much as praise Louis's work.

[134] Among the *enquêteurs'* favorite phrases to describe their master was *rex serenissimus*: Michel, *Beaucaire*, p. 410 no. 20; *HF*, XXIV, 619. The appellation seems to have caught on. The charters, for example, of the lords of Posquières in Languedoc in which allusion is made to the king show an increased frequency in the use of *serenissimus* after the 1240s; Falgairolle, "Chartes . . . des seigneurs de Vauvert," pp. 20-37.

[135] E.g., *HF*, XXIV, 362 no. 10, 363 no. 14, 406-7 no. 78. See also Appendix Three.

[136] The informality of the investigations, as demonstrated by the motley variety of petitions they accepted (preceding note) was also partly built into the system which required the *enquêteurs* to proceed *simpliciter et de plano*—simply and in the vernacular; *Layettes*, V, no. 490. (Both Wyse, "*Enquêteurs*," pp. 54-59, and Labarge, *SL*, p. 185, appear to accept this interpretation of the phrase. Cf. Berger, *Encyclopedic Dictionary of Roman Law*, s.v. "De Plano" and "Simpliciter.")

[137] Thus, *aula domini regis*; *in platea ante domum regis*; etc.; Michel, *Beaucaire*, pp. 412-15 nos. 20-22. The possible significance of the *enquêtes* drawing large crowds in the open air has been raised in personal conversation with my student, Richard Landes.

[138] Above n. 136. Even though case summaries are abbreviated (cf. *HF*, XXIV, 386, 692 no. 1, 705, 719 no. 125) and usually in Latin, it seems clear to me that the instructions to hear cases in the vernacular were carried out to the letter: In the first place there are a few *enquêtes* in dialects of OF (e.g., Carolus-Barré, "Richard Laban, sergent du roi"). Moreover, I have now had the opportunity to examine excellent photographs of an original *enquête* (AN, J 1028[A] no. 4; partly published, with reference misnumbered, in *HF*, XXIV, "Preuves de la Préface," no. 152); the Latin was clearly written but in a rapid hand: there are long tails at the ends of words and frequent *et cetera* for witnesses who gave similar testimony. This suggests that the translation was instantaneous from the vernacular; cf. Le Roy Ladurie, *Montaillou*, p. 18 n. 3, for his analysis of later ecclesiastical *enquêtes*. This fact further suggests, contrary to the views of Langlois, "Doléances," p. 5, that the *enquêteurs'* scribes or notaries were local men. For example, Petrus de Mandolio who worked for the *enquêteurs* in the south in 1254 and 1255 had been a local notary in Languedoc since at least 1249—Michel, *Beaucaire*, pp. 407-14 nos. 16, 20-21.

[139] That is, no reviews of decisions were allowed; Molinier, *Correspondance*, II, p. xxxv. A review system did function over Alfonse's *enquêtes*: see Fournier and Guébin, *Enquêtes administratives*, pièce 52. Dossat, "Alfonse de Poitiers et les clercs," has summarized the role of the *enquêteurs* of the count in the overall government of his territories.

[140] Lecoy de La Marche, *France sous SL*, p. 79; Strayer, "Conscience du roi," pp. 726-27. See also Appendix Three.

Even when, after the crusade, the *enquêteurs* were reintroduced as a permanent feature of royal administration, and their courts became slightly more formal,[141] Louis's belief that the *enquêteurs* should have a "mendicant" cast of mind, a deep compassion, never faltered. Arguments to the contrary, based largely on the fact that the post-crusade commissioners had a smaller proportion of friars among them, miss the point. Even after 1254 about half the royal *enquêteurs* were drawn from the mendicant orders,[142] and those that were not—like the royal counselor and future pope, Gui Foucois[143]—seem to have been chosen because they shared the evangelical conception of justice which the original friar-*enquêteurs* are famous for. They were certainly just as lenient as their predecessors.[144] In short the considerable elevation of the king's reputation by the work of his *enquêteurs* was as potentially important and far-reaching as the substantial improvement they brought to the administration of his kingdom on the eve of the crusade.

The activities of Louis IX described in this chapter constitute almost the whole of his administrative achievement in the three and one-half years of his preparations for crusade. Indeed, I may have slightly exaggerated his accomplishment since the last wave of appointments to the rank of *bailli* in 1249 (that is, after the reception of the final reports of the pre-crusade *enquêteurs*) would have to have been made by his mother, who reassumed regnal powers in her son's absence. Certainly, however, he had advised her on her duties in this regard and trusted her to make able choices.

The administrative reforms of the pre-crusade period could be considered part of an ongoing reform of the kingdom which would be resumed after the crusade (as with the reintroduction of the *enquêteurs*). But even assessed in this way—as but one phase in a more comprehensive program—Louis's accomplishment before the crusade was distinguished: by the end of 1247 and increasingly thereaf-

[141] This meant more screening of cases (cf. *HF*, xxiv, 619) although in some areas preliminary screening of petitions was introduced before the crusade (*Layettes*, iii, no. 3623). See also Appendix Three on the secular change in the status of petitioners.
[142] Using the data in *HF*, xxiv, "Préface," pp. 8-9, there are twenty-one certainly identifiable royal *enquêteurs* after the crusade: ten mendicants, nine secular clerks, two laymen. Among the scholars who have interpreted this shift in the occupational background of the *enquêteurs* as evidence that the original friar-*enquêteurs* were too lenient and thus were supplanted, see Langlois, "Doléances," pp. 3-4; Little, *Frater Ludovicus*, pp. 173-74 (citing Petit-Dutaillis, *Feudal Monarchy*; the point is reiterated in Little's "SL's Involvement with the Friars").
[143] There are two recent studies of the mentality and early career of Pope Clement IV; see Chazan "Archbishop Guy Fulcodi," and Dossat, "Gui Foucois" (see also Carolus-Barré, "Grand Ordonnance de 1254," p. 92).
[144] See Appendix Three for a fuller discussion of this point.

ter his demands on his kingdom could be made through men whose fundamental loyalty was to him, who owed their positions directly to him, and who were dealing with a population that for the first time, as a result of the friar-*enquêteurs*, may have desired genuinely to help him in the great crusade he planned. When Louis had first sworn the crusader's vow in December 1244, it is unlikely anyone would have ventured to believe that these developments were possible. In subsequent chapters we shall have the chance to evaluate the results of these developments in sustaining the Holy War and in upholding the king's reputation after his defeat.

•4•

WAR FINANCE:
MEN, MATERIEL, AND MONEY

Like the bear and the beetle in the medieval French folktale who could not "make" war until they had "made" their armies,[1] Louis IX had no instrument immediately at hand to invade the East. Nor did he have the apparatus to transport an army to its destination. And armies must be fed and provided with equipment; they must have support staff, especially medical personnel. In the War of the Animals, all the bear had to do was enlist the panther, the fox, and the wolf in his entourage. The beetle did little more. After a brief and unfortunate sortie by the fox, the one and only battle ended in utter defeat for the "great big animals." The outcome of Louis IX's crusade was not much different, but he put so much more effort into his preparations, he carried out his plans with such minute precision, that the final and unqualified failure was to send a shock wave through Western European society.

The best estimate of the number of troops that eventually fought under Louis IX's command is fifteen thousand.[2] For the period the figure is a sizable one. In the early twelfth century the standing army of the kingdom of Jerusalem had numbered about thirty-five hundred troops in total.[3] In Louis's army according to three informed contemporary estimates—one by Joinville; another by Gui Mauvoisin, a baronial commander; and a third by Jean Sarrasin, a royal chamberlain—there were twenty-five or twenty-eight hundred knights.[4] There was a substantial number, perhaps ten thousand, of well-equipped but lower ranking troops such as crossbowmen and mounted sergeants. Jean Sarrasin estimated the number of crossbowmen at five thousand, and Strayer believes there were two mounted sergeants on the average for every knight, that is, five thousand or fifty-six hundred mounted sergeants in total.[5] The remainder of the army was

---

[1] "The Bear and the Beetle, or the War of the Animals," in Massignon, *Folktales of France*, no. 49.

[2] Strayer, "Crusades of Louis IX," pp. 166-67, summarizes the views of several historians on the size of the army and wages paid the troops upon which this figure is based.

[3] Ben-Ami, *Social Change*, p. 38.

[4] For Joinville's estimate, chap. xxxii; for Lord Gui's, see Joinville, chap. lxxxiii; and for the chamberlain's, "Letter of John Sarrasin," Hague ed. of Joinville, p. 243. See also Strayer, "Crusades of Louis IX," p. 166.

[5] "Letter of John Sarrasin," p. 243; Strayer, "Crusades of Louis IX," p. 166.

comprised of less well-armed infantry, approximately four foot for every knight, or about ten thousand.[6] A large proportion of these various troops—probably in roughly equal proportions in the ranks—were provided from the very beginning by Louis himself.[7] The other half was supported by ancillary leaders of the crusade.

More is known about Alfonse of Poitiers and his war effort than about any of the other ancillary leaders of the crusade including Louis's two other brothers, Robert and Charles. Both Robert and Charles participated actively in the crusade and brought fair-sized contingents,[8] but Alfonse's forces are more extensively documented. A summary assessment of his expenditures from Purification (February 2) 1250 until Christmas details expenses of 1,300 pounds for wages for his *barones* and *milites* and 2,500 pounds for their horses which had been lost in battle. He paid out an additional 400 pounds or thereabouts to mounted crossbowmen and 381 pounds to foot soldiers. Bows, arrows, crossbow bolts cost him 180 pounds.[9]

Fortunately it is also possible to get some idea—qualitative and, at times, quantitative—of other sorts of contributions such as those of the great fiefs and their seigneurs. The men of Champagne, for example, lost approximately thirty-five knights banneret in battle in Egypt during the crusade,[10] and since normally a banneret led a group of knights bachelor (four would seem to be standard),[11] the men of Champagne provided at least 175 *milites*. Using Strayer's estimates (two mounted sergeants and four foot soliders for each knight) the county of Champagne would thus have contributed over one thousand troops to the war. Even if Joinville, who provides the information on the Champenois losses, exaggerated slightly the number of bannerets killed in battle, the basic point is that a very large contingent of Champenois knights was on crusade.[12]

[6] Strayer, "Crusades of Louis IX," p. 166.

[7] Ibid., p. 167.

[8] Joinville's *Histoire* is the best source here; see also Loisne, "Catalogue des actes de Robert . . . d'Artois," p. 198 no. clvi.

[9] *Layettes*, v, no. 548.

[10] See Joinville, chaps. XXIV, LXXXVI, XCII. See also the "List of Knights" in Johnes, *Memoirs*, II, 226. This list of knights accompanying Louis on crusade is dated variously by different authors. Johnes refers it to the first crusade, 1248; the editors of volume XX of *HF* to the eve of the second crusade (1269). Part of the list must go back to 1248, however, since it records a loan to Guillaume, titular count of Flanders, who died in 1251 (below chapter 5 n. 125). Other data for the later crusade may have been added subsequently to the original list, so that the transcription which has come down to us is an amalgam.

[11] "List of Knights," Johnes, *Memoirs*, II; *HGL*, VIII, c. 1222. See also "Notes," in the Hague ed. of Joinville, pp. 256-57. Joinville may be introducing nomenclature more typical of the very late thirteenth century by using the word *banneret*; however, the term became fairly common after 1240; cf. Contamine, *Guerre, état, société*, p. 14 n. 21.

[12] Cf. Prévost, "Champenois aux croisades," pp. 163-65.

Evidence is less rich on the Burgundians, Flemings, and Bretons, but what there is indicates that important contingents were raised by the seigneurs of these counties. Burgundian sympathy with the French royal house was a given almost throughout the century, and the duke of Burgundy took a prominent part in the military events of the late 1240s.[13] The Flemish contingent, though raised by the designated successor to the county, Guillaume Dampierre, was largely financed by Louis IX. The sums Louis invested were considerable and suggest, if in only the vaguest terms, that Guillaume's force was large.[14] On the Bretons we have little evidence. But since the old count had turned his county over to his son and had decided or been urged to go on crusade with Louis, it is probable that the king's appeals to the Breton baronage had a significant impact. The most recent historian of Breton events of this period has shown that all the substantial seigneurs in the county joined the king's crusade.[15]

The former rebels from the south contributed somewhat smaller contingents. Goceran de Pinos furnished five knights and twenty sergeants; Bernard de Caracilles and Olivier, lord of Termes, contributed the same.[16] Raymond Trencavel came up with five knights but he could muster only five sergeants.[17] Raymond, the count of Toulouse, and Hugh Lusignan, the count of La Marche, were greater men. The first, in the codicil to his will, offered fifty knights for the war;[18] the latter, in his will, five thousand pounds *tournois*.[19]

The Lusignans had pledged themselves to join the crusade,[20] but Hugh in fact died in late 1248.[21] I am thus using his bequest of five thousand pounds as an approximation of the actual initial outlay of the family in carrying out his testament. In terms of men, Hugh's oblation is rather tricky. Yearly earnings for knights varied from about 160 to 200 pounds *tournois*.[22] Sergeants, who made as much as

[13] Briefly the Burgundians *had* supported the rebels (circa 1230) not because of dislike for Louis, but because of the duplicity of Thibaut of Champagne; see Joinville, chap. XVIII. On the duke's crusading vow, chap. XXIV; and on his and his company's activities during the crusade, chaps. XXXII, XLV, XLVII, XLVIII, LIII, LV, LIX. See also MP, V, 143.

[14] On the loans, see below figure nine. The actual size of the Flemish knightly class in the first half of the thirteenth century has been established by Warlop, *Flemish Nobility*, I, pt. 1, p. 307, as one thousand.

[15] Martin, *Ordres mendiants en Bretagne*, p. 18.

[16] *HGL*, VI, 786; VIII, cc. 1222, 1224. These references are to records of loans made to the barons which indicate the size of their contingents.

[17] Ibid., VIII, c. 1223; see also, VI, 792.

[18] *Layettes*, III, no. 3803. See also *HGL*, VI, 788, and above chapter 3 n. 31.

[19] *Layettes*, III, no. 3705.

[20] MP, V, 158, 204, and VI, 159; *Layettes*, V, no. 529; Joinville, chap. XXIV.

[21] Molinier, *Correspondance*, p. 420 n. 1.

[22] "List of Knights," Johnes, *Memoirs*, II, 224. See also Strayer, "Crusades of Louis IX," p. 166; and Contamine, *Guerre, état, société*, pp. 95, 619.

90 pounds per year, usually accompanied them,[23] and it is not unlikely that cost of passage to the fighting was intended to be covered
from Hugh's five thousand pounds.[24] Ten knights, at the outside fifteen, joined the French king's army by means of Hugh's money.

One of the most peculiar features of the period of Louis's preparations for crusade was the large number of his barons who took the
vow but died before they ever left. Raymond of Toulouse died almost
on the eve of departure. Hugh Lusignan, as it has just been pointed
out, passed away in 1248. The count of Saint-Pol who was eagerly
making preparations died just before they were completed.[25] We
know about some of their efforts because of the wills they left behind,
copies of which were sometimes kept in the royal archives. This careful planning was a natural outgrowth of the provision of the Council
of Lyon that urged those who took the cross to adjust their wills in
order to make a pledge to the crusade.[26]

It is from another of these contingency bequests that we can estimate the size of the force furnished by the count of Boulogne.[27] Evidently he had intended to invest 1,500 pounds *parisis* (1,875 pounds
tournois) into the Holy War. Using the same sort of calculation that was
employed in the case of Hugh Lusignan's will, we conclude that this
bequest could not have provided more than five knights and their
companies for a full year.

We have only bits and pieces of information on the other contingents. Joinville's cousin, the count of Saarbrücken, financed ten
knights; Joinville also ten (counting himself).[28] The king's sister, the
devoted Isabella, took the money left her by her father and financed
ten knights for her brother's crusade.[29] A few petty seigneurs could
do little more than bring themselves.[30] But middle-class or even
lower-middle-class persons gathered up enough to join the king as
well. One ought not overemphasize this last point—the data are ex-

[23] Strayer, "Crusades of Louis IX," p. 166.
[24] On the desire of Louis IX to have the barons supply transportation for their contingents, see below nn. 45-47.
[25] MP, v, 93; Lépinois and Merlet, *Cartulaire de Notre-Dame de Chartres*, III, 84.
[26] Purcell, *Papal Crusading Policy*, p. 28, discusses this provision (canon 15 of the decrees of the council). See too the "Letter of John Sarrasin," p. 243.
[27] Delisle, *Cartulaire normand*, no. 1186.
[28] Joinville, chap. XXIV.
[29] Garreau, *Bienheureuse Isabelle*, p. 40; giving money was the normal way for women
to fulfill their vows, Brundage, *Medieval Canon Law and the Crusader*, pp. 77, 102.
[30] See the lists of seigneurs who accompanied the king prepared by several contemporary or near-contemporary observers: Guillaume de Nangis, *HF*, XX, 353; Baudoin
d'Avesnes, *HF*, XXI, 165; MP, IV, 489-90, and v, 1; Joinville, chap. XXIV; and Minstrel of
Reims, p. 334. Cf. "List of Knights" in Johnes, *Memoirs*, II. See also the early works of
those scholars who may have had access to scraps of information now lost such as Colliette, *Vermandois*, II, 630; and Essigny, *Roye*, p. 26.

ceptionally sparse—but one finds evidence of a Vermandois butcher in the army, of middle-class Germans, and eventually of French and Flemish peasants.[31]

A large number of prelates took the vow (a certain proportion also failed to fulfill it). They too were grand seigneurs and might have sent large contingents in their behalf even when they personally did not leave the country. The roll call of bishops who took the cross is impressive: the archbishops of Bourges and Reims, the bishop of Beauvais, the bishop of Noyon, the bishop of Orléans, the bishop of Clermont, and the bishop of Soissons.[32] (The absence of southerners should be noticed.) Taking a sample of the abbots and priors of the French church, one can identify a peak in the turnover of these officers—with incumbents presumably joining the crusade—before both of Louis's expeditions.[33]

There was less success in turning the crusade into an international enterprise, a conclusion which follows from what we have seen of Louis's failure in "foreign policy." Some northern Europeans came—a handful of Norwegians;[34] a somewhat miscellaneous group of Germans who may not have got any further than Italy;[35] two hundred or so Englishmen;[36] and perhaps a few Scots.[37] Some Italians came, but the number of them and who paid for them are problematic.[38] Fundamentally, Louis's crusade was a French crusade.

It would be misleading to suggest that the contingents raised by the ancillary leaders of the crusade were financed without help from the king. In the beginning, it is true, most were, but as time went on they required generous injections of money from Saint Louis to sustain them (see table eight). Indeed, for certain contributors the king even underwrote the initial effort. This was particularly the case with former rebels. Whatever may have been their protestations of pov-

[31] Colliette, *Vermandois*, II, 630; and below n. 35 and chapter 5 n. 48.
[32] See the sources adduced above n. 30. See also *GC*, II, cc. 276-77; Joinville, chap. LXXVII; and Colliette, *Vermandois*, II, 633. Among those who were allowed to renounce their vows were the archbishop of Bourges and the bishop of Orléans; below chapter 5 n. 80.
[33] I took my sample from volume two of *GC*. Leaves of absence were evidently granted normally to such prelates; cf. Brundage, *Medieval Canon Law and the Crusader*, p. 178.
[34] Joinville, chap. XCVI; they seem to have arrived rather late.
[35] At least 452 Germans, most of whom seem to have been rather middling people, trekked to Italy to find a way to the Holy War. In 1250 they were still arguing with the Italians about booking passage; *Layettes*, III, no. 3883.
[36] MP, v, 76. See also Tillemont, *Vie de SL*, III, 265; and Strayer, "Crusades of Louis IX," p. 162.
[37] Potthast, *Regesta*, II, 1188; and MP, v, 93, for the fact that Scots were building a ship for the French crusader, the count of Saint-Pol.
[38] Italian crews must have manned many of the ships Louis hired; below n. 44, and Joinville, chap. LXXVIII.

erty—and consistent failure in rebellion induces poverty—the most important rebels were still persuaded to join the crusade. To accomplish this, Louis lent Goceran de Pinos 50 pounds, Bernard de Caracilles 50 more, and Trencavel 290.[39] Blanche of Castile lent the count of Toulouse 20,000 pounds *parisis* (25,000 pounds *tournois*).[40]

Estimates vary on the total size of Louis's expenditures for troops (and for the horses[41] and medical personnel[42] which accompanied them). But despite all he did to encourage his barons to finance their efforts on their own, the estimates of his personal expenses, for the army alone, begin at 500,000 pounds; a better estimate, perhaps, is one million pounds for the first two years, the most active militarily of the war.[43]

To have raised an army was a notable achievement, but it was only the opening act in a continuing drama. The army had to be transported. From the beginning Louis intended that the burdens incurred for overseas transport were to be shared between him and the other leaders of the crusade. In 1246 he had contracted for thirty-six fully outfitted ships from Genoa and Marseilles.[44] His associates worked on a smaller scale. His friend John of Joinville together with John's cousin, the count of Saarbrücken, hired a vessel at their own expense.[45] The count of Saint-Pol who died in 1248 had earlier commissioned a ship that was to be built at Inverness in Scotland.[46] Its ultimate disposition, as far as I can tell, is unknown. The count of

[39] For the first two, *HGL*, VIII, c. 1224 (December 1247); for Trencavel, *Layettes*, III, no. 3700 (July 1248).

[40] For the loan, *Layettes*, III, no. 3672. See also *HGL*, VI, 787. The count's testament directed that the money be returned in the event of his death and that his contingent of fifty knights be financed from his estate (above n. 18).

[41] The French crown traditionally accepted responsibility for its men's horses lost in battle (cf. *HF*, XXIV, 258 nos. 45-46), and on the crusade each leader assumed responsibility for horses lost in passage or in battle. See, for example, the account for Alfonse (1250): *Summa pro deperditis equorum baronum et militum*: $II^M V^C XV$ lb. (*Layettes*, V, no. 548). See also "List of Knights," Johnes, *Memoirs*, pp. 222-26; and Contamine, *Guerre, état, société*, pp. 103-6.

[42] *Layettes*, III, no. 4022. See also Stein, "Pierre Lombard, médecin de SL," pp. 63-65; Lohrmann, "Pierre Lombard, médecin de SL," *passim*; and Daumet, "Femme-médecin," pp. 69-71.

[43] Strayer, "Crusades of Louis IX," pp. 166-67.

[44] For these contracts and references to them, see *Layettes*, II, no. 3537; *Une Charte de Nolis*; and *Formulaires*, no. 6, item 317. Most of these documents and some others are published with a few variations in Champollion-Figeac, *Documents*, I, 605-9, and II, 51-67. The record in vol. I was edited by A. Jal and is well done, but the bulk (in vol. II) appear to have been edited by Champollion who has been called "le plus inexact des éditeurs" by the compilers of the works of Marguerite d'Oingt; see Duraffour et al., *Oeuvres*, pp. 23-24 n. 6 (citing Mayer). For a brief discussion of Louis's hiring of ships, see Strayer, "Crusades of Louis IX," p. 165; and for a short discussion of the religious obligations of the suppliers of ships in relation to Louis's first crusade, see Purcell, *Papal Crusading Policy*, p. 55 n. 13.

[45] Joinville, chap. XXIV.

[46] MP, V, 93.

Toulouse negotiated successfully with contractors in Marseilles,[47] but his unexpected death probably terminated the contracts. In an eleven-month period in 1250, the king's brother, Alfonse, paid out over six thousand pounds in wages for sailors and for leasing ships and galleys.[48] In the end, however, Louis had to subsidize him and other barons heavily. He lent Alfonse forty-six hundred pounds *pro navibus*,[49] and he also aided the lord of Termes in securing transportation to the East.[50]

The question of sea transport leads naturally to the problem of supplies and port facilities. Louis's agents began purchasing perishable stores and other supplies for the king's ships before the crusade, but, of course, additional purchases were made as the crusade continued.[51] One fourteenth century government estimate put Louis's naval costs above thirty-two thousand pounds *tournois* for three or four years (1250-1253) of the six-year crusade.[52] This figure cannot include galley rations for the crews or expenditures for upkeep and repairs which predate the period for which the estimate was made. Yet food supplies for the crews before embarkation of the crusaders cost him nearly two thousand pounds *tournois*, and an entry in the royal accounts of 5,926 l. for "canvas, hauling line, rope, towing gear, yard arms and rudders" at the port of Aigues-Mortes, the agreed-upon point of embarkation, makes it clear that the Italians had never outfitted Louis's ships properly or that bad weather at the port, probably the winds, had damaged them severely.[53]

Certain conditions in the port itself, aside from the heavy winds that buffeted loading craft and large ships alike, were also alarming. Not the least of these were the recurrent silting of the inner harbor and the lack of fresh water for the embarking troops.[54] One might wonder why Aigues-Mortes was ever chosen as the site for the departure. But this little village, which some have supposed had a distinguished classical history,[55] was in one of the few coastal areas, with a natural harbor, under direct royal control. Rather than use Montpel-

---

[47] Guillaume de Puylaurens, *HF*, xx, 771. [48] *Layettes*, v, no. 548.
[49] Ibid., iii, no. 4310, and iv, no. 5722. [50] *HGL*, viii, c. 1222.
[51] *Layettes*, ii, no. 3537; Champollion-Figeac, *Documents*, ii, 62-63 no. 30. See also Tillemont, *Vie de SL*, iii, 111.
[52] *HF*, xxi, 515.
[53] For the figures, ibid., 283. The money of account here was *viennois*; it ran considerably less than *tournois* in the fourteenth century, but as far as can be determined it ranged from about .75 to .88 of *tournois* in commercial transactions in the mid-thirteenth century; Cartier, "Remarques," p. 127; Fournier and Guébin, *Enquêtes administratives*, p. 475 n. p. Tillemont (*Vie de SL*, iii, 171) mentions payments of eleven thousand pounds for diverse naval stores.
[54] In general, see Labarge, *SL*, p. 102; and Morize, "Aigues-Mortes."
[55] Cf. Albaric, *Aigues-Mortes*, pp. 12-15; Pietro, *Aiguesmortes*, pp. 11-12; and Mahoudeau, *Croisade*, p. 18.

lier, Marseilles, Saint-Gilles, or even Narbonne—and something could be said against each town[56]—Louis chose to pursue an independent policy which would relieve him and future Capetian kings of the necessity to go begging to haughty municipal oligarchies. Given the peculiarities of Aigues-Mortes's ecology, this decision was a questionable experiment in royal policy.[57]

It devolved on the king's agents to solve the problems: the common theme in all their efforts, as it had been in raising the army and procuring transportation for it, was the endeavor to circumvent direct expenditures. But the ideal was rarely achieved. Under their supervision workmen apparently extended the system of natural channels with the construction of an artificial canal, which allowed egress from the port for small loading craft.[58] It is also a reasonably good hypothesis that fresh water, *aqua dulcis*, was shipped into the town of "Dead Waters" to supplement its inadequate supplies;[59] similar shipments for other nearby coastal towns were not unknown during peak activ-

[56] Because of its infection with heresy and rebellion, Louis took temporary control over Narbonne in the early 1240s, but he reinstated self-government after 1243 (cf. Emery, *Heresy*, pp. 101, 147). Besides its dubious loyalty and its status as a species of free city like Marseilles, Narbonne was also too close to Aragon. On these points, see Labarge, *SL*, p. 102; Pietro, *Aiguesmortes*, p. 12. Montpellier was partly under the suzerainty of the king of Aragon; *HGL*, VIII, cc. 1429-30. Sablou, "SL et le problème de la fondation d'Aiguesmortes," pp. 259-65, has an interesting argument that the small harbor of Saint-Gilles, near Aigues-Mortes, was also not chosen because it was in the proximity of imperial territories.

[57] More could be said on this issue, especially with regard to Aigues-Mortes's lagoon-indented shoreline. For centuries it has not allowed easy access to the open sea. Consequently scholars since Tillemont have striven to show that the coast line degenerated after the time of Louis IX. There is some truth in this, but whether one accepts the idea of massive degeneration or not, the harbor was always inferior; for a variety of opinions, see Pietro, *Aiguesmortes*, p. 12; Reclus, *Nouvelle géographie universelle*, II, 248-49; Fliche, *Aigues-Mortes*, p. 6 n. 1; Mahoudeau, *Croisade*, pp. 44-45; Lasserre, *Aigues-Mortes*, p. 2; Perry, *SL*, p. 144. It is a fact that Louis's improvements were constantly in need of restoration in subsequent reigns; cf. Henneman, *Royal Taxation*, pp. 109-10.

[58] Cf. Lasserre, *Aigues-Mortes*, p. 2 n. 1 and map p. 63. See also, Reclus, *Nouvelle géographie universelle*, II, 249. Cf. also Germain, *Histoire du commerce de Montpellier*, map for vol. I; and Fliche, *Aigues-Mortes*, p. 7.

[59] On the lack of fresh water, see Lasserre, *Aigues-Mortes*, p. 7; cf. Reclus, *Nouvelle géographie universelle*, II, 247 n. 2; *Times Atlas*, p. 17. The name Aigues-Mortes suggests the quality of the water in the immediate area. The closest river with fresh water which Louis controlled (AD: Gard, H 106, fol. 59 recto; *GC*, VI, "Instrumenta," c. 202 no. xxxi) was the Vidourle. The delta-like Rhônes-Mortes are actually closer (Reclus), but the name again suggests the quality of the water. An undated petition (AD: Gard, SS 17 Nîmes) contains both a lament of the population of Aigues-Mortes over the "horrible and odious name" of their town and a request that the king divert a fresh water river to it: "quod dominus noster rex faciat fieri ut fluvius aque dulcis veniat, seu dirivetur, seu ducatur ad dictam villam"—cf. Ménard, *Nismes*, 1, "Preuves," p. 78. An archivist's notation on the original dates the petition to the thirteenth century. Some researchers (Marquet, Lasserre, Ménard) specify 1248, but Michel, the best of the lot, argued for a date closer to 1270.

ity.[60] There was nothing to be done about the winds, but the large ships could anchor in calmer waters at a distance. The improved system of channels would simplify supplying them.[61]

Aigues-Mortes also had no traditional system of provisioning. Being a new town (at most, only a small and insignificant fishing village existed on the site before Louis's building program began), trade routes bypassed the port. Merchants found the established depot at Nîmes and the bustling metropolis of Montpellier, with its easy access to the sea, much more attractive trading centers. To Louis and his agents this was a fundamental problem because these two great cities and a host of smaller towns were not eager to have their livelihood adversely affected in the interest of the king's new port.[62]

There seems to be no doubt that Louis found the problem more vexing and more time-consuming than he had anticipated. First it was necessary to plan the new routes of access to the town and to divert merchants and ships to the port.[63] As usual he (or his men) found a helpful tool in the coercive pressures that could be applied to former rebels—buying their land at strategic points, requisitioning products from their land without very much concern for the niceties of law (as he was to admit several years later when he made restitution to the despoiled lords).[64] The city of Nîmes fits in well with this analysis. Because it had a history of opposition to the royal presence in the south, the reaction of the city to the building of Aigues-Mortes could be ignored or, rather, severe measures could be threatened against it if it refused to go along with Louis's plans.[65]

The king's men had to be more careful in their dealings with other powers. Montpellier, for example, had a strong tradition of independence and was not susceptible to the forms of coercion practiced against defeated rebel seigneurs. If Louis had pushed too hard, the resistance of the Montpellierans to the building of Aigues-Mortes could have had international complications since the lord of part of the city was the king of Aragon. Thus, concessions went to Montpellier. As long as they did not directly impair the vitality of Aigues-Mortes, these were passed out rather freely. Moreover, Louis's men used the city fathers' love of liberty to the king's advantage: they offered protection to the notables of the town, including its bishop,

---

[60] For water shipped to Montpellier in the mid-thirteenth century, see (Berthelé) *Archives cartulaires*, pp. 505-12; for Béziers in 1247, see Sabatier, *Béziers*, p. 451.

[61] On the winds—a problem noted by Joinville and even the pope—see Joinville, chap. CXXX; *HGL*, VII, 108. See also Tillemont, *Vie de SL*, III, 113. On the vagaries of anchoring in the Mediterranean near Aigues-Mortes and the relative calm of waters to the southeast of the town, see Reclus, *Nouvelle géographie universelle*, II, 250.

[62] Jordan, "Supplying Aigues-Mortes," pp. 165-69.

[63] Ibid., pp. 169-71.   [64] Ibid., pp. 170-72.   [65] Ibid., p. 169.

against the possible encroachments of the Aragonese crown.[66] Simultaneously, they eliminated tolls throughout royal Languedoc on many types of goods that were handled by merchants from Montpellier and certain other smaller towns.[67]

Despite the amount of effort, the short period between Louis's swearing of the crusading vow in December 1244 and his departure from Aigues-Mortes in August 1248 was hardly enough time to complete the harbor facilities. Negotiations for redirecting trade dragged on until June of 1249.[68] Only enough stone had been brought into the town by 1248 to build the Tour de Constance, the military tower protecting the port;[69] the ramparts were made of wood hastily requisitioned from the timber lands of former rebels and put into place by conscripted carpenters.[70] Yet, when all this is said, it remains true that in the short space of three and one-half years a royal port had been constructed in the south of France, an imposing symbol of the authority of the Capetian kings. It was to retain its importance until Montpellier could be annexed in the fourteenth century.[71]

I have called the port an "imposing" symbol—and that it was. Now, with the wooden ramparts replaced by the stone wall of Philip III,[72] it is perhaps more imposing in its architectural lines than it was in August 1248. On the other hand, today there are few people. One can hardly imagine the present sleepy town with perhaps five thousand troops[73] and their hangers-on—the servants, the horses and grooms,[74] and the prostitutes who no doubt tried to keep out of the king's sight.[75] All of the human activity took place in the shadow of the Tour de Constance.

Art historians—even the most distinguished of them—have been frankly uninterested in the military architecture of the magnificent tower.[76] The best descriptions are those of Protestant historians who

---

[66] Ibid., pp. 166-67; and above n. 56.

[67] Jordan, "Supplying Aigues-Mortes," pp. 166-67. [68] Ibid., p. 171.

[69] The tower was constructed between 1246 and 1248; Morize, "Aigues-Mortes," pp. 321-22; *Histoire d'Aiguesmortes,* "Notes et pièces justificatives," no. II, pp. 60-61; Pietro, *Aiguesmortes,* p. 15; Fliche, *Aigues-Mortes,* p. 7 (cf. Millerot, *Lunel,* p. 71).

[70] *Histoire d'Aiguesmortes,* pp. 62-63; *SL,* Exposition, p. 48; Jordan, "Supplying Aigues-Mortes," pp. 171-72.

[71] Henneman, *Royal Taxation,* pp. 109-10. See also Dainville, *Archives . . . Montpellier: Documents omis,* II, 85 no. dclix et passim.

[72] Above n. 70.

[73] In coming to this figure I am simply assuming that a sizable proportion of the troops actually engaged by Louis were at the port in August 1248. Most of the ancillary efforts departed later.

[74] Jordan, "Supplying Aigues-Mortes," p. 171 n. 47.

[75] Louis's stern attitude toward crusaders who consorted with prostitutes is recorded in Joinville, chaps. xxxvi, xcli. They did not always keep out of his sight (chap. xxxvi).

[76] Branner, *SL and the Court Style,* p. 7.

1. The Tour de Constance, Aigues-Mortes, with the gate known as La Gardette to the left. The wrought-iron cone atop the tower is modern.

remember the tower as an austere and dreadful prison in the Wars of Religion[77] or those of nineteenth century antiquaries, like Prosper Mérimée, the eccentric inspector-general of historical monuments.[78] But the tower offers a great deal to the careful observer. It was deliberately constructed at a short distance from the original walls and stood out from the surrounding landscape (see the accompanying illustration). It was Louis's *palatium*; it was where he stayed with his wife when he arrived at the port.[79] It was built of special stone imported from the Rhône Valley near Beaucaire,[80] and it was from this citadel

[77] On its use as a prison, see Berthelé, *Répertoire numérique*, I, 411. See also Néel, *Tour de Constance*.

[78] Mérimée, *Notes de voyages*, pp. 187-90, 356.

[79] *HGL*, VIII, cc. 945, 1247. The question of whether *palatium* in these instances has more than a conventional signification is problematical. Griffiths, *Counselors of Louis IX*, p. 2, has shown that chancery formulae often included the word in the reign of Saint Louis. Lépinois and Merlet (*Cartulaire de Notre-Dame de Chartres*, I, 123 n. 1) and Brühl (*Fodrum*, I, 248-50) have shown that the term sometimes had no relation to a real building at all.

[80] *Histoire d'Aiguesmortes*, "Notes et pièces justificatives," no. II, pp. 60-61; cf. Tillemont, *Vie de SL*, III, 114. Albaric, *Aigues-Mortes*, suggests that stone began to be brought to Aigues-Mortes as early as 1241 (cf. Morize, "Aigues-Mortes," p. 321). Louis certainly may have been thinking about building a defensive port in the hostile south this early, but major shipments are unlikely since he did not own the village of Aigues-Mortes then and since the south was in rebellion in 1240 and again from 1241 to 1243. Certain sources report that stone for the fortifications at Aigues-Mortes came from the moun-

that Louis would have had his first panoramic view of the Mediterranean Sea. In one sense, the tower—so severe in its architectural style—symbolized both the hard work which had already been done and that which still lay ahead of the determined monarch.

As he looked out upon the sea from Aigues-Mortes, Louis's thoughts must have turned to Cyprus, the secondary point of rendezvous for the various divisions of the crusading army. Sicily, owing to its imperial connection, had had to be discounted. When he finally arrived on Cyprus, Louis would engage shipwrights to build light attack and landing craft for the invasion of Egypt which was to be the first theater of military operations.[81] But long before this he had sent his agents to the island to prepare for the final arrival of the crusaders' forces. With Aigues-Mortes's facilities scarcely completed, the king surely worried about his agents' success in a foreign land. What of the enormous quantities of salted pork, of wheat, and of wine that would be required for the army? Had his men received the cooperation they so desperately needed?[82]

In fact, the situation on Cyprus, for all the clutter of domestic politics, was to turn out as well as the king could have hoped. A vision met Joinville on his arrival:

> There was such a supply of wine that in the middle of the fields by the seashore . . . [the king's] men had built great piles of barrels of wine which they had been buying for two years before his arrival; they had put them one on top of the other, so that when you looked at them from the front you would have thought that they were great wooden barns.

tainous region north of Beaucaire known as les Castillones (the evidence on this is criticized by Lasserre, *Aigues-Mortes*, p. 14 n. 1). This area, near the town of Aramon, was a region in which Louis exercised some immediate suzerain rights; Michel, *Beaucaire*, pp. 16, 72, 75. Lasserre, *Aigues-Mortes*, p. 14, believed that stone for the tower came from quarry sites on the Rhône, even nearer Beaucaire. Whatever the case, the cost of transporting the stone to Aigues-Mortes must have been very high indeed (cf. Jordan, "Supplying Aigues-Mortes," p. 169 n. 29), for both les Castillones and Beaucaire are about forty kilometers on a straight line from Aigues-Mortes. Why stone was not taken from closer sites is not difficult to determine. The regional stone is rather weak sandstone. Even though stone from around the town of Mus, which is close to Aigues-Mortes and in which Louis had some suzerain rights, was used to build the contemporary walls of Aimargues (Vidal, *Aimargues*, p. 31; Michel, *Beaucaire*, p. 75) and stones from the county of Melgueil were used to repair the walls of Aigues-Mortes in the early fourteenth century (Fawtier, *Comptes royaux*, I, no. 13797), the king's agents originally took no chance on the quality of the tower.

[81] Johannes de Columna, *HF*, XXIII, 119: the Christians landed in Egypt *in vasis parvis quae in insula Cypri fabricata fuerunt*.

[82] Joinville, chaps. LX, LXXII, LXXIX, talks about the salted meat (pork) a product obviously unrequisitionable from the native Moslem population of North Africa. It must either have been accumulated at Aigues-Mortes or Cyprus. On wheat and wine, below n. 83. The unsettled conditions in the internal politics of Cyprus have been alluded to before, chapter 2 n. 122.

The wheat and barley were also heaped out in the fields. At first sight you thought they were hills; the rain had made it sprout on the outside so that all you could see was green grass. But when they were ready to ship it to Egypt they tore off the outside crust of grass, and inside the wheat and barley were as fresh as if they had been newly threshed.[83]

It seems to me inevitable that a large portion of the supplies—both perishable and nonperishable—was lost to pilfering or even transported to the Moslems and resold at inflated prices. Establishing effective controls over a thousand-mile supply line was no more easy in the thirteenth century than in the twentieth. The royal archives assiduously kept records (*verba nunciorum*) concerning military equipment, contraband, given over to the sultan in the era of the crusades (*tradendo soldanc aliqua quibus se contra dominum regem juvare poterat*).[84] No estimate of Louis's losses to deceit can be made, but if the pilferers of military equipment in modern wars are any standard, they were very large indeed. That Louis, despite all the possible problems, still managed to keep his army well supplied[85] is probably evidence of overpreparation (expecting more troops to join the war than actually did) rather than of effective supervision of resources. This preparation for an overly generous estimate of troops gave him just the margin he needed to provision his own troops through the worst period of the crusade.

The raising of a large and powerful army and the transport of that army, with its supplies and stores, from a recently constructed harbor facility to Cyprus and thence to Egypt were no mean accomplishments. And the expenditures which they required—in spite of the efforts to cut costs—were considerable. But this is not the end of the story, for like every enterprise of these proportions major unexpected costs aggravated the financial problem: armies encamp and cross rivers; men must be hired to build bridges and look-out towers; spies must be engaged and loyalties suborned. Nothing is accomplished without money.[86] But the capture of the king by the Moslems at Mansourah and the rout of his army which ensued introduced the most unwonted expense, the ransom: money for his army, the city of Damietta for him. His captors demanded immediate payment of half of the money ransom, the total having eventually been fixed at

---

[83] Ibid., chap. XXIX.
[84] *Formulaires*, no. 6, item 399.
[85] Strayer, "Crusades of Louis IX," p. 165.
[86] Joinville's *Histoire* (e.g., chaps. XLI, XLIV, XLV, LIII, LVIII) often provides the crisp narration of such activities, and various financial records usually corroborate his impressions. See, for example, *Layettes*, v, no. 548, detailing Alfonse's expenses "pro liciis et fossatis factis ultra passum Mansoriam": II^c XVII lb. x s. and "pro gagiis carpentariorum": XLVII lb. XII d.

800,000 gold bezants (400,000 pounds *tournois*). Although the other half, by mutual consent, was never paid, the amount allocated for the army's release finally came to 208,750 pounds.[87] In addition Louis evidently redeemed many other troops later for relatively large sums.[88]

Even though the pace and enthusiasm of the crusaders, especially of his brothers, fell off after the defeat at Mansourah,[89] the king, obsessed with his mission, continued to pour his resources into the shattered crusade. For fortifications constructed in the Holy Land after he left Egypt, he spent ninety-five thousand pounds according to one governmental estimate.[90] It is unlikely that "fortifications" include military equipment like horns and glue which he purchased at about the same time for making crossbows.[91] Nor did the "end" of the crusade in 1254 bring his expenses to a close. To fulfill traditional etiquette, he gave pensions and gifts to some of the men who served him,[92] and he also spent an average of four thousand pounds *tournois* per year from 1254 until 1270 for a contingent of knights who remained in Acre after his departure for France.[93]

It is known that the total cost of the crusade or, rather, the outlay of money by Louis himself amounted to 1.5 million pounds *tournois*.[94] At the same time, the average annual income of the French monarchy

[87] I have converted the figures, which are often given in pounds *parisis*, to *tournois*. Minstrel of Reims, p. 338; Joinville, chaps. LXVII, XCII; MP, v, 204; and the governmental records in *HF*, XXI, 404, 515. See also Blancard, *Bésant d'or*, pp. 36-37; and Strayer, "Crusades of Louis IX," p. 177 (the latter author suggests tentatively that the excess beyond 200,000 pounds may have been interest).

[88] Cf. Joinville, chaps. LXXXIV, XCI. An early fourteenth century estimate of this (*HF*, XXI, 515) is 1,050 pounds *tournois*. Cf. MP, v, 342; and the chronicle of Limoges, *HF*, XXI, 767.

[89] Louis's brother Robert was killed in the battle; the other two brothers, Alfonse and Charles, later left the crusade. In general see the summary of evidence on this point in Purcell, *Papal Crusading Policy*, p. 77 nn. 120, 122; I also deal with this important matter below chapter 5 nn. 166-69.

[90] *HF*, XXI, 515. See also Tillemont, *Vie de SL*, III, 403-4, 413, 489-90; Sayous, "Mandats," p. 273.

[91] Joinville, chaps. LXXXVIII, XCII, CXX, CXXI.

[92] *Layettes*, III, nos. 3986, 4022, and perhaps 4334; v, no. 519; *HGL*, VIII, c. 1276. See also Daumet, "Femme-médecin," pp. 69-71.

[93] MP, IV, 459-60; Borelli de Serres, "Comptes d'une mission," p. 255 n. 6. See also Servois, *Emprunts*, pp. 1-8; Strayer, "Crusades of Louis IX," p. 181.

[94] Two different early fourteenth century governmental estimates (analyzed by Strayer and Schaube) may be found in *HF*, XXI, at p. 404 and at pp. 512-15. The first is for the duration of the crusade and amounts to 1,537,570 l. 13 s. 5 d. *tournois*. The second is for the period 1250-1253 and amounts to 1,053,476 l. 17 s. 3 d. (*tournois?*). Schaube in a brilliant two-part study, "Die Wechselbriefe König Ludwigs des Heiligen," suggested that this last sum was *parisis*: "Die 1053 476.17.3 paris der Gesamtausgabe des Königs 1250/3 sind gleich 1316 846 lb. turon" (p. 616). He also computed a mean daily cost of one thousand pounds for the crusade (p. 617). See also Strayer, "Crusades of Louis IX," pp. 166-67.

was about 250,000 pounds;[95] and most of that was earmarked for domestic use.[96] Therefore, to meet the expenses of the Holy War, the king attempted to increase the profits from his traditional sources of revenue and to call upon other sources explicitly conceived for the crusade. What these sources were and how he exploited them in order to achieve his goal are the concerns of the remaining part of this chapter.

The church had long taxed itself "voluntarily" in the interest of the crusades.[97] The proceeds of this taxation would then be turned over to the appropriate secular leaders to support their enterprises.[98] But the particular situations in which these agreements were made were always difficult. Arrears tended to mount up; ecclesiastics had to be "compelled" to carry through on their so-called voluntary efforts; and so forth.[99] It was no different for Louis. Originally the church in the province of Gaul had promised to give the king a twentieth of its annual income for three years, but Louis evidently put pressure on the papacy and selectively launched out against reluctant dioceses and, thereby, succeeded in coercing the hierarchy into granting him a tenth for three years.[100]

What sort of pressure he brought to bear is problematical. The suggestion that he might seize church property, which is found in the "Protest of St. Louis," would have been useful, but that document reports an embassy which must have post-dated negotiations for the tenth.[101] Louis might have threatened to squeeze vacant bishoprics for their income (at least, the eve of the crusade was marked by this type of activity),[102] but an explicit threat of this sort seems uncharacteristic of him. Although people sometimes do uncharacteristic things, it would be more reasonable to argue that the most extreme statements and actions were those of his subordinates. Nonetheless, they were not wholly to blame. If they went too far—if the ambassador to

[95] This figure is based on the computations of various accounts for the first half of the reign brought together by the editors of *HF*, xxi (p. lxxvi; convert to *livres tournois*). For a short general overview on royal finances under Saint Louis, see Favier, "Finances de SL."

[96] Schaube, "Wechselbriefe," p. 614, calculated expenditures after the crusade—when domestic expenses were the rule—at a little over 180,000 pounds.

[97] Lunt, *Papal Revenues*, p. 71; Purcell, *Papal Crusading Policy*, pp. 137-81. The royal government considered the levy an *auxilium*; *Formulaires*, no. 6, item 172.

[98] See the records of Louis's levy, *HF*, xxi, 532-40. Cf. Lunt, *Papal Revenues*, p. 76.

[99] *HF*, xxi, 532-40. The following form letter in the royal archives was inventoried by Jean de Caux: "Ut persone ecclesiastice compellantur solvere decimam pro subsidio Terre Sancte" (*Formulaires*, no. 6, item 6, also 171). Lunt, *Papal Revenues*, pp. 75-76, seems to have underestimated the difficulties with the levy.

[100] MP, iv, 561-62. See also Strayer, "Crusades of Louis IX," pp. 162-63.

[101] Above chapter 2 nn. 46, 54-56.   [102] Below nn. 152-76.

the Court of Saint Peter said too much in the "Protest"; if a royal *bailli* took too much from a vacant diocese—it is probably because they understood or thought they understood how important success on the crusade was to the king. The same royal attitude which impressed them must also have impressed reluctant churchmen to raise their contribution to the Holy War.

In 1251, in the aftermath of her son's capture, the regent secured an additional two-year tenth.[103] Combined with the earlier levy, the best estimate—and it is a very rough best estimate—is that 950,000 pounds *tournois* were eventually collected from clerical taxes in Gaul for the king's crusade.[104] This was almost two-thirds of the revenue ultimately expended by Louis for the war.[105]

The obstacles to getting hold of what was due, however, were numerous and exasperating. The collection mechanism was the first problem. Papal officials were authorized to collect the tenths,[106] but they often delegated their tasks to local churchmen.[107] The king, not quite satisfied with the eagerness or reliability of local prelates, used the *baillis* as watchdogs.[108] On numerous occasions they seem to have intruded themselves into the collection process. A notorious example during the regency involved one *bailli*'s confiscation of the property of the abbot of Cluny who claimed, on behalf of his monastery, an historical exemption from the tenth,[109] but a curious entry in the royal accounts suggests a more subtle role for the *baillis*.[110] The entry, in the Account for the Ascension term 1248 for Sens, indicates that sometimes only the formality of collection by churchmen was preserved:

[103] *Layettes*, III, no. 3924; *Reg.* of Innocent IV no. 6067 (as cited in Berger, *SL et Innocent IV*); cf. *HF*, XXI, 532-40; *Layettes*, V, no. 497; Potthast, *Regesta*, II, no. 14645.

[104] Strayer, "Crusades of Louis IX," p. 163.

[105] Although Louis IX had the right to the tenth, he sometimes distributed portions of it to ancillary leaders of the crusade. For Alfonse's access to this income, see *Layettes*, III, nos. 3679, 3725, 4081; for Raymond of Toulouse's, no. 3624. On the son of the duke of Burgundy, cf. Purcell, *Papal Crusading Policy*, p. 130. It is therefore impossible to determine how much of the 950,000 pounds went toward offsetting Louis's expenses. The current assumption is that the vast majority stayed with the king. But the matter is more than of pedantic interest.

[106] MP, V, 171. See also Lunt, *Papal Revenues*, p. 40.

[107] Or so the records indicate; *HF*, XXI, 533, 537, and elsewhere. Of course, despite Lunt's general statement to the contrary (above n. 106), these local men may have been the original delegates of the papal curia rather than appointees of the curial collectors.

[108] Cf., for example, the *baillis* noted in *HF*, XXI, 537-38; and in the fragmentary Candlemas 1250 (n.s.) Account, *HF*, XXII, 739.

[109] *HF*, XXIV, "Chronologie," p. 173. There were, on the other hand, many legitimate exemptions, notably the Cistercians; see the documents published by Petit, "Jully-les-Nonnains," pp. 771, 781; *Formulaires*, no. 6, items 132-33; and the chronicle of Limoges, *HF*, XXI, 766-67 and n. 7. The exempted religious seem to have given gracious grants (under pressure?) before Louis's second crusade; Huchet, *Chartrier . . . Fontmorigny*, p. 277; *Formulaires*, no. 6, item 353.

[110] *HF*, XXI, 273 (with marginal note).

after acknowledging the *bailli*'s collection of one such levy, the *bailli*'s clerk had second thoughts and tried to eradicate all reference to the impropriety. The erasure was not simply an attempt to rectify an unimportant clerical error, for the *bailli* involved in this case was none other than Thibaud Clairambaut, one of the small group of troubleshooters that Louis was employing on crusading matters.[111]

Plagued similarly by problems of collecting the levy, Louis encountered a second obstacle in his attempt to receive the tenth in southern Gaul, lower Languedoc. The new factor was legal. In territorial terms lower Languedoc was a relatively recent and certainly unstable acquisition, an inheritance from the Albigensian confiscations. Rights, privileges, and obligations were at best ill-defined and often profoundly different from northern customs.[112] Led by the archbishop of Narbonne, the hierarchy of the region employed an array of legal technicalities stressing the historical independence of the ecclesiastical province from lay power and its lack of obligations to the state—all aimed at avoiding having to pay the clerical levy.[113] Although the resistance was unsuccessful in most cases,[114] it is hardly surprising that the king ordered the *sénéchal* of Carcassonne in 1247, when the resistance first came to light, to keep close watch over the collection of the tenth in the south.[115]

Thus far I have been talking about the church in Gaul, only one department of the Church Universal. The papacy granted the king the return from a tenth on the cardinalate and from a twentieth on the clergy in other Catholic *regna*,[116] but these grants appear to have been completely ineffectual. No crusading revenue came to the support of Louis from England,[117] from Germany or from the Spanish kingdoms *ultra fines Galliae*.[118] In Norway King Haakon squeezed the

[111] Above chapter 3 nn. 72, 77.
[112] Cf. Bisson, "Negotiations for Taxes," pp. 80-81.
[113] *GC*, VI, "Instrumenta," c. 64 no. lxviii. See also Strayer, "Crusades of Louis IX," pp. 161-62 n. 3; and Purcell, *Papal Crusading Policy*, p. 150.
[114] I do, perhaps, find one example of success. Rouquette and Villemagne's *Cartulaire de Maguelonne*, II, 659 no. dlxxii, includes a papal document according the bishop of Maguelonne (Montpellier) exemption from the tenth, 12 December 1249. But a fragmentary royal account for Candlemas (2 February) 1250 (1249 old style) refers to the *decima deposita* at the major sees of Languedoc, including Maguelonne; *HF*, XXII, 739. It is possible that the papal order had not yet been received when the deposits were demanded.
[115] *HGL.*, VIII, c. 1222.
[116] *MP*, IV, 458.
[117] Thus, Strayer, "Crusades of Louis IX," p. 163 (citing Lunt and Powicke). But in fact this view can be made more precise. The levy was evidently collected in England; it was not distributed. See Brundage, *Medieval Canon Law and the Crusader*, pp. 186-87.
[118] The province of Gaul included, for example, part of Navarre; cf. *Layettes*, III, no. 4047, but on the general point, see Strayer, "Crusades of Louis IX," p. 163.

church for a third of its income, but used the money for his own personal needs.[119]

Granted that the church or, more properly, the French church gave 950,000 pounds for the Holy War (and presumably most of this went to the royal forces), that still left 550,000 pounds at the very minimum, equivalent to more than two years crown revenue, which ultimately Louis had to contribute. Here the refreshing efficiency of the new administrators played the decisive role. They were responsible for substantial increases in royal revenue in the late 1240s. Characteristically, the documentation is sketchy: reasonably full and comparable financial accounts for the monarchy exist only for the Ascension terms 1234, 1238, and 1248. Balance sheets and fragments of accounts for other terms and other years provide only a partial picture of the financial situation.[120] The problems of interpretation are also numerous: there is no assurance that the three fiscal terms (Ascension, All Saints', Candlemas) returned approximately equal income.[121] There is no way to correct for inflation. And the fiscal system in Normandy, for which documentation of income is even more fragmentary, differed markedly in some respects from that in other parts of the domain.[122] Nonetheless, the broad patterns of activity of the new administrators in meeting the urgent financial demands of their king emerge quite clearly from surviving fiscal records.

Bailliages were not unchanging units. New ones could be and were created; old ones disappeared or their "boundaries" were redefined.[123] Several however were relatively stable in the critical period that I am concerned with. I have compared the income of the six *bailliages* of this type for which records exist from the Ascension term 1238[124] and the Ascension term 1248.[125] In every case the comparisions demonstrate that more income was being collected in the latter term (table two) and that there were decreases in traditional expenses. The increases appear to arise from three developments:[126] (1) the more meticulous collection of nonfeudal sources of traditional revenue, (2) the deliberate and sustained exploitation of hitherto occasional extraordinary revenue, and (3) the creation of new sources of revenue explicitly in the interest of the crusade. Decreases in tradi-

[119] MP, IV, 458. See also Tillemont, *Vie de SL*, III, 151, and above chapter 2 nn. 113-15.
[120] The major royal accounts for France, outside of Normandy, are in *HF*, XXI and XXII; equally important accounts for Normandy are in *HF*, XXIV, "Preuves" and *Layettes*, V, no. 581.
[121] Gravier, "Prévôts," p. 572.   [122] Above chapter 3 nn. 15-19.
[123] Above chapter 3 nn. 68-71; see also Laurent, "Bailliage de Sens," pp. 322-29.
[124] *HF*, XXI, 252-60.   [125] Ibid., pp. 262-84.
[126] Total crown revenue in 1248 was less than that in 1238 because Poitou, Saintonge, Auvergne, and part of Touraine as well as Maine and Anjou were given over as appanages to Alfonse and Charles in the interim. For the totals, see *HF*, XXI, lxxxvi.

TABLE 2 ● Increases in Income:
Ascension 1238 to Ascension 1248, pounds *parisis*

Bailliage	Ascension 1238			Ascension 1248			Increase
Gisors	1227 l.	16 s.	10 d.	5571 l.	11 s.	3 d.	4344 l.
Amiens	322 l.		13 d.	6092 l.		10 d.	5770 l.
Vermandois	8928 l.	14 s.	11 d.	16040 l.	14 s.	4 d.	7112 l.
Sens	4793 l.	8 s.	10 d.	4924 l.	11 s.	2 d.	131 l.
Orléans	836 l.	13 s.		4735 l.	15 s.	9 d.	3899 l.
Bourges	589 l.	4 s.	11 d.	1852 l.	6 s.	11 d.	1263 l.

NOTE: The accounts for 1238 are listed in *HF*, xxi, under the name of the *bailli* alone; the accounts for 1248 under the *bailli* and *bailliage*. Part of the total for the *bailliage* of Gisors listed in the account of 1248 in pounds *tournois* has been adjusted to pounds *parisis*.

tional expenses primarily affected outlays for certain types of charity, for public works, and for salaries for lower echelon administrators.

The increase in collected revenue in the *bailliage* of Gisors[127] provides evidence that the new administrators were more meticulous than their predecessors in their attention to their work. Time after time one finds small increases in specific items over the ten-year period, three pounds more from the town of Villeneuve de Saint-Mellon, forty-two pounds more from the sales of lumber from the royal wood at Pacy, and so forth. Decreases were rare. It is possible, of course, that the increases occurred gradually and were independent of the needs of the crusade. In a sense, there is no way to test this hypothesis, but it is partly negated by the king's express reminder to the *baillis* in the late 1240s to farm out the appropriate parts of the royal domain at the highest possible levels.[128] Such a policy was not strange in itself; it must always have been the ideal procedure. But the fact of the reminders suggests that Louis intended the *baillis* to be more demanding than they had been in the past. In any case, the evidence from Gisors demonstrates that there were increases in successful bids for farms.[129]

Slightly more evidence pertains to the second method of increasing revenue, that is, the sustained, even abusive, exploitation of irregular

[127] On Gisors as a "border," that is, Franco-Norman *Bailliage*, which rendered its accounts in various monies of account, see Goineau, *Gisors*, pp. 129, 196-97 (he also discusses similar features of the financial records of Verneuil).

[128] Ménard, *Nismes*, I, 317; *HGL*, VIII, cc. 1235-36. See also Wallon, *SL*, II, 71.

[129] For example, profits from the sale of lumber at Pacy during the Ascension term 1238 were 191 l. 13 s. 4 d.; *HF*, xxi, 253. During the Ascension term 1248, they were 233 l. 6 s. 8 d.; *HF*, xxi, 277. That these profits were the proceeds of farms seems to be proved by the fact that if one multiplies each figure by three (since there were three terms per year) total annual profits would come to the elegant figures of 575 pounds in 1238, 700 pounds in 1248.

income:[130] confiscations of heretics' property in the south, the taking of the Jews, and profits from temporal regalia. With regard to the first, there are no adequate figures, but in an order dated July 1246, Louis announced his decision to pay the expenses of the Inquisition in the south of France as it ferreted out heretics.[131] By this action the Inquisition was urged to pursue a wider field of activity and more investigations. A year later Louis endowed two Dominican convents in the heartland of the Cathar heresy—at Béziers and at Carcassonne.[132] Far from being a new departure in French religious politics, however, Louis's order of 1246 and his endowments of Dominican houses were but the culmination of the traditional alliance between the militant church and the royal government in the south.[133] The political implications of this alliance—the conquest and absorption of Languedoc—have already been dealt with,[134] but the religious aspects, especially as they bear on fiscal matters, have not.

The French crown could always get some "moral capital" out of its defense of orthodoxy in the south. The eve of the crusade threw this issue into high relief, for in a sense the crusade for Jerusalem had to begin at home. The Dominicans who ran the Inquisition in the south seem to have got it into their heads that the sternest measures were called for in this period. They tended to transfer the king's enthusiasm for the crusade to their execution of his policies. In other words, if the Dominicans of the Inquisition were particularly stringent on the eve of the crusade, as some historians seem to suggest,[135] it was probably because they thought the king desired them to be. His efforts to control the institution much more closely after the crusade, his admission that he had been too rigorous, is reasonably good evidence that those who carried out his orders went too far.[136]

Of income from the taking of the Jews, we also have very little direct fiscal data, but the picture of a particular royal policy taken to

[130] I am using the traditional terms, but I agree with Henneman that there is a certain artificiality in the dichotomy regular/irregular or ordinary/extraordinary. Cf. Henneman, *Royal Taxation*, p. 18.

[131] *HGL*, VIII, c. 1206: the order provided, among other things, for the establishment of prisons for heretics, the confiscation of their property to reimburse providing them with bread and water, and the paying of the expenses of the inquisitors. See also Douais, "Sources de l'histoire de l'Inquisition," pp. 420-21 and 421 nn. 2-6.

[132] Above chapter 3 n. 110. Dossat, *Crises de l'Inquisition*, p. 190, has shown that the foundation of the Dominicans of Carcassonne was directly related to the inquisitorial activities of the friars.

[133] Guillaume de Chartres, *HF*, xx, 33. See also Dossat, *Crises de l'Inquisition*, pp. 173-96; Lacger, "Albigeois," p. 42; Delaruelle, "SL devant les Cathares," pp. 274-76. Cf. Dossat, "L'Établissement de l'Inquisition."

[134] Above chapter 2 nn. 6-10 et passim.

[135] Cf. Molinier, *Inquisition*, p. 462; and Dossat, *Crises de l'Inquisition*, pp. 173-96.

[136] Below chapter 6 nn. 129-35. Cf. Guiraud, *Histoire de l'Inquisition*, II, 237-38.

extreme by its administrators is the same as for confiscations of heretics' property. Louis was no friend of Judaism or of the Jewish population in France.[137] The monarchy had consistently made efforts to
denigrate the practice of Judaism.[138] As the fulfillment of royal anti-
Jewish polemics, the Talmud was condemned and burned on the eve
of the crusade perhaps even over the mild objections of the pope.[139]
Equally important, the profession of a large number of French Jews,
money-lending at interest, was extremely disagreeable to the pious
monarch and his mother who had made such business patently illegal
since 1230.[140] Again, however, the eve of the crusade may be regarded, at least partly, as a culmination of this policy as well.

Canon seventeen of the General Council of Lyon (1245) urged secular princes to take the usury of Jews for use in the Holy War.[141]
There are indications throughout the late 1240s of the king taking the
appropriate steps to raise money in this way. In July 1246 he commanded his chief officer of Carcassonne-Béziers to take stern measures against royal Jews.[142] In the late forties the Norman Exchequer
vigorously pursued a policy against Jewish moneylenders "for the salvation of (the king's) soul and the souls of his father and his predecessors." One-third of the money owed the Jews was pardoned; two-
thirds was remitted to the crown.[143] Throughout 1247 and into 1248,
the *enquêteurs* assiduously investigated usury in the provinces.[144] Finally, in 1248 or 1249 the Jews—or at least those who lent money at
interest and had not fled already—were expelled from France[145] and
their property confiscated: a Norman account for the Easter term

---

[137] The only book dealing in detail with royal policy toward the Jews (in this case of
northern France) is Chazan, *Medieval Jewry*. See, *inter alia*, the criticisms of Zimmer,
"Medieval Jewry," and Strayer's review, p. 385. Two short studies are those of Labarge,
"SL et les juifs," and Riquet, "SL et les juifs." See also Jordan, "Jews on Top" and Nahon, "Ordonnances."

[138] Labarge, "SL et les juifs," pp. 269-70. All authors now agree that the anti-Jewish
policies of Blanche and Louis were fundamentally different from those of their more
lenient predecessors; cf. Chazan, *Medieval Jewry*, pp. 32-33, 43-44, etc.

[139] *CUP*, nos. 172, 173, 178; Jourdain, *Index chronologicus*, no. LX. See also Labarge,
"SL et les juifs," p. 271; and, for background, Chazan, *Medieval Jewry*, pp. 126, 129-31,
and Rabinowitz, *Social Life of the Jews*, p. 105. Cf. Nahon, "Ordonnances," p. 22.

[140] Langmuir, "*Judei nostri*," pp. 203-39, discusses the history of royal legislation culminating in the ordinance of 1230. See also Labarge, "SL et les juifs," p. 269.

[141] MP, IV, 459. See also Berger, *SL et Innocent IV*, p. 136.

[142] *HGL*, VIII, c. 1191. An important additional measure in the south, taken against
Jewish vendors of meat, is discussed in Jordan, "Problems of the Meat Market of
Béziers."

[143] Delisle, *Jugements de l'Echiquier*, nos. 735-36.

[144] Above chapter 3 n. 120; and cf. Chazan, *Medieval Jewry*, pp. 119-20.

[145] Unfortunately the only reference to the expulsion of 1248/9 is an allusion from a
post-crusade ordinance; *Ordonnances*, I, 85 (1257/8). See also Strayer, *Administration of
Normandy*, p. 50; Roth, in *Cambridge Medieval History*, VII, 657. Cf. Nahon, "Pour une
géographie administrative," p. 326. That only usurers were expelled is evident from

1252 confirms the royal administrators' partial success in dispossessing the Jews.[146]

These actions undoubtedly had a directly deleterious effect on the Jewish population in royal France, but there were inportant indirect consequences as well. Although Louis would not have condoned everything that happened in the wake of his pronouncements, the general enthusiasm aroused by a "campaign" against the Jews could not have been entirely disagreeable to him. All that had to be done was to channel the enthusiasm against the Jews (the enemy of Christianity at home) into enthusiasm for the crusade (against the enemy abroad). The financial gains that the king's barons could expect from "taking" the profits of Jewish usury if they joined him on crusade were the material link between the two.[147]

These actions—whether on Louis's part or his barons'—fanned nascent popular anti-Judaism in any number of instances. In 1247 in the eastern town of Valréas, not far from the present Swiss border, wandering Franciscans dredged up the libel of ritual murder and would have wreaked havoc on the Jewish population of the town but for the timely intervention of the local lord.[148] While Louis was actually on crusade, a motley group of his supporters in France on their way to join him, took some time out to plunder the goods of the Jews of Bourges, to burn their books, and to desecrate their synagogue.[149] When a group of contemporary English Jews asked the king of England for permission to leave his oppressive rule, he wondered aloud where they would go: "Behold the king of the Franks hates you and persecutes you, and has condemned you to perpetual exile; avoiding Charybdis (England) you have desired to sink in Scylla (France)."[150] Perhaps the most knowledgeable student of Franco-Jewish relations, Bernard Blumenkranz, put it best when he wrote, "pour les Juifs, Louis IX n'est pas Saint Louis."[151]

Besides confiscations of heretics' and Jews' property, temporal re-

---

the Michaelmas account of Normandy 1252 in which a Jew at Alençon is recorded as living peaceably and paying his customary rent of twenty shillings.

[146] The confiscations of Jewish chattels took place at Falaise, Caux, and (Château-)Vire. The total amount was small, about one hundred pounds, but the record at least confirms the actual confiscation of property; *Layettes*, v, no. 581. See also *QNor*, no. 67. Cf. Lazard, "Revenues tirés des juifs," p. 233.

[147] Taxes were imposed on the Jews, for example, by Alfonse of Poitiers, and he also threatened to expel them (below nn. 213-14).

[148] Molinier, "Enquête sur un meurtre"; Berger, *SL et Innocent IV*, pp. 306-10. Langmuir, "Absence d'accusation," p. 243, seems to tie this event to the atmosphere created by Louis's condemnation of the Talmud.

[149] Below chapter 5 n. 72.

[150] MP, v, 441. Either the king or the reporter (Matthew Paris) has confused Scylla with Charybdis.

[151] "Louis IX ou SL et les juifs," p. 21.

galia constituted another source of irregular income. This was the king's recognized right to an undefined portion of the revenues of certain vacant benefices.[152] Many kings abused this privilege by design;[153] but there is no indication that Louis IX did.[154] What did occur from about 1245 on, however, was a close inspection of the archives in preparation for the departure for crusade. A new inventory of records (known as Register F) was prepared for the king's use abroad.[155] The search of extant inventories and documents in making this register probably had a byproduct in the review of rights and obligations between the crown and its dependents. No institution was affected so much by this as the church. One happy result may be seen in the remarkable peak in the number of royal confirmations of ecclesiastical liberties on the eve of the crusade.[156] On the other hand, in certain instances, in which rights were disputed and in which the king or his men thought the crown had the better case, "settlements" only served to antagonize the churchmen.

So it was with temporal regalia and the right that often led to the sustained exploitation of temporal regalia, the *licentia eligendi*. The *licentia* was the face-to-face permission which certain chapters and monastic communities had to seek from the king before electing their bishop or abbot.[157] Failure to apply for the *licentia*—a formality that was sometimes ignored before 1245—became a point of contention between lay authorities and churchmen after that date. Needless to say, failure to apply for the *licentia* invalidated the election and inevitably prolonged vacancies. As a result, the king's men collected ecclesiastical revenues longer than they would normally have anticipated from those benefices where the right of temporal regalia also

[152] Campbell, "Temporal and Spiritual Regalia," and idem, *Ecclesiastical Policy*, pp. 64-77. See also *Formulaires*, no. 6, items 71-75. As I use the adjective *regalian* in the following paragraphs, I mean, always, temporal regalia not "royal." There is less evidence on spiritual regalia, the king's right to fill benefices *sede vacante*, but the conclusions with regard to the history of temporal regalia that I come to in the text apply in general to spiritual regalia as well. On spiritual regalia, besides the article by Campbell, see also Mollat, "Application du droit régale spirituelle," pp. 430-31. Cf. *Layettes*, II, nos. 3211-13.

[153] Cf. Knowles, *Monastic Order*, pp. 612-13.

[154] Campbell, *Ecclesiastical Policy*, p. 77; idem, "Temporal and Spiritual Regalia," p. 371; Berger, *SL et Innocent IV*, p. 373 n. 2.

[155] Delisle, *Catalogue des actes de Philippe-Auguste*, pp. xviii-xx; (Delaborde) *Layettes*, v, ix-x; Berger and Delaborde, pp. xxxvii-xxxix.

[156] The easiest way to verify this numerically would be to have a collection of the extant charters of Louis IX; there is no such collection. But the Norman charters have been brought together by Delisle (*Cartulaire normand*), and it can be demonstrated from them that the number of *conventiones* with ecclesiastics from 1246 through June 1248 was about the same as that for the whole first twenty years of the reign; pp. xxviii-xxx. Cf. above chapter 3 n. 86.

[157] Berger, *SL et Innocent IV*, pp. 42 n. 3, 44 n. 2, 373-76; Campbell, *Ecclesiastical Policy*, pp. 66-68.

applied. In 1245 failure to apply for the *licentia* was grounds for keeping the bishopric of Châlons vacant.[158] In 1246 failure to apply for the *licentia* was cause for discord between the crown and the bishopric of Limoges.[159] In 1250, formal disagreements over the *licentia* also placed Clermont in a difficult position after the death of its bishop on crusade.[160]

In several other instances disputes arose over the nature of regalian powers over sees which claimed and, in some cases, could prove an earlier exemption. It is not always possible to know the basis of the king's demands for the revenues of a vacant diocese, especially where there is strong evidence of a previous royal cession.[161] For example, it is difficult to explain the attempt to collect the regalia of Langres in February 1245 (it had been ceded in 1203),[162] or that of Auxerre in February 1247 (it had been ceded in 1206).[163] Perhaps we may take our cue from the situation in the diocese of Limoges. Louis claimed the regalia there in 1246 probably because an earlier concession of the right had been invalidated on political grounds.[164] No doubt, some such occurrence, although not necessarily similar in detail, affected the situation in the other sees as well.

Concurrent with the preparation of the new Register F, an effort—a very unsuccessful one according to Delaborde—was made to detail, also in register form, the documentary records of the king's relations with Languedoc.[165] But the royal government simply did not yet know very much about its rights (such as regalia) over the church in Occitania.[166] For different reasons, the crown's rights of regalia in the

---

[158] *Layettes*, II, nos. 2940, 3353. Cf. *Layettes*, II, nos. 3122, 3150. See also Campbell, "Temporal and Spiritual Regalia," pp. 360-61.

[159] *Layettes*, II, nos. 3466, 3472. Cf. *GC*, II, c. 529.

[160] *Layettes*, III, no. 3906; cf. no. 3894. See also *GC*, II, cc. 276-77.

[161] Cf. Campbell, *Ecclesiastical Policy*, p. 77; Benson, *Bishop-Elect*, p. 368.

[162] Delisle, *Catalogue des actes de Philippe-Auguste*, no. 791; *GC*, IV, "Instrumenta," c. 197; *Reg.* of Innocent IV no. 1056 (as cited and discussed in Campbell, *Ecclesiastical Policy*, pp. 70-77).

[163] *Reg.* of Innocent IV no. 2386 (as cited and discussed in Campbell, *Ecclesiastical Policy*, pp. 70-77); Gaudemet, *Collation . . . des bénéfices vacants en régale*, p. 14 n. 2.

[164] *Layettes*, II, nos. 3466, 3472. The cessions of the regalia of Limoges (in 1203; confirmed 1224) may be consulted in *GC*, II, c. 527; and Petit-Dutaillis, *Louis VIII*, App. VI, nos. 158-59, 262. The crown was again exercising the right of regalia in 1238 (Account of the Ascension term 1238, *HF*, XXI, 258). The original cession of 1203 had not eliminated the regalian obligations of the bishopric per se but had translated the rights of collection of the count of La Marche. The support for and participation in rebellions against Louis by his house had probably invalidated the original grant.

[165] The so-called Register XIII which should be dated before 1254 according to Delaborde's remarks in *Layettes*, V, x.

[166] On the eve of the crusade, Louis authorized investigations into the regalian rights applicable to Le Puy as well as throughout the south; *GC*, II, 742, and *HGL*, VIII, c. 1196. See also Campbell, *Ecclesiastical Policy*, pp. 72-73; Boutaric, *SL et Alfonse*, p. 436; and Bisson, "Organized Peace," pp. 296, 310-11.

appanages were unclear; the issue unfortunately seems to have been left vague at the time of the institution of the system. Again, however, an attempt was made to delimit the powers of the appanage princes and the king and to avoid or lessen possible tensions.[167]

The inquiries into royal rights suggested by the problems we have seen with regalia were not all completed by the time of the king's departure; many points still in contention when he left for crusade would not be settled before his return, and some, indeed, would be aggravated during his absence.[168] More pertinent at this point in our discussion is the fact that the new administrators apparently took their jobs even more seriously than the king would have hoped. During the king's exercise of his right of temporal regalia over Châlons in 1248 the income of the bishopric during the Ascension term was 323 pounds of which 200 went into the royal treasury as a tidy profit. The mendicants received 40 pounds as an episcopal charity; the royal guards 45 for their work. The operations of the diocese were maintained—if that is the word I want—for a paltry 35 pounds.[169]

The case of Châlons was hardly exceptional. Income at Chartres, during approximately four months of a vacancy in 1248, came to 860 pounds. Ten pounds were allocated for the operating expenses of the diocese; 850 went into the royal treasury.[170] Alas, only a final 70 pounds are mentioned in the documentation for Rouen for the last portion of its vacancy in 1248.[171] But the exploitation suggested by the examples from Châlons and Chartres must necessarily inform scholars' conclusions about what took place in Rouen, in Amiens, in Soissons, in Sens, in Thérouanne, in Jumièges, and other places during vacancies in the late 1240s and early 1250s.[172] One thing is certain: royal administrators were not allocating sufficient funds for the spiritual work of the communities in this period.[173]

This state of affairs may have been the administrators' fault. Chosen for their loyalty to the crown, encouraged no doubt by an en-

---

[167] The king had not specifically reserved the right of regalia in the grants in appanage to Robert in 1237 or Alfonse in 1242; *Layettes*, II, nos. 2562, 2926, and *Ordonnances*, XI, 329. However, in August 1246, when Louis granted Charles the appanage of Anjou-Maine, he reserved regalia; d'Achery, *Spicilegium*, III, 623, and *Ordonnances*, XI, 329-30. In 1246 in a grant of privileges to all three brothers, he again retained regalia over churches affected by the grant; *Layettes*, V, no. 482. In 1247, he continued this pattern in a grant to Alfonse; *Ordonnances*, IV, 206, 646-47, 663-64. Cf. Wood, "*Regnum Francie*," p. 129.

[168] Below chapter 6 nn. 95-96.   [169] *HF*, XXI, 282.   [170] Ibid.

[171] Ibid., XXII, 739. Eudes Rigaud had been elected in March 1248.

[172] Ibid., 740; *GC*, "Monitum," p. ii (on the coupling of Morinensia with Amiens); Delisle, *Cartulaire normand*, no. 488; Boutaric, *Actes*, I, "Arrêts . . . antérieurs aux *Olim*," no. 37. See also Berger, *SL et Innocent IV*, pp. 393-94.

[173] *Olim*, II, 183, xxxviii, as cited and discussed by Phillips, *Regalienrecht in Frankreich*, p. 63.

thusiastic king to do their best for the crusade, and instructed to be just but thorough in the exploitation of royal revenue, many of them probably erred on the side of thoroughness. Perhaps as a group they were too quick to use the needs of the crusade as justification for a certain preemptoriness and insensitivity on their part. But to be fair, it could not have been easy to walk the fine line described by the king when the administrators so often came into contact with stubborn prelates whom they rightly suspected of a certain lack of enthusiasm in paying for the Holy War.

If the administrators were directly responsible, it was obviously the king on whom churchmen themselves put the blame. The church felt wrung out by the tenth.[174] Still, it was something that had become traditional and it was explicitly for the Holy War. But the exploitation of temporal regalia, pushed to the limits we have seen, was infuriating. The sees which eventually gave some of the greatest difficulties in the regency were just those which lost their life's blood to regalia.[175] The pope himself protested the royal government's exploitative policies in 1252.[176]

Thus far we have observed the royal government try to augment its revenue by a new thoroughness in collecting ordinary income and in squeezing as much as possible from extraordinary income. Before discussing the third method of increasing revenue—the creation of new sources of income—it may be wise to consider the fall off in traditional expenditures achieved in the late 1240s. I associate the decrease with three trends: the king's restrictions on charitable giving, his suppression of some public works projects, and his decision to reduce the amount of money paid as wages to lower-echelon administrators.

With regard to charity, at first glance the situation does not appear to favor the interpretation that expenditures were even contained, let alone reduced. First, annuities such as perpetual rents that had been assigned for pious reasons suffered no reduction because reducing them would not only have constituted breach of contract in the purely legal sense but also an irreligious breaking of the oaths that had sealed the contracts.[177] Second, the mendicant orders received grants from the king for additional foundations in 1247[178] (fortunately, these did

---

[174] MP, v, 170-71; Joinville, chap. LXXXIII. See also Tillemont, *Vie de SL*, III, 116-17.
[175] Below chapter 5 n. 108.
[176] Berger, *SL et Innocent IV*, p. 376 n. 2 citing *Reg.* of Innocent IV 6131 no. 274, 7 December 1252; see also below chapter 5 nn. 82-89.
[177] That there were no diminutions is evident from a comparison of the relevant accounts; see, for example, the alms for *Sanctus Lazarus*, the *Domus Dei* of Paris and Senlis, and the *Leprosi Trium Domorum* in 1248 and 1234: *HF*, XXI, 261-65, and XXII, 566-69.
[178] Above chapter 3 n. 110.

not require very much direct outlay).[179] It should be said, third, that the late 1240s may have seen the continuation of the rather lavish expenditures for the Sainte-Chapelle.[180] I am inclined to doubt this. Most of the construction of the building was achieved, apparently, by the mid-forties even though the finishing touches, the endowment of the religious personnel and the dedication of the chapel, were later.[181] The only other expenditures for religious devotion in the late 1240s that could not have been anticipated from the regular pattern of annual gifts were the small special donations in early 1248 to mark the king's departure for crusade.[182]

With these observations, especially the remote possibility that large expenditures for the Sainte-Chapelle were still being made after 1246, one might argue that there was no decrease in royal charity or expenses for religious devotion. But this is simply not true. For example, royal investments in the construction of elaborate Cistercian houses, which were proceeding apace until 1245, came to an end on the eve of the crusade (see table three).[183] Although the Cistercians, in general, were closing their expansionary period,[184] the order remained especially close to the French royal house, particularly to Blanche of Castile.[185] It is probably the case, therefore, that the diminution of foundations that can be identified after 1245 is signifi-

---

[179] See the discussion by Dossat ("Opposition des ordres anciens," p. 264) of the benefaction of Louis IX for the Dominicans of Carcassonne in 1247 and, especially, its "site mediocre et défavorisé": "La génerosité des bienfaiteurs n'était pas sans limite, même lorsque le bienfaiteur était le roi de France." Cf. Jordan, "Contrats d'acquisition royaux," n. 5; and Louis's own cautionary remarks apropos of Thibaut of Navarre's indulgent endowment of the Dominicans of Provins, Joinville, chap. v.

[180] There are two estimates on the cost of the building, 40,000 pounds and 100,000 pounds; Tillemont, *Vie de SL*, II, 413, and v, 308.

[181] In general see the discussion below chapter 5 nn. 12-20. The discrepancy in the cost estimates (above n. 180) may be that the purchase price of the relics for the chapel was added to the expenditures for construction (Gébelin, *Sainte-Chapelle*, p. 9). If so, then a large part of the 100,000 pounds would have been expended in the late 1230s and probably a good deal of the remaining in 1244 when the building was begun in earnest. This would mean that the brunt of the expenditures had been made before Louis IX took the crusading vow in December 1244.

[182] Below chapter 5 nn. 2-28.   [183] Cf. Dimier, *SL et Cîteaux*.

[184] Compare the chart indicating only the most trivial Cistercian expansion in thirteenth century England, prepared by Knowles and Haddock, *Medieval Religious Houses*, p. 490.

[185] I believe, as apparently Little does, that Dimier should have entitled his book *Blanche et Cîteaux*. Cf. Little's criticisms in "SL's Involvement," p. 135. This is not to say that Louis had no interest in the Cistercians. He exempted them from the levy to pay for the crusade (above n. 109); he gave a gift or two to individual Cistercian houses on the eve of his departure (below chapter 5 n. 25); and he asked the order to pray for his success in the Holy War (MP, v, 203; cf. 596). The Cistercians later enrolled him among the saints special to their order (BN MS. latin no. 1882, thirteenth century; cited by Deville, *Manuscrits*, p. 42).

TABLE 3 • Foundations of Cistercian Abbeys in France, 1226-1269

Years	Number
1226-1229	5
1230-1234	6
1235-1239	3
1240-1244	4
1245-1249	0
1250-1254	1
1255-1259	0
1260-1264	1
1265-1269	0

SOURCE: Dimier, *Saint Louis et Cîteaux*, index and chronology

cant—both in terms of what it says about the overall pattern of royal expenditures on the eve of the crusade and about the transfer of royal authority, this time control over modes of religious devotion, from the Queen Dowager to her son. Louis himself seems to have felt that his mother's lavish giving was a problem: he was reluctant to give her the power to distribute royal charity when he assigned her the regency.[186]

But more can be said. From an intensive study of the architectural evidence, the most astute of art historical scholars, the late Robert Branner, showed that in the course of the "(c)rusade of 1248-1254 most building operations in the capital were suspended or slowed down."[187] He also demonstrated that, at practically every major construction in northern France with which the monarchy had associated itself and invested its resources, reductions in outlays can be associated with Louis's preparations for the crusade. And no new efforts were undertaken once he took the vow.[188] It was crusading projects, like the building of Aigues-Mortes, which consumed these savings in a dramatic trade-off.

I would also argue that outlays for public works were reduced in the period immediately before the crusade. In the broad general sense that construction of religious buildings was a public work, this proposition follows from the foregoing discussion. In the equally broad sense that the construction of Aigues-Mortes and certain other crusading projects were public works, one sees again a trade-off of sorts. But expenditures for public works in the more restricted modern sense, such as roads and bridges, at least those whose upkeep was

[186] This is my interpretation of the fact that this power was assigned by a separate instrument; *Layettes*, v, no. 514 (*vers* June 1248).

[187] Branner, *SL and the Court Style*, p. 86.

[188] Ibid., pp. 65-67.

dependent on the king and which did not play a special role in Louis's preparations for crusade, also decreased in the late forties. Perhaps the king had cautioned his *baillis* or one of them about unnecessary expenses or about spending money on certain public thoroughfares that were properly the concern of seigneurs or municipalities.[189] Whatever the case, the Account for the Ascension term 1234 records expenditures for public works with other expenses as lump sums.[190] The Account for the Ascension term 1238 also records expenditures of this sort as lump sums, indeed over several *bailliages*.[191] Together these early accounts suggest that some sort of lumping process was a traditional feature of royal bookkeeping. In the Account for Ascension 1248, however, specific types of expenses were detailed precisely.[192]

The precision itself might have been a clerical response to a royal admonition to be careful about expenditures. However that may be, it should also be pointed out that despite the difficulty of making comparisons between the precise categories of expenses in 1248 and the largely undifferentiated expenses of the 1230s, the entries *pro operibus* in 1248 are almost ridiculously small. Perhaps, again, royal officers overdid their zeal.[193]

A final diminution in "traditional" outlays was brought about by reducing wages for lower-echelon administrators or, rather, since that possibility seems to be outside certain accepted norms in the Middle Ages, by the reduction in the number of administrators receiving wages. The method of remuneration would have been replaced by revenue farms. Few lower-level functionaries received wages anyway, so Louis's savings could not have been great; but the stress he put on farming the domain in the late 1240s may have been the impetus for the *baillis* to replace assistants who received wages with those who could be convinced to accept revenue farms. Because of data, again all that one can say for sure is that wages, *liberationes*—either paid by or to the *prévôts*—decreased from 669 pounds at Ascension 1238 to 534 pounds during the Ascension term 1248.[194] I suspect that the shift actually took place around 1247 on no better grounds than that other

---

[189] The fact is the French crown tried traditionally to burden the users of public thoroughfares with their upkeep; Pirenne, *Economic and Social History*, p. 88.

[190] *HF*, XXII, 565-78.

[191] Ibid., XXI, 259-60. [192] Ibid., pp. 262-84.

[193] Henri Gravier accounted for the drop in terms of the lessening competence of the *prévôts* who had normally controlled such expenditures. Indeed by 1285 the *prévôts* were to be stripped completely of the duty of allocating money for public works. But there is no indication in the accounts that the *baillis* began expending progressively more on public works in the 1240s, and this is my point. There was, therefore, a net decrease in royal expenses for public works. Cf. Gravier, "Prévôts," pp. 562-63.

[194] *HF*, XXI, 259, 270. See also Gravier, "Prévôts," p. 562.

adjustments in fiscal matters, such as the order to farm *prévôtés* at the highest level, occurred about that time.

In all the discussions so far, the evidence, though suggestive, has not allowed us to assess the relative importance of these methods of raising revenue and lowering expenses to the financial needs of the crusade. But the final method of raising money—the creation of special new sources of revenue—provides much more data on which such assessments might be based. To begin with, the Account for Ascension term 1248 records not only customary sources of revenue which had been collected annually for decades, but many "new" sources of income in the *bailliages*, new, that is, since 1238. For example, in Gisors the *bailli* collected from 17 different sources at Ascension 1238, from 47 at Ascension 1248. Indeed in the royal accounts for the six comparable *bailliages*, the number of sources of revenue totaled 88 in 1238 and 208 in 1248, an average increase of twenty in each district (table four).

I may not be able to justify saying that each of these new sources was conceived in the interest of and orchestrated to coincide with the coming of the crusade, but for eighty-two important examples from the Account of the Ascension term 1248 there is no doubt. These were the gifts from the towns *pro auxilio regis* or *pro auxilio viae transmarinae*.[195] Some towns had given gifts in the previous term (Candlemas 1248, new style) or were scheduled to give supplementary gifts in the next term (All Saints 1248); the clerks' notations explain this. This series of collections constituted the original benevolence for the crusade (see table five).[196]

All the towns listed in the Account for the Ascension term 1248

TABLE 4 ● Increases in Sources of Income:
Ascension 1238 to Ascension 1248

Bailliage	Ascension 1238	Ascension 1248
Gisors	17	47
Amiens	6	22
Vermandois	27	69
Sens	25	39
Orléans	6	23
Bourges	7	8

[195] The word *auxilium* means aid, but *donum* was also used to describe the communal levy. It was just at this time—in the mid-thirteenth century—that the weight of tradition was finally succeeding in turning what evidently had been the benevolences from the towns into aids. See Petit-Dutaillis, *Feudal Monarchy*, p. 252; Stephenson, "Aides"; Henneman, *Royal Taxation*, pp. 6, 104; cf. Dupont-Ferrier, "Histoire . . . du mot aides."

[196] Cf. Strayer, "Crusades of Louis IX," p. 164.

TABLE 5 • Crusading Grants from the Towns circa 1248

Town	Amount (in l. p.)		Explanation	Reference
Paris	10,000 l.		total gift	*HF*, XXI, 270
Amiens	1,500 l.		latter half of gift	Ibid., 271
Beauquesne	150 l.		latter half	Ibid., 271
Doullens	200 l.		latter half	Ibid., 271
Montreuil-sur-Mer	350 l.		latter half	Ibid., 271
S. Ricquier	500 l.		latter half	Ibid., 271
Corbie	500 l.		latter half	Ibid., 271
Péronne	1,000 l.		latter half	Ibid., 271
Bray-sur-Somme	100 l.		latter half	Ibid., 271
Cappy	30 l.		latter half	Ibid., 271
Athies	60 l.		latter half	Ibid., 271
Bourges	1,000 l.		total gift	Ibid., 272
Aubigny-sur-Nère	120 l.	100 s.	latter half	Ibid., 272
Dun-le-Roi	160 l.		latter half	Ibid., 272
Orléans	750 l.		latter half	Ibid., 272
Checy	60 l.		latter half	Ibid., 272
Châteauneuf-sur-Loire	25 l.		latter half	Ibid., 272
Neuville-aux-Bois	50 l.		latter half	Ibid., 272
Courcy	15 l.		latter half	Ibid., 272
Janville	50 l.		latter half	Ibid., 272
Montlhéry	180 l.		latter half	Ibid., 272
Sens	1,000 l.		latter half	Ibid., 273
Pont-sur-Vannes	50 l.		latter half (?)	Ibid., 273
Dixmont	20 l.		latter half (?)	Ibid., 273
Pons (Latin)	20 l.		latter half (?)	Ibid., 273
Bois-le-Roi	50 l.		latter half (?)	Ibid., 273
Yèvre-le-Châtel	80 l.		latter half (?)	Ibid., 273
La Bussière	40 l.		latter half (?)	Ibid., 273
Samois	50 l.		latter half (?)	Ibid., 273
Moret-sur-Loing	50 l.		latter half (?)	Ibid., 273
Champigny-sur-Yonne	4 l.		latter half (?)	Ibid., 273
Bonnevaux	4 l.		latter half (?)	Ibid., 273
S. Clément	20 l.		latter half (?)	Ibid., 273
Rouvres		100 s.	latter half (?)	Ibid., 273
Gron	20 l.		latter half (?)	Ibid., 273
Recourart		100 s.	latter half (?)	Ibid., 273
Nailly	10 l.		latter half (?)	Ibid., 273

TABLE 5 • Crusading Grants from the Towns circa 1248

Town	Amount (in l. p.)		Explanation	Reference
Gisy-les-Nobles	10 l.		latter half (?)	Ibid., 273
Rigny-le-Ferron		60 s.	latter half (?)	Ibid., 273
Lailly.		100 s.	latter half (?)	Ibid., 273
Chapelle-sur-Oreuse		40 s.	latter half (?)	Ibid., 273
Armeau } S. Aubin-sur-Yonne }		100 s.	latter half (?)	Ibid., 273
Gien	12 l.	10 s.	latter half (?)	Ibid., 273
Montargis	140 l.	100 s.	latter half (?)	Ibid., 273
Cepoy	25 l.		latter half (?)	Ibid., 273
Villeperot		30 s.	latter half (?)	Ibid., 273
Grange-le-Bocage		100 s.	latter half (?)	Ibid., 273
Grès et La Chapelle-la-Reine	60 l.		latter half (?)	Ibid., 273
Villeneuve-le-Roi (Yonne)	1,200 l.		latter half (?)	Ibid., 274
Laon	1,500 l.		latter half	Ibid., 275
Vailly-sur-Aisne	150 l.		latter half	Ibid., 275
Noyon	750 l.		latter half	Ibid., 275
Villeneuve-le-Roi (Oise)	50 l.		latter half	Ibid., 275
Crépy en Laonnois	100 l.		latter half	Ibid., 275
Compiègne	1,250 l.		latter half	Ibid., 275
Chaudardes	120 l.		latter half	Ibid., 275
Cerny-les-Bucy	150 l.		latter half	Ibid., 275
Montdidier	500 l.		latter half	Ibid., 275
Chauny	200 l.		latter half	Ibid., 276
Beauvais	1,750 l.		latter half	Ibid., 276
Bruyères-sous-Laon	250 l.		latter half	Ibid., 276
Ham	150 l.		latter half	Ibid., 276
Chambly	200 l.		latter half	Ibid., 276
Roye	600 l.		latter half	Ibid., 276
Soissons	1,000 l.		latter half	Ibid., 276
S.-Quentin	1,500 l.		latter half	Ibid., 276
Senlis	1,250 l.		latter half	Ibid., 276
Beaumont-sur-Oise	100 l.		latter half	Ibid., 276
Asnières-sur-Oise	50 l.		latter half	Ibid., 276
Tournay	500 l.		one-half	Ibid., 277
Crépy	1,000 l.		total gift	Ibid., 277
Les Andelys	60 l.		latter half	Ibid., 277.

TABLE 5 • Crusading Grants from the Towns circa 1248

Town	Amount (in l. p.)	Explanation	Reference
Vernon	60 l.	one-half	Ibid., 277
Longueville (now			
S. Pierre-d'Autils)	20 l.	one-half	Ibid., 277
Pacy-sur-Eure	40 l.	one-half	Ibid., 278
Evreux	150 l.	latter half	Ibid., 278
Nogent (-le-Sec)	15 l.	latter half	Ibid., 278
Mantes	1,000 l.	total gift	Ibid., 278
Gisors	60 l.	latter half	Ibid., 278
Chaumont en Vexin	200 l.	latter half	Ibid., 278
Tours			
(2,000 l. t.)	1,600 l.	total gift	Ibid., 280
village near			
Paris (?)	10 l.	first half	Ibid., 262
Totals: (1) of "total gifts" listed	14,600 l. p.		
(2) of "one-half," "latter half" or "first half" gifts: multiplied by two to give total amount	42,884 l. p.		
Grand Total	57,484 l. p. (71,855 l. t.)		

which gave to the crusade were from north or central France where Louis's suzerain rights as a "feudal" lord were well defined. Naturally, since income was collected in Normandy at different terms, no Norman towns are listed in this account,[197] but it has always been assumed that the Norman records, if they had survived, would reveal similar substantial grants in the period.[198] No gifts are recorded in the section of the accounts for Languedoc, and Strayer is probably mistaken in saying they contributed.[199] Custom was different, and Louis did not overcome this barrier until the 1260s.[200] This is evident from the fact that much later certain participants in a contention over these grants

[197] The towns of the border (Franco-Norman) *bailliage* of Gisors were included; *HF*, XXI, 277.

[198] Strayer, "Crusades of Louis IX," p. 164.

[199] Ibid.

[200] Thus, the levy before Louis's second crusade did extend to the southern towns; below chapter 8 n. 12. It was not until 1269 that a decent register was established for documents recording royal rights in Languedoc; see Teulet's remarks in *Layettes*, I, p. vi; Delaborde's in *Layettes*, v, p. xvii; and Delisle, *Catalogue des actes de Philippe-Auguste*, pp. xxix-xxx. Cf. Bisson, "Negotiations for Taxes," pp. 80-82, on Alfonse's inadequate knowledge of his rights in the south and especially of whether the towns had to give *dona* for a crusade.

forged a reference to such a grant for the town of Cahors for 1245.[201] If there had actually been a southern benevolence in the late 1240s, it is unlikely that a thirteenth century man would have been unable to prove it by legitimate records.

My estimate of the *original* return of the benevolence from the towns, not counting the Norman towns, is 71,855 l. t. This is an easy figure to arrive at. All one needs to do is add up the individual gifts listed in the Account for the Ascension term 1248 and supplement that sum with the information the clerks have left, namely, that the "first half" of a two-part gift had already been paid or the "latter half" was scheduled to be paid.

But the towns were called upon again and again for subsequent benevolences. Certain municipal accounts refer to these gifts (table six). This evidence—rather extensive—provides the data for a very valuable comparison. I have aggregated the complete data for six towns for which I know the amount of the original benevolence and the total amount of all subsequent gifts for the crusade: in 1248 these towns gave 4,500 pounds *tournois* to the king; in various supplements they contributed 4,470 pounds (see table seven). This suggests that a multiplier of two would give a reasonable approximation of the total amount collected from municipal benevolences for the crusade, or in numbers, 2 × 71,855 l. t. = 143,710 l. t.

This might be only half or, rather 55 percent of the story since the Norman towns—it is assumed—also contributed to the crusade. Income from Normandy usually constituted 45 percent of total crown revenue.[202] If one assumes that this percentage is a useful approximation of Normandy's relative contribution to the total return from municipal benevolences and if the non-Norman towns gave about 144,000 pounds, then the Norman towns added 130,000 pounds to this. The sum total of all such gifts was, therefore, about 274,000 pounds *tournois*. This is a rough estimate, to be sure, but it is probably in a respectable range of accuracy.

The grants of the church, the extraordinary revenue from the confiscations of heretics' property and Jewish chattels and from temporal *regalia*, and the benevolences from the towns provided most of the money for Louis's crusade. Indeed, coupled with the traditional small profit margin on ordinary income, increments from the greater efficiency of a revitalized upper-level administration, from a restricted program of large-scale expenditures for religious devotions, from cuts in wages for the few salaried lower-echelon administrators, and from greater restraint in outlays for public works, the amount of

[201] Cf. Bisson, *Assemblies . . . in Languedoc*, p. 131.
[202] That is, not including Languedoc; *HF*, xxi, lxxxiv table 18.

TABLE 6 • Municipal Grants for the Crusade,
Supplemental to the Original Benevolence

Town	Amount	Reference
Noyon (1249-1252)	600 l. t.	*Layettes*, III, no. 4598
Chauny (1248-1254)	1,100 l. t.	Ibid., no. 4609
Montdidier (during the crusade)	1,000 l. t.	Ibid., no. 4662
Montdidier (on the king's return)	200 l. t.	Ibid.
Cerny (during the crusade)	200 l. t.	Ibid.
Cerny (on the king's return)	160 l. t.	Ibid.
Villeneuve-le-Roi in Oise (during the crusade)	110 l. t.	Ibid.
Roye (during the crusade)	1,100 l. t.	Ibid.
Paris (1253)	4,000 l. t.	*HF*, XXII, 740

TABLE 7 • Municipal Grants for the Crusade: Comparisons

Town	Original Grant	Supplemental Grants
Noyon	1,500 l. t.	600 l. t.
Chauny	400 l. t.	1,100 l. t.
Montdidier	1,000 l. t.	1,200 l. t.
Cerny	300 l. t.	360 l. t.
Villeneuve-le-Roi	100 l. t.	110 l. t.
Roye	1,200 l. t.	1,100 l. t.

money ultimately available to the king may have exceeded the 1.5 million pounds he expended on the crusade. Of course, the money did not come in at once: the first gifts from the towns entered the royal treasury in 1248, but supplementary gifts were requested during and immediately after the crusade. Income from regalia depended on unpredictable vacancies in the church hierarchy. The tenths were paid annually beginning in 1247, but recalcitrant prelates delayed their collection for years. Running down the Jews and the debtors who owed the Jews in order to make assessments on the profits of usury was a process which was never completed.[203] There were, then, problems; and yet, it is the relative ease with which the money was collected that strikes the scholarly observer.

As in the case of the army, however, the raising and collection of revenue in such amounts were not the only problems. Money, too, had to be transported to the East. In preparation for the crusade the

[203] Roth in *Cambridge Medieval History*, VII, 657.

king deposited his funds with the Templars as was becoming customary for the French crown.[204] And transfers of funds through the military order functioned smoothly.[205] Direct shipments of specie, with an occasional mishap, arrived at the correct locations in the East.[206] And the fact of Louis's financial solvency in the Levant, at least until 1253, is proof of the smooth working of the coordinated government he had left behind him in France.

Not everyone was so fortunate as the king. The ancillary leaders of the crusade did have access to much the same sources of revenue, but it should probably be assumed, with the possible exception of the administrative genius, Alfonse of Poitiers, that they had not streamlined the administrations of their principalities as effectively as Louis IX. I will use the sources Alfonse drew upon as an illustration of the barons' access to revenue although this gives the French aristocracy more credit than it deserves.

Alfonse received a portion of the tenth:[207] the grant in Auvergne amounted to seventy-five hundred pounds.[208] He exacted money for the war from "uninheritable" legacies, those for which no proper successor survived,[209] from the profits of usury,[210] and from confiscations of heretics' property in the southern portions of his territories.[211] He received permission to levy a hearth tax on the townsmen of Poitiers by promising to expel the Jews.[212] And then he promised the Jews not to expel them if they gave him one thousand pounds.[213] He also made money from the fines imposed on crusaders who failed to fulfill their vows.[214] Yet despite all this, Alfonse was borrowing from his brother in 1248.[215]

[204] Sayous, "Mandats," p. 263 (also citing Delisle, *Templiers*). See also *Formulaires*, no. 6, items 102-3.

[205] Cf. Sayous, "Mandats," pp. 290-304.

[206] MP, v, 116-17; vii, 205.

[207] Above n. 105 for the access of Alfonse, Raymond of Toulouse, and the scion of the house of Burgundy to such revenue.

[208] Strayer, "Crusades of Louis IX," p. 164.

[209] *Layettes*, iii, nos. 3723, 4043. Technically this fell within crown revenues. Louis simply assigned the proceeds from the appropriate properties to his barons; cf. Berger, *SL et Innocent IV*, p. 207, and Purcell, *Papal Crusading Policy*, p. 147.

[210] *Layettes*, iii, nos. 3720, 4042.

[211] Ibid., no. 4054.

[212] Ibid., no. 3782.

[213] So conclude Boutaric, *SL et Alfonse*, pp. 319-20, and Bisson, "Negotiations for Taxes," p. 79. This conclusion is based on the fact that the Jews did pay one thousand pounds, but cf. Nahon, "Juifs . . . d'Alfonse."

[214] *Layettes*, iii, nos. 3721, 3724, 3726, 4047, 4095. Again, this fell technically within crown revenues but was alienated as Louis saw fit. On access to this revenue by the duke of Burgundy, see no. 3923²; by Robert of Artois, see Loisne, "Catalogue des actes de Robert d'Artois," p. 198 no. clvi. On the legal background to redemption of vows, consult Brundage, *Medieval Canon Law and the Crusader*, pp. 77-78, 92, 102, 133-35; on the theological background, see Purcell, *Papal Crusading Policy*, pp. 99-132.

[215] Above n. 49.

If Alfonse had to borrow from Louis, it is not surprising that other barons found themselves owing the king sizable sums. Even when they spared him the direct drain on his resources, they succeeded in getting him to stand surety when they sought loans from bankers (see table eight). Certain consequences of the latter privilege were remarkable. Some barons, for example, deliberately provoked their own excommunication so that, given the spiritual economy of the age, their creditors could not have relations with them.[216] As a result they had a ready-made excuse for not paying off their debts. Other barons, however, simply defaulted without this ruse.[217] Alfonse evidently suffered under similar liabilities whenever impecunious barons managed to borrow money from him.[218]

Neither the king nor his brother seems to have anticipated the full range of these problems. Alfonse apparently just stopped lending money. Louis did not go quite this far. It is true that he persuaded the pope to prohibit excommunications of those for whom he stood surety,[219] but he continued to give loans, gifts, and assurances when they were requested. The reason for this must be sought among the methods the king employed in raising his army in the first place. Jean de Caux, for example, inventoried in the 1280s a form letter encouraging participation in the crusade;[220] we can be reasonably certain of what it contained. Besides all the other privileges offered crusaders,[221] it would have appealed to the impecunious by informing them that during their preparations for crusade they had temporary (as many as three years') relief from their debts.[222] Louis had known the value of the privilege;[223] he had issued a circular letter to his *baillis* as early as 1245 reminding them to be particularly protective of crusaders who were being pestered to pay their outstanding debts.[224]

During the crusade itself, then, Louis was at least partly reaping

---

[216] *Layettes*, III, no. 3869. The reverse was not true: as a special privilege, crusaders could engage in commercial or other mutual relations with excommunicated individuals; Brundage, *Medieval Canon Law and the Crusader*, pp. 155-56.

[217] *Layettes*, III, no. 3960.

[218] Alfonse stood surety for at least one loan which he had to repay on default; ibid., nos. 3827, 3907. Cf. II, no. 3789, and V, no. 548.

[219] Ibid., III, no. 3869.

[220] *Formulaires*, no. 6, item 10: "pro querendis militibus et balistariis pro negocio Terre Sancte."

[221] Above chapter 2 n. 27.

[222] The OF text of the chronicle of Reims specifically points out that the relief was for debts owed to townsmen (*as bourgeois*); *HF*, XXII, 311, 331. See also Brundage, *Medieval Canon Law and the Crusader*, pp. 179-83.

[223] *HF*, XXII, 311. Purcell, *Papal Crusading Policy*, p. 165, describes Louis as "particularly exigent" in getting the privilege put into effect.

[224] *HF*, XXIV, "Preuves," no. 118. See also *HF*, XXIV, "Chronologie," p. 68; *Formulaires*, no. 6, items 43-45, 174; cf. 402.

TABLE 8 • Sureties, Loans, Gifts

Name	Amount (l. t.)	Type	Reference
(At Cyprus, 1249)			
Yolande de Châtillon	3,750	surety	L-III 3760[a]
Raoul de Coucy	3,500	surety	L-III 3769
Erard de Chassenay	1,000	surety	L-III 3771
Guillaume de Dampierre	650	surety	L-III 3770
Jean de Joinville	800	gift	Jv. chap. XXIX[a]
(Near Damietta, 1249)			
Guillaume de Dampierre	5,000	surety	L-III 3800
Gaucher de Châtillon[b]	1,696	surety	L-III 3810
Gaucher de Châtillon[b]	3,750	surety	L-III 3823
Gui, Count of Forez	1,000	surety	L-III 3811
Guillaume de Chauny	400	surety	L-III 3821
(At Acre, 1250)			
Guillaume de Dampierre	3,300	surety	L-III 3875[2]
Guillaume de Beaumont[c]	230	surety	L-III 3879
(At Cesarea, 1251)			
Philippe de Toucy	500	surety	L-III 3954
Jean de Beaumont[d]	1,500	loan	L-III 3948
(Date and place unknown)			
Paillart[e]	180	surety	L-III 4319
Johannes-Poillevillain	60	?	L-III 4335

NOTES:

[a] L-III and Jv are abbreviations for *Layettes*, III, and Joinville, *Histoire*.

[b] The first of Gaucher's requests for the king to stand surety occurred in September (for the residual amount listed); a second request came in November 1249.

[c] Guillaume de Beaumont's surety was through Peter the Chamberlain, the king's agent.

[d] Jean de Beaumont was another of the king's chamberlains.

[e] Paillart was a royal sergeant.

what he had sown. He became a creditor or surety for men who had joined the crusade hoping to make financial gains on the crusade; in most cases they had not the means and, in a few, perhaps not the intention of paying him back.[225] From the table I have prepared on the king's grants and assurances (table eight), it should be obvious that the supplications of the barons coincided with the very beginning of the crusade and accelerated as time progressed, that is, until most of them got disgusted and went home. Yet the fact that Louis could sustain these men at all is fundamental evidence of his own financial solvency.

[225] I cannot footnote intentions in this case, but a few chroniclers make clear that some barons were ruined financially by their expenses for Louis's crusade. Cf. Minstrel of Reims, p. 334; and Joinville, chap. XXIX.

This remarkable solvency came to an end in 1253. In that year alone, the king himself borrowed, at low interest,[226] 100,000 pounds from the Italians, especially the Genoese.[227] Why? Later commentators thought they knew the answer. Like the ransom of Richard I, the ransom of Louis's army (which they equate with Louis's ransom) had bankrupted France. Some very striking, if perhaps fanciful, stories were told to illustrate this theory. A sixteenth century chronicler reported that the stone mortuary-vessel at Rouen, containing the heart of Richard I, was a replacement for the original silver casket that had been taken away "aider a paier la renson du roy sainct Lois."[228] In another narrative, an annalist-abbot of Saint-Riquier under the year 1248 recalled that "Saint Louis prisonnier, pour sa ranchon payer, fit courir monoie de cuir bouly en son dit royaume," that is, he allowed the circulation of coins made from boiled leather because France was denuded of specie after paying the ransom.[229] Perhaps impressed by such stories, at least one scholar has argued that the great monetary reforms of the last half of Louis's reign are traceable to the insufficient money supply of the mid-thirteenth century.[230]

I do not mean to underestimate the financial strain of the crusade. It was certainly severe. But up until and including the year 1252, the administrators of the fiscal system seem to have been doing their jobs effectively. They were collecting money and it was being sent to the king. Indeed, the ransom had been paid with surprisingly little difficulty from funds already on deposit in the East and a small supplement squeezed from the Templars.[231] Neither in size nor in importance did the ransom of Louis's army (200,000 French pounds; less than one year's income in France) compare to that of Richard I of England (the equivalent, without considering inflation, of at least 500,000 French pounds and four years' English revenue). The break came in 1253; this is the significance of the fact that Louis's personal need to call upon the Italian credit monopoly in the Holy Land was expressed with such force in that year.[232]

If there had been money from home to come to Saint Louis in 1253, it could have reached him easily, or relatively so, since the mili-

---

[226] Sayous, "Mandats," p. 279.

[227] Schaube, "Wechselbriefe," pp. 604-8, 733; Sayous, "Mandats," p. 279. Cf. Lopez, "Back to Gold," p. 228.

[228] Héron, *Deux chroniques de Rouen*, p. 37.

[229] Hénocque, *Saint-Riquier*, I, 513 n. 2. On the use of leather coinage in general in medieval Europe, see Courtenay, "Token Coinage," pp. 281-82.

[230] Barthélemy, "Essai sur la monnaie parisis," p. 155; also below chapter 7 nn. 133-74.

[231] Joinville, chap. LXXV; cf. MP, VII, 205. See also Sayous, "Mandats," p. 270.

[232] Sayous, "Mandats," p. 273. See also Branner, *SL and the Court Style*, p. 145.

tary situation was comparatively calm. But it did not come. On the way back to France in early 1254, Louis told Joinville that "his treasury was so ill-supplied that he had drained it to the dregs."[233] It is the timing, as I have intimated before, that is crucial here. In military terms supply might have been easy in 1253 or 1254. No one would have had to break through enemy lines or rescue the king from prison to deliver desperately needed money; but other factors were at work. In November of 1252, after a month's illness, Blanche of Castile had died. The resulting crisis could not but have an impact on the administrative and fiscal system. In short, the collapse of Louis's financial position in the East was the result of a major political breakdown in France.[234]

[233] Joinville, chap. xxx.
[234] Even the news of Blanche's death took an incredibly long time to reach Louis (about six months); this has led some commentators to suggest that Joinville simply did not remember his dates correctly; cf. Shaw's translation of Joinville (p. 315 n. 1).

·5·

THE REGENCY

In laying such stress on the emotional component and the material side of Louis IX's preparations for crusade, we should not be misled into thinking that the spiritual character of this war went unappreciated. It has already been shown that the king's piety played an important role in strengthening the ecclesiastical Inquisition in the south, that it was behind his stern measures against the Jews, and that, more favorably, it was the foundation for his establishment of the *enquêteurs*.[1] Indeed, it is precisely because these three levels of behavior—the emotional, the practical, and the spiritual—were intertwined that it is sometimes so difficult to know what was really in the mind of the king when he pursued any particular policy. Consider, for example, the quality of the ceremonial *gestes* which Louis carried through on the eve of his departure. Spiritually, I believe, these *gestes* were expected to provide symbolic assurance of the heavenly favor with which the earthly kingdom of France had been graced. Practically, they served to underscore the strength and stability of the royal power in the very course of its transmission to a regency government. Emotionally, they served as another vehicle to express the feeling of power and freedom which had emerged so dramatically with the swearing of the crusader's vow.

The first of these "ceremonial" acts was a tour of the royal domain which the king undertook in early 1248.[2] (He had spent most of 1247 in the voluntary confinement of Paris while the *enquêteurs* carried out their commissions.)[3] This *tournée* has a certain cartographic elegance about it:[4] Louis set out from Paris in late February or early March moving briskly in a northwesterly direction. He crossed the Oise at Pontoise and passed through Gisors and Gournay-en-Bray in March. From Gournay he traveled eastward probably crossing the Oise for

[1] Above chapters 3 (nn. 103-10) and 4 (nn. 131-51).
[2] The itinerary prepared by the editors of *HF* (above chapter 3 n. 23) has been used to provide the basic outline of the discussion of the royal progress which follows. Specific supplementary sources will be noted as appropriate.
[3] Above chapter 3 nn. 94-95.
[4] See the map. (A map prepared by Bruhl, *Fodrum*, II, no. 7, indicating royal residences, is useful for determining the frequency of royal travel to particular places but not the patterns of travel.) Beugnot in his *Essai* (pp. 101-2) on Saint Louis's government, which he published in 1821, thought he noticed a formal *tournée* of the domain somewhat earlier in the reign, but he based his conclusion on the sketchy itinerary of Tillemont.

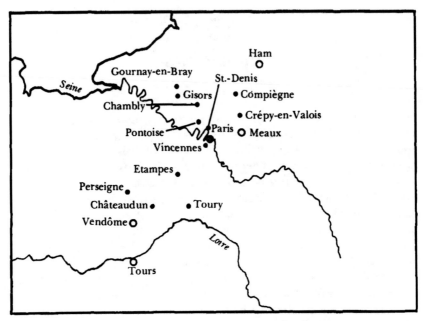

MAP 2: The *Tournées* of Louis IX in the North
  • = places probably visited on the *tournée* of 1248
  ○ = places probably visited on the *tournée* of 1269/70

the second time at Compiègne. He was in Crépy-en-Valois (Oise) in April and in Paris later in the month. In geopolitical terms this journey constituted a schematic version of a circuit of the royal domain in the north.[5] An analogous and equally brisk circuit was undertaken almost immediately: heading south from Paris through the woods of Vincennes in late April, the king passed through Étampes and Toury (Eure-et-Loire) in May. Turning west or southwest at Toury he reached the abbey of Perseigne (Sarthe) later in the same month. From there he returned to Paris. He was in the capital before the end of May. Geopolitically he had completed a southern circuit, also schematic and clipped, of the old domain.[6]

The *tournée* of 1248, despite its rapidity, was the occasion for doing or promising justice. At Pontoise in March, Louis confirmed the privileges of Guillaume Perceval in lands held of the king at Ver, Eve, and

[5] In establishing this northerly route I have used the itinerary of *HF* and supplemented it with Faivre d'Arcier, *Gournay*, p. 41; Lecocq, *Histoire . . . de Saint-Quentin*, p. 86; Colliette, *Vermandois*, II, 573, 629, 687; Potin de la Marie, *Gournay*, I, 408. I have, where necessary, adjusted dates for new style.
[6] In establishing the southerly route I have employed the itinerary of *HF* as well as Thoison, *Séjours*, p. 181; Pompon, *Toury*, p. 12; Delisle, *Cartulaire normand*, p. 78 no. 468, and pp. 323-24.

Ermenonville.[7] Probably at Châteaudun in May 1248, the viscount of Châteaudun presented evidence of his right to the fief of *Castrum Mons Dupelli*, his title to the fief being confirmed by charter dated at Paris in June.[8] Also in May, Louis granted the abbey of Perseigne a charter of liberties during his brief stay. To judge from this charter, the general quality of the *conventiones* of this period differed from what was normal. They were unusual especially with respect to their concessive character.[9]

The ceremonies surrounding the agreements were also exaggerated, or so it would seem. It is enough to recall that the *enquêteurs* had prepared the way for the advent of the king while his artificially enforced absence from the provinces, which their work demanded, heightened awareness of the special character of the *tournée* that followed. The flavor of the royal progress is suggested in the local traditions of the town of Chambly which recall the king's visit there on the first Sunday in Lent, 8 March 1248.[10] The king's visit is supposed to have been the occasion of the very first celebration of *Bois-Hourdy*, a festival replete with torchlight parade and bonfire.[11] If we let our imaginations go, we shall conjure up a picture of the king leading this procession—perhaps it has come together from various neighborhoods to the central square; and at the moment when the torches are put to the straw for the bonfire, the royal visitor is illuminated: soon he will take leave of this town and his kingdom to do battle with the enemies of Christ.

At the center of the *tournée*, in the brief interlude in April between Louis's completion of the northern half of the circuit and his commencement of the southern half, he attended the dedication of the Sainte-Chapelle.[12] The building had been commissioned about four

---

[7] Müller, *Analyse*, p. 126. See also Potin de la Marie, *Gournay*, I, 388-89.

[8] All that with certainty survives is the confirmation in June at Paris (Lépinois and Merlet, *Cartulaire . . . Notre-Dame de Chartres*, pp. 138-39 no. ccxcii); but Châteaudun is on the route of the *tournée*, and it was frequently necessary to discuss matters *in situ* before issuing formal documents from Paris. See, for example: Delisle, *Cartulaire normand*, pp. 75, 321 no. 459 n. 1 and no. 1172, and pp. 321-22 nos. 1175-76. See also *Olim*, I, 530-31 xii, and below chapter 6.

[9] Fleury, *Cartulaire . . . de Perseigne*, pp. 59-61, 85-86 nos. 21, 44-45; Bellée and Duchemin, *Inventaire-sommaire des AD: Sarthe*, III, p. 403. See also Fleury, *Guide*, pp. 185-86.

[10] Lecotté and Marguet, *Fête*, pp. 10-11; Bisson de Barthélemy, *Beaumont-sur-Oise*, p. 193 n. 996. The visit fits the *tournée* perfectly.

[11] On the festival itself (and its association with Brandons), above n. 10. See also Hénocque, *Saint-Riquier*, III, 59 n. 1; Melleville, *Histoire de Chauny*, pp. 58-59; and *Dictionnaire de l'Academie*, I, s.v. "Brandon": "Le dimanche des brandons, se disait anciennement du Premier dimanche de carême, parce que, ce jour-là, le peuple allumait des feux, dansait à l'entour et parcourait les rues et les campagnes en portant des brandons ou des tisons allumés."

[12] The dedication took place on 25 or 26 April 1248 in the presence of Louis and the

years before the king had taken his vow to go on crusade and was probably finished two years before he left, but the dedication was delayed to coincide with his departure for the East.[13] Built to house the relics of the Passion which Louis had purchased in 1238 from his cousin, the financially pressed Baldwin, emperor of Constantinople,[14] the edifice was a kind of architectural parallel to the king's crusading zeal. The relics of the Passion symbolized that earthly Jerusalem which it was Louis's deep desire to reconquer for Christ. The windows of the chapel in their original parts depicted the king as a barefoot pilgrim and in pilgrim's habit.[15] Contemporary written sources, of course, described his departure for the crusade as a barefoot pilgrim and in pilgrim's habit.[16] Frenchmen, from the first moment they received the relics, considered them something which gave their kingdom a special connection with the heavenly kingdom,[17] but—it seems to me—the relics did not find their true place in the religion of French monarchy until Louis IX swore the crusader's vow. So deep was the association, indeed, in men's minds, that the legend grew up and was memorialized in art that Louis, the crusader, had personally brought back the relics of the Passion from the Holy Land.[18]

---

papal legate who was preaching the crusade. See *Layettes*, III, no. 3652. See also Gébelin, *Sainte-Chapelle*, p. 9; Paravicini Bagliani, *Cardinali*, I, 204; Branner, *Painted Medallions*, p. 5. Cf. Beaurepaire, *Saint-Germain-en-Laye*, p. 215.

[13] Art historians differ on the precise dates of construction: Branner, *SL and the Court Style*, pp. 64-65, esp. n. 26, says 1241-1248 with most of the building completed by 1246 (indulgences for visitors were granted beginning in November 1246; Riant, *Exuviae*, II, 132). Most recent authorities are in agreement that the building was conceived in the early 1240s and more or less finished by 1246; cf. Gébelin, *Sainte-Chapelle*, pp. 8-9; Frankl, *Gothic Architecture*, p. 102; Deschamps, in *SL*, Exposition, p. 9.

[14] The purchases included the crown of thorns, a piece of the true cross, the holy sponge, lance, purple vestments, and sepulchral stone. Some bones of Saint Mary Magdalene, the occipital of John the Baptist, the mantle of the Virgin, and the sponge with which Jesus washed the disciples' feet rounded out the collection (Riant, *Exuviae*, II, 133-35). See also Tillemont, *Vie de SL*, II, 413, and V, 308; Gébelin, *Sainte-Chapelle*, p. 9.

[15] Gébelin, *Sainte-Chapelle*, p. 75. The windows (and, for that matter, numerous manuscript illuminations) illustrate the narrative sources. Among the manuscript illuminations, one of the most famous is found in the fourteenth century French life of the king, British Museum (now British Library) MS Royal 16 G VI, fol. 365 (the library kindly supplied me photographs; see also Eydoux, *SL*, p. 43). The most important narrative sources of the reception of the relics are the descriptions by the eyewitness Gautier Cornut, the archbishop of Sens, *HF*, XXII; and the anonymous "De susceptione" in Miller, Review. Riant, *Exuviae*, II, 241-59, has twenty-six other relevant extracts from various sources.

[16] See, for example, the chronicle of the Norman abbey of Lire, *HF*, XXIII, 469; and cf. below nn. 23, 28.

[17] On popular appreciation of the relics, see the description by Gautier Cornut, *HF*, XXII, 29-30; and in Miller, Review, p. 300.

[18] Thus, at Versailles Saint Louis is depicted as a pilgrim returning to France from the Holy Land with the relics of the Passion; *Revue d'histoire de l'église de France*, XXIV

The Sainte-Chapelle also took its place as part of the traditional ceremonial apparatus for a French royal crusader. In late May and the first two weeks of June, after the *tournée* of the domain had been successfully concluded, the king initiated the traditional ceremonial events that should precede his departure for the south. The first of these was probably the exposition of the relics of the Passion—the True Cross and the Crown of Thorns—to the faithful at the Sainte-Chapelle. This seems to follow from two facts. First, additional indulgences, beyond those granted visitors in April for the dedication, were granted in May.[19] Second, also in May the king gave a precious relic—a thorn of the Crown of Thorns—to representatives of the Castilian monarchy; surely this took place at a ceremony in the Sainte-Chapelle.[20]

In the same month Louis solemnly declared the concession of special jurisdictional immunities to the bell ringers of the cathedral of Notre-Dame. He had originally promised them this concession during his illness in December 1244 when he took the crusader's vow, and it seemed appropriate to declare it formally at the moment of his departure for the Holy War.[21] The cathedral was also where he received the pilgrim's scrip and staff.[22] From the magnificent episcopal setting of the cathedral he journeyed barefoot to the royal abbey of Saint-Denis where he accepted the *oriflamme*, the battle-flag of Charles the Great.[23]

Thereafter, the king seems to have undertaken a ritual *tournée* of the city of Paris as his last formal act: he proceeded to the abbey of Saint-Antoine on the outskirts of old Paris, to whose nuns he gave a charter of privileges.[24] It is likely that he duplicated this ritual progress for the Cistercian nunnery of Pourrais, also on the outskirts of the city, since the sisters there received a similar solemn confirmation of their privileges in June.[25] The reception of the generous monarch

---

(1938), 540. Potin de la Marie, *Supplément*, p. 455, seems to have accepted a version of this legend. In general on the pilgrimage quality of Louis's first crusade, see Labande, "SL pèlerin."

[19] *Layettes*, III, no. 3666.

[20] Above chapter 2 n. 103.

[21] Vidier, "Marguilliers," pp. 213-14.

[22] See the French text of the Minstrel of Reims, *HF*, XXII, 311; cf. an anonymous chronicle of Flanders, *HF*, XXII, 331.

[23] Ibid. (both texts); Baudoin d'Avesnes, XXI, 165; the chronicle of the Norman abbey of Lire, XXIII, 469; and MP, v, 22. Interestingly, Charlemagne's battle-cry, *Montjoie*, was used as the name of Louis's sailing vessel on the crusade; "Letter of John Sarrasin," pp. 241-42.

[24] *GC*, VII, c. 901, and "Instrumenta," c. 107; the chronicle of Saint-Denis, *HF*, XXI, 113; the chronicle anthology *E Floribus chronicorum*, *HF*, XXI, 696; and the chronicle of Limoges, *HF*, XXI, 766.

[25] *GC*, VII, "Instrumenta," c. 107 no. cxlv; *Layettes*, III, no. 3682.

was impressive; one chronicler related that the journey to Saint-Antoine's proceeded *multis processionibus*. At the end of May he went to Corbeny where, possibly, he touched for scrofula.[26]

Although there were to be other ceremonial acts as he traveled to the south[27]—he would act the pilgrim and dine with the Franciscans during their Provincial Chapter at Sens, for example[28]—the performance of the Paris ritual really marked the culmination of Louis's work in France. From the time he swore the crusader's vow in December 1244 until early June of 1248, he had striven mightily to prepare for the Holy War. Henceforth, it would be up to the regent, his mother, Blanche of Castile, to see that his accomplishment would endure.

Queen Blanche did her best. Although she had opposed the crusade from the day her son first swore the vow until the day he left, she did not let this interfere in her regency, which she exercised vigorously from 1248 until 1252. She brought the reforms in the administration, begun by Louis in 1245, to completion in 1249 following the review of the information amassed in the last *enquêtes* before the crusade. She harried churchmen reluctant to pay the tenth and supervised the collection of ecclesiastical revenues in her son's name up until her death. She completed the negotiations for the permanent provisioning of Aigues-Mortes a few months after her son's departure. In every way, Blanche followed Louis's policies faithfully.[29]

This tendency to complete the work of her son remained the theme of government for the first year or so of the regency, but from 1250 on it was displaced as new problems and issues developed. Most important was the crisis produced at home by the changing fortunes of the crusade. The people most affected, from one point of view, were Louis's ordinary subjects—peasants, craftsmen, and burghers—who were firm allies of the monarchy. Louis's *enquêteurs* had sustained and strengthened this alliance by popularizing and giving substance to the notion that the interests of the crown were identical with the people's well-being. Thus, Louis's crusade became their crusade. He himself

[26] Bloch, *Royal Touch*, p. 283.

[27] In determining the route and sojourns in the south I have supplemented the itinerary in *HF* with information in *HF* furnished by Guillaume de Nangis, xx, 551-52; Guillaume de Puylaurens, xx, 771; *E Floribus chronicorum*, xxi, 696; and *La Branche des royaus lingnages*, xxii, 186. Also valuable were Thoison, *Séjours*, pp. 16, 18, 95-97, 152-53, 180; Delisle, *Cartulaire normand*, p. 78; Durand, "Beaucaire sous SL," p. 14; Eysette, *Consulat*, p. 46. It hardly needs to be stated that the further south Louis went the less warmly he was welcomed.

[28] See, *inter alia*, Salimbene, *Cronica*, I, 321: Porro illa die rex fecit expensas et comedit cum fratribus.

[29] All these issues have been discussed or documented in the appropriate places; see chapters 3 and 4.

had articulated this theme in 1248. At one of the workaday sessions of
the curia in Paris, held in the open air, a crowd of Parisian citizens
bustled around as Louis personally judged the case of a cleric who
had killed three royal policemen notorious for their oppression of the
local population. After ritually defrocking the clergyman, Louis re-
warded his "prowess" by making him a soldier for Christ in the royal
army. The crowd cheered while wishing the new crusader and his
master success in the Holy War.[30]

Blanche, by carrying out Louis's reforms, benefited too from the
rising identification of the rural and urban population with the
monarchy. Her own reputation enhanced this identification. She was
remembered as the defender of her son in the early struggles with the
baronage.[31] She was known for emancipating serfs, and an anonymous northern chronicler reported that out of pity she pardoned
some paupers held in prison for not paying their taxes.[32] Then there
were the mendicants—especially the Franciscans—who penetrated
French society in the first half of the thirteenth century, who captured
the devotional loyalties of the lower classes, and to whom Blanche had
evidently shown especial favor.[33] Blanche, thus, represented a convenient and comfortable object of devotion for the French people.

The crusaders' defeat in Egypt in 1250 and the news of the king's
capture accentuated popular loyalty to the monarchy. It was perhaps
ironic that this should have been the case. After all, when rumors
began to circulate about the slaughter of the crusaders by the Moslems,[34] critics might have blamed Louis himself. Perhaps his absence,
certainly the feeling that it was time for reevaluation rather than re-
crimination, helped insulate him from scorn. The first reactions to the
plight of the army were more like despair and a feeling of impotence
than criticism. An example of this is the verbalized scream of the
chronicler of Saint-Étienne of Caux, *Hoc anno* (1250), *peccatis nostris
exigentibus, heu, proh dolor! captus est. . . .*[35]

Screaming was not enough. After his release, Louis addressed a
public letter to churchmen and nobles in France seeking aid from
those among them who could or might help.[36] Reaction to this request

[30] Joinville, chap. XXVI, I say "ritually defrocking." In fact, Louis may simply have
barred him from taking major orders; Joinville's French is a bit imprecise.
[31] Above chapter 1 nn. 3-5.
[32] *HF*, XXI, 141. See also Beugnot, *Essai*, p. 91; and Labarge, *SL*, pp. 149-50. Bloch,
"Blanche de Castille," p. 248 and passim, has shown that some of our sources are
tainted with the deliberate propaganda of overenthusiastic panegyrists.
[33] Above chapter 3 nn. 106-7.
[34] Baudoin d'Avesnes, *HF*, XXI, 169; "St. Louis's Letter," p. 254. Cf. Joinville, chap.
LXV.
[35] *HF*, XXIII, 492.
[36] The Latin text may be found in Duchesne, *Historiae*, V, "Epistola sancti Ludovici."

was negative or indifferent. It might not have been polite to criticize, but it was stupid to invest scarce resources in an already collapsed enterprise. Recently ransomed troops felt the same way; they too returned home refusing to undertake the more prosaic work of salvage that Louis planned for the Christian crusader states.[37]

Writers often insinuate that the aristocracy displayed its true colors in failing to come to Louis's aid. This opinion is substantially correct; yet, an argument can be made that a second spurt of crusading activity was impossible in the absence of the planning mentality of the king. What could have been done without active leadership in Aigues-Mortes, without additional ships, supplies, and stores? Although Blanche was willing to provide the leadership in her efforts to aid her son, the demands of the original venture handicapped her. Much of the available revenue had already been spent by the end of 1250, and knowing of the defeat churchmen were just as reluctant or more reluctant to contribute the tenths they owed. Alone she could do little more than provide Louis with the resources to sustain a very reduced enterprise in the East; and it seemed for a while that she was utterly alone.

The king's brothers, Alfonse and Charles, returned home to find the pope unwilling to increase his efforts on Louis's behalf. Although Frederick II died in 1250, his heirs continued the struggle. Victory might be in sight, but it demanded all the pope's resources.[38] It is a mark of Blanche's determination that in these circumstances she managed to negotiate a two-year extension of the tenth, but its collection was difficult.[39] Moreover, the papacy had long been diverting spiritual resources and, as it were, encouraging the diversion of material resources originally earmarked for the crusade in the East to the German business instead.[40] And the prospect of success in Germany induced some French knights to sign up with papal forces and seek the closer rewards of the political crusade in the empire. Enraged, Blanche exiled them from France forever! "Those who fight for the Pope," she said, "should use the Pope's resources and they should leave (France) never to return."[41]

The two brothers, Charles and Alfonse, fell under Blanche's accus-

---

It has been translated into English in the Hague version of Joinville and published in modern French by O'Connell, *Propos de SL.*

[37] Joinville, chaps. LXXXIII-LXXXV.

[38] MP, v, 175, 188. See also Strayer, "Political Crusades," pp. 137-38.

[39] Above chapter 4 n. 103.

[40] Purcell, *Papal Crusading Policy,* pp. 75, 77; Strayer, "Political Crusades," p. 136.

[41] MP, v, 260: "Qui Papae militant, de Papalibus sustineantur et eant irredituri." See also Purcell, *Papal Crusading Policy,* p. 79.

ing eye for leaving the war in the East, an act which had left a bad impression on many. It had saddened the king and had disappointed some of the close friends of Alfonse and Charles.[42] Louis's other brother, Robert, had been killed at Mansourah; this too eroded Blanche's hopes and expectations. But it did not turn her away from her primary task—whatever possibilities of future deaths that might mean. She urged Alfonse and Charles to return to the Holy Land; this was the only path which seemed morally acceptable to her. Alfonse eventually came around to the opinion that his place was with his brother,[43] but Charles never seriously considered turning aside from the more fruitful possibilities which were likely to spin off from the death of Frederick II. Blanche, while she lived, managed to restrain the count of Anjou,[44] but she failed to persuade him or the great mass of nobles and prelates to help her son in the East. One is reminded of the sententious pessimism of Jude the Obscure in Hardy's novel: "nobody did come because nobody does."

It was the *pastoureaux* who transformed some of the despair into hope. In northern France and in Flanders,[45] a movement began in the spring of 1251 which is known as the crusade of the shepherds.[46] The *pastoureaux* are substantive proof that the lower levels of society equated or could be convinced to equate their social and political well-being with the king's welfare. The avowed aim of the leadership of the *pastoureaux* was to join Louis's forces in the East.[47] Some adherents of the movement made it to the Holy Land and entered Louis's service.[48] The mass of them, however, estimated by the chroniclers at one hundred thousand (a way of saying a very large number), never reached Palestine.[49]

In its earliest stages the movement was free of violent hostility to-

[42] Joinville, chaps. LXXXIX, LXXXIII, LXXXVII; MP, v, 281. And see also below nn. 167-69.

[43] Cf. Purcell, *Papal Crusading Policy*, p. 77.   [44] Wallon, *SL*, II, 409.

[45] The fact that the *pastoureaux* were strong in Flanders reinforces the feeling that Louis had easy access to the Flemish population as a result of his close friendship with Guillaume Dampierre; above chapter 3 nn. 40-48.

[46] The specialized bibliography on this movement is not extensive: Tillemont, *Vie de SL*, III, 429-38; Wallon, *SL*, I, 431-37; Berger, *Blanche de Castille*, pp. 392-400; Kerov, "Vosstanie 'pastushkov' "; Lerner, "Uses of Heterodoxy," pp. 198-202; Röhricht, "Die Pastorellen"; Delalande, *Extraordinaires croisades*. The lamb symbolism of the movement has recently been discussed in Jordan, "Lamb Triumphant," pp. 81-82. Hilton, *Bondmen*, pp. 100-102; Cheyney, *Dawn of a New Era*, pp. 111-15; and Purcell, *Papal Crusading Policy*, p. 78, try to put the movement into a European perspective.

[47] Salimbene, *Cronica*, II, 645-46; MP, v, 247; chronicle of Saint Laud of Rouen, *HF*, XXIII, 395. See also Röhricht, "Die Pastorellen," p. 292.

[48] MP, v, 253; chronicle of Saint-Denis, *HF*, XXXI, 116.

[49] MP, v, 248; chronicle of Saint Laud of Rouen, *HF*, XXIII, 395. See also Rohricht, "Die Pastorellen," pp. 292-93; Kerov, "Vosstanie 'pastushkov,' " p. 121.

ward prelates and nobles. Not altogether correctly, the *pastoureaux* did blame the aristocracy for the disaster in Egypt, and the natural object of their hatred was the large group of nobles and prelates who had stayed behind in France while the king fought.[50] Even so, there are no recorded physical attacks on lay and ecclesiastical barons by the *pastoureaux* before they reached Paris in early June 1251.[51] In Paris or its environs Blanche confirmed their faith in the crown. She welcomed them and gave them supplies.[52] I do not believe that she regarded the movement as a revolutionary force; I do not believe she subtly used their "heterodox" religious opinions to frighten other Frenchmen. Of course, among the thousands of shepherds some talk of a new social and religious order must have been in the air, but she would not have destroyed a movement whose fundamental purpose was to help her son simply because of idle talk.[53] It was not until threatening statements started coming from the leadership of the movement, and the demagogue known as the Master of Hungary urged his followers to take a violent path against the upper levels of society,[54] that Blanche decided, albeit hesitantly, to suppress the shepherds.[55]

An argument contrary to this opinion assumes that the *pastoureaux* were violent before reaching Paris, and by making this assumption, suggests that Louis's plight traumatized Blanche to such a degree that she ignored the rapacity and strange notions of the shepherds.[56] To sustain this interpretation there must be evidence that the shepherds committed significant acts of violence prior to their arrival in Paris. A contemporary chronicler refers to an attack by the *pastoureaux* on a Pentecost synod held by the archbishop of Rouen.[57] This is taken as proof that the shepherds were violent before reaching Paris,[58] but a Pentecost synod may refer to the time period before or after Pente-

---

[50] Röhricht, "Die Pastorellen," pp. 292-93. Cf. Kerov, "Vosstanie 'pastushkov,' " p. 121.

[51] Röhricht, "Die Pastorellen," p. 293; Delalande, *Extraordinaires croisades*, pp. 41-51.

[52] Chronicle of Saint Laud of Rouen, *HF*, XXIII, 396; MP, v, 248. See also Delalande, *Extraordinaires croisades*, p. 49; Röhricht, "Die Pastorellen," p. 294.

[53] *CUP*, no. 198 (a letter written by a Franciscan observer reporting some of the wilder statements of certain adherents of the movement; I use this edition of the letter instead of that in the *Annals of Burton*, p. 291, because of the critical apparatus to the text).

[54] Röhricht, "Die Pastorellen," p. 294; Lerner, "Uses of Heterodoxy," pp. 200-201. The Senonais chronicler, Geoffroy de Courlon, among others, attributes special powers to the Master of Hungary; he was a *nigromaticus*, a necromancer—Julliot, *Chronique*, pp. 525-26.

[55] Röhricht, "Die Pastorellen," p. 294; Delalande, *Extraordinaires croisades*, pp. 41-51.

[56] Lerner, "Uses of Heterodoxy," p. 200; Labarge, *SL*, p. 148.

[57] Chronicle of Saint Laud of Rouen, *HF*, XXIII, 396.

[58] Lerner, "Uses of Heterodoxy," p. 200. Cf. Röhricht, "Die Pastorellen," p. 293.

cost, not necessarily to the day of the feast itself.[59] At least, this is the case in the registers of Eudes Rigaud, the archbishop of Rouen, who knew something about the attack since he was its principal victim.

Eudes dated the disruption on the third and second of the ides of June,[60] or, since the ides of June fall on the thirteenth, the *pastoureaux* were in Rouen on the eleventh and twelfth of June.[61] This is precisely the same time that a faction of them were in Orléans (11 June).[62] Since the Orléans disturbances occurred after the *pastoureaux* left Paris,[63] the disruption in Rouen—whose violence historians tend to exaggerate[64]—also occurred after the *pastoureaux* left Paris. In other words, from Paris some of the shepherds went into Normandy or stragglers arrived there from farther north[65] and some headed south, toward Tours and Orléans. Both of these groups were in these places on the eleventh of June.[66]

Blanche, therefore, in greeting the *pastoureaux*, in giving them gifts, and in supplying them, was being beneficent to what had so far been an essentially peaceful movement whose avowed aim was to fight for her son. The chroniclers, in hindsight, thought she had been duped.[67] As it turned out hers was certainly a false hope, but before long she recognized the incapacity or unwillingness of the leaders of the movement to keep order.[68] When the shepherds began the murderous pillage of Paris which the chroniclers record, Blanche determined to suppress them. She hesitated—either because she still cherished the illusion that responsible leadership would reassert itself or because she did not want to risk a pitched battle in the city, that is, at the very heart of royal government—but when the so-called mob[69]

---

[59] *New Catholic Encyclopedia*, XI, "Pentecost Cycle," p. 100; Giry, *Manuel de diplomatique*, p. 270, s.v. "Pentecôte"; Cheyney, *Handbook of Dates*, p. 59 n. 1.

[60] *HF*, XXI, 575.   [61] Giry, *Manuel de diplomatique*, p. 132.

[62] MP, v, 249; *CUP*, no. 198 n.

[63] Cf. ibid.; all the reporters of the events put the Paris-Orléans sequence in the order described.

[64] Cf. Lerner, "Uses of Heterodoxy," p. 200. See also some of the primary evidence on the violence not heretofore cited: chronicle of Rouen, *HF*, XXIII, 335; and the chronicle of Saint Catherine of Rouen, *HF*, XXIII, 401-2.

[65] I am almost certain that one of the leaders of this band reached England (MP, v, 253). Many others took ship at Rouen (*HF*, XXIII, 396).

[66] Cf. Delalande, *Extraordinaires croisades*, pp. 41-51; Berger, *Blanche de Castille*, p. 397.

[67] For example, the chronicler of Saint Laud of Rouen, *HF*, XXIII, 396.

[68] Lerner, "Uses of Heterodoxy," p. 201, and Labarge, *SL*, p. 148, interpret the delay as proof of Blanche's despair and inability to act. But Labarge seems to go back on this view when on the next page (149) she says despair never interfered with Blanche's steadfast ("imperious") wielding of power and "maintenance of the royal rights."

[69] Mob is a loaded word which has been thrown around too easily (e.g., Chaillou des Barres, "SL à Sens," p. 204; Andrieu-Guitrancourt, *Archevêque Eudes Rigaud*, p. 401). See Kerov, "Vosstanie 'pastushkov,'" p. 116. Cf. the description of the shepherds as "whores, thieves, magicians, and *malefici*," by the Franciscan chronicler of Erfurt, *MGH*, *Script.*, XXIV, 200.

was sufficiently far from Paris so that it was no longer a threat to the capital, the thorough repression took place.[70]

Perhaps because the counterattacks commenced in earnest only after their departure from Paris, the *pastoureaux* themselves never associated Blanche with their opponents. The contemporary rhetoric accused them of being antinoble, anticlerical, and too violently anti-Semitic, but never antiroyal.[71] The chroniclers' reports of their actions, indeed, fall in line with traditional royal policies. The attacks on the Jews which they refer to, for example, were a continuation of the process begun by Louis IX.[72]

Whatever may be said of Blanche in all this—that she was slow to see or slow to act—she finally did see and did act. And the revolt of the *pastoureaux* was only one area in which she proved herself. She may have been slipping; she was old and tired. But time after time she met the challenges that pressed upon her.[73] Whether controlling disturbances at the University of Paris, transferring the county of Toulouse to the appanage system after the death of Count Raymond, or dealing with the papacy, she was hard and tough.[74] Her long and successful career came to an end in November 1252. The pent-up forces that were released on her death put considerable strain upon the equilibrium that she and her son had tried so earnestly to bring to French political life in the first half of the thirteenth century.

Four patterns of disorder emerged after Blanche's death, each contributing to the others and making their solution more difficult. First came disorganization at the summit of government, for *ipso facto* the passing of the queen-mother caused a crisis in the regency. The formal choice for regent was Louis IX's ten-year-old son, Prince Louis (d. 1260). Real political power was concentrated in the hands of a regency council.[75] This in itself was a curious development. The natural foci would, of course, have been the king's two brothers. Charles,

[70] Delalande, *Extraordinaires croisades*, pp. 41-51; Guillain de Bénouville, *SL*, p. 216.

[71] *CUP*, no. 198; Salimbene, *Cronica*, II, 117-18. See also Petit-Dutaillis, *Feudal Monarchy*, p. 319; Röhricht, "Die Pastorellen," pp. 294-95. Kerov, "Vosstanie 'pastushkov,'" p. 120, argues—wrongly in my opinion—that although the movement was antiroyal (a proposition for which there is absolutely no evidence) Blanche successfully used the *pastoureaux* to thwart the "separatist, decentralizing tendencies of the great feudatories" (*separatitskie, detsentralizatorskie tendentsii krupnikh feodalov*).

[72] The burning of Jewish holy books at Bourges and the desecration of the synagogue there are noted in the chronicle of Saint Laud of Rouen, *HF*, XXIII, 396; and by Johannes de Columna, *HF*, XXIII, 124. See also above chapter 4 n. 139.

[73] Labarge, *SL*, p. 149.

[74] For documents and discussion illustrating these issues, see *CUP*, nos. 195, 197, 215; *HGL*, VIII, cc. 1260-68; and above n. 41.

[75] Delisle in *HF*, XXIV, "Preuves," observations following no. 134; Berger, *SL et Innocent IV*, p. 386; Boutaric, *SL et Alfonse*, pp. 87-88; Olivier-Martin, *Régences*, p. 91. Cf. Boutaric, *Actes*, I, cccxxiv n. 1.

however, took no interest in the regency; after Blanche's death he immediately immersed himself in Flemish affairs.[76] Alfonse's failure was less complete: he was in Paris (he governed his own territories from there), and he was normally a conscientious, even brilliant administrator. But he was handicapped by the development of a paralytic illness which probably involved pressure on the optic nerve inducing temporary blindness. And after his recovery, most of his time was taken up with his preparations to rejoin his brother. Both these facts tended to shut him out from the day-to-day administration of the royal government.[77] His prestige was available, however, when problems reached crisis proportions.[78]

The government of the country therefore fell to a group of prelates (the archbishop of Bourges and the bishops of Senlis, Evreux, Paris, and Orléans) with whom Blanche had taken counsel during her regency.[79] Louis had chosen these men before the crusade, for two of the five had taken the crusader's vow yet were permitted to renounce it, and this could not have occurred without the king's approval.[80] The selection of prelates to give counsel to the queen-mother and, by inference, to guide the kingdom in the event of her incapacity was, I would argue, a consequence of Louis's distrust of the nobility. The history of royal power in his reign had been a history of armed resistance to the attacks of hostile barons. He had not lived through that history for nothing. He believed, no doubt, that the interests of the clergy were less selfish than the interests of his lay nobles.

He may have been right. Nonetheless, he underestimated the harmful consequences of a purely episcopal council. (The solution the king opted for in 1270 during his second crusade—a mixed lay and ecclesiastical regency council—shows that he understood his original error.)[81] Despite their loyalty to Louis the bishops were devoted to the political interests of the church, and the two did not always coincide.

[76] Below nn. 123-30.
[77] Boutaric, SL et Alfonse, pp. 86-87; Berger, SL et Innocent IV, pp. 391-93; Delisle in HF, xxiv, "Preuves," observations following no. 134. Bisson, "Negotiations for Taxes," details his financial preparations for crusade.
[78] Berger and Boutaric, perhaps, overemphasize his role, but there is no doubt that others appealed to his authority in very trying conditions; see, for example, below n. 103. See also Carolus-Barré, "Prince héritier," p. 594.
[79] Delisle discovered the regency council; HF, xxiv, "Preuves," following no. 134. Berger, Blanche de Castille, pp. 403-4, also concluded that the governing council had no lay nobles at this time. Cf. Tillemont, Vie de SL, iii, 467; Griffiths, "New Men," p. 237; Carolus-Barré, "Prince héritier," p. 594.
[80] The pastors of Bourges and Orléans had taken vows (MP, iv, 490; Guillaume de Nangis, HF, xx, 353), but had remained in France. On canonistic views of bishops' renunciation of the crusader's vow for government service, see Brundage, Medieval Canon Law and the Crusader, pp. 99, 133-35.
[81] Below chapter 8 n. 17.

Pope Innocent IV aggravated the discrepancy. He seems to have recognized quite early that the informal council of the five bishops constituted the effective authority in France after Blanche's death, and he repeatedly called upon the bishops in what he felt was the church's best interest. This may be demonstrated rather easily. Although it would be absurd to consider every letter and every suggestion which the pope made to the conciliar bishops to be part of a nefarious scheme to subdue them to his will, the fact is that Innocent's requests regularly called upon the prelates to act in matters outside their episcopal competence but within what may be considered their *de facto* competence as regents.[82]

In 1253, for example, he ordered Guillaume, the bishop of Orléans, one of the conciliar bishops, to use the threat of ecclesiastical censure to effect the return of the regalia of Thérouanne to capitular authorities despite the obvious resistance of royal officials to cease collecting the revenues of the diocese.[83] Since the matter clearly was not one which touched Guillaume in his episcopal capacity (the two sees were utterly unconnected), it seems reasonable to conclude that the pope turned to him because of his position in the royal government. It is equally significant that the policy which the pope directed him to pursue was one which was opposed to long-standing royal traditions: the French crown regarded the use of ecclesiastical censures against its officials to be an unfair interference in the legitimate exercise of royal authority.[84] If we ask ourselves why Bishop Guillaume would have accepted the charge laid on him by the pope, the possible answers are numerous. He may have felt it was his duty to act simply because he was ordered to do so by his superior, or he may have shared ecclesiastical opinion that Louis IX was wrong in his views on ecclesiastical censure.[85] Whatever the case, this instance of Innocent IV's intrusion into the governance of France through the medium of the conciliar bishops was only one of many. He can be seen subtly exceeding his pastoral powers in such matters as his advice to them on the turmoil at the University of Paris in 1253, on jurisdictional squabbles between the two powers, and on the payment of the tenth.[86]

Simultaneously the pope began to renege on promises he had made before the crusade. Thus, the abuse of papal provisions (here imply-

[82] Berger, *SL et Innocent IV*, pp. 374-81, 393-96.
[83] Ibid., pp. 393-94.
[84] Campbell, "Attitude of the Monarchy toward . . . Ecclesiastical Censures," pp. 553-54. Cf. on contemporary English attitudes, Jordan, "On Bracton and *Deus Ultor*," pp. 27-28.
[85] Cf. the apparently representative views of Bishop Gui of Auxerre recorded in Joinville, chaps. xxxv-xxxvi.
[86] *CUP*, nos. 218, 223, 226.

ing the papal appointment of a foreign clerk to a French benefice), which was in part the target of the "Protest of St. Louis" in 1247 and upon which Innocent capitulated, appeared with a "new persistence" by the time of the king's return from the East.[87] In every sense, according to Élie Berger, after Blanche's death the pope put himself at the head of those who defied royal officials in the name of the church in France.[88] Only Innocent's death in late 1254 brought an end to this new assertiveness of the papacy and staved off a confrontation with the crown.[89]

The difficulties of the regency council and the resentment caused by the clerical direction of its policies gave rise to a second type of political disorganization, conflicts and confusion in the technical administration of government. Royal *baillis* and *sénéchaux* who opposed or defied the council in what they thought were the king's best interests left office. If the prelates of the regency council expelled them with Prince Louis's permission (and this seems to be the only reasonable hypothesis), they were not, in the ordinary sense, being disloyal to the king for doing so. Their perceptions of the welfare of the kingdom differed from those of royal officers on important points. And they were the governors; they had to exercise supervisory responsibility, in the boy-prince's name of course, over the whole administration. That the bishops had problems in doing so—that they allowed themselves to be coerced by a strong pope; that they never seem to have found an effective method for making final decisions; and that their ecclesiastical persuasion left them open to the hostility of Louis's reformed *baillis*, many of whom were getting reputations for harrying the church—to repeat, that they had problems in keeping the gov-

---

[87] Berger, *SL et Innocent IV*, pp. 293-94 n. 5.   [88] Ibid., p. 393.

[89] A dispute in 1253 in which the bishop of Beauvais, a returned crusader (above chapter 4 n. 30), served as chief judge illustrates something of the dynamics of Pope Innocent's role. With the assistance of two lesser prelates, the bishop, who had become involved in squabbles with local royal officials not long after his return to Beauvais (*Layettes*, III, no. 4084; also Tillemont, *Vie de SL*, II, 260), rendered a judgment in favor of the Benedictine abbey of Saint-Valéry against the inhabitants of the town of the same name; see Durand, *Inventaire . . . Somme . . . G*, v, 329 (notation in an eighteenth century inventory). Since the violence at the heart of the litigation occurred in 1234, twenty years before the townsmen agreed to the bishop's arbitration, it may be that they were urged by the conciliar regents, themselves bishops, to accept episcopal arbitration. The likelihood of coercion is supported by the fact that the burghers evidently attempted to have the matter retried somewhat later before laymen. This is my interpretation of a papal bull of 10 Kalends August 1254, issued for the diocese of Amiens (where Saint-Valéry is located). Innocent's bull not only prohibited religious in the region from appearing before secular judges but recommended that jurisdictional disputes between the two powers be adjudicated before bishops, an argument that legitimized *ex post facto* the arbitration of the Saint-Valéry case by the bishop of Beauvais; Durand, p. 330; Potthast, *Regesta*, II, nos. 14674-75. Cf. Gandilhon, *Inventaire . . . Cher . . . Archevêché de Bourges*, I, c. 19.

ernment in smooth working order is hardly surprising, but the immediate administrative consequences of this fact are worth noting.[90]

The evidence on administrative disorder comes from a variety of sources. In the first place, the conciliar regents may have introduced or reintroduced into the royal administration men who would treat the church with greater deference than was true of the classic type of the reform appointee.[91] Secondly, conflicting opinions at the center apparently found expression in the accumulation of vacancies in other administrative slots: the *bailliages* of Rouen, Caen, Caux, the Cotentin, Orléans, and the *sénéchaussées* of Languedoc all lacked chief officers on the eve of the king's return.[92] The conciliar regents were not hesitating simply in order to permit the king to make his own appointments although this may have played a part in their slowness to act. For example, it cannot explain why, at the same time, there was the most rapid succession of suspensions and appointments of top administrative officials in Gisors, Paris, and Sens that had ever been seen.[93] The year 1253 also witnessed the abandonment of royal guidelines on the geography of *bailliagère* jurisdictions. Probably because they had not appointed a sufficient number of *baillis*, the conciliar regents had to make temporary adjustments in the political geography of the *bailliages* of Bayeux, Étampes, Senlis, and Artois. So much can be said for this part of their work: they tended to resurrect traditional units or traditional associations of joint administration rather than create entirely new administrative districts.[94]

The crisis in the regency after Blanche's death and the unsettled conditions in the administration which sprang from it aggravated, in turn, a third type of disorder. More vivid than the first two, it was precipitated by members of the nobility. Annoyed by the new government's emphatic defense of ecclesiastical privileges, a group of barons

[90] One of the reasons for their weakness as administrators is that no one had clear precedence over the others in these lay matters. The opinion of Maurice, *Angerville*, pp 16, 83, that the bishop of Paris was "Vice-Roi de France" in 1253-1254 seems to be unsupported by the sources.

[91] This may explain the reappointment of André Le Jeune in Amiens and Guerne de Verberie in Paris, both of whom had left royal service in the late 1240s. See Appendix One, s.v. "Amiens," "Paris." Bloch, "Blanche de Castille," p. 227 n. 4, constructed a hypothetical chronology of the *prévôts* of Paris which, if accurate, would exclude Guerne as an illustration of this.

[92] Appendix One under relevant headings. See chapter 3 figures one and two, which show relative stability in the turnover of administrative personnel in 1250-1252 and a disequilibrium in 1253.

[93] Appendix One. The list for Gisors should be supplemented by additional data in *HF*, xxiv, "Chronologie," on other doubtful *baillis* appointed there in 1253. That such appointments were for "training" purposes seems farfetched; but, cf. Griffiths, "New Men," p. 252.

[94] Appendix One. For Arras, see also *HF*, xxiv, "Preuves," no. 138. Cf. d'Hérbomez, "Baillis d'Arras," p. 456.

grew surly and demonstrated their discontent in various ways. A few seem to have refused to do homage to the king's son in 1253.[95] Others sought to call in a strong regent to replace the council. Simon de Montfort, then known only as a capable leader, was suggested as a possibility to rescue the "desolate" realm. But this did not materialize.[96] Less peaceful barons turned violently against the church.[97] What happened to the great monastery at Cluny in 1253 is instructive.[98]

The problem had begun before Blanche's death. Cluny claimed to be exempt from the tenth and refused to pay. Unimpressed by the monastery's claim, Baudoin de Pian, the royal *bailli* in the Mâconnais, seized the goods of the abbot in retaliation.[99] Blanche, who was perhaps exasperated by the monks' reluctance to pay, seems to have supported this and similar seizures.[100] Thus Cluny appealed to its overlord, the pope. With Blanche apparently unresponsive to his entreaties, Innocent IV wrote to the crusading king.[101] I have seen no record of the king's reply, but it is not unreasonable to suspect that he referred the case right back to his mother who would have had much more direct information on the matter. The dispute thus remained alive.

In 1253 the monastery successfully settled the matter or, at least, the seizure of its goods seems to have come to an end, for in that year Baudoin de Pain ceased to be *bailli* of the Mâconnais. Apparently, not everyone was satisfied at the rightness of Baudoin's dismissal or the justness of the monastery's cause.[102] Perhaps this is why the returned crusader, the duke of Burgundy, needing money as badly as the king,

[95] See the list of feudal homages, HF, XXIII, 680, and the cases of Johannes de Calniaco and Symon de Foullosis, 5 April 1253.
[96] MP, v, 366, 371-72, 415. Berger looked upon this evidence with suspicion because he was influenced by the history of the revolutionary events of 1258-1265 in England and by Simon's role in them. French barons certainly could be disagreeable, but did they really want such a man to take control of the state? Powicke, *Thirteenth Century*, p. 114, correctly recognized that in 1253 Simon was known only as an effective administrator. Powicke was mistaken, however, in his opinion that the barons called upon him because Louis's brothers were still on crusade. In fact, they had already returned, which is itself powerful additional evidence that Charles and Alfonse were either unwilling or unable to direct government effectively themselves; cf. above nn. 76-77. I assume, however, that they made it plain to the baronage that whatever their limitations they needed no help from Simon de Montfort.
[97] Berger, *SL et Innocent IV*, pp. 414-17, is helpful on this general subject.
[98] *Layettes*, v, nos. 643-47; Boutaric, *Actes*, I, "Arrêts . . . antérieurs aux *Olim*," no. 40. See also Berger, *SL et Innocent IV*, pp. 415-16.
[99] *HF*, XXIV, "Chronologie," p. 173.
[100] Varin, *Archives administratives*, I, 727 n. 1 (in the diocese of Reims).
[101] *HF*, XXIV, "Chronologie," p. 173. Cf. Tillemont, *Vie de SL*, IV, 41-42.
[102] Cf. Appendix One. Administrative records show that Louis IX sought him out and reemployed him as a royal official after the crusade; *HF*, XXI, 381.

turned against Cluny. Neither the regency council nor Alfonse could stop the duke's invasion of the sanctuary or his retainers' physical abuse of the monks.[103]

When Louis returned from crusade in 1254, he was greeted by the abbot of Cluny who, it is reported, gave the king two beautiful and expensive ponies as homecoming presents. The next day they talked about the trouble in the Mâconnais. There can be no doubt that the gift of the ponies was intended to get Louis in the right mood for the discussions; he rather naively recognized it as such later on. His subsequent order forbidding officials who were adjudicating litigation from receiving gifts was tied, in the opinion of Joinville, to his own remorse over accepting the abbot's ponies. That Louis coupled this *mandement* with an equally binding restriction against members of the council accepting gifts might also be evidence that the actions of the conciliar regents in 1253 were not simply the result of their well-intended, albeit confused and misguided, efforts to govern properly but also of their susceptibility to bribery.[104]

Be that as it may, the king had done wrong in accepting the ponies. Did he also do wrong in accepting a loan of five thousand pounds from the monastery at a time when his treasury was "drained to the dregs?"[105] It is hard to say. The monastery made the loan in December 1254, a few months after the king's return to France but only one month after the curia at Paris gave judgment (November 1254) against the duke of Burgundy for his attack on the monastery.[106] Possibly the loan had nothing to do with the judgment. More likely, it had been promised at the original meeting between the abbot and the king, a gesture, perhaps, on the abbot's part to demonstrate that even though the monastery was justly exempt from paying the tenth it had always wanted to do its share to help the financially pressed king. Louis may have regretted ever having agreed to accept the loan; he paid it back extremely quickly.[107]

Cluny was illustrative of the sort of disagreeable problem, culminating in violence, that disturbed domestic order in 1253. There are many other examples. In the dioceses of Thérouanne and Chartres which had already had nasty confrontations with royal officials over regalia the atmosphere was poisoned with murderous attacks on the

---

[103] Berger, *SL et Innocent IV*, pp. 415-16.
[104] On the events and commentary, Joinville, chap. CXXXI. With regard to the corruption that might be attributed to the conciliar regents, compare Bellamy, *Crime and Public Order*, pp. 12,18, who has found just such a pattern of bribery in England during royal absences.
[105] *Layettes*, III, no. 4133.
[106] Boutaric, *Actes*, I, no. 1.
[107] It was repaid by 1256; *Layettes*, III, no. 4294.

king's men and on churchmen in that year.[108] The diocese of Albi was the scene of disorder centering on the bishop,[109] who led troops in a private war that threatened to tear that part of the south asunder:[110] royal authority was curtailed by the bishop's excommunication of the royal *viguier*[111] and by the ineffective investigations ordered and reordered by the regency council.[112] There is either something sad or mocking—I cannot decide which—in the addressing of a petition on the violence in Albi in 1253 to the ten-year-old boy-prince.[113] Violence in and around Paris, emigration of frightened residents,[114] the strike at the university where mendicants and seculars resented each other's power[115]—all this surfaced uncontrolled. The realm was in great danger wrote one chronicler;[116] it was "desolate" wrote another.[117] The otherwise enthusiastic defender of the crusades, the poet Rutebeuf, was deeply dismayed by events.[118] Scholars, in hindsight, have even suggested that the period was one of anarchy.[119]

The lack of strong authority which was becoming increasingly evident probably had its influence on the emergence of a fourth and final type of "disorder," one whose repercussions basically affected the position of the French kingdom vis-à-vis foreign powers.[120] Henry III of England (or his advisers) very likely saw the worsening situation in France as an opportunity to recover the Angevin inheritance. It

[108] Berger, *SL et Innocent IV*, pp. 425-26.

[109] *Layettes*, II, no. 3008, IV, nos. 4786, 4799, 4820, and V, nos. 561-62, 594-605, 607-12, 614-30, 632; *HGL*, VIII, cc. 1358-60, 1364, 1455-63; Boutaric, *Actes*, I, no. 379. See also *Cahiers de Fanjeaux*, 6 (1971), 313-15.

[110] *Layettes*, V, no. 607.　　　　　　　　　　　[111] Ibid., no. 602. Cf. above n. 84.

[112] Ibid., nos. 607, 632.

[113] Ibid., no. 607. For similar examples of petitions on violence to the boy-prince, see III, no. 4057 (on Cluny); and Carolus-Barré, "Prince héritier," p. 595 n. 1 no. 5 (on Clermont).

[114] Joinville, chap. CXLI. Joinville gives no year for the incidents in Paris, but he opens his discussion with the words "at that time" (the time of the event just described). That event was the issuance of the ordinance on administrative reform (dated by independent authority immediately on Louis's return from crusade in the summer of 1254; below chapter 6 n. 136). So it seems entirely appropriate to conclude that he is talking about events in Paris which occurred in 1253 or early 1254.

[115] *CUP*, nos. 224-25, 227, 231, 237.

[116] Anonymous of Saint-Denis, *HF*, xx, 56.　　　　　[117] Above n. 96.

[118] Bastin and Faral, *Onze poèmes*, p. 31.

[119] Thus, Pacaut, "Louis IX," p. 415. Strayer, "Crusades of Louis IX," p. 178, provides a useful corrective to some of the more excessive of these views, but his statement that Louis's prolonged absence was "not greatly to the detriment of France" cannot be admitted without qualification. It was not only a commonplace of anti-crusade sentiment that *regna* suffered in the absence of *reges* (cf. Brundage, *Medieval Canon Law and the Crusader*, p. 104), it was a fact (see, for example, Bellamy, *Crime and Public Order*, p. 10). The very capture of the king in 1250 had set off a brief wave of violence in anti-French Languedoc, a wave of violence of which Delisle himself—a man not given to exaggeration—stressed the importance; *HF*, xxiv, "Chronologie," p. 249.

[120] Blanche had alerted Louis to the possibility of danger from foreign princes before the war; MP, v, 3-4.

was unlawful to attack a crusader's lands, Henry was a notorious failure at war, and he could not get his barons to pay for the expedition; so, the attack did not come off.[121] But the threat caused some trepidation in France: the feudal host was summoned and part of it assembled for war.[122]

Louis's brother, Charles of Anjou, capitalized on the situation in his homeland in quite a different way: he was freed by the death of his mother to go to war. He threw in his lot with the Dampierre family in an effort to secure their inheritance of the county of Flanders from their stepbrothers, the d'Avesnes, who were trying to seize the county by force. Louis and the papal legate's settlement, in 1246, of the succession to Flanders and Hainaut (Flanders to the younger set of sons of Margaret of Flanders; Hainaut to the older set by an illicit marriage)[123] had been called into question owing to the death of the heir-designate to Flanders, Guillaume Dampierre. Guillaume, like the king's brothers, had returned from crusade in late 1250.[124] During a tournament in 1251, he was killed.[125] Although his death was probably accidental, rumor had it that the d'Avesnes were responsible. They seized upon the slander as the excuse to undo the entire judgment of 1246.[126] With Louis IX in the Holy Land, they had felt little or no constraint on their actions.

From the first the Dampierres had tried to enlist the support of France on their side. Blanche could not have been happy at events in Flanders and Hainaut, but the most effective way to deal with them was uncertain. Margaret, the countess, offered Hainaut to Charles of Anjou if he would raise an army in behalf of her Dampierre offspring.[127] The count of Anjou was willing, but Blanche was not. She considered Charles's first responsibility to be to return to the Holy Land with help for Louis.[128] When his mother died, however, Charles promptly accepted the title count of Hainaut and began to raise an army. Showing a remarkable loyalty to the Capetians, the towns of

[121] Above chapter 2 nn. 66-69; also Joinville, chap. LXXXII.

[122] For the summons, see HF, XXIII, 730-31. See also Coët, Roye, I, 183, 185. While in the East in 1250, Louis had expressed his belief that Blanche "had ample forces to defend" France from English attack; Joinville, chap. LXXXV.

[123] Above chapter 3 nn. 40-48.

[124] Wallon, SL, II, 408-12; Labarge, SL, pp. 151-54.

[125] Wallon, SL, II, 408. Of course, tournaments were banned during the crusade; see Purcell, Papal Crusading Policy, p. 29. But the Flemings had a special privilege granted by Innocent III and apparently still in effect in the mid-thirteenth century: they could hold tournaments if they would at the same time "pay something in subsidium Terrae Sanctae"; Warlop, Flemish Nobility, I, pt. 1, pp. 299-300.

[126] Wallon, SL, II, 408-9; Duvivier, Querelle des d'Avesnes et des Dampierres, I, 204-5, 212-13.

[127] Wallon, SL, II, 409-10; Duvivier, Querelle des d'Avesnes et des Dampierres, I, 238.

[128] Wallon, SL, II, 409. Cf. Duvivier, Querelle des d'Avesnes et des Dampierres, I, 236-37.

northern France that had already given enormous sums for the king's crusade also gave large loans to Charles.[129] Nobody could or did stop Charles from pursuing his goal. Only the battles were indecisive. The d'Avesnes matched the future hero of Tagliacozzo in generalship, and an uneasy truce prevailed on the lines by the spring of 1254.[130]

There was a different tone of life among the French crusaders in North Africa and the Levant during the years of the regency. After the collapse of the crusade at Mansourah in 1250, owing to the rash commitment of the crusaders' forces by Robert of Artois, who died in the assault, events became progressively more dismaying. Yet it had all started out very differently.

From the moment they had landed in Egypt the crusaders had swept all before them. Egypt, they well knew, was where Moslem power had to be confronted if Jerusalem was ever to be regained. They had successfully taken the fortified stronghold of Damietta and, from there, hoped to continue their advance.[131] Damietta became, very briefly, a symbol of the crusaders' optimism. Materially, it served as the major depot for the supplies that had been accumulated at Cyprus and Aigues-Mortes.[132] Spiritually, Damietta was elevated into a Christian see. Louis endowed the newly converted cathedral of Damietta immediately after the victory and had it dedicated to the Virgin.[133]

But the period of elation was incredibly short. With equal courage and tenacity and better generalship, the Moslems succeeded in stopping the French advance in the vicinity of Mansourah. The battles around the small town which lasted from February to the beginning of April 1250 went back and forth for several days, but by the end of February the tide had turned decisively in favor of the Saracens.[134] Strayer has written that "prudence dictated a retreat, but at this point the piety of Louis overcame his generalship. He could not believe that the army had been brought so far, through so many dangers, only to fail at the last."[135]

The rout of the Christian army ensued; large numbers of troops were taken prisoner, others were slain. The king and his surviving

---

[129] See the municipal accounts in *Layettes*, III, nos. 4583, 4592, 4597-98, 4609, 4629, and elsewhere.

[130] Wallon, *SL*, II, 410; Duvivier, *Querelle des d'Avesnes et des Dampierres*, I, 251.

[131] Strayer, "Crusades of Louis IX," pp. 167-69.

[132] Ibid., p. 169.

[133] Joinville, chap. XXXVIII; "Letter of John Sarrasin," p. 245. See also Richard, "Fondation de l'église de Damiette," pp. 39-40, 52-54.

[134] Strayer, "Crusades of Louis IX," pp. 171-76; Oman, *Art of War*, p. 59.

[135] Strayer, "Crusades of Louis IX," p. 175.

brothers were captured. (Louis had wisely left his pregnant wife in Damietta with its small garrison.) Ironically, only the religious leader of the crusade, the legate, and a small group of his men managed to escape. Louis was sick in body with dysentery; he was probably a great deal sicker in spirit. The crusade had failed. The crusade had failed.[136]

For reasons largely of the internal politics of Islam it was decided that the best course of action was the release of the king's army for a heavy ransom (although not all factions favored this approach). It was also agreed that Louis would concede Damietta as the price for his own release. When these agreements were finally reached, there was a revolt in the Moslem army. Though order was ultimately maintained and the treaty confirmed, for a brief period the fate of the crusaders and the king was in jeopardy.[137] It is no doubt from this period, when the king's life was in the greatest danger, that the legend arose that he found comfort in the visit of the Dove, the Holy Spirit, Who brought the Roman breviary to the fallen ruler.[138]

Through all the trials of the few weeks of his imprisonment, the king bore up well. At least, this is the picture painted by his contemporaries. He may have betrayed something like despair during the first negotiations for his release as, for example, when he expressed to the sultan his uncertainty whether the queen would pay his ransom, but this could have been bluff.[139] There are no other examples of such self-pitying. He defiantly made the sign of the cross with his whole body, lying prostrate on the ground in the presence of his captors.[140] He showed no fear before the tortures with which he was threatened by the sultan's council.[141] The Saracens, in general, were deeply impressed by his behavior.[142] Moreover, though the thought of returning home immediately after his release passed his mind or

[136] Certainly the best narration of these events is in Joinville's *Histoire*, chaps. LVIII-LXXIV. See also Strayer, "Crusades of Louis IX," pp. 175-76.

[137] Joinville, chaps. LXVII-LXXIV. See also Strayer, "Crusades of Louis IX," pp. 176-77.

[138] *Hours of Jeanne d'Evreux*, fol. 154 verso. Sometimes the tradition speaks of an angel bringing the book; Delisle, "Testament de Blanche de Navarre," p. 29 no. 196. It was also said that Louis received the gift of healing at this time; Bloch, *Royal Touch*, p. 397.

[139] Joinville, chap. LXVII.

[140] Ibid., chap. LXXII.

[141] Ibid., chap. LXVII. Du Cange reports having seen royal coins from Louis's reign which apparently bore symbols of the instruments of torture and imprisonment; his opinion has been contested. Nonetheless, according to Tillemont, certain coins with these symbols did exist and were accompanied by the legend *etiam reges*, "even kings"; Du Cange, "On the Torture of the Bernicles," pp. 164-65, and "Notes" in Hague version of Joinville, pp. 279-80 (citing Tillemont). I, too, have doubts as to whether these descriptions are accurate, but the opinion of such great scholars cannot be dismissed lightly.

[142] Joinville, chap. LXXII; MP, V, 425; Geoffroy de Beaulieu, HF, XX, 16-17; "Chronique de Primat," HF, XXIII, 14. Tillemont, *Vie de SL*, III, 359-60, 363-66.

was urged on him, Louis was so far from despair that he was ready to begin anew. His concern, as he expressed it, "for the miseries and sufferings of the Holy Land . . . determined us to delay our departure and stay some time longer in the Kingdom of Syria, rather than entirely to abandon the cause of Christ."[143] When he arrived by boat in Palestine in mid-May, it was for a stay of four full years.

Matthew Paris, the English monk, has left the most sensitive portrait of the king and of his personal growth after the military collapse of 1250.[144] Behind this portrait is the unquestioned belief that the reason for the failure of the crusade was not to be sought in the peculiar circumstances of military tactics or strategy, but in the moral failures of Louis himself. No doubt impressed by the vigor of the king's exploitation of revenue in France before his departure, Matthew asserted that the judgment of God had descended on Louis as the plunderer of the poor and the church.[145] Joinville recognized, even in the circle of crusaders, the feeling that the king had ruthlessly used the church's material resources.[146] Whether for these specific reasons or not, Louis himself acknowledged in the conventional but extraordinarily important formula of his time that the crusade had failed because of his sins.[147]

To answer the objections of his contemporaries and his own conscience, Louis changed. This is easy enough to prove: everyone—from his intimates to his enemies to the pope who would eventually canonize him—recognized and either criticized or praised the change.[148] Louis did not become "more religious" in the superficial sense of that phrase. However, the manifestations of his religious devotion were transformed. What was new in this transformation was not the types of religious devotion the king practiced but the intensity, almost obsession, with which he practiced them. He went through or, rather, the remainder of his life was, in a certain sense, a long penance.[149]

Penance implies both punishment and absolution. The punishments came in several forms. The acceptance of flagellation, in the tradition of the martyrs[150] and in remembrance of the failure of 1250,

---

[143] "St. Louis' Letter," p. 253.

[144] MP, v, 107-8. See also Kienast, *Deutschland und Frankreich*, III, 634-38.

[145] MP, v, 170-71, 254, 260, 280-81.

[146] Joinville, chaps. LXXXIII, LXXXIV. Cf. Tillemont, *Vie de SL*, III, 116-17.

[147] "Epistola sancti Ludovici," p. 429: *peccatis nostris exigentibus*.

[148] Geoffroy de Beaulieu, *HF*, XX, 18-19; Guillaume de Nangis, *HF*, XX, 650; *E Floribus chronicorum*, *HF*, XXI, 698; Boniface VIII's canonization sermon, *HF*, XXIII, 150. See also Tillemont, *Vie de SL*, v, 324-74; and O'Connell, *Propos de SL*, pp. 48-49.

[149] Cf. O'Connell, *Propos de SL*, p. 22. See also Labande, "SL pèlerin."

[150] Normally one finds the phrase (*usque*) *ad sanguinem* used to describe the discipline of the saints (for example, above chapter 1 n. 43 and below n. 160); it is borrowed from

was one of these.[151] There was also the touching—the insistent touching—of the ugly, the diseased, the filthy, which revolted his friends. It started in Palestine when he insisted on burying with his own hands the corpses of fallen crusaders and refused to hold his nose when he had to touch their putrid bodies.[152] These sense aberrations were one aspect of his personal punishment.

This motif would endure long after the crusade. According to Joinville, for example, Louis constantly surrounded himself with the poor.[153] Joinville also speaks of the king's later gifts to lazar houses, the *leprosaria*,[154] and Pope Boniface VIII in his canonization sermon was to cite Louis's compassion for the leprous as a quality of his saintliness.[155] Wall paintings and miniatures provide us with arresting evidence of the king ministering to lepers and especially of holding them and feeding them.[156] After the crusade, he laid it down as an ordinance that wherever he sojourned the right of the lepers to share his table would be observed.[157]

Louis's self-punishment took the additional form of a kind of intentional mockery of the vanities of his early life and style of ruling. Most important was the self-centered humiliation of wearing the pilgrim's habit and the forsaking of spicy foods and wines.

---

early Christian descriptive terminology of martyrdom. Cf. Vermeulen, *Semantic Development of Gloria*, p. 115.

[151] Guillaume de Saint-Pathus, *HF*, xx, 83. Louis's flagellum is on display at the *trésor* of the cathedral of Notre-Dame in Paris. The flagellation was depicted on the windows of Saint-Denis (now destroyed); see the drawings in Montfaucon, *Monumens*, pl. xxiv. The scene was also represented in the wall paintings of the Franciscan nunnery at Lourcines founded by Louis's widow in 1289; see Longnon, *Documents*, pl. v and p. 17 (ix). A fourteenth century *vita* of Saint Louis has an excellent miniature of the scene; Paris, BN MS fr. 2813, fol. 265. The library kindly supplied me photographs. The king's sister, Isabella, also adopted flagellation as a penance (above chapter 1 n. 43).

[152] Joinville, chap. cxiii. See also Folz, "Sainteté," p. 34 n. 10; Auzas, "Essai d'un répertoire iconographique de SL," pp. 17-18.

[153] Joinville, chaps. cxxxv, cxxxix, cxlii. There is much more evidence from a wide variety of sources that could be adduced here: see the anonymous chronicle of Saint-Denis, *HF*, xx, 51-53; the descriptions of the wall paintings of Lourcines and the lower chapel of the Sainte-Chapelle, Longnon, *Documents*, pp. 19-20 and pl. iv; and several illuminated manuscripts of the king's *vita*, Paris, BN MS fr. 5716 fol. 137, and MS fr. 2813, fol. 265. See also Folz, "Sainteté," p. 39 n. 48; Auzas, "Essai d'un répertoire iconographique de SL," p. 17.

[154] Joinville, chap. cxxxix.

[155] *HF*, xxiii, 150. See also Folz, "Sainteté," p. 39 n. 50.

[156] For such scenes at Lourcines, see Longnon, *Documents*, p. 18 (x); in the lower chapel of the Sainte-Chapelle, pl. vi. The destroyed windows of Saint-Denis bore the motif of Louis feeding a leprous monk; Montfaucon, *Monumens*, ii, pl. xxv. A fine example of this scene in an illuminated *vita* is Paris, BN MS fr. 2813, fol. 265. See also Auzas, "Essai d'un répertoire iconographique de SL," p. 17.

[157] Le Grand, "Maisons-Dieu," pp. 330-31 n. 4. See also, Boullé, "Maison de Saint-Lazare," pp. 130, 134.

After his return from overseas [Joinville writes], the king led so devout a life that he never again wore ermine or miniver, or scarlet, or gilt stirrups or spurs. His clothing was of undyed or dark-blue wool. The lining of his blankets and clothing was of doeskin, or fur from the legs of hares, or lamb's-wool; he was so temperate at table that he ordered no dishes beyond what his cook prepared; it was placed before him, and he ate it. He mixed his wine with water in a glass goblet, adding water in proportion to the strength of the wine, and while the wine was being watered behind his table, he held the glass in his hand. Every day he fed his poor, and after dinner provided money to be given to them.[158]

One runs the risk of forgetting the humor and embarrassment of such exaggerations. Mid-thirteenth century holy people were constantly chided for their immoderation.[159] Louis's contemporary, Blessed Thomas Hélye, the Norman saint, also put away luxurious clothes and underwent discipline and was firmly criticized by his biographer for his extremes.[160] The author of the life of Saint Beatrice, Marguerite d'Oingt, with some chagrin found her heroine to be overzealous in her penances.[161] Louis's wife was thoroughly ashamed of the way he dressed,[162] and his subjects, at least the more sophisticated among them, laughed at him when they saw him dressed like a friar, acting like a friar, and constantly associating with friars. "Fie, fie" on you, said one old woman in disgust.[163]

In 1250 one finds still deeper and even more arresting evidence of the king's abundant self-analysis. He began to wish for death. There is an undercurrent of striving for martyrdom, not in quite the same heroic or "adolescent" way that can be identified before the crusade;

[158] Joinville, chap. CXXXV. See also Geoffroy de Beaulieu, HF, XX, 5-6; two anonymous chronicles, HF, XX, 53, and XXI, 84; Boniface VIII's canonization sermon, HF, XXIII, 150. Cf. Deslandres, "Costume du roi SL," on the iconographic conventions of the saint-king's clothing.

[159] Geoffroy de Beaulieu, HF, XX, 10, explains that Louis's desire to wear a hairshirt had to be restrained.

[160] Acta Sanctorum, VIII October, 606-8. See also Lemaître, Gloire normande. (With regard to his discipline, his hagiographer, a personal friend, wrote, "Frequenter viderunt sui socii sanguinem ad pedes ejus usque manantem.")

[161] Duraffour, Oeuvres, pp. 161-62.

[162] Guillaume de Saint-Pathus, HF, XX, 106. Cf. the king's remarks (are they ironic?) that men should wear clothes that make their wives love them more; Joinville, chap. VI.

[163] HF, XX, 106. Cf. the story retold by Coulton, From St. Francis to Dante, p. 405 (citing Ana. Fra., I, 413) of Louis's servants' derisive use of the epithet, "Brother Louis," and the king's decision to bear their jibes with patience. See also Little, Frater Ludovicus, pp. 174-78; Bastin and Faral, Onze poèmes, pp. 31-32; Ham, Rutebeuf and Louis IX, pp. 13-14; McDonnell, Beguines, p. 471; and Congar, "Église et l'état," p. 263. Cf., again, the probably ironic remarks of the king (Joinville, chap. VI): a man's dress should make his "people think the more" of him.

something much more subtle was at work. It is reported that he wanted to remain forever in Palestine as a pilgrim, but his duty as a king prevented him. He wanted to abdicate and join the friars, but, again, his obligations as king stood in the way.[164] These obligations were themselves essentially religious, for Louis had been consecrated with holy oil from the Dove, an act which laid tremendous responsibilities on him and from which he did not dare retreat.[165]

Not everyone reacted in the same fashion as the king to the failure of the crusade. Many barons departed for France in the very first days after their release from captivity.[166] Joinville, without much enthusiasm, relates incidents in 1250 which compel us to conclude that the attitude and eventual departure of Louis's two surviving brothers, Charles and Alfonse, had struck deep into the king's consciousness. Neither visited him during the illness he had contracted in early 1250, and Louis compared their behavior unfavorably with what he could have expected from his now dead brother, Robert.[167]

Joinville has also recorded the king's great disappointment over Charles's gambling on the ship taking them to the Holy Land: "tottering with weakness from his disease, the king took the dice and the board and threw them into the sea. He was very angry with his brother for so soon taking to playing with dice." And then the brothers left; they (or Charles) displayed some sorrow at the parting which "astonished" everyone, "but none the less [they] went back to France."[168] Matthew Paris, writing in Europe after the two brothers' return, had the impression that they had only hate for the king.[169]

A few barons, like Joinville, did stay with the king in the Holy Land to the end. Of all the sources which attest to the feelings of the king and his supporters in that critical period, none are more revealing than the illuminated manuscripts produced for this small band of determined crusaders. So dramatic was the achievement of the hastily established royal *atelier* in this period that art historians recognize these years as a distinct phase in French aristocratic book production.[170]

[164] For his desire to renounce kingship either in order to remain a pilgrim or to join the friars, see Geoffroy de Beaulieu, *HF*, xx, 7; the anonymous of Saint-Denis, *HF*, xx, 55; and MP, v, 466.

[165] I am arguing that this was his opinion on the basis of remarks he made to his son late in life on the significance of the royal unction. See O'Connell, *Teachings*, pp. 56-57 no. 15.

[166] Joinville, chap. LXXIV; see also chaps. LXXXII-LXXXVI.

[167] Ibid., chap. LXXIX.

[168] Ibid.; see also chaps. LXXXII-LXXXIV, LXXXVI, LXXXVII, in which Joinville speaks of the idea of returning in 1250 as a "disgrace" and the choice of "broken-down hacks."

[169] MP, v, 281.

[170] Buchtal, *Miniature Painting in the Latin Kingdom of Jerusalem*, pp. 66-68. The

2. The King Beckoned to the Friars.

Among the works was Joinville's "Credo," a statement of his personal faith in God, which he commissioned in 1250 with the advice and counsel of the king. The book has come down to us in a revised edition of 1287, but scholars agree that the revisions did not affect the fundamental form or content of the work.[171] The "Credo" is suffused with themes of affirmation in the face of defeat. Its principal *imago* was the Old Testament Joseph whose failures and humiliations at the hands of his brothers were a perfect parallel to the crucifixion of Christ, and whose eventual triumph prefigured the resurrection of the Lord.[172]

Similar themes were expressed in a great many other media. One of the works commissioned by Louis in this period was a *Bible abrégé* with glosses and sumptuous decoration.[173] It may have been commissioned

achievements in book production were not to cease when the focus of royal power returned to Paris; see Branner, *Manuscript Painting*.

[171] The critical text of the "Credo" is appended to Natalis de Wailly's text of Joinville. An English version follows Hague's Joinville. On the dating of the manuscript and the three sets of miniatures that were made for or from it at different times, see the introductory notes in Hague, and also Friedman, *Text and Iconography for Joinville's "Credo,"* pp. 2-3.

[172] See especially paragraphs 772-76 in the Hague version (pars. XIII-XVIII in the Natalis de Wailly text). This particular metaphor was very common: it is prominent in Louis's post-crusade psalter (*Psautier de saint Louis*). See also Friedman, *Text and Iconography*, p. 61; Hughes, *Oxford History of Music*, II, 176; Gébelin, *Sainte-Chapelle*, p. 77. The interpretation I have offered was standard: see Vermeulen, *Semantic Development of Gloria*, p. 112; and the moralized Bibles at Oxford, Lib. Bod. MS 270b, fol. 24, and Paris, BN MS fr. 167, fol. 167 (photographs consulted at the Index of Christian Art, Princeton University).

[173] New York, Pierpont Morgan Library MS 240 (I wish to thank the library for excel-

in memory of Blanche of Castile, at the news of whose death the king had been almost overwhelmed with grief,[174] for portraits of his mother and him adorn the Bible. But among its most interesting illuminations is that appended to the discussion of the phrase *sponsa*, *uxor agni* (bride, wife of the Lamb) in the Book of Revelation. It depicts a haloed king being beckoned to the friars (see accompanying illustration). The commentary to the passage interpreted the *sponsa* or *uxor agni* as a person who renounces all earthly considerations for a life serving God.

We have from this period explicit statements of the king himself that reveal his full commitment to the attitudes expressed in the artistic productions. Besides his letter home indicating his determination to stay in the Holy Land,[175] there exists the evidence of the so-called *sarrazinas*, a coin minted by the Christian settlers to help facilitate commerce with their Moslem neighbors. The *sarrazinas* bore inscriptions praising Mohammed and Islam. Louis reproved the Christians for this expediency and had the coin restruck. The new inscription, also in Arabic, praised Christ as the Life, the Salvation, the Resurrection, and the Redemption of the World.[176]

It is also from this period that we can date the association of the French royal house with the motto *Christus Vincit, Christus Regnat, Christus Imperat*. In certain media the legend was commonplace,[177] but it is found on a gold coin for the first time in the crusader principality of Antioch around 1253.[178] The coin was minted by Louis's young friend Bohemond VI of Antioch, for whom the king had tried to convince the prince's mother to end her regency. He then permitted Bohemond to bear the symbolic "arms of France."[179] In 1266, when Louis undertook to reform his own coinage at home and for the first time since the Carolingians issued a gold coin for the realm, he would

---

lent photographs of the manuscript). See fol. 8 for portrait and fol. 4 for illumination to be discussed here. The scripture from Revelation (21:9) for the latter reads: "Et venit unus de septem angelis habentibus phialas plenas vii plagiis novissimis et locutus est mecum dicens. Veni et ostendam tibi sponsam uxorem agni." The commentary follows: "Quelibet anima fidelis mundo renuncians cum ad serviendum deo consecrata fuit uxor agni id est sponsa Christi." Cf. the ordinary gloss; *PL*, CXIV, 746.

[174] Joinville, chap. CXIX.   [175] Above n. 143.

[176] Balog and Yvon, "Monnaies"; Blancard, *Bésant d'or*, pp. 24, 26-27; idem, *Gros tournois*, p. 2 n. 1; and Kantorowicz, *Laudes regiae*, p. 5 n. 14.

[177] Kantorowicz, *Laudes regiae*, pp. 1-2, 11-12.

[178] Grierson, "Rare Crusader Bezant"; Schlumberger, *Numismatique de l'Orient latin*, p. 495 and pl. 19 n. 9; Blancard, "Sur l'Agnel d'or." The coin also bore the emblem of the lamb triumphant. The affirmational quality of this symbol should not be ignored; cf. Jordan, "Lamb Triumphant."

[179] Joinville, chap. CI; above chapter 1 (text to n. 45). See also Balog and Yvon, "Monnaies," pp. 137-39; and Du Cange, "On the Granting of Armorial Bearings," p. 195.

find its appropriate motto in the Antioch gold of Bohemond: *Christus Vincit, Christus Regnat, Christus Imperat.*[180]

When the king finally returned to France in 1254, it is said that he uttered these words: "If I alone could bear the opprobrium and adversity and my sins did not redound upon the universal church, I could endure with equanimity. But woe is me; by me all Christendom has been confused."[181] It may have been that the return to France reemphasized for a moment the feelings of despair that must have initially accompanied his defeat and capture; and yet the hopelessness implicit in these words was only temporary. The lasting effect of the crusade, indeed of the defeat of the crusade, was affirmative: as the mortal Christ had suffered, was humiliated and mocked, so Louis IX would endure his *poena*, but endurance promised joy.[182]

[180] Kantorowicz, *Laudes regiae*, pp. 3-4; Grierson, "Rare Crusader Bezant," pp. 176-77.
[181] MP, v, 466.
[182] Cf. Joinville, chap. xv, to whom the deaths of the king and other crusaders on Louis's two crusades were occasions of great mourning but "in Paradise there is great joy" (*maintes grans joies en sont en paradis*). The sentiment is ancient; one is reminded of the tombstones of early Christians that bore the single word *chará*, joy; Galaveris, *Bread and the Liturgy*, p. 51. Salimbene, *Cronica*, ii, 117-18, in one of his most savage attacks against the *pastoureaux* chides them for their rage which, to him, contrasted so markedly to the defeated king's *patientia*.

MAP 3: The *Tournée* of Languedoc, 1254 (with other associated locations)

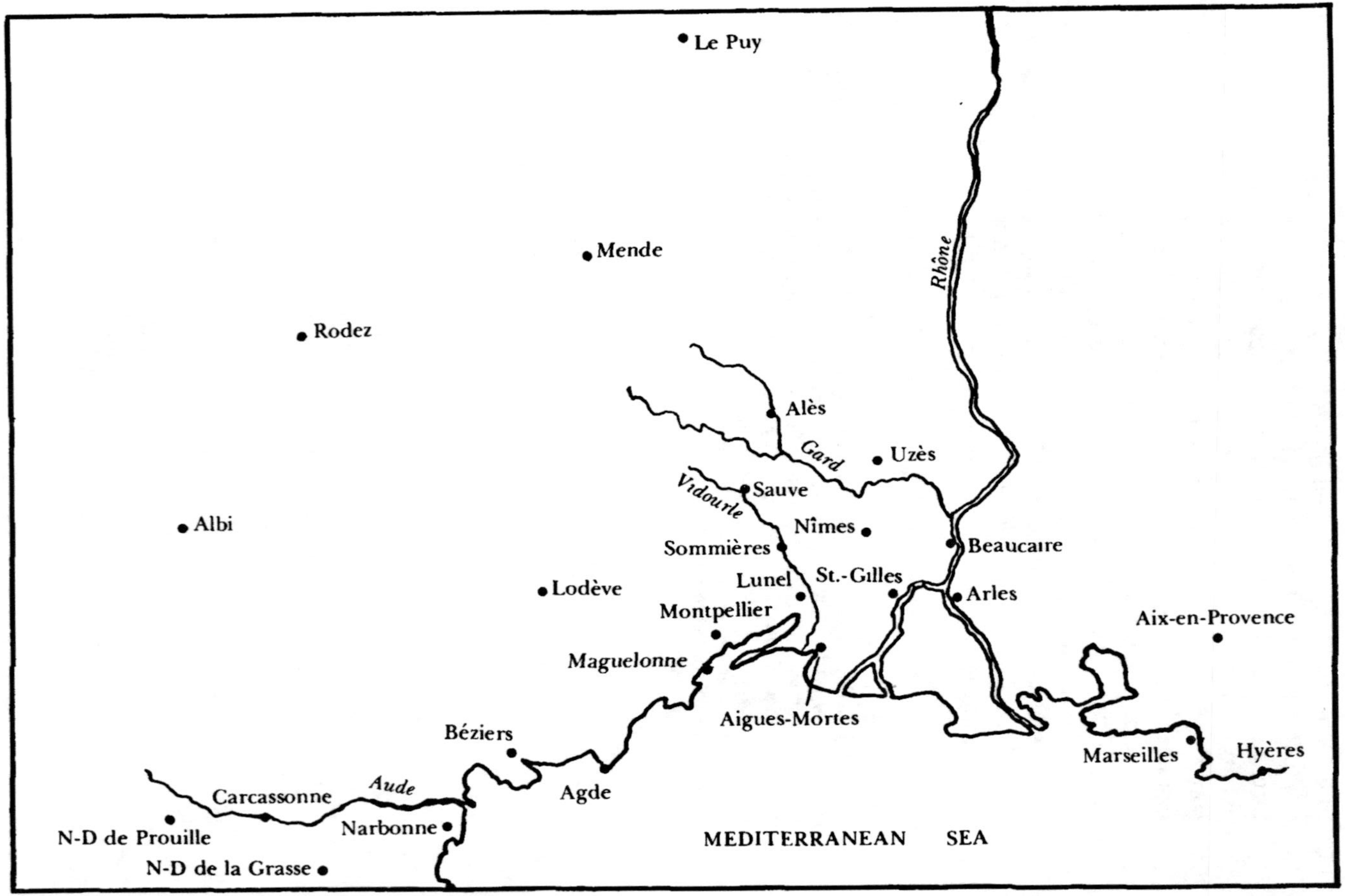

• Le Puy

• Mende

Alès •

Rhône

Gard

Uzès •

Beaucaire

Arles •

• Rodez

Sauve

Vidourle

Nîmes •

Sommières

Lunel

St.-Gilles

Aigues-Mortes

• Albi

• Lodève

Montpellier •

Maguelonne

Agde

Béziers •

Aude

Carcassonne •

Narbonne •

N-D de Prouille •

N-D de la Grasse •

MEDITERRANEAN   SEA

Aix-en-Provence

Hyères

Marseilles

·6·

THE NEW SPIRIT OF REFORM

Choosing to delay his return to Paris, Louis made a slow and deliberate progress through eastern Languedoc after his debarkation at the port of Hyères in July 1254. From the port, which is east of Marseilles, he set out for Aix-en-Provence and from there continued in a northwesterly direction for Beaucaire on the Rhône. Later in the month, following the Rhône Valley, but south from Beaucaire, the king traveled the dry, narrow roads leading to Saint-Gilles, near Aigues-Mortes. Soon after, he again set out northward, this time for the old Roman city of Nîmes, and northwesterly from there in August through the cooler and more pleasant valleys of the Cevennes to Alès and Le Puy.[1] The zigzagging itinerary of the summer of 1254 found him at each stop along the way trying to bring order out of chaotic situations "par des actes de justice, de bienveillance et de sollicitude paternelle."[2]

At Beaucaire and Nîmes, this meant taking steps to affirm these cities' reentry or, rather, entry for the first time into the community of the realm after the long legacy of rebellion and mistrust inherited from the Albigensian Crusades. The municipal government of Nîmes was restored,[3] and the gap which has distressed local patriots—the failure of the saint-king to confirm the liberties of the Languedocian cities during his first trip to the deep south in 1248[4]—was rectified by successive grants of charters to Nîmes and Beaucaire during this summer.[5]

The trips to Saint-Gilles and Alès began a series of negotiations further clarifying the measures taken to build Aigues-Mortes. The monastery at Psalmody, which held lands at Saint-Gilles and which

[1] I have utilized the published itinerary (above chapter 3 n. 23); but see also Joinville, chap. CXXXIV; Viguier, *Anduze*, p. 167; Eysette, *Histoire administrative de Beaucaire*, II, 160-61; idem, *Consulat*, p. 46. Carolus-Barré would add a trip to Aigues-Mortes after Saint-Gilles, but there is no explicit evidence for this supposition ("Grand Ordonnance de 1254," p. 93).

[2] Eysette, *Consulat*, p. 46.

[3] AD: Gard, oo 91 Nîmes (incorrectly dated to 1250 by Bessot de Lamothe, *Inventaire . . . AC . . . Nîmes*, II, no. 00.91). See also Michel, *Beaucaire*, pp. 231-39, 250; Ménard, *Nismes*, I, "Preuves," pp. 80-81.

[4] CF. Durand, "Beaucaire sous SL," pt. 1, pp. 402-3.

[5] Ménard, *Nismes*, I, "Preuves," pp. 79-80, 85. See also Michel, *Beaucaire*, pp. 259-61; Eysette, *Histoire administrative de Beaucaire*, II, 160-61; Durand, "Beaucaire sous SL," pt. 2, pp. 16-7.

had conceded property to the king for his expansion of the port facilities of Aigues-Mortes before the crusade, received assurances that outstanding disputes over the concession would be handled as quickly and as fairly as possible.[6] The Alésiens commenced discussions regarding the government's reformulation of regional trade routes for provisioning Aigues-Mortes and the forced requisition of material used to fortify the port.[7] These negotiations, both with Psalmody and the municipal, ecclesiastical, and baronial authorities of Alès, were to go on with the king's proctors for months, even years before final decisions were reached. But ultimately decisions were made, and in them Louis acknowledged the exploitative character of his pre-crusade policies, gave compensation where it was required, and made a few additional concessions to encourage good relations in the south.[8]

At Le Puy, where jurisdictional disagreements plagued the crown's relations with the bishop, the king initiated discussions leading to a formal settlement of mutual claims. The disagreements, a clear legacy of the pre-crusade period, involved conflicting assertions on the nature of the king's regalian rights in the diocese.[9] Although a preliminary convention was achieved in 1254,[10] following the typical pattern in the south, the formal settlement was delayed, in this instance until 1258, and minor points of contention continued to upset the equilibrium until 1267.[11]

At Nîmes, Beaucaire, Saint-Gilles, Alès, and Le Puy, it is quite likely that notables from neighboring regions came and had audiences with the king. His meeting with the abbot of Cluny has already been considered.[12] As with this contact, however, final resolutions of the matters discussed were probably made at Paris. This explains (or helps to explain) the spate of conventions over disputed rights and confirmations of contested privileges which crop up from 1254 through 1260 with such southern notables as the bishop of Uzès in 1255,[13] the bishop of Mende in 1257,[14] the archbishops of Arles and Narbonne in

---

[6] (Bessot) de Lamothe, *Inventaire . . . Gard . . . H*, pp. 41, 47-48 (H. 142, H. 167, H. 170); *Layettes*, III, no. 4202. See also (Bessot) de Lamothe, p. 1 H. 1; and Bligny-Bondurand, *Inventaire-sommaire AD: Gard—supplément . . . H*, p. 14 H 785, f. 88.

[7] There is useful material in *HF*, XXIV, 531-41. See also *HGL*, VIII, cc. 1335-36 no. 2; and Michel, *Beaucaire*, pp. 261-62.

[8] See especially *HF*, XXIV, 531-41; similarly in *Layettes*, III, no. 4202.

[9] Above chapter 4 n. 166.

[10] *Layettes*, III, no. 4505; *GC*, II, 742, and "Instrumenta," c. 234 nos. xviii-xix. See also Tillemont, *Vie de SL*, IV, 208.

[11] Tillemont, *Vie de SL*, IV, 126-27; Delcambre, "Paréage," p. 123.

[12] Above chapter 5 nn. 104-7.

[13] Bligny-Bondurand, *Inventaire-sommaire . . . Gard—supplément . . . G*, p. 89 (AD: Gard 1631 peaux IX) has July 1255; *GC*, VI, "Instrumenta," cc. 306-7 no. xvii, has July 1254. See also *Olim*, I, 52-53 xxxix.

[14] AD: Hérault, B 23 fols. 190-91. Cf. Michel, *Beaucaire*, pp. 176-81, 353, 457-58; Germain, *Sauve, cité*, p. 143.

1259 and 1260.[15] Municipalities, like Sauve, Sommières, and Montpellier, also received formal acknowledgment of aspects of their relationship with the crown after the summer of 1254.[16]

In some instances, we know little about the details of the preliminary negotiations and hardly more about the final decisions since there are only the briefest hints in the available sources. A convention restoring a *péage* in Lunel in 1255, for example, is indicated in passing in a local inventory, the original documents apparently being lost; but it is likely that the *péage* which was restored in that year had been suppressed about 1248 because it hampered the provisioning of Aigues-Mortes.[17] Some sort of discussions also probably took place with officials or notables from Béziers during the king's southerly progress; this may account for the (apocryphal) legend that Louis visited there on his return from crusade and took the Franciscan nuns (the Clarissines) of the city under his protection.[18] There are many other suggestive examples, like these, in which the insufficiency of data presently accessible limits our knowledge of the role the king played in the initial negotiations in the summer of 1254.[19]

In any case, the negotiations were not particularly easy. Perhaps this is why the formal settlements were delayed in many cases. Two examples, the negotiations with the bishop of Maguelonne and the

[15] *GC*, II, "Instrumenta," cc. 235-36 no. xx, and VI, "Instrumenta," cc. 60-61 no. lxv.

[16] The records of agreements with the men of Sauve and Sommières are scattered through *HF*, XXIV, 531-42. Among secondary sources, Germain, *Sauve, cité*, pp. 139, 142, gives a rather inexact résumé of the available information on Sauve; Boisson, *Sommières*, p. 69, has a valuable summary of issues relating to Sommières. Evidence pertaining to Montpellier may be consulted in (Berthelé) *Archives . . . cartulaires*, p. 101 nos. 708, 711; cf. idem, *Archives . . . Montpellier*, I, 2d fasc.: *Grand Chartrier*, p. 45 nos. 339 à 341, 342-43, p. 208 no. 2559, pp. 381-82 no. 4269.

[17] AM: Lunel, AA 1, 1639 (*Le Livre Blanc*), fol. 28. See also Jordan, "Supplying Aigues-Mortes," p. 168 n. 21.

[18] Soucaille, *État monastique de Béziers*, pp. 172-73. Cf. Julia, *Béziers*, p. 309 n. 5.

[19] Thus, among such settlements which possibly began with preliminary discussions with the king during his passage through Languedoc are the following: (1) With the abbey of Notre-Dame de La Grasse, see *GC*, VI, "Instrumenta," cc. 454-55 no. xlvii; cf. cc. 453-54 no xlvi. See also Tillemont, *Vie de SL*, IV, 98; and Michel, *Beaucaire*, p. 351. (2) With the city of Carcassonne, see Poux, *Carcassonne*, I, 81, 152. (3) With the see of Agde, see AD: Hérault, G 4426, the records of a jurisdictional dispute, 1292-1298, between Philip IV and the bishop of Agde relating to the cession of secular jurisdiction to the bishop by Amaury de Montfort. This cession had been reconfirmed by Louis IX—my suggestion would be in the 1250s—but the document, of several hundred pages (paper), is faded, worm-eaten, and damaged by moisture. For reference—such as it is—see Gouron, *Répertoire numérique AD: Hérault, série G*, p. 203. (4) With the abbey of Prouille near Carcassonne, see Guiraud, *Cartulaire de . . . Prouille*, I, 59-61. Negotiations with certain communities leading to shared administration (*paréages*) may also have been commenced during Louis's sojourns in Languedoc in 1254. On these *paréages*, see Michel, *Beaucaire*, p. 189 (the dating of them is imprecise; in 1294 men recalled that they took place about thirty years before). See also AM: Puissalicon, AA 1, lost as of 1971 but reported in Berthelé, *Répertoire . . . AC*, I, "Puissalicon, AA 1." Cf. Bisson, *Assemblies*, p. 195, on the *paréage* with Mende.

arrangements with the bishop of Albi, may help to illustrate some of these difficulties. The fundamental question in Maguelonne was the bishop's right to exercise secular jurisdiction in his capacity as count of Melgueil. When Innocent III had proclaimed the Albigensian Crusade, he had insisted that principalities conquered by orthodox Frenchmen would be transferred to their administration with the same powers as their former lords. On occasion, bishops in residence seized these powers before the party of Simon de Montfort had a chance to take them. This had happened in Melgueil where the bishop took the title *count* and was confirmed in that title by the pope.[20]

Originally, specific usurpations such as the bishop of Maguelonne's action would have mattered little to the French crown, but eventually the Albigensian Crusade came under the direction of the French kings. Inheriting Simon's conquests, they inherited his problems as well.[21] If one considers the mood of Louis IX in 1254, however, it seems reasonable to suppose that the king would seek a compromise with the bishop. What was finally hit upon was an acknowledgment of the bishop's claim to the county of Melgueil in return for his submission to the sort of relationship, with its duties and obligations, that characterized the relations of the crown with the count-bishops of the north.[22] The fact that Louis's agents in the south—in building and fortifying Aigues-Mortes—had tended to be excessive in curtailing unquestionably legitimate rights of the bishop also disposed Louis to reach an amiable agreement on the matters at issue.[23]

On the bishop's side there was also sentiment for reaching a compromise because his relations were deteriorating with the king of Aragon who had jurisdictional claims throughout Languedoc and especially strong ones over Melgueil and Montpellier. Since the bishop of Maguelonne was actually the bishop of Montpellier (he simply retained until 1536 an old and outmoded ecclesiastical title), the problems he had with the Aragonese inclined him to make an accommodation with the French. By 1255, probably as a gesture of defiance to the Spanish monarch, Bishop Pierre de Conques as count of Melgueil voluntarily became a vassal of the king of France and thereby officially entered into that relationship with the French crown already commonplace in the north.[24]

[20] *HGL*, VI, 456-57, 895.

[21] Louis's negotiations in and after the summer of 1254 often went back to the first phase of the Albigensian Crusade; above nn. 9, 13-15; also nn. 3-5, 19.

[22] For Louis's general attitude on matters of this sort (he preferred precise divisions of responsibility), see the Anonymous of Saint-Denis, *HF*, XX, 49. See also Bunger, *Beziehungen Ludwigs IX . . . zur Curie*, p. 17.

[23] Cf. Rouquette, "SL," p. 195; Michel, *Beaucaire*, pp. 183-85.

[24] For the incidents recalled in this paragraph, see Germain, *Histoire . . . commune*, II,

Yet, below the surface, forces were at work to upset the compromise. Royal officials were slow to give up rights that had been exercised before the crusade,[25] and the fact that the regency council had allowed lapses to occur in the administrative hierarchy of the *sénéchaussées* prevented quick and smooth transitions. Beginning with Innocent IV and continuing into the later 1250s, the interference of concerned prelates, who tried to use their influence to protect the bishop from zealous royal functionaries, made the king's men feel all the more unfairly pressured and gave inspiration to their attempts to put technicalities in the way of restoring the bishop's claimed privileges.[26] Whether basic agreement was reached or not in 1255,[27] it can be argued that complications marred the settlement right down to 1269.[28]

One of the most important of these complications arose from the fact that the pressure from the king of Aragon was substantially removed in 1258 after negotiations between the French and the Aragonese produced the Treaty of Corbeil which effectively drew the border between the two kingdoms at the Pyrenees.[29] The bishop became more self-confident and more exacting about his rights from that time on. This naturally provoked a more antagonistic response on the royal side—if not from the king directly then from his officials on the spot. The bishop's involvement in striking coins with inscriptions favorable to Mohammed on them, a method of facilitating commercial prosperity in the port city of Montpellier,[30] could have been an additional major complication in his relations with the crown.[31] Only the secret counsels to the bishop of an old *enquêteur*

"pièces justificatives," no. vi; *Layettes*, III, nos. 4156, 4160, 4325, 4312, 4285. See also Morlhon and Lacaze, *Cathédrale et l'île de Maguelone*, p. 59; Michel, *Beaucaire*, pp. 183-85.

[25] For examples of these kinds of tensions, see AD: Hérault, G 1475 (MS numbered by clerk "#20"); Rouquette and Villemagne, *Cartulaire*, II, 729-70 nos. dcv, dcxiii. See also Jordan, "Supplying Aigues-Mortes," p. 463 n. 38; and above n. 23.

[26] AD: Hérault, G 1477 (MS with clerk's notation "GRQ-No. 26"); Rouquette and Villemagne, *Cartulaire*, II, 663-771 nos. dlxxiv, dcix, dcxiv, dcxvii.

[27] Rouquette and Villemagne, *Cartulaire*, II, 728 no. dci; cf. Michel, *Beaucaire*, p. 412 ("pièces justificatives," no. 20).

[28] For varied examples of such—often petty—squabbles, see Germain, "Notice . . . cartulaire seigneurial," pp. 446-47; Rouquette and Villemagne, *Cartulaire*, III, 58-115 nos. dclxxiv, dclxxxvi, dclxxxix, dcxcviii, dcci, dccix; AD: Hérault, G 1302 (packet entitled "Louis VII renouvelle en faveur de Jean de Montlaur").

[29] Below chapter 7 nn. 93-94.

[30] See Bisson, "Coinage," pp. 465-66. These and similar problems with feudatories who struck such coins at the same time, and Louis's vehement denunciation of them are treated by Boutaric, *SL et Alfonse*, p. 217; Balog and Yvon, "Monnaies à légendes arabes"; Kantorowicz, *Laudes regiae*, p. 5 n. 14; Germain, *Monnaie mahométane*; and especially the fine works of Blancard: *Bésant d'or*, pp. 24, 26-27; *Gros tournois*, p. 2 n. 1; "Le 'Millarès,' " pp. 5-6; *Essai sur les monnaies*, pp. 480, 487. See also *SL*, Exposition, p. 53 no. 71.

[31] If the bishop was minting the coin as count of Melgueil, then even after his feudal

turned pope, Clement IV, saved him before Louis had time to un-
cover the truth.[32]

As with Maguelonne the situation in Albi was complicated. In 1253
private war had erupted in which the bishop took part. An interim
solution had been reached in 1254, but it was very tenuous. The
bishop, like many of his peers in the south, claimed that the king had
little jurisdiction over him or in his diocese, and problems intruded
themselves continually into the ad hoc arrangements that had
brought peace to the region. These problems are recounted with rep-
etitious insistence in the sources.[33] Either the bishop was claiming
that the *sénéchal* of Carcassonne, despite Louis's prescriptions, was
humiliating him and seizing his legitimate rights or the chapter was
claiming the rights of the bishop as its own.[34]

A final compromise was not reached until December 1264.[35] Although both the bishop and the crown had been claiming high justice,
most of it was conceded to the prelate at that time. However, riots in
the town remained within the royal competence. Overlapping or
common rights were to be exercised, according to the compromise, as
the parties to disputes requested. No new privileges were to be
granted the bishop, nor would the king authorize any attempt to lessen
the stated privileges. Included among these were the immunity of
the diocese from the feudal military levy (although certain men in the
diocese remained obliged) and the right of diocesan authorities to
one-half the confiscations of the property of heretics in the diocese
(this provision was made retroactive, presumably to the diocese's advantage). The really fundamental concession by the bishop had been
his acceptance of the royal view that in matters of private war the
king's curia was competent to judge him.[36]

---

submission to Louis IX and the treaty of Corbeil, the immediate lord of his coinage
privileges was still the king of Aragon; AD: Hérault, G 1302 (MS in packet entitled
"Privilèges de l'Evêque, Monnaie de Maugio 1272, 1282, 1590"). Rouquette and Villemagne, *Cartulaire*, 11, 847-53 no. dcli, give similar evidence for the year 1263. Louis IX,
however, would have retained supervisory responsibilities; cf. below chapter 7 n. 135.

[32] Rouquette and Villemagne, *Cartulaire*, 111, 81 no. dclxxxvii. Griffiths, *Counselors*, p.
125, suggests that the pope was under the king's thumb. On Clement IV's independent
spirit, however, see the recent articles by Chazan, "Archbishop Gui Fulcodi"; and Dossat, "Gui Foucois" (esp. p. 51).

[33] On the situation in Albi prior to the king's return, above chapter 5 nn. 109-13; for
further evidence of disputes, see Gandilhon, *Inventaire-sommaire . . . Cher*, cc. 134, 58
(records of arguments in 1258 and 1263), and the following note.

[34] *GC*, 1, "Instrumenta," pp. 8-9 no. xviii (circa 1259); Tillemont, *Vie de SL*, iv, 345-46.

[35] *GC*, 1, "Instrumenta," pp. 9-10 no. xix. See also Lacger, "Albigeois," p. 45.

[36] Boutaric, *Actes*, 1, no. 379; *Layettes*, iii, no. 4578. This assertion of royal authority
may be considered part of a broader attempt to control private wars throughout the
kingdom, on which see below chapter 7 nn. 119-25. On continuing problems with Albi,
see *Cahiers de Fanjeaux*, 6 (1971), 314-15.

The fact that every convention was probably disturbed by different but perhaps equally vexing issues as those in the cases of Maguelonne and Albi does not detract, however, from the main point. The king's progress through the south in the summer of 1254 is the first clear indication we have that the experience of the crusade had led him to reevaluate policies and working relations with his subjects.

The king reached Paris in late August 1254, and he remained in the city for more than a month while taking stock of the situation in the north. The clearest threat to the peace, as far as he could see, was the situation in Flanders in which he intervened straightaway.[37] It took time, of course, to bring the disputants to agreement, but by 1255 they were prepared to return to the *status quo ante bellum*, the arbitrated judgment of 1246, as the framework of peace. Louis meted out some punishments to both sides of the dispute. By adhering to the earlier compromise as the basis for a just and lasting peace, he necessarily invalidated the claim of his brother, Charles of Anjou, to the county of Hainaut. He indemnified Charles for this loss of status, probably a matter of form, and Charles accepted the settlement and indemnity rather than antagonize his brother.[38]

The king, as it has been said, stayed in Paris in August and September 1254, reviewing the state of affairs, listening to reports from the departments of government, hearing, no doubt, the conciliar regents' account of Prince Louis's administration, and going over the records of their actions carefully.[39] It would be hard to put a specific date to them, but it was probably at this time that he gave serious thought to minor reorganizations of the structure of central government. Some of the changes of this type that have been noticed by historians were merely repercussions from reform in other spheres. Thus the increase in paperwork engendered by Louis's reintroduction of the *enquêteurs* almost immediately on his arrival in the south in July 1254[40] surely helped speed up the establishment of a permanent and organizationally superior archival depository for incoming documents[41] and

[37] MP, v, 561; *Layettes*, III, nos. 4138-39, 4290-92.
[38] Duvivier, *Querelle des Dampierres et des d'Avesnes*, I, 270-71.
[39] This follows, at least partly, from the reworking of (archive) Register F (which the king had taken with him on crusade) by the addition of notations from the Register left behind—and vice versa. Delisle, *Catalogue des actes de Philippe-Auguste*, pp. xviii-xx; Delaborde in *Layettes*, v, ix-x; Berger and Delaborde, *Recueil . . . Philippe-Auguste*, I, xxxvii-xxxix.
[40] On the reintroduction of the *enquêteurs*, below n. 107. That there was a burdensome increase in clerical work owing to the first (pre-crusade) wave of *enquêteurs* has been argued by Langlois, "Doléances," pp. 4-5.
[41] The basic studies, drawing together bits of documentary and architectural evidence, are those of Delaborde, "Bâtiments" (p. 161), "Classements du Trésor"; and his remarks in *Layettes*, v, x. See also Lot and Fawtier, *Histoire*, II, 94; Bloch, *Feudal Society*, II, 422; and Carolus-Barré, "Apparition de la langue française," pp. 148-55. Cf. For-

possibly led to an expansion of the number of functionaries in the chancery.[42]

One can also see in the post-crusade period a marked increase in the status of the chamberlains.[43] The duties of these men were primarily financial,[44] and as individuals they seem to have taken on important special functions during and immediately before the crusade when the king regularly employed them on delicate missions.[45] The belated improvement in their status probably owes itself primarily to these facts.

Except for these instances of a kind of "reactive" reform, organizational change at the very center of royal government was slow, and in a sense it remained slow precisely because of the crusade. Louis learned from the crusade; or, at least, its fate was linked in his mind to his failure to be as careful in his governmental responsibilities as he ought to have been. It followed from this that what his sins as a personal ruler tainted, his virtues in personal rulership might redeem. Therefore, whenever possible, government had to remain immediately in his hands. If he used the traditional instruments of central government, he did so because they were traditional (and, hence, right to use), but he made no innovations which delegated more power than was absolutely necessary. He was not a seeker after convenience.

How then ought one account for what might appear to be a remarkable exception to this conclusion, the fact that the central judicature, the *Parlement* of Paris, reached organizational maturity in 1254? In the first place, this development, if it could be proved, would only support the previous argument because Louis never let the institution operate "impersonally"; he was always the vital center of *parlement*. He was consistently in attendance at its sessions; the professional judges were there too, but to their dismay he would intervene and reverse a decision in their presence or arbitrate in a spirit that transcended the legalisms that were too often stressed in court.[46] Above all, he en-

mulaires, no. 6, items 57, 348 (on the royal clerks—their privileges and pay; other information on these subjects is scattered through the royal accounts). On the royal library established after the crusade in imitation of Moslem practices, see Gabriel, *Vincent of Beauvais*; and Delisle, *Manuscrits*, I, 8.

[42] This may explain the increase in the number of laymen in the chancery. Cf. Ullmann, *Law and Politics*, p. 260 n. 1 (citing Griffiths, "Pierre de Fontaines").

[43] Griffiths, *Counselors*, pp. 62, 290 n. 1.

[44] Cf. Viollet, *Histoire des institutions*, II, 124-25.

[45] The chamberlain Jean Sarrasin, for example, seems to have filled a supervisory role for the army; above chapter 4 nn. 4-5. See also Jordan, "Supplying Aigues-Mortes," pp. 168 and 462 n. 24, on the chamberlains in Aigues-Mortes.

[46] Joinville, chap. XII. *Olim*, I, 286 viii, 699-700 ix. On his attendance, see Shennan, *Parlement of Paris*, pp. 16-17; Griffiths, "New Men," p. 269.

deavored to downplay the very formality which was essential to the depersonalization and institutionalization of *parlement*. Thus, while on the one hand even the ushers, the *huissiers*, of *parlement* were assigned clerical duties including the task of formally screening petitions, the king, according to Joinville, deliberately held court under the oak at Vincennes or at the foot of his bed (no *lit de justice*) or on the ground in one of the royal gardens "without the interference of any usher or other official."[47]

In any case, the achievement of organizational maturity by the central judicature has been, at times, notoriously exaggerated. Of course, given the fact that the king always wanted to bring difficult matters to judicial decision rather than permit them to fester and provoke discontent, it is certainly true that he relied heavily on his *parlement*.[48] Inevitably, its members and servants (for example, the *huissiers*) improved their ability and became more specialized in some of their functions. However, persuasive evidence of technical maturity coinciding with the mid-century is thin: insofar as possible, "appellate" procedures, which should be a useful yardstick, had already been worked out in the 1220s and 1230s, but they still had a confusion about them throughout the mid-century which only Philip the Fair's men succeeded in smoothing out.[49] The "legislative" process was not new in 1254,[50] nor was the use of lay counselors in the *curia judicialis*.[51] Why then the emphasis on *parlement*?

Certain scholars have stressed the maturity of *parlement* because the continuous report of its records appears to begin with the year 1254. Moreover, the fact that those records improve after 1254 is regarded as further proof that Louis's reforms were ongoing. Unfortunately, the two facts are not related. The improvement in the record-keeping, as I have tried to show, came about largely from the fact that the *curia judicialis* did so much work after the crusade. Its clerks, with

[47] Joinville, chap. XII. On the ushers' remuneration, *HF*, XXI, 358. Further on the *huissiers*, Aubert, "Huissiers"; and Lot and Fawtier, *Histoire*, II, 404-5.

[48] Louis's commitment to the law is discussed by Buisson, *Ludwig IX und das Recht*; and Verdier, "Origine . . . des legistes."

[49] Cf. Griffiths, "New Men," p. 265; Mortet, "Constitucions," pp. 28-31. See also Fustel de Coulanges, *SL et le prestige de la royauté*, pp. 37-39. See also *Olim*, I, 706 xii.

[50] It probably went back to 1230; see Langmuir, "*Judei nostri*" (followed, happily, in the survey by McGarry, *Medieval History*, pp. 443-44). Griffiths ("New Men," pp. 270-71) regards "legislation" as appearing later, about 1269, but his view in this instance seems to me to be lacking in evidence and unconvincing. Whether my feeling is right or wrong and however important the personal role of Louis IX may have been in beginning the legislative process in French history (cf. Fustel de Coulanges, *SL et le prestige de la royauté*, pp. 37-39), both Griffiths and I would probably agree that 1254 is unacceptable as the date for Louis's achievement.

[51] These are Griffiths's "New Men"; they are seen in the curia long before the crusade.

experience, improved their style (*stylus*). One of them thought it would be a good idea to get together a collection of the most vital decisions of the court. Looking back from the 1260s he began his collection with an important case from 1254. He might have started in 1202 or 1229 or 1250 or 1253, but he did not. Yet we know that records were being kept before because many of these earlier reports have come down to us in bits and pieces.[52] There is, in other words, almost no significance that can be attached to the year 1254 in the institutional history of the *Parlement* of Paris.

Louis remained, in short, an active king, one who, if it had been possible, would have done everything by himself. *Parlement*, important as it was, was not an impersonal institution in the modern sense of the word and showed none of that precocious independence of spirit which the English royal court manifested from time to time. The *Parlement* of Paris was the king's own court whether meeting solemnly on the *Ile de la Cité* or informally in his bedroom. Of course, Louis IX recognized the limitations of personal rule, and especially in provincial administration he took steps to overcome them. Like his grandson he could have exclaimed, "We cannot be everywhere! That is why we send men into the provinces."[53] But it is significant that even in the provinces Louis strove to uphold the reality of his position as an immediate lord and judge. We have watched him perform part of this role in the deep south; we must now turn to the north where this mode of rulership reached its culmination.

In October 1254, after his brief stay in Paris, Louis undertook a series of trips in the north reflecting a desire on his part to display the royal person and dignity to his subjects. During the remainder of 1254, this parading was confined to the regions nearest Paris,[54] but in early 1255 the king descended into the Loire Valley.[55] Later that year he went to the far north visiting Ghent in present-day Belgium,[56] and in 1256 he progressed tirelessly throughout Normandy.[57]

The pattern of Louis's movements from 1254 through 1256 corre-

[52] Most general books stress the date 1254; even Boutaric, who published some "arrêts antérieurs," was led into error (*Actes*, 1, p. lxv). But see Langlois, "Origines du Parlement"; Aubert, "Nouvelles recherches sur le Parlement," pp. 62-63, 67; and Shennan, *Parlement of Paris*, p. 15.
[53] Cited and translated in Fesler, "French Field Administration," epigraph.
[54] Besides the published itinerary as cited above chapter 3 n. 23, see Thoison, *Séjours*, pp. 30, 34-35, 82-83, 95-97, 152-53. Cf. Poulain, *Séjours*, p. 30.
[55] See also Thoison, *Séjours*, pp. 30, 95-97. Béziers, *Bayeux*, p. 29; and also Pompon, *Toury*, p. 12 (convert the date to new style).
[56] See also Thoison, *Séjours*, pp. 26, 30, 95-97; Coet, *Roye*, 1, 184; Vanhaeck, "Cartulaire . . . Marquette," 1, 178 no. 185.
[57] See also Thoison, *Séjours*, pp. 18, 30, 41-42, 79-80, 95-97, 152-53; Coet, *Roye*, 1, 184; Béziers, *Bayeux*, p. 158; Poulain, *Séjours*.

sponds perfectly with the unfolding of new appointments at the *bailli* rank. It has long been recognized that from 1254 through 1256 a dramatic personnel shift once more occurred in the upper-level field administration.[58] Hitherto, and incorrectly, this introduction of new officials has been tied directly to the *enquêteurs* of 1247 and 1248. I tried to show earlier why this view leaves out a critically important intermediate phase of adjustments in personnel. The work of the pre-crusade *enquêteurs* already yielded fruit in 1247, 1248, and 1249.[59] It may even have been the case that the radical reevaluation of personnel in those years was conceived as a one-time and one-time only expedient (after all, such overhauls, for all their usefulness, can be enormously disruptive of effective administration). Stability marked the rule of Blanche. When a *bailli* died, a new appointment was made, but, as far as I can tell, nothing more radical was undertaken.[60]

Confusion set in after the regent's death in 1252. The rate of turnover of top-level field administrators became excessive.[61] Louis, therefore, seems to have been reacting to the administrative breakdown of the later regency when he introduced new personnel into the provinces upon his return to France. He was no doubt guided by some of the same considerations that had first made him reevaluate administration;[62] he may even have reread the summaries of the *enquêteurs'* original reports. But the immediate problem was that the provincial government was out of kilter; and it was that problem which he set himself to solve immediately after his return.

In the Mâconnais, which he traversed in 1254, a new *bailli* was appointed in 1254. In the regions nearest Paris through which he traveled in late 1254, one dates new appointments at the *bailli* rank in the same year—in Amiens, in Sens, in Orléans, in Senlis. Moreover, the cartography of *bailliagère* administration which had been disturbed, for example, in Étampes by the tampering of the regents in 1253 was corrected the next year when Louis traveled in the *bailliage*. The king visited Tours in 1255; the old *bailli* of Touraine was removed in 1255.[63]

The rhythm in Normandy was the same. In 1254, for the vacancy in the wildest *bailliage*, the Cotentin,[64] Louis appointed his friend and fellow crusader, Jean de Maisons.[65] Jean had returned from crusade

[58] See, for example, Fietier, "Choix des baillis," pp. 258-59, 261.
[59] Above chapter 3 nn. 125-30. For the traditional interpretation, see Labarge, *SL*, p. 185.
[60] Above chapter 5 n. 92.   [61] Above chapter 5 nn. 92-93.
[62] Cf. Carolus-Barré, "Grand Ordonnance de 1254," pp. 90-94.
[63] Appendix One under relevant headings for the data in this paragraph.
[64] Strayer, "Viscounts and Viguiers," p. 224.
[65] Appendix One, s.v., "Cotentin."

before the king, but he had not found a place in the administration of the conciliar regents. Alfonse, however, used his services as a comital *enquêteur*.[66] When Louis appointed him in 1254 it was with the knowledge that he could handle conditions in the Cotentin. He had been *bailli* there before the crusade;[67] he could go in confident of putting matters straight. Aside from the appointment of Jean, however, the basic shake-up of personnel in Normandy coincided with Louis's inclusive progress through the duchy in 1256: Caen, Caux, and Verneuil received new *baillis* at that time while the *bailliage* of Mantes was separated from Gisors.[68]

Normandy, in yet another way, reveals that the king's personal effort to settle problems in a conciliatory manner characterized government in the north as it had in Languedoc. The sorts of problems at issue were different to be sure. Many were of more recent origin than those in the south. Others arose from a local abbot's or prior's attempt to get some formal statement of the vague privileges of his house. In 1256, for example, Louis confirmed the *libertates plurimas* of the abbey of Bec;[69] in July 1257 he declared the abbey of Bon-Port free of all royal tolls.[70] But time and space will be wasted by going through such concessive grants one by one. Delisle's Norman cartulary records eighty examples of confirmations and reconfirmations of charters by royal grant from 1254 through 1259 in the duchy, the vast majority, of course, coming during the progress in 1256 or formally in Paris a short time after.[71]

In comparison to the period before the crusade, it cannot be said that Louis actually traveled more after 1254. This is because there were no rebellions to suppress, but the ordered character of his progresses in the post-crusade period is remarkable. The first two and one-half years after his return, which we have been discussing thus far, are really only the introduction to this subject.[72] The opportunity for personal review of affairs in Normandy was commonplace: he penetrated deeply into the province in most years from 1257 through 1269; he traveled rather more on the periphery in 1260, 1262, and

[66] Fournier and Guébin, *Enquêtes administratives*, p. xl; Carolus-Barré, "Grand Ordonnance de 1254," p. 92.
[67] Appendix One, s.v. "Cotentin."
[68] Ibid., under relevant headings.
[69] *Chronique du Bec*, p. 37 with notes.
[70] Andrieux, *Cartulaire de Bonport*, p. 218 no. ccxvi.
[71] Delisle, *Cartulaire normand*, pp. xxxii-xxxiii.
[72] In general see the published itinerary and Thoison, *Séjours*; also Mathon, *Creil*, pp. 4-5; Lecocq, *Histoire . . . Saint-Quentin*, p. 86; Colliette, *Vermandois*, ii, 643; Rocher, *Saint-Benoît-sur-Loire*, pp. 337-38; Sulpice, *Hôtel-Dieu*, p. 11; Chardon, *Auxerre*, pp. 199-200; Charpentier, *Séjour*, p. 183. Subsequent references in this paragraph are to the published itinerary unless otherwise noted.

1264.[73] Normandy was not an exception. No area close enough to be visited with regularity was allowed to be without the king for very long. Orléans received him in 1257, 1259, and 1266;[74] Saint-Quentin and Noyon in 1257; Bourges and Reims in 1258; Ligueil in 1261; Hesdin in 1263.

Certain regions, because of distance, were not susceptible to this mode of rulership even in the north. Nonetheless, the king realized his own importance as a symbol of unity for these areas. In this regard, it is worth considering the nature of his itinerary on the eve of his second crusade, in late 1269 and early 1270. His travel at that time constituted a *tournée* of sorts, but unlike the *tournée* of 1248 (see map 2) it was neither abbreviated nor schematic.[75] Louis reached out to districts which had rarely seen him: the people of Meaux, who had not entertained him since 1260, those of Tours, who could not have recalled a visit since 1255, those of Vendôme who had not welcomed the king since he was a boy in 1227, and those of Ham who had never received their lord, all found themselves the hosts of the royal court.

Not unlike the episcopal visitations of his friend, the Franciscan archbishop of Rouen, Eudes Rigaud,[76] the visits of Louis IX, whatever their avowed intent, for example *translationes* of saints' bodies,[77] gave him firsthand information on local conditions. This information continuously fueled the machinery of effective government because the king held court during his sojourns and made far-reaching decisions which affected the structure of his administration.[78] In January 1257, for instance, he visited Senlis and Saint-Quentin, the *chef-lieu* of the *bailliage* of Vermandois;[79] this trip coincides with the suppression of the *bailliage* of Senlis and its incorporation into Vermandois.[80]

The middle-aged but restless peripatetic was welcomed by his hosts (or so I have claimed); yet, royal progresses were notorious witherers of the land. Something like this sentiment is in back of the alliterative catch phrase about the unwelcome visitor who eats his host "out of house and home" and the Russian folk saying that compares the un-

[73] In general see Petit-Dutaillis, *Feudal Monarchy*, p. 321. Complementary information on Normandy for the years 1257-1270 is scattered through Poulain, *Séjours*. See also Charpillon, *Gisors*, p. 261; Colliette, *Vermandois*, II, 645; Potin de La Marie, *Gournay*, I, 410; idem, *Supplément*, p. 123; and the *Register of Eudes of Rouen*.
[74] For the trip in 1259 see Rocher, *Saint-Benoît-sur-Loire*, pp. 337-38.
[75] Cf. above chapter 5 nn. 2-28.
[76] *Register of Eudes of Rouen.*
[77] Carolus-Barré, "SL et la translation des corps saints." See also below chapter 7 nn. 65-70.
[78] *HF*, XXIV, "Preuves," no. 102. See also Louat, *Senlis*, p. 52; Dupuis, *Senlis*, p. 114; and the arguments advanced in the opening pages of this chapter.
[79] See the published itinerary; Lecocq, *Histoire . . . Saint-Quentin*, p. 86; and Colliette, *Vermandois*, II, 643.
[80] See Appendix One under the relevant headings.

invited guest unfavorably to the Tatar.[81] A common enough theme in pre-modern societies, it had possibly reached its zenith in the medieval period, for the Middle Ages found itself bound at several levels by a tangle of custom justifying the exploitation of one stratum of society by another. Inherited, perhaps, from the conqueror-conquered mentality of early feudalism,[82] this so-called right of hospitality had become a form of oppression whose chief exponents, throughout the feudal age, were the protectors of society, the kings and prelates themselves.[83]

Louis IX became sensitive to this oppression after the crusade. In its earliest manifestation he concentrated on his own customary right to *gîte*, the revenues paid to provide hospitality on the visit of a superior and his entourage.[84] What appears to have happened after 1254 was the initiation of a policy limiting, in selected cases, the amount of royal *gîte* levied against ecclesiastical corporations. Whether the several clustered examples of this selective limitation point to the existence of a unified directive is uncertain. It is probable only that Louis was more receptive to charges of his agents' and his abuse of the privilege of hospitality, and that churchmen got his ear first. One fact stands out clearly and undeniably, and that is that out-and-out elimination of the levy, a "proper" custom when properly exploited, was never intended.[85]

There are many examples of reductions. In 1255 the levy of *gîte* on the cathedral chapter of Saint-Hilaire of Tours for royal visits to the archdiocese was limited to one hundred pounds *tournois* per year.[86] (It is noteworthy that the timing of this reduction coincides with a royal visit to Tours during which the king made or confirmed a new appointee as *bailli* of Touraine.)[87] This started a trend. In the same year restrictive limits were put on the amount of *gîte* levyable on the churches of Saint-Thierry, Saint-Basil, and Saint-Pierre of Hautevillier for royal visits to the archdiocese of Reims.[88] When Louis acquired the overlordship of the abbey of Marmoutier from the count of Blois in 1258, he voluntarily limited his maximum yearly *gîte* to

[81] *Oxford Dictionary of English Proverbs*, p. 215; and Pushkin, *Kapitanskaya Dochka*, in *Sobranie sochineniǐ*, IV, 354 (epigraph, cap. 8).

[82] Cf. Bloch, *Feudal Society*, II, 297-98.

[83] Cf. Petit-Dutaillis, *Feudal Monarchy*, p. 249.

[84] On the general history of this subject, see Brühl, *Fodrum*, and for documents relevant to the French experience, see *HF*, XXI, 272, 275, 277; Brussel, *Usage général des fiefs*, I, 552-65. See also *Olim*, I, 458 i, 486 v.

[85] Cf. Boutaric, *Actes*, I, no. 489. See also Bourgin, *Soissons*, p. 21 n. 9; Wood, *Apanages*, p. 78 n. 34.

[86] *Layettes*, III, no. 4163; Grandmaison, *Cartulaire . . . Tours*, II, 201-2.

[87] Above n. 63.   [88] *Layettes*, III, nos. 4226-27.

sixty pounds *tournois*.[89] In August 1259 in an agreement with the bishop of Chartres *gîte* was eliminated, the bishop paying a token grant of fifty pounds *tournois* for the concession.[90] Also in 1259 the abbey of Saint-Denis was recognized to be free of the obligation.[91]

A financial record detailing the collection of *gîte* between 1254 and 1269 also indicates various adjustments of the levy.[92] From it, one learns that there were two ad hoc eliminations of the levy (recorded as 110 pounds)[93] for the diocese of Chartres in 1255 and 1258, that is, before the permanent suppression of the levy in 1259. More typical adjustments took place for the abbey of Saint-Mesmin in the diocese of Orléans in October 1261 when *gîte* levied at over ninety-four pounds was reduced to seventy pounds and for the diocese of Nevers in June of 1262 when *gîte* levied at one hundred pounds was reduced by more than 55 percent. This same record, in addition to confirming the intermittent selective reduction of *gîte* for ecclesiastical corporations, also reveals the apparent expansion of the policy into selective reductions for villages and towns beginning in 1261. In general, the established assessments were small—they ranged from 68 to 160 pounds; reductions varied too: from 12 percent to 69 percent.

Concurrently there was a progressive lessening of the sheer number of collections of *gîte*. Following the divisions of the published manuscript in its old-style dating, the figures are these: in 1254 there were twenty-two collections of the levy, twenty-two more in 1255; but after 1255 such collections never exceeded twenty and rarely ten.[94] If,

[89] Trouillard, *Inventaire-sommaire . . . AD: Loir-et-Cher . . . H*, I, 159; Metais, *Marmoutier . . . Blésois*, no. 287; also Chevalier, *Marmoutier*, II, 227-29.

[90] *GC*, VIII, "Instrumenta," cc. 369-70 no. c; Lépinois and Merlet, *Cartulaire de Notre-Dame de Chartres*, II, 169-72 and no. cccxxxi, and III, "Necrologium," p. 8; Molinier, *Obituaires . . . de Sens*, II, 29.

[91] Brussel, *Usage général des fiefs*, I, 541.

[92] "Gista quae dominus rex Ludovicus cepit," *HF*, XXI, 397-403. Except where indicated, I have converted all dates to new style.

[93] But cf. *gîte* in 1248 of only one hundred pounds in Chartres; *HF*, XXI, 277.

[94] The raw data are summarized chronologically in accord with the old-style dating of the manuscript in column one of the table which follows. The figures in column one were able to be improved slightly first by adjusting for multiple entries (those in which separate notations were made for two or three different institutions which paid *gîte* for a visit to a single location) and second by removing all entries which simply noted the suppression of a specific payment of *gîte*. Column two, by incorporating these corrections, more accurately reflects the frequency of the crown's actual collection of *gîte*.

Year	Column 1 (unrevised)	Column 2 (revised)
1254	22	16
1255	22	19
1256	2	2
1257	7	4
1258	15	14
1259	4	4

as seems entirely probable, Louis's travel followed a rather consistent pattern in most years after his return from crusade, the fall off in collections of *gîte* might indicate that even though he frequently visited regions near Paris, as far as possible he avoided repeated sojourns in particular localities that owed him *gîte*.

As I have said before, the initial motivation for the policy of reducing *gîte* or excusing its payment for ecclesiastical corporations is problematical. It is nice that the first example of the policy coincides with Louis's visit to the bishopric which benefited from it. We might conclude that the representatives of the see told him *gîte* was oppressive there, that he believed them and reduced it, and that henceforth he was sensitive to the question of *gîte* whenever it came up. But this is all surmise; it is not proof.

For what it is worth an argument can be made that Louis's leniency with *gîte* was part of a broader attempt to atone for his and his agents' exploitation of church revenues before and during the crusade. Temporal regalia, the royal right to the revenue of vacant benefices, which was vigorously exploited between 1245 and 1252, might possibly be the key here, for the king recognized that his officials had overstepped the bounds of propriety in the vigor of their collection of such revenues. As a result he undertook (or continued) a policy after the crusade both to settle his regalian rights[95] and also, probably, to supervise more closely the officials who looked after them (by making known to them in one instance, for example, that they could not appropriate more than one-half of diocesan revenue during a vacancy).[96] His selective reductions of *gîte*, some of which correspond nicely with the bishoprics at loggerheads with the king before the crusade, may be an extension of this policy.[97]

1260	5	4
1261	8	8
1262	6	6
1263	0	0
1264	6	6
1265	5	3
1266	13	13
1267	3	1
1268	2	2
1269	10	7

[95] *Layettes*, III, nos. 4102, 4116-17, 4119, 4127, 4505; Boutaric, *Actes*, I, no. 125; *GC*, II, 742, and "Instrumenta," c. 234 nos. xvi, xix, and x, "Instrumenta," cc. 65-66 nos. lxvii and lxix. See also Berger, *SL et Innocent IV*, p. 376 n. 1; Tillemont, *Vie de SL*, IV, 126-27, 192-99, 208, 410-16; Phillips, *Regalienrecht*, pp. 67, 81; and Mollat, "Application du droit de régale spirituelle," pp. 432-33.

[96] See the agreement with Evreux; Delisle, *Cartulaire normand*, no. 1195. See also Phillips, *Regalienrecht*, p. 63.

[97] For example, Chartres and also Nevers, where there were problems in the collection of the tenth; *HF*, XXI, 539, and XXIV, "Chronologie," p. 120. On the exploitative

The further manifestation of the government's concern with matters of hospitality was Louis's interest in the gift-giving of his communes and other municipal corporations under his suzerainty. The direct motivation, in this instance, can be inferred from the so-called communal accounts of circa 1260 which the king had ordered prepared to provide the basis for a reassessment of the indemnity due the English after their official recognition of the loss of Normandy and certain other provinces in 1259.[98] The accounts revealed the widespread practice by towns of giving gifts to great visitors to the apparent detriment of their financial integrity.

The problem was not unreal:[99] Saint-Riquier had spent perhaps as much as 50 pounds in 1259 on presents of wine; its total budget was 900 pounds. Poissy had expended almost 20 pounds out of a total budget of 157 pounds, largely on gifts to ecclesiastics. The municipality of Chauny spent 20 shillings 6 pence on fish and over 35 pounds on wine for presents to "good men" from a total budget of 880 pounds. Roye made purchases of approximately 25 pounds for wine and 17 pounds for fish, capons, and cakes from its budget of 776 pounds during the visits of the archbishop of Reims and the bishop of Amiens to the town. Beaumont-sur-Oise expended 30 pounds for various gifts, 15 percent of its budget; the account of Crépy-en-Laonnois is hardly more than an extended list of its obligations in presents.[100]

This information must have conjured up in the king's mind the *tournée* of 1248 and the material effect it had on places he visited. It was reinforced by the episcopal complaints he had already received and which we have discussed above. His initial reaction to the information appears to have been a self-conscious limitation of his own customary exploitation of the towns and communes. This would ex-

---

application of the right of temporal regalia in the diocese of Chartres, above chapter 4 n. 170. For full discussions of problems over the regalia of Reims, which may be applicable to the argument in the text since Remois churches benefited from Louis's reductions of *gîte* (above n. 88), see Tillemont, *Vie de SL*, IV, 192-99, and Mollat, "Application du droit de régale spirituelle," pp. 432-33.

[98] Once the subject of heated discussion, this is now the reason accepted by scholars for the making of the accounts; Borrelli de Serres, *Recherches*, I, 100-105. Among recent scholars, Wood, *Apanages*, pp. 94-95 n. 31; Schneider, "Villes," p. 47; and François, "Bonnes villes," p. 552, have suggested an earlier dating of the reforms inspired by the accounts based on a marginal notation in the ordinance of reform, but this was simply one clerk's suggestion about the date; and, as Borrelli has shown, it is in error (pp. 95-99).

[99] For discussions touching various towns, see Beauvillé, *Montdidier*, I, 105-6; Hénocque, *Saint-Riquier*, III, 60 n. 1; Labande, *Beauvais*, p. 242; Lot, "Evolution," *Recueil des travaux*, III, 267; Coet, *Roye*, II, 124-25; Duchaussoy, *Beauquesne*, p. 74.

[100] These data may be found in *Layettes*, III, nos. 4583, 4591, 4609, 4611, 4630, 4644. For other examples see nos. 4610 (Beauvais), 4629 (Rouen), 4633 (Pont Audemer), 4636 (Chambly), 4645 (Vailly-sur-Aisne).

plain why the reductions in *gîte* levied against municipalities, according to the official enumeration of the income, did not begin until 1261 rather than, as in the case of ecclesiastics, in 1255.[101] But if the dates differed, the underlying principle was the same: selective, not across-the-board, reductions in the levy were authorized. There was no sense that the levy itself was wrong, merely that it had been abused. Guided by the same principle, Louis took steps to make sure that in legitimately entertaining other visiting dignitaries, the municipalities could not impoverish themselves: they could offer their visitors no more than wine "in cups or in flasks."[102]

The effect of Louis's policies regarding *gîte* on the prestige of government after the crusade was obvious: they gave government—as it followed the king around the country—the benefit of being welcomed or at least they defused a potential source of conflict and bad feeling. I have the impression, based on the records of petitions presented to the crown for the remainder of Louis's reign, that there was even a marked diminution over time in the frequency of complaints by the lowest segment of the population over the problem of royal visits. Before 1248 this had been a favorite point of contention as small town dwellers and peasants decried the rapacity of local officials and notables burdened with providing hospitality; they denounced the latter for stealing pillows, quilts, and mattresses whenever the king and the court visited in regions under their influence. Later petitions hardly mention such excesses,[103] a fact which suggests—as much as silence can—that the king was making sure his wishes were effective even at the local level.

In sum, the intent of royal government was made clear immediately after the crusade. A spirit of compromise and decency, implying no sacrifice of legitimate prerogatives,[104] was carried directly to the governed. Louis imposed order through his personal presence in the field. He started investigations into more difficult problems after local discussions in which he personally took part. He made appointments to administrative posts based on firsthand observations of field administration. He redrew the cartography of *bailliagère* jurisdictions based on the evidence of his own eyes and ears. Personal government, peripatetic government, direct government—this was the nature of

---

[101] Cf. *HF*, XXI, 397-403.

[102] Cf. Giry, *Documents*, pp. 85-88, clause three of the ordinances of communal reform for *Francia* and Normandy.

[103] Petit-Dutaillis, "*Queremoniae normannorum*," p. 112, drew attention to this problem in the early records. It is only fair to add that the post-crusade records are less extensive for the north, and, therefore, my conclusion should be regarded as tentative.

[104] Cf. Anonymous of Saint-Denis, *HF*, XX, 49. See also Bünger, *Beziehungen Ludwigs IX . . . zur Curie . . . 1254-1264*.

political relations in the immediate post-crusade era, and it became a permanent feature of Louis's personal rule.

Nonetheless, Louis obviously felt that a great deal more was required of him to assure the effective governance of his kingdom. There are at least two fundamentally important considerations which force me to make this statement. In the first place, the king had apparently decided even before his return from crusade that the *enquêteurs* were to become a permanent institution in royal government. Indeed, new appointees to the dignity began another wave of work within months after his return. In the south they started work actually in 1254 pursuing themes developed before the crusade such as dealing with the complaints of women abused during the Albigensian Crusade or the rebellions incident to it,[105] but they also carried forward the effort at reconciliation commenced during the king's progress, receiving petitions, for example, from those aggrieved by royal measures for Aigues-Mortes.[106] In the south commissions were renewed at intervals so that that region was visited by *enquêteurs* regularly through 1262.[107] In the north the commissions seem to have got started almost as quickly but to have been limited, more or less, to supervision of local administrators, an activity which thereafter became cyclical and a commonplace of administrative discipline in Capetian history.[108]

To their work in the south the new *enquêteurs* (mendicants about half the time) brought slightly more formality than their predecessors. This was inevitable since they were bound to learn from the mistakes of the former. But they brought equal dedication to equitable justice.[109] They were instructed to do so by the king. They were told to seek out the innocent victims of oppression—widows, orphans, the sick.[110] And they did so with sincerity and verve. For example, upward of 40 percent of all the petitions they accepted in the south came from widows. Well nigh to 90 percent of these petitions were disposed in favor of the petitioners. The orphans who brought their petitions

---

[105] Cf. Strayer, "Conscience du roi."   [106] See especially *HF*, xxiv, 531-41.
[107] Ibid. (years 1254-1257); pp. 545-614 (circa 1258), 619-95 (year 1262). Besides these case summaries in the basic collection, see also Michel, *Beaucaire*, pp. 410-15 nos. 20-22 (years 1254-1256), 432-33 no. 34 (year 1262); and below Appendix Four (records of a case held in 1256).
[108] The records of the extant commissions are printed in *HF*, xxiv, "Preuves," no. 152 (year 1261); pp. 698-728 (before 1269). But Wyse has summarized the evidence showing that *enquêteurs* were also commissioned in the *bailliage* of Sens, in Picardy, in Bourges, Tours, and Orléans from 1255 to 1257; "Enquêteurs," pp. 52-54. Precisely when any of these commissions were carried out is problematic.
[109] Above chapter 3 nn. 141-44.
[110] *HF*, xxiv, 620-21. Cf. Alfonse's similar sentiments, but less effective action, Fournier and Guébin, *Enquêtes administratives, pièces* 24 and 64.

before the commissioners were consistently treated with gentleness and understanding.[111]

I have said that the rapid reintroduction of the *enquêteurs* was one clear proof that the king had given a great deal of thought to the operation of domestic government even before his return and that he came home armed with a coherent program which went far beyond his commitment to "personal" rule per se. The second, equally clear, and massive proof of this proposition is the extraordinary series of ordinances for reform that accompanied his return. First in time was a draft of an ordinance on the Jews that had been forwarded to the regency government in 1253; a final version of it was issued in December 1254. Second was probably to have been a directive for the operation of the ecclesiastical Inquisition to be issued in conjunction with the royal *enquêteurs'* reception of petitions on the unjust actions of certain Albigensian crusaders. In this case, however, the death of Innocent IV in August 1254 apparently delayed the issuance of the directive for several months. The third group of ordinances comprised the major administrative reorganizing measures for the realm which were issued in 1254 with subsequent additions as the king toured the kingdom (1254-1256). The fourth and final set of reforms concerned the proper administration of the city of Paris; the earliest glimmerings of these reforms occur also in 1254. All four of these legislative efforts were to have a fundamental impact on the governance of medieval France.

Concerning the first, we know that a draft ordinance which Louis sent to France in 1253 exiled Jews who lent money at interest.[112] On his return he reissued this ordinance, apparently revised, and it set out in very careful terms the limits of anti-Jewish activity which he would tolerate.[113] (This was presumably a reaction to the wave of violent anti-Judaism that had accompanied his crusade.)[114] By the ordinance, the Talmud, considered a source of anti-Christian polemics, continued to be proscribed. Jewish usurers were condemned to exile (a fate which would soon overtake Christian usurers as well).[115] How-

[111] Appendix Three supplies analysis for the statistical statements.

[112] MP, v, 361: "venit de Terra Sancta mandatum domini regis Francorum, ut omnes Judaei . . ." Cf. Lazard, "Revenues," p. 233; Michel, *Beaucaire*, appendix 2, esp. p. 319; Chazan, *Medieval Jewry*, p. 121. Cf. also the imprecise remarks of Parkes, *Jew in the Medieval Community*, pp. 326, 361, 380. Matthew Paris attributed the ordinance to the Saracens' taunts, during Louis's brief captivity, to the effect that the king allowed the murderers of Christ to live among the Christian Franks; MP, v, 361-62.

[113] *Ordonnances*, I, 65. [114] Above chapter 4 nn. 47-50.

[115] Matthew Paris, who died in 1259, thought Jewish money-lending had been wiped out by the expulsion and expected the Cahorsins (an epithet for Christian usurers, many of whom were originally from Cahors) to take up the slack; MP, v, 362. In the

ever, it was specifically laid down that practicing Jews, who were otherwise innocent of crime (usury, blasphemy, sorcery), were under the protection of royal law, a protection that they often had recourse to in the closing years of the reign.[116] Later, in 1257, traditional provisions of ecclesiastical programs regarding Jews were incorporated into the royal program: Jewish liturgical books, cemeteries, and old synagogues were put under royal protection and could not be confiscated as a punishment for engaging in usurious activities.[117]

The king had singled out old synagogues, a traditional qualification. The very idea of the construction of new synagogues, signifying the continuation of Judaism as a strong subcurrent in France, was abhorrent to him.[118] His piety in this respect found an outlet in a comprehensive program to convert the Jews. There had been some of this before the crusade, but not much.[119] Things changed after 1254, a fact recognized by several historians[120] and by contemporary Jews, some of whom emigrated voluntarily.[121]

Conversion was represented as an attractive alternative to remain-

---

short run he may have been correct: this appears to be Nahon's view ("Crédit") and Labarge's opinion ("SL et les juifs," p. 270). The so-called communal accounts (discussed above n. 98) bear them out that Christians were active usurers in the postcrusade period, at least for a while. But whether the Jewish money-lending business was crushed completely is really not so obvious—it was no doubt eclipsed, but it may have survived by going more underground (cf. Jordan, "Jews on Top," p. 52). However that may be, Chazan, *Medieval Jewry*, p. 103, seems to misinterpret a story told by Louis's confessor-biographer, Guillaume de Chartres, on these and similar issues. Chazan implies that Louis never interfered with the lending carried out by Christian usurers because the king is reported to have said that Christian usury was a matter of concern to the clergy while usury by Jews (who were his men; cf. Langmuir, "*Judaei nostri*") was his personal concern. This was true in a strictly legal sense, and it may in part account for the "Jewish emphasis" of Louis's anti-usury policies, especially before the crusade. But as the crown could legitimately come to the aid of the church over matters of heresy (below n. 130), so too it could help ecclesiastics deal with the issue of Christian usury. In 1268 and 1269 Louis ordered his *baillis* to expel all usurers from the royal domain, including Lombards and Cahorsins, that is, Christian usurers. Cf. Nahon, "Ordonnances," p. 20 n. 16. He also compelled his *baillis* to expel the usurers operating in his barons' lands. See also Grunwald, "Lombards," pp. 396-97. Cf. *Olim*, I, 51 xxxii.

[116] Boutaric, *Acts*, I, no. 508; cf. also nos. 1462, 1465, 1522, 1531; and *Layettes*, v, no. 849.

[117] *Ordonnances*, I, 85. See also Nahon, "Ordonnances," p. 22.

[118] The implicit prohibition against new synagogues had a long history, stretching back to late antiquity; cf. Giraud, *Droit*, I, 334-35 (text). Cf. Chazan, *Medieval Jewry*, p. 122, who has argued that the king's regulations on synagogues show that despite the exile of Jewish moneylenders (see Nahon, "Ordonnances," pp. 20, 24; cf. below n. 121) a "substantial segment of the Jewish community remained" in royal France. On Alfonse's similar prohibition of new synagogues, see Saige, *Juifs*, p. 21.

[119] Below nn. 123-24, 126.

[120] Labarge, "SL et les juifs," p. 273; La Serve, "Juifs à Lyon," pp. 308-9 (a very old but still strong article).

[121] Kahn, "Juifs de Posquiéres et de Saint-Gilles," pp. 20-21 (evidence of the Jews of Saint-Gilles, Languedoc, migrating to Marseilles, not at that time under royal control).

ing Jewish.[122] In the first place pensions were offered to converts.[123] They could also choose new names, royal names, that put them under the protection of the king as their godparent.[124] Such inducements were traditional, but in 1260 a royal directive removed all residual restrictions on converts.[125] As to the methods used to bring the propaganda of conversion to the Jews, we are not very well informed. Originally, learned disputations were held between Christians and Jews as in 1240 when Nicholas Donin, a converted Jew, defended the Christian case for the royal family. But this never proved effective.[126] On the other hand, sermons may have become the preferred method later in the reign. For example, a Jewish convert, Lombard by birth, who had become a Dominican friar, was commissioned by the king during a trip to Paris to preach to all the assembled Jews of the need to abandon the Old Law in favor of the New Covenant.[127]

Whatever the methods, the results were significant. There are no good figures on this, but the early antiquary, Vyon d'Hérouval, who was an important royal functionary in the seventeenth century and who may have had access to a more complete set of data than is presently obtainable, believed that he had discovered a massive conversion of Jews after Louis IX's first crusade. At that time, according to the evidence before him and which his friend Tillemont utilized, *baptisati*

---

[122] Labarge, "SL et les juifs," p. 273. Cf. Louis's support, in 1248, for Christians to learn Arabic to aid them in the conversion of the Moslems; cf. *CUP*, nos. 180-81; and his attitude toward the Tatars, above chapter 2 following n. 120.

[123] Labarge ("SL et les juifs," p. 273) seems to place the first pension payment in 1253, but during the Ascension term 1248 there is a record of a payment to *Ludovicus de Pissiaco, conversus* of 6 l.16 s.; *HF*, XXI, 261. See also Rabinowitz, *Social Life of the Jews*, p. 103.

[124] See Rabinowitz, *Social Life of the Jews*, p. 106 n. 7; Grayzel, *Church and the Jews*, p. 285 n. 1.

[125] Boutaric, *Actes*, I, no. 479. Parkes, *Jew in the Medieval Community*, p. 143, confuses the intention of this decree with its potential effect; the normalization of the status of converts might have been seen by certain Frenchmen as a downgrading of the converts' special protection and, therefore, an opportunity to release their hatred against the converts.

[126] Rabinowitz, *Social Life of the Jews*, p. 105; Chazan, *Medieval Jewry*, pp. 124-28. Joinville (chap. x) records the famous remark of Louis, namely that a Christian layman should not hear the faith maligned (by a Jew) but should punish the malefactor by the sword. Interestingly, the remark follows a story told by the king in which an organized disputation between Jews and Christians was criticized by a knight as a bad method of strengthening the faith. Louis's agreement with this criticism (as recorded by Joinville) is strong evidence of a change in his views about the best methods of conversion. Unfortunately, this change cannot be dated precisely because the king's remark occurs only in that part of Joinville's book which treats of Louis's virtues (not in the chronological part).

[127] Delisle, "Notes sur quelques manuscrits," p. 189, publishes the anonymous Paris chronicle with this information. See also Chazan, *Medieval Jewry*, pp. 149-51; and his "Barcelona 'Disputation,'" pp. 828-29.

and *conversi* began to permeate the sources.[128] Louis IX was doing his job effectively.

With regard to the second group of directives mentioned above, those dealing with the operation of the Inquisition, the piety of Louis IX, tempered by the lessons of the crusade, stimulated another adjustment in royal policy. Institutionally, the old division of the Inquisition into two provinces, northern and southern, was suppressed with the support of the new pope, Alexander IV. The institution itself was directed thereafter from the University of Paris.[129] No doubt the reorganization was designed to smooth out the operations of the Inquisition, to give it a kind of overall unity and relative functional efficiency.

But more important than institutional change was the change in style. The Inquisition could not carry on its work without the king's support.[130] It was he who allowed its courts to function and paid for their administrative expenses.[131] But he expressed his belief after the crusade that he had been "too rigorous" before.[132] No individual's property ought to be violated simply because he was accused of heresy,[133] and every effort was made—through his own royal *enquêteurs*—to return goods and lands illegally or insensitively confiscated.[134] It is not that Louis had deliberately said, "Be ruthless!" before the crusade. On the contrary, the interesting thing is that one can find formulaic statements made by him before 1248 urging restraint in investigating a subject as complex as complicity in heresy;[135] yet, he

[128] Bruel, "Notes de Vyon d'Hérouval," pp. 611-18; Tillemont, *Vie de SL*, v, 296-98. See also Labarge, "SL et les juifs," p. 273; Nahon, "Pour une géographie administrative," p. 312 n. 8. Cf. Chazan, *Medieval Jewry*, p. 146 n. 148. *Baptisati* were infants born Jewish but baptized during infancy into the Christian faith; *Conversi* were adult converts. See also Nahon, "Ordonnances," p. 22.

[129] Haskins, "Robert le Bougre," p. 243, esp. n. 6.

[130] The assertion that the crown had a duty to intervene in the matter of heresy is explicit in the early ordinance *Cupientes* which established the Inquisition in France circa 1230. See Campbell, "Attitude of the Monarchy toward . . . Ecclesiastical Censures," pp. 544-45. The original *Cupientes* or, rather, the version that historians know about was specifically intended for the south of France, but since the Inquisition also operated in the north—if somewhat less consistently (cf. Grigulevich, *Istoriia inkvizitsii*, pp. 95-96; Guiraud, *Histoire de l'Inquisition*, II, 185-218); it has been assumed that there was a version of *Cupientes* for the north as well (Haskins, "Robert le Bougre," p. 242 n. 5). Whatever differences there were between the two ordinances must have been erased by the uniting of the two provinces of the Inquisition.

[131] *HGL*, VIII, cc. 1435-36 (order to pay the expenses of the inquisitors dated 1258).

[132] *HF*, XXIV, 620-21. See also the discussion by Guiraud, *Histoire de l'Inquisition*, II, 237-39.

[133] *HGL*, VIII, cc. 1440-41.

[134] Above nn. 109-11; and below Appendix Three. See also Boutaric, *Actes*, I, nos. 429, 574, 995A.

[135] *HGL*, VIII, c. 1206 (order dated July 1246).

still thought it necessary after the crusade to say that he had been too rough. An attitude has changed here, a tone: after 1254 much more effort was put into making the pious formulas ring true in practice.

The third part of the program of reform, the administrative regulations on local government that were issued in 1254 (with subsequent additions thereafter), had much wider implications for French history than the Jewish ordinances or the reorganization of the Inquisition. The provisions of the regulations are well known:[136] every royal official transferred from one office to another would be liable for a specified period of time to investigation of his conduct by his replacement. In the ban of their administrations, *baillis* could not hold property, acquire benefices, enroll their younger children in abbeys or priories, or permit their older ones to marry local inhabitants. The judicial responsibilities of provincial authorities were also regulated. Judges who failed to do good justice were made answerable directly to the king. They were not to accept gifts from their litigants, sell their offices, show bad faith to subalterns, impose secret fines, make justice expensive, or cause it to be delayed. Inferior officials—foresters, sergeants, and the like—received vaguer instructions. They were obliged merely to take public oaths to uphold the king's justice and to promise to be just in carrying out their own duties.[137]

Too often, these regulations alone have been taken as the chief evidence of a kind of Holy Monarchy in the reign of Saint Louis.[138] Now, there is some truth in this, but virtue, or the pious proclamation of virtue, was not limited to Louis IX. Men always have ideals and they express them tirelessly; but they almost always fail to live up to them. If Louis IX was the symbol of moral progress for his age as Fustel de Coulanges once eloquently argued,[139] it was not only, perhaps not even predominately, because he spoke morally or even lived morally himself. It was because, as far as possible, he made others behave morally. In other words, the administrative regulations of 1254 may have been less important because they were stated than because they worked.

---

[136] Carolus-Barré, "Grand Ordonnance de 1254," discusses the technical features of the regulations and their elaboration (pp. 86-88); he plans a new edition of the ordinance (p. 96). See also his "Grand Ordonnance de réformation." All the major biographies have discussions of the regulations. For other more specialized or idiosyncratic remarks, see Delisle, *HF*, xxiv, "Préface," p. 22; Bisson, *Assemblies*, pp. 187-91; Rogozinski, "Counsellors," p. 423; and Fiétier, "Choix des baillis," pp. 258-59, 261. See also *Formulaires*, no. 6, items 320-21.

[137] Specific references to these provisions will be made in subsequent paragraphs.

[138] See the pointed remarks of Fesler, "French Field Administration," p. 91 n. 23, apropos of this subject.

[139] Fustel de Coulanges, *SL et le prestige de la royauté*, p. 41.

To illustrate this blanket statement, we may take several aspects of the ordinances. To begin with, every official transferred from one position to another was liable to investigation of his conduct in office by his replacement.[140] Evidently, at the time of transfer the new *baillis* made inventories of important royal possessions in the charge of former officials. Most of these, no doubt, took place orally, but perhaps in important instances (or more generally in the south where written records were a regular feature of administration) the results of the inventories were committed to parchment. A *quittance* of this type now in the royal archives, dated at Nîmes 8 September 1260, records the transfer of the castle at Sommières from Geoffroy de Roncherolles to Geoffroy de Courferaud, the new *sénéchal* of Beaucaire and Nîmes.[141] The inventory, taken in the new official's presence with the castellan of Sommières attending, does not indicate whether the former *sénéchal* was there. In any case, he did not have to be, for the ordinance speaks of the privilege of transferred agents acquitting themselves by proxy.[142]

This inventory was not originally intended for transmission to Paris: the *sénéchal*'s clerk did not address it to the central government nor did a notary public certify it as was common in Languedoc. The new *sénéchal* might have found a discrepancy and forwarded the document to Paris, or *enquêteurs* who had access to the document at a later time may have referred it to the capital. But the fact that such records existed at all and could be used as check lists is good evidence of the functioning of supervisory review. In other words, the oversight of the *baillis* was dependent on no one particular system. Audits (the periodic verification of accounts) helped; the *enquêteurs* helped; and in the north the king's regular visits were useful. But if these devices failed to alert the central government to the corruption or ineptitude of local officials, the investigatory mechanisms which accompanied transferral would come into operation.

Even the combination of these measures was deemed insufficient by the seemingly uneasy monarch. It is for this reason that the reform ordinances included provisions designed to inhibit the formation of local loyalties by royal officials. These provisions, as it will be shown, were also successfully applied. Their drawback was that in certain particulars, notably the sections on marriage, they pertained only to

[140] *Ordonnances*, I, 67, 76, 77-81; Joinville, chap. CXL.
[141] *Layettes*, IV, no. 4626. Demay reported in 1874 (*Bulletin de la Société des antiquaires*, pp. 43-44) that this inventory antedated by several years similar surviving documents. This judgment, as far as I have been able to determine, is still definitive.
[142] Cf. Joinville, chap. CXL.

the chief administrators of provincial government, the *baillis* and *sénéchaux*. Inferior officials were exempted.[143]

It has long been recognized that the *baillis* and, with more exceptions, the *sénéchaux* were selected from a geographically restricted area, preferably the old royal domain. The exhaustive studies of Henri Stein have established this point incontrovertibly.[144] But over time such men adopted their new areas, and when supervision was limited, such as before 1245, they became deeply integrated into provincial society. It is clear that the personnel revolution of 1247, 1248, and 1249 fractured this relationship, without, however, providing any special mechanism to prevent its reemergence.

The return of the king provided several such mechanisms. For one thing, transfers from one *bailliage* to another became relatively more frequent from the time of the crusade on. In Normandy, for example, terms of administration generally ranged from eight years to eleven years before 1248 whereas in the whole reign of Saint Louis average length of service in one district in Normandy was a little over six years.[145] It is difficult to be more precise (the data for Normandy are the most complete available), but some sense of the total picture is suggested by them. A few instances, from outside Normandy, will underscore the point: before the crusade, in the *bailliage* of Sens, Nicolas de Hautvillers served for at least twenty-two years; in Étampes Adam Héron and Galeran d'Escrennes were *baillis* for twenty-two years and ten years respectively. In Senlis before the crusade there were *baillis* who served fifteen years, twenty-six years, thirteen years, eleven years.[146] Only three or four *baillis*, in the entire country, served in one place as long as ten years after Louis's return from crusade.[147]

Long rule was potentially dangerous, and yet in specific cases it might have been to the king's advantage to use a functionary in one role in one district for a considerable length of time. This probably accounts for the few instances of long administration after the crusade noticed in the previous paragraph. What could not be allowed, at least in theory, was a dynastic succession of *baillis* such as characterized some provinces before the crusade.[148] For example, in

[143] Cf. Vidier, "Origines de la municipalité parisienne," pp. 281-82.
[144] Stein's various contributions, under the title "Recherches," still constitute the best and most thorough work in the field, with the possible exception of Delisle's "Chronologie" in *HF*, xxiv. Some scholars have complemented their work (Wacquet, Michel, Strayer, Goineau, and Griffiths). The bibliography on this question may be appreciated best through the notes in Appendix One.
[145] Appendix One. See also Fesler, "French Field Administration," p. 91.
[146] Appendix One. Also, on Senlis, see Laurain, "Renaud de Béronne."
[147] For the most conspicuous exceptions—Gautier de Villers in Caux (fourteen years) and Jean de Criquebeuf in Verneuil (fifteen years)—see Appendix One.
[148] Above chapter 3 n. 62.

pre-crusade Caux, Guillaume de La Chapelle was succeeded as *bailli* by his son Geoffroy, Geoffroy by his brother Thibaud. Together the three ruled the *bailliage* for thirty-five years from 1210 to 1245.[149] It is not that these men were corrupt. In fact the career of Geoffroy de La Chapelle continued long after the end of his administration in Caux.[150] On the other hand, no single family was allowed to direct the administration of any *bailliage* for a sustained period after the crusade. There may have been families, administrative families like the de La Chapelles, that regularly contributed their members to the pool of royal officials, but at the rank of *bailli* they were under control.[151]

What was true of top-level field administrators in terms of the success of supervision was less true of lower-echelon officials. I have hinted at this before. Nonetheless, it would be wrong to believe that the latter were as free from oversight after the crusade as they were before. Let me begin with the *prévôts* and the *prévôtés*.

Speaking generally, the *prévôts* (or *bayles* or viscounts or *viguiers*, depending on the regional vocabulary) were a varied and in many ways disturbing group of people. Traditionally (that is, from the eleventh century) their principal duty was the collection of domain revenue in the towns and their *banlieux*; with this duty they also carried limited judicial powers and responsibilities.[152] In towns which were owned by the king these traditional functions persisted unmolested. In more autonomous urban centers, like the communes and free towns, circumstances could be different.[153] In a few instances, for example, the dignity of *prévôt* had been ceded to or bought up by a commune for a set annual payment in which case the municipality would delegate an official on its own (also called *prévôt*) who would collect the necessary revenues to pay the king.[154] In most instances, however, the *prévôts* remained royal agents concerned with the crown's residual rights even in the communes and free towns.

The royal *prévôts* and viscounts in the north (unlike their southern counterparts) were usually *bourgeois*[155] but not always or even usually of the same *bourg* as their charge. Jean de Callois, a case in point, who

[149] Appendix One.
[150] Stein, "Recherches," *ASHGâtinais*, XXIV, 30-32; Griffiths, "New Men," pp. 236-37.
[151] Cf. Griffiths, "New Men," p. 236; Carolus-Barré, "Baillis de Philippe III," pp. 239-40; and Vidier, "Origines de la municipalité parisienne," pp. 281-82.
[152] Above chapter 3 nn. 51, 54-56.
[153] The best juridical treatment of the communes is Petit-Dutaillis, *Communes*. See also Viollet, *Histoire des institutions*, III, 1-142.
[154] Cf. Gravier, "Prévôts," pp. 650-60; Melleville, "Notice sur la commune de Laonnois," p. 209; Bourgin, *Soissons*, p. 255; Lachiver, *Mantes*, pp. 69-70 no. 99 and n. 9.
[155] Strayer, "Viscounts and Viguiers," pp. 221-22.

was a *bourgeois* of Chambly, became *prévôt* of Beaumont-sur-Oise in 1261.[156] What other *prévôtés* he may have held are unknown, but typically during his career a *prévôt* would exercise his office in several different towns. Of course, one rarely finds a Norman viscount as a Picard *prévôt*, but within Picardy or within Normandy a *prévôt* or viscount might serve in any number of royal districts:[157] Beauquesne and Doullens;[158] Roye and Crépy-en-Valois;[159] Roye, Saint-Quentin, and Chauny;[160] etc. Although it was much more unusual, as mentioned above, to find a *bourgeois* serving his own bourg as *prévôt*, the pattern was not completely unknown. Stephanus de Berron, for example, who was a communard of Crépy-en-Valois with important financial interests in the town which could have led to conflicts of interest, served the king as royal *prévôt* there in the 1250s and 1260s.[161]

Within the rather narrow geographical limits in which the *prévôts* pursued their careers, their network of relations reached deeply into the local population. Since the marriage provisions of the ordinances did not apply to them,[162] they freely intermarried with the local inhabitants. Inevitably there were little dynasties of *prévôts* throughout the country, but especially in the north. These families, in a sense, would have a special chief town whose *prévôté* they kept under their own control, but they also had influence over other somewhat lesser *prévôtés* nearby and put cadet members of their families into the posts. A few illustrations will bear this out.

Radulfus (dictus) Clergie, the *prévôt* of Crépy-en-Valois about 1248, probably had a son-in-law Petrus de Say who would not only become *prévôt* of Crépy but later *prévôt* of Pierrefonds and Ferté-Milon.[163] Robertus de Paregni served as *prévôt* of Laon, perhaps intermittently from 1227 through 1240. His brother Jacquerus farmed cognate positions in the late thirties and in the forties in Laon as well as in Ribemont and Saint-Quentin.[164] Other families showing elements of this informal hereditary succession to the *prévôtés* in the north were the "de Brueriis"—Johannes and Thomas—and the "Tourgis"—Albertus and Johannes.[165]

---

[156] Simon, *Beaumont-sur-Oise*, p. 43.

[157] For Normandy, see Strayer, "Viscounts and Viguiers," pp. 218-19.

[158] Johannes ad Dentes; *HF*, XXIV, 707-9 nos. 17, 19-20.

[159] Michael dictus Matons; ibid., "Preuves," no. 152 pt. 65.

[160] Ibid., pt. 71.

[161] *Layettes*, III, no. 4592; *HF*, XXIV, "Preuves," no. 152 pt. 237, and XXIV, 700 no. 10.

[162] Above n. 143.

[163] For this example, *HF*, XXIV, 740 no. 103 n. 6.

[164] Ibid., pp. 275-93 (especially no. 47).

[165] Ibid., pp. 272-96 (especially no. 63), 698 (no. 3), 733-35. In these examples I am using the surnames as the men themselves used them, there being independent evidence that they were related.

I have been somewhat careful so far to speak of the north because what I do not find is that these men were mediators between local and external forces cushioning the blows from the outside as Le Roy Ladurie has found in Occitania in the late thirteenth century.[166] This difference may not be accidental. The royal and comital *prévôts* or *bayles* of central France and the *viguiers* of Languedoc were far more localized in individual districts and towns than, exceptions aside, their northern counterparts.[167] As such they were in some sense the protectors—often at a high price—of their *menu peuple*. This level of the administration was also staffed in the south with nobles rather than *bourgeois*.[168] If there is any truth to the notion of noble paternalism, this may have affected the southern officials' relationship to the local population. "*Bourgeois* acquisitiveness" functioned in the north; and the *prévôts* were hated almost as much as the police.[169]

How then were the *prévôts* to be controlled? A possible answer lay in their method of remuneration. Here, an important difference between the viscounts and *viguiers* on the one hand and the *prévôts* and *bayles* on the other is pertinent. The former were remunerated by wages, the latter were revenue farmers.[170] Discipline, to speak generally, finds a natural whip in the wage. I do not doubt that the government recognized this fact and seriously considered expanding the number of wage-earners at the expense of revenue farmers in the ranks of second-level field administrators. Although the fact has been denied,[171] there is, as we shall see, reasonably good evidence on the point.

According to the inventory of Jean de Caux, the royal archives, already in 1286, included form letters *de prepositura non vendenda*,[172] which might have been drafted as early as 1260. The wife of the *prévôt* of Beauquesne in Picardy in testimony before the *enquêteurs* in the 1260s had petitioned them to make payment of fourteen pounds for the horse her husband once used in his royal service. To buy the expensive animal she had sold a portion of her land, and since the horse had expired in the king's service she believed that she was entitled to reimbursement. It might be necessary, she said, for the *enquêteurs* to inquire of Master Jean de Duillac, a royal clerk, on this matter since

[166] Le Roy Ladurie, *Montaillou*, p. 106.
[167] Cf. Strayer, "Viscounts and Viguiers," pp. 219-20.
[168] Ibid., pp. 221-22. See also Julia, *Béziers*, p. 304.
[169] Lot and Fawtier, *Histoire*, II, 151; Langlois, "Doléances," pp. 25-27.
[170] Strayer, "Normandy and Languedoc," p. 54; idem, "Viscounts and Viguiers," pp. 214, 230; Gravier, "Prévôts," pp. 557-58; Dossat, "Tentative de réforme," p. 506. (The statement knows a few exceptions but not many.)
[171] Gravier, "Prévôts," would certainly disagree with my view; above chapter 3 nn. 53-54. He argued that wages were paid only in exceptional circumstances.
[172] *Formulaires*, no. 6, item 317.

he had formally "appointed her husband G. *prévôt* of Beauquesne at the time when the king removed *baillivos* who were in service by purchase and replaced them by his own money."[173]

If as this text suggests Louis carried through on the first phase of making the *prévôts* wage-earners after the crusade, he did not pursue the reform with determination. Except for the *prévôts* in Picardy there is little evidence that the experiment was tried with *bayles* or that it continued for very long. Perhaps the king felt he could not do more. Even though the financial demands of the crusade had largely disappeared, it would have been difficult for him to finance administration at all levels. Moreover, although there was some feeling against the evils of revenue farming (especially where major administration of justice was concerned),[174] there was a sincere attachment to the efficacy of the traditional system when purely fiscal matters were involved. In other words, it was possible to like the idea of paying the *prévôts* wages, to experiment a while and assess the value of the change, and yet to come to the conclusion that no permanent change was necessary. It was possible to do so even in full conscience if other mechanisms of supervision were adequate.

The elaborate system of supervision described earlier was, therefore, the key. But did it always or even usually work at this level, and more particularly did it work in the south? The case of the abbot of the Cistercian monastery of Salvanès (in the old diocese of Rodez) is germane here.[175] At Nîmes in July 1256 he presented a petition to the *enquêteurs* for the return of certain woodlands and usages in and around the forest of Anglès in the western extension of royal territory in Occitania.[176] These had been seized, unjustly according to the abbot's petition, by the former *bayle* of Anglès, Ancellus de Ortolio, and his men,[177] probably one of whom was the present *bayle*, a retired forester named Arnaud Catusse.[178] In a previous investigation, referred to in the records of the case, the *sénéchal* of Carcassonne-Béziers had collected the necessary information so that the *enquêteurs*

---

[173] *HF*, XXIV, 712 no. 48. *Baillivus* is functioning as a generic here for one who accepts a *bail à ferme*. This text is representative of many others in the post-crusade *enquêtes*.

[174] Cf. Strayer, *Royal Domain*, p. 20.

[175] A full summary of the case from transcriptions in the BN Collection Languedoc-Doat, vol. 151, fols. 237-41 verso, is given in Appendix Four. Salvanès (Silvanès or Sylvanès in the present *département* of the Aveyron; the Latin *Salvanesium*) became part of the diocese of Vabres after 1317. The monastery was established circa 1132; *GC*, I, cc. 286-87.

[176] Fol. 238. Anglès, *département* of the Tarn.

[177] Fol. 238 verso; the text *specialiter* accuses Ancellus but it implicates other unspecified royal officials.

[178] Arnaud Catusse had been a forester of Angles about the time of the seizure; *HF*, XXIV, 374.

could make a quick decision.[179] On 13 July they ruled in the abbot's favor.[180] Only a few days later, 21 July 1256, the conscientious *sénéchal* issued an order to Arnaud Catusse, the *bayle*, to enforce the *enquêteurs'* decision.[181]

He did not do so. Having very likely been involved in the original seizure of the abbot's rights, he felt that the *enquêteurs'* decision was wrong. Arnaud, like his predecessor, Ancellus, seems to have been one of those officials whose zeal in office, whose desire to protect the royal rights at all costs, made many of his actions appear criminal to his opponents. The abbot of Saint-Pons-de-Thomières, for one, had brought criminal charges of abuse of power against him and Ancellus before another panel of *enquêteurs*, and though neither man could be accused of leniency in his handling of matters in dispute with the abbot, it is significant that both were exonerated.[182] To Arnaud it was his proper job to give extremely narrow interpretations to ecclesiastical claims on contested property. If he felt that the *enquêteurs* had erred in their judgment, then it was his duty to use all the influence he had to hinder their decision from being carried out. In the case of the abbot of Salvanès, by technical means he was successful for nearly three years.[183]

I would argue that the most important reason for his success in thwarting the *enquêteurs'* decision was the fact that he was a southerner. Louis knew about the situation only through letters and reports. He did not have that personal intimacy with the details of litigation and disputes that made his rule in the north so effective. Eventually he realized that the *bayle* was being wrongly protective of dubious royal rights: "even Louis IX," we have been told, "could not keep his officials from being more royalist than the king."[184] When Louis made this realization he reacted with characteristic probity. He

---

[179] Fol. 238 verso. [180] Fols. 238-238 verso.

[181] Verlaguet, *Cartulaire . . . de Sulvanès*, p. 443.

[182] *HF*, xxiv, 663-65 (Saint-Pons is in the *département* of the Hérault). As a forester before the crusade Arnaud had been convicted of accepting a bribe, but in that case he had simply followed the lead of his superiors—the whole staff of a former *sénéchal* of Carcassonne-Béziers had been found guilty; *HF*, xxiv, 374. His offense, evidently, was not sufficiently serious to lead to his dismissal or to prevent him from being promoted later on.

[183] That he tried to have the decision reversed is implicit in the use of the word *ulterius* on fol. 237 verso. The means are not explicitly stated in the records of the case although he probably brought objections to the witnesses offered by the abbot for the perambulation of the lands which were in dispute; cf. fols. 239 verso and 240. There are several instances of delays in enforcing the decisions of the southern *enquêteurs* after the crusade, but these other delays were the result of the cases being reviewed at Paris before orders of enforcement were issued. In the case of the abbot of Salvanès, the decision was impeded for three years *after* the order of enforcement.

[184] Strayer, *Royal Domain*, p. 19; idem, *Albigensian Crusades*, p. 170.

personally commanded, on 15 July 1259, that the *enquêteurs'* original decision be enforced and that all the profits from the lands and usages at Anglès, which had gone to the royal government during the three years that Arnaud Catusse had managed to delay the execution of the *enquêteurs'* decision, were to be restored immediately to the abbot of Salvanès and his monastery.[185] Once Arnaud learned the king's will, he obeyed quickly; by December the monastery was in full possession of all that rightfully pertained to it.[186]

In the north, as I have suggested, this sort of situation could never have developed. Not only was the king more aware of the operation of government, his *baillis* in the north, being under close personal scrutiny, were unwilling to have their records tarnished by obdurate assistants and subordinates. They were, of course, required to regulate the behavior of lower-level functionaries: *et seront li baillif puni par nous* (the king), *et li autre par les bailliz*.[187] To find the evidence to punish (or reward) them, there were formal methods of investigation such as the regular courts or special inquiries. Among the latter, the great and evidently personally commissioned survey of administration in the *bailliage* of Rouen circa 1260 by the *bailli* Julien de Péronne, stands out.[188] It shows that the *baillis* and their clerks had an impressive machinery for thoroughly inspecting their subalterns' financial activities. But certain informal methods of supervision were perhaps more significant. The *baillis*, urged on by their administrative *élan* and the knowledge that the king would become aware of their style of governance, often took as personal an interest in the work of their *prévôts* as the king took in them.

Consider Mathieu de Beaune, the *bailli* of Vermandois, and the evidence on his relations with his *prévôts* from the investigation launched into his administration of the *bailliage* from 1256 through 1260. The size of the inquiry is itself an indication of the general methods of royal supervision, in this instance by the *enquêteurs*: 508 witnesses and 245 depositions on 63 folios.[189] But the subject now is not the central government's supervision of the *bailli*; it is his informal supervision of his *prévôts*. Mathieu was, first and foremost, familiar to them; he had got to know them and they respected him. "I never saw a better *bailli*," said Philippe d'Ambleny, the *prévôt* of Chauny.[190] More to the point, he was always on the move, much like his peripatetic king, partly to carry out his official judicial circuit but also to visit,

---

[185] Fol. 237 verso.   [186] Fol. 241 verso.   [187] Joinville, chap. CXL.
[188] Strayer, *Royal Domain*, has edited this extraordinary record.
[189] Only part of this has been published; *HF*, XXIV, "Preuves," no. 152, and Jordan, "Jews on Top," n. 34. Cf. Langlois, "Doléances," pp. 32-40.
[190] *HF*, XXIV, "Preuves," no. 152 pt. 31.

to keep abreast of local conditions. Michael Matons, who had served as *prévôt* of Saint-Quentin, Chauny, and other places in the *bailliage* of Vermandois was accustomed to receiving Mathieu in his official capacity, but the *bailli* simply "used to come and sojourn" at the house of Stephanus de Berron, the *prévôt* of Crépy, as well.[191] Not everyone found this intense scrutiny to his liking, but Mathieu seemed so concerned with his reputation that there was little, in terms of bribes or gifts, that one could do to influence him to restrain it. Exasperated, Jean Mahonmes, the *prévôt* of Roye and formerly of Crépy, tried to protect himself by sending his clerk to bribe Mathieu's wife, a possible weak link in his armor of respectability.[192]

Surely not all *baillis* were so conscientious in their different fashions as Julien de Péronne and Mathieu de Beaune. Julien, a brilliant administrator, was attached to the regency of 1270.[193] Mathieu was less the policy maker than the ideal functionary. As the prior of Saint-Sulpice of Pierrefonds put it, "I have never seen a *bailli* who guarded the rights and property of the lord king and his *patria* as well as lord Mathieu."[194] In this he was seconded by the mayor of Montdidier who "had never seen a wiser or better *bailli* among all those he had observed in Vermandois"[195] and by the abbot of La Victoire according to whom Mathieu always acted sensibly.[196] More important, there are plenty of indications that contemporary *baillis*, about whom personally we know much less than Julien or Mathieu, were also becoming more conscientious supervisors and that their subalterns were more closely watched than ever before.

The evidence on this point, while sufficient in one respect, is deficient in another since it comes from the *enquêtes* where the possibility of perjury looms large. But the fact that there are complaints from *conciergerii regis* over *baillis*' seizures of gifts which the latter considered bribes speaks in favor of this increased supervision.[197] Perhaps the gifts were legitimate; nonetheless, the fact that the *baillis* knew enough about what was going on to act is significant in itself. Or consider the remarks of a sergeant who, in passing, speaks of some *prévôts*' loss of their revenue farm during the same term it was granted. He claimed that the deprivation had had adverse effects on him that

---

[191] Ibid., pts. 65, 237, and elsewhere.

[192] Ibid., pts. 71-72; Jordan, "Jews on Top," n. 34.

[193] For discussions of Julien's career, see Strayer, *Royal Domain*; and Griffiths, "New Men," pp. 259-61.

[194] *HF*, xxiv, "Preuves," no. 152 pt. 113.   [195] Ibid., pt. 77.

[196] This remark is in an unpublished portion of the MS, Paris AN J 1028^A no. 4 fol. 61 verso: "idem dominus Mathaeus bene se habuit in ballivia tanquam sapiens homo prout sibi videtur."

[197] See, for example, *HF*, xxiv, 703 no. 18.

should be rectified. Perhaps it did, but from our point of view what is revealing in this case is the evidence that the *bailli* kept close tabs on his revenue farmers.[198] I do not mean to whitewash the *baillis* or to assume that the "domino" effect of supervision—from one level to another—was completely successful. But there was this lower-echelon supervision after 1254, and to exaggerate slightly, there was almost none before the crusade, most especially before 1245.

Did the royal ordinances on the reform of field administration work even below the level of *prévôts*? It is extraordinarily difficult to say. The sergeants (*servientes*, *bedelli*, *gardes*, *custodes*) constituted the most visible of these lower levels. Though their duties varied depending on the environment in which they worked, the sergeants are most readily thought of as police agents,[199] something like the sheriff's deputies in the American West of the nineteenth century. Whether the majority received pay directly from fines is an open question.[200] Some certainly worked for wages.[201] Others possessed farms of low justice: thus, in Normandy there are examples circa 1260 such as Thomas de Baalie who farmed the justice of Foulbec and Ferri du Mesnil who farmed that of Berville-sur-Mer.[202] Still other sergeants were enfeoffed, that is, their offices were heritable; they received no wages but collected a customary amount of the revenues or produce of the property they protected.[203] Whatever the inconsistencies in the ways sergeants were paid, the rate of pay was generally low and, if customary, was being constantly eroded by the steady inflation of the thirteenth century. In many instances they supplemented their inadequate incomes by extortion.[204]

As long as sergeants continued to be chosen at the discretion of local men, it is hard to think what effective controls could have been placed upon them by the central government. Certainly the regulations never attacked the idea of the local selection of sergeants; the regulations simply reiterated the traditional view that *prévôts* should exercise this power with care.[205] Patterns of selection in existence before the crusade were, therefore, likely to continue after it. Merit

[198] Ibid., p. 701 no. 12.

[199] Michel, *Beaucaire*, pp. 56-93, and elsewhere. Decq, "Administration des eaux et forêts," pp. 68, 96-97, 100-102, 104; on the sergeants of Paris, below nn. 264-81.

[200] Decq, "Administration des eaux et forêts," p. 96.

[201] See the fiscal records printed at *HF*, XXI, 278.

[202] Strayer, *Royal Domain*, pp. 114, 117 and note *sub* Berville-sur-Mer.

[203] *HF*, XXIV, 14, 21, 34-35 nos. 87, 141, 267. See also Goineau, *Gisors*, pp. 208-9. Cf. Decq, "Administration des eaux et forêts," pp. 100-102; and, for England, Kimball, *Sergeanty*, pp. 84-89.

[204] Below n. 214. Cf. on this, the well-delineated portrait by Fédou of sergeants as "un type social" in a slightly later period, "Sergents à Lyon."

[205] Joinville, chap. CXL; *Ordonnances*, I, 65, 76ff. See also Gravier, "Prévôts," p. 808, cf. p. 806.

yielded before ties of family, friendship, and geography. One sergeant might convince his local *prévôt* to employ his brother;[206] another, his local viscount to employ his son.[207] Although it was not unknown for a *prévôt* to hire his own brother as his sergeant,[208] this was unlikely since the sergeants were usually drawn from men of lower social status than *prévôts*; and once a sergeant always a sergeant.[209] Often sergeants would themselves informally choose assistants drawn from among their friends and cronies;[210] indeed, this was such a common practice that sub-sergeants became a recognized grade in the field administration.[211] Nothing, of course, could have been more natural than for sergeants to seek help from their long-time friends because they were so readily available: a sergeant was rarely appointed to an area beyond the limit of his native *patria*. If he changed locality at all, the change was geographically trivial— Ribemont to Laon;[212] the forest to the town.[213]

The question that must be answered is whether, given the persistence of these patterns after the crusade, it was still possible to control the sergeants, whose abusive actions were the underlying cause of most of the complaints against the French government in the thirteenth century.[214] It may be assumed that the *enquêteurs* supervised them closely since their records are quite often divided into sections isolating the misdeeds of individual sergeants.[215] It would be logical to expect the well-supervised *baillis* and *prévôts* to keep closer watch on the sergeants than had been usual. The king and the central court, as if recognizing the lack of precision of the reform ordinances which

[206] Galcherus de Vernolio and his brother served the *prévôt* of Laon simultaneously in the 1240s; *HF*, XXIV, 271-95 nos. 2, 24, 32, 49, 106, 142.
[207] Johanninus de Lira and his father Aufredus worked in succession as sergeants in the ban of Breteuil; ibid., pp. 34-35 no. 267.
[208] Gautier served briefly in 1242 as sergeant in Laon under his brother Guillaume Pilate, the *prévôt* there from 1237 to 1247; ibid., pp. 271-95 especially no. 2.
[209] *HF*, XXIV, 703, 727, nos. 18, 228. Cf. Decq, "Administration des eaux et forêts," p. 97.
[210] The texts are a bit vague: P., a sergeant of the *prévôt* of Cappy in 1243-1244, was probably hired by Petrus de Causni, another sergeant, on his own; *HF*, XXIV, 736 no. 46. Imgerranus, a sergeant in the Laonnois circa 1242, was very likely an auxiliary of the regular sergeant, Johannes de Bocunville; p. 280 no. 46. Unless *Prior* was a nickname, how, except by informal cooption, could a churchman like the prior of Saint-Nicolas-aux-Bois have become a royal sergeant (pp. 84 no. 77 and 286 no. 91)?
[211] Decq, "Administration des eaux et forêts," p. 97.
[212] Colardus de Sissi; *HF*, XXIV, 292-93, 296, nos. 135, 137, 157.
[213] Wyetus: at different times, *desarcinator vinorum* (he put out the fires in the royal vineyards) and sergeant, forester of a seigneur, guard of the *prévôt*'s court; ibid., pp. 268 no. 69, 275-93 nos. 22-23, 136.
[214] *Olim*, I, 343-47 xiv, 532 xv. Langlois, "Doléances," pp. 25-27; Strayer, "Viscounts and Viguiers," p. 229; Lot and Fawtier, *Histoire*, II, 151, 154.
[215] See, for example, Carolus-Barré, "Richart Laban"; also *HF*, XXIV, various *enquêtes*.

did little more than require the sergeants to promise to be good,[216] formulated more specific guidelines for various categories of sergeants at irregular intervals. The discretionary power of *servientes forestae* in the matter of fines was limited after 1259;[217] residence requirements were imposed in 1260;[218] and, as we shall see, systematic scrutiny of the sergeants of Paris was enforced at about the same time.

What is also apparent is that the crown felt that it was doing an adequate job policing its police. Vigilante action against sergeants, almost tolerated in the pre-crusade period as a necessary evil,[219] was severely punished after 1254.[220] Yet the frequency of popular vigilante attacks or, more properly, the frequency with which litigation concerning them reached Paris could bear two interpretations. To some it might suggest strongly that the government, even if it refused to admit it, still lagged in restraining its enforcers of the peace. To others it might be taken as evidence that the government had channels open to the localities which should have been used and were available for use in preference to popular retribution. This is a tricky problem, as similar efforts to assess the effectiveness of police review boards in every major city in the United States testify: they exist as a deterrent to corruption; yet, if they find corruption to punish, then there is evidence that existing supervisory mechanisms (of which they are the chief part) are inadequate.

On balance, however, it seems to me that the evidence presented on provincial reform supports the view that it was effective. The *baillis* and *sénéchaux* were appointed by a carefully selective king; this was the first check. Their accounts would be audited two or three times a year at the Exchequer or at Paris. They submitted themselves after 1254 both to cyclical investigations of their conduct in office by the *enquêteurs* and, except in the south, to the inquiries of an almost constantly mobile king. (These two methods of supervision probably did not overlap, for, just as before the crusade, it is likely that the king avoided traveling in areas while the *enquêteurs* were at work there.)[221] The likelihood of their succumbing to local pressures was reduced by

---

[216] Joinville, chap. CXL.
[217] Guillemot, "Forêts de Senlis," p. 192 (citing *Olim*, I, 93 no. vi; this was a special case in which the king's court undid a bad custom. It may have set a precedent elsewhere.)
[218] *Olim*, I, 474 i.   [219] Cf. above chapter 5 n. 30.
[220] Boutaric, *Actes*, I, nos. 44, 495, 679, 1002.
[221] Owing to the sparseness of the evidence, this statement is only partly verifiable, but, for example, the investigation of Vermandois by the *enquêteurs* in 1261 coincided with a period in which Louis did not visit the province except for Compiègne on the southernmost edge; *HF*, xxi, 419. There is also no indication that *enquêtes* were held in Normandy after the crusade (above n. 108; cf. the remarks of Thomson, *Friars in the Cathedral*, p. 75) probably because the king regularly traversed the province doing justice (above n. 73).

the frequency of transfer after 1254; and every such transfer was probably accompanied by at least a cursory inventory of possessions in the *bailliage* or *sénéchaussée*.

Concurrently, the *baillis* seem to have increased their formal and informal supervision, financial and otherwise, of their subordinates—men like the *prévôts*, *bayles*, *viscounts*, and *viguiers*. Such second-level functionaries were themselves susceptible to control by the *enquêteurs*. The royal government experimented with ways, such as paying wages, as a further preventive against corruption. Below this level discipline was perhaps less effective although the *enquêteurs* had cognizance over sergeants, foresters, and the like, and the government did take a series of steps to keep even the most minor functionaries in harness.

Thus far we have described and attempted to evaluate the king's reforms, that is, the program whose outlines he had conceived on the crusade itself, as they affected the Jews, the ecclesiastical Inquisition, and the field administration. The fourth and final set of directives that was part of this program concerns the administration of Paris. Despite Louis's residence in the city, Paris in some respects had a certain independence or autonomy which it was proper for him to respect.[222] After 1254 he set about, or so I shall argue, to define the limits of this autonomy and to do what he could to make sure of three things: first, that the limits were respected on both sides; second, that the aspects of municipal life not coming under direct royal control remained responsive to the needs of the community; and third, that those aspects of city life under royal authority would enjoy the same good government which he was trying to impose in the provinces. To understand how he achieved these goals, inasmuch as they were achieved, we shall briefly have to describe Parisian government before his great reforms.

Up until about 1260 Paris was under the administration of two royal *prévôts* as far as matters pertinent to the crown were concerned. This anomalous situation can be traced to the reign of Philip II Augustus during whose lifetime a *petit bailli*, a judicial agent paid a salary, was employed to complement the work of the then singular *prévôt*, a farmer of royal revenue. But the *petit bailli* was never permitted to become a *grand bailli* either in name (the preferred title of the *petit bailli* of Paris was also *prévôt*) or in fact (no large administrative region was carved out for him as for the provincial *baillis*). The reason appears to

[222] For a charming overview of life in Paris under Saint Louis—stressing the paradox of the king's immanence yet spiritual distance—see Cazelles's brief note "Le Parisien au temps de SL."

have been political. Philip Augustus, the man who did not trust *grands sénéchaux* and *grands chambriers* in his capital, was not likely to trust a *grand bailli* in his city.[223]

The judicial *prévôt* (*petit bailli*) of Paris did not amalgamate his responsibilities with that of the original or, if you will, financial *prévôt*. The judicial *prévôt* had cognizance of royal justice in the city, imposed fines, and supervised administration in a broad sense. The financial *prévôt*, on the other hand, remained a revenue farmer with only limited judicial responsibilities. Historians have always been confused and exasperated about the exact competence of two men with the same title, but from a medieval perspective there was not a significant problem. The tendency, in order to avoid disagreeable tensions, was for united actions in matters of importance. A letter dealing with a prominent judicial affair would be issued in the name of both *prévôts*, and the seal of the *prévôté* was in fact the seal of the *prévôts*, *sigillum prepositorum parisiensium*.[224]

The financial *prévôt* was a second-level functionary whose status duplicated the revenue-farming urban *prévôts* in the provinces of the north—although his location in Paris must have made him the first among equals.[225] The judicial *prévôt*, while lacking the title *grand bailli* and, obviously, the omnicompetence of that agent, for example, in military affairs, was a great royal administrator nonetheless. Paris was so important that from the 1230s onward the judicial *prévôt*, seems to have carried the status *de facto* of the provincial *baillis*. Through his sergeants he controlled most, but not all, police power in Paris. And in this he was, as it were, ahead of the provincial *baillis* most of whose sergeants remained under the direct control of urban *prévôts*.[226] The judicial *prévôt* of Paris also had a very prestigious court, the *Châtelet*, which compared favorably to the courts of the provincial *baillis*. The original jurisdiction of the *Châtelet* extended to cases in and for the *prévôté* (or viscounty as it was sometimes called) of Paris; it had appellate jurisdiction over the several castellanies situated in the viscounty and over petty seigneurial jurisdictions in the city and *banlieue*. Appeals from the *Châtelet* were heard at the *parlement*, paralleling resort from the high courts of the *bailliages* and *sénéchaussées*.[227]

[223] On the developments described in this paragraph, see Borrelli de Serres, *Recherches*, I, 552-56, 558, 570. He described the administration of Paris, on reflection, as *fort bizarre*. See also Cazelles, *Nouvelle histoire de Paris*, p. 177.

[224] Boüard, *Études de diplomatique*, pp. 92-95, 162-63 no. xv.

[225] Borrelli de Serres, *Recherches*, I, 558; Gravier, "Prévôts," p. 551.

[226] Joinville, chap. xxv. See also Strayer, *Administration of Normandy*, p. 103; Gravier, "Prévôts," pp. 665-72, 807 n. 5.

[227] Mortet, "Constitucions," p. 10 nn. 2-3, pp. 13-19; Cazelles, *Nouvelle histoire de Paris*, pp. 183-86. In Normandy, exceptionally, resort from the assizes of the *bailliages* was to the Exchequer; above chapter 3 n. 17.

While Louis was on crusade and after Blanche of Castile's death, public order had degenerated in Paris.[228] This pattern of violence—not anarchy but petty crime during royal absences—appears to have been typical for Western Europe.[229] The king's return, by implication, helped stifle crime,[230] and this may be the reason that there was such rejoicing, *espéciaument* among *li bourgois*, at the king's *entrée* in 1254.[231] Joinville carefully affirms that the king's immediate efforts in 1254 were designed to eradicate "the evil customs by which the people could be oppressed."[232] To do so he used the wage again as a lever. In Joinville's words, "he gave a generous salary to those who should hold [the *prévôté*] in future."[233] This suggests that the appointments of the first *prévôts* after 1254 were contemporary with efforts to reevaluate personnel in the field administration, which certainly seems to have been a reasonable course of action.[234]

Joinville also says that Louis "refused . . . to have the provostship of Paris sold," that this underlay the necessity of paying the *prévôts* salaries.[235] In fact, Joinville's statement can be improved upon. What actually occurred in the first place was that the annual farm of the *prévôté*, which was in the hands of the financial *prévôt*, was transformed into a multi-year farm, a perpetual farm of sorts. It no longer presumed bidding and, often, annual change in the personnel.[236] While

[228] Joinville, chap. CXLI (with the argument on dating, above chapter 5 n. 114). See also *CUP*, nos. 224-25, 227, 231, 237.

[229] Cf. Bellamy, *Crime and Public Order*, pp. 10, 12, 18.

[230] Cf. ibid., p. 11, on a similar pattern in late medieval England.

[231] "Chronique anonyme," *HF*, XXI, 83. See also Tillemont, *Vie de SL*, IV, 45.

[232] Chap. CXLI. Joinville is usually faulted for his compressed narrative of events in Paris (Borrelli de Serres, Cazelles; below n. 236). It is true that if his remarks are used loosely, they will be misleading. But it is also true that what he says, when examined carefully, conforms quite closely to the information obtainable from other more objective records.

[233] Joinville, chap. CXLI.

[234] This conclusion seems to put to rest Borrelli de Serres's argument that Joinville overlooked the early crucial phase in the reform of the *prévôté* in order to follow the hagiographic traditions which emphasized Louis's selection of Étienne Boileau as *prévôt* somewhat later (below n. 240). For discussions of this early phase of reform, 1254-1259, see Borrelli de Serres, *Recherches*, I, 556; Cazelles, *Nouvelle histoire de Paris*, p. 178; Lot and Fawtier, *Histoire*, II, 373-74.

[235] Joinville, chap. CXLI. Formerly scholars supported this view without qualification; see Lespinasse and Bonnardot, *Livre des métiers*, p. x; Huré, "Étude sur les origines du notariat," pp. 30, 34; cf. Gravier, "Prévôts," p. 554 n. 3. This now outmoded view coopted to it the idea that the gracious jurisdiction or voluntary jurisdiction of the notaries of the *Châtelet* began to function about this time (cf. Huré). Latter-day critics have seldom differentiated the two arguments, the first having some truth, the second having none; see, for example, Boüard, *Études de diplomatique*, pp. 49-56. The best recent study is by Carolus-Barré, "Juridiction gracieuse," pp. 418, 434-35 and passim. Cf. also Colliette, *Vermandois*, II, 652.

[236] Borrelli de Serres, *Recherches*, I, 552-53, 556, 558-59 n. 1. Showing that this was what actually occurred was an important accomplishment of Borrelli; his ranting

there was certainly a period of transition involved,[237] this innovation was rather rapidly followed by the absorption of the functions of the financial *prévôt* by the judicial *prévôt*, that is, by the combination of the two offices into one.[238]

Louis was careful in making his selection of the man who would first bear the burden of the combined offices: "everywhere throughout the Kingdom he had enquiries made to find a man who would deal out fair and firm justice, sparing the rich no more than the poor."[239] The man he finally found was Étienne Boileau.[240] With this appointment, tentative efforts came to an end and a full-scale reorganization of royal administration in Paris was undertaken. Étienne, beginning in 1260 or 1261, was in office for over eight years, received a large annual salary (perhaps three hundred pounds), identified himself closely with the rank and status of provincial *baillis*, and, indeed, by the end of his term of office, was even called *bailli* occasionally.[241]

Louis could hardly have made a superior choice. Joinville's praise is exuberant. To hear him speak, Étienne was the perfect administrator and people flocked to Paris to live under his benign rule.[242] Scholars, historians particularly, have a healthy constitutional distrust of exuberance, but in this case the objective evidence shows with extraordinary clarity that Étienne's impact on Parisian government and life was profound. The crown's fiscal accounts for the city become much more detailed around 1260;[243] and about the same time the diplomatics of the *prévôté* begin to show improvement. Verbal formalities led to the standardization of *prévôtine* documents in the 1260s; a modified seal must have been issued concurrently.[244] Unfortunately the precise date of the latter is unknown except that it occurred after 1246 and before 1276. The most logical date, since the seal had originally carried a plural legend, would be about 1261. Additional support for this date is the fact that by 1261 in the provinces income from the use of the seal and the control of its uses were taken

---

against Joinville in other places was, however, unnecessary. I suspect from the tone of his remarks that the judicious Delisle also thought that Borrelli's criticisms were a bit overdone; cf. *HF*, xxiv, "Chronologie," p. 24.

[237] Preceding note, and Lot and Fawtier, *Histoire*, ii, 373.

[238] Borrelli de Serres, *Recherches*, i, 564-65.

[239] Joinville, chap. cxli.

[240] Ibid. See also Borrelli de Serres, *Recherches*, i, pp. 548, 563-65; Cazelles, *Nouvelle histoire de Paris*, p. 179; Lespinasse and Bonnardot, *Livre des métiers*, pp. ix-xvi; Wallon, *SL*, ii, 54-57. Cf. Gravier, "Prévôts," p. 551.

[241] Borrelli de Serres, *Recherches*, i, 566-67; Lot and Fawtier, *Histoire*, ii, 374.

[242] Joinville, chap. cxli.

[243] Cf. Borrelli de Serres, *Recherches*, i, 568.

[244] Boüard, *Études de diplomatique*, pp. 95-97. Cf. *Formulaires*, no. 6, item 323.

over by the *baillis* from the urban *prévôts*. If the crown was giving thought to the proper employment of the seal in one context, arguably it was doing so at the same time in another.[245]

The new *prévôt* also attempted to systematize the practical administration of the *prévôté*. It is not simply that he united the financial and judicial functions of two distinct offices, a customary means of administrative innovation in the Middle Ages.[246] He did much more. Paris was a great commercial community. It was Étienne who systematized royal controls over the merchant sector of the city. He formalized the position of the head of the merchants, the so-called *prévôt* of the merchants, in the formal statement of regulations of the crafts and gilds, the *Livre des métiers*.[247] According to Joinville, although he does not mention the role of the *Livre* specifically, Étienne's actions led to a significant increase in the commercial prosperity of the city.[248]

The details of craft activity related in the *Livre* are not directly relevant here. (Lecaron has discussed them masterfully.)[249] But the sense of order which permeates the book is pertinent. It was the *Livre des métiers* which first attributed the title *prévôt* to the head of the merchants.[250] Although the duties associated with this office went back very far,[251] the importance of their formalization in writing and the imposition of a model, the office of *prévôt royal*, from current administration ought not to be underestimated. These words imposed self-perceptions. It is likely that the "new" *prévôt* of the merchants (one is known by name within three years of Étienne's appointment)[252] acted like the *prévôt royal*, imitated, that is, the obvious model, Étienne Boileau himself. The *Livre* called the four counselors of the *prévôt* of the merchants *échevins*, again borrowing terminology but from a different administrative system, the royal communes.[253] The head of the merchants had advisers long before Étienne Boileau chose to call them *échevins*, but the choice reinforces the idea, if it needs reinforcing, that the king and Étienne were determined to make administration in Paris as clear, orderly, and neatly hierarchical as possible.

[245] Cf. Gravier, "Prévôts," pp. 560-61.
[246] Cf. Ben-Ami, *Social Change*, p. 184.
[247] Lecaron, "Origines de la municipalité parisienne," pt. 1, p. 110.
[248] Joinville, chap. CLXI.
[249] Lecaron, "Origines de la municipalité parisienne." Lespinasse and Bonnardot published the *Livre*. See also Mahieu's brief treatment ("Livre des métiers") in the recent *Siècle de SL*, and the specialized remarks of Geremek, *Salariat*, pp. 27-44.
[250] Lecaron, "Origines de la municipalité parisienne," pt. 1, p. 110; Cazelles, *Nouvelle histoire de Paris*, p. 200.
[251] Lecaron, "Origines de la municipalité parisienne," pt. 1, pp. 110-11; Boüard, *Études de diplomatique*, p. 18 n. 4.
[252] Boüard, *Études de diplomatique*, p. 18 n. 4.
[253] Lecaron, "Origines de la municipalité parisienne," pt. 1, p. 111; Cazelles, *Nouvelle histoire de Paris*, p. 201.

Following from the remarks in the preceding paragraph, the relative powers of the crown and the merchants were carefully defined. High justice was the crown's monopoly, but otherwise mercantile administration was comparatively autonomous. The *prévôt* of the merchants or, rather, his tribunal, whose composition, unfortunately, is uncertain, had direct jurisdiction over the commercial activities of the merchants of the corporation of the city and, possibly, seigneurial jurisdiction as the owner or representative of the owners of certain streets in the city.[254] Insofar as the *prévôt royal* was involved in these matters at all, it was to adjudicate abuses of power by municipal authorities.[255] When merchants of Paris came into conflict with feudatories or corporate bodies outside the *prévôt royal*'s competence, the court merchant of Paris or the court ordinarily having jurisdiction over the other party might exercise authority depending on the nature of the dispute, but the decision of either could be appealed to *parlement*.[256]

Just as purely administrative and judicial aspects of city government were neatly blocked out in the post-crusade period, so too was the division of responsibility in the execution of public works projects. The royal *prévôt* had cognizance of the primary thoroughfares while the *prévôt* of the merchants had oversight of the works which were more directly limited to the commercial sector. Louis was surely behind this careful division, which put ultimate supervisory powers into the *prévôt royal*'s hands.[257]

I am arguing in favor of Louis's personal role because already in the period before the crusade the king had cautioned his *baillis* to exercise restraint in funding public works projects.[258] There is also evidence that he remained very attentive to questions raised by such projects after the crusade.[259] In 1266, for example, he visited the Auxerrios, a trip which coincided with the approval of the petition of the burghers of Auxerre that Parisians having property in the town should contribute to the municipal bridge works just as the Auxerrois

[254] Buché, "Essai sur l'ancienne coutume de Paris," p. 47; cf. Lombard-Jourdan, "Fiefs," pp. 301-58, and Lot and Fawtier, *Histoire*, II, 374 n. 2. For comparative purposes (England), see Hemmeon, *Burgage Tenure*, pp. 104-5 and 106 n. 1. There were other independent jurisdictions—churchmen, of course, and for that matter, the maintenance crew for the bells of Notre-Dame (Vidier, "Marguillers laics de Notre-Dame").

[255] Lecaron, "Origines de la municipalité parisienne," pt. 1, p. 118.

[256] Ibid., pp. 141, 145-67, 171-74. Cf. below n. 260 on Louis IX's intervention in a dispute between the *bourgeois* of Paris and the *bourgeois* of Auxerre.

[257] Lecaron, "Travaux publics de Paris." See also idem, "Origines de la municipalité parisienne," pt. 1, pp. 136-38.

[258] See the argument advanced in chapter 4 nn. 189-93.

[259] Lachiver, *Mantes*, p. 63 no. 91.

who had property in Paris made contributions to public works there.[260]

No separation of responsibilities and spheres of influence could have worked perfectly. Inevitably, the crown's or the merchants' legitimate activities would come into conflict. An important illustration of this concerns the king's building program in Paris after the crusade. In the 1250s, Louis (and his brother Alfonse) recommenced the construction projects and initiated new ones that had been delayed since he swore the crusader's vow.[261] A fragmentary financial account for 1261 details some of the king's expenditures, many of which, significantly, were for the expansion of the *prévôt royal*'s headquarters, the *Châtelet*.[262] Although the building program must have affected certain trades very favorably, expansion also ran the risk of disrupting the shops and, therefore, livelihood of merchants in the vicinity of the construction. Characteristically, in 1263 Louis adjusted his building efforts in favor of these men and women, the *merciers*.[263]

To a degree, this adjustment was not simply a reaction to the complaints of the *merciers* but was part of a broader sensitivity to the uncertainties of commercial life.[264] I do not want to overstress this point. Louis IX did not understand economic trends (who did in the High Middle Ages?). He had deeply seated religious and aristocratic prejudices against business activity as his views on usury show. But he could and did recognize the need for some sort of agreed upon procedures in commercial relations, a fact emphasized by his sponsorship of the *Livre des métiers*. He could appreciate that certain exactions might be harmful to the prosperity of his city. Thus, in 1256 he suppressed royal levies on fodder entering Paris by boat.[265] In other words, the separate jurisdictions and responsibilities which suffused life in Paris were not used as an excuse by Louis to retreat from the burdens of rulership. He never let himself find comfort in the proposition that if

[260] On the trip to the Auxerrois, see Chardon, *Auxerre*, p. 199 (Louis was at Regennes on 24 July). For the *conventio* of 1266, see Lebeuf, *Auxerre*, II, "Recueil de monumens, chartes, etc." (separate pagination), p. 63 no. 136.

[261] See the argument advanced in chapter 4 nn. 183-88.

[262] *HF*, XXII, 744-45. Besides these financial records we have deeds of purchase and miscellaneous material detailing the building program; *Layettes*, III, nos. 4342, 4351-53, 4391, 4477. See also Tillemont, *Vie de SL*, IV, 117. Alfonse had purchased several tracts of land for the construction of a palace in Paris; *Layettes*, III, nos. 4106-8, 4140, 4200, 4603, 4622-24, 4649-50. See also Boutaric, *SL et Alfonse*, pp. 96-97, and Jordan, "Contrats d'acquisition royaux," n. 10.

[263] Biollay, "Anciennes halles de Paris," pp. 297, 307, 338.

[264] He evidently gave alms to unemployed craftsmen; cf. below chapter 7 n. 32.

[265] Lecaron, "Origines de la municipalité parisienne," pt. 1, p. 106. Note the date—before Étienne's appointment—and notice also that Joinville refers to the abolition of such levies in Paris *before* he discusses Étienne's appointment; chap. CXLI.

something went wrong it was someone else's fault. He could be hard on those who failed to fulfill their obligations, but he never left it at that: he corrected their mistakes.

In no sphere would this be more clearly demonstrated than in the king's attempts to quell violence in Paris. Uppermost in Louis's mind on the very morrow of his return to the city in 1254 was not administrative confusion, public works projects, building programs, or commercial prosperity; it was order. And whatever his presence itself in Paris may have accomplished, he felt—after the problems of 1253—that something had to be done with the institutional arrangements by which criminals were brought to justice. The center of his concern was the police of the city. The royal *prévôt* employed sergeants.[266] Parallel to the royal police in the city was the commercial watch, *guet*, which was financed by a levy imposed by the royal government on the merchants or the merchant gilds.[267] Despite the assertions of earlier scholars, it is unlikely that this differentiation was purely a matter of accounting. That is, there were indeed two police forces in Paris—although, as might be expected, ultimately they were both under the control of the *prévôt royal*.

If Paris, despite the existence of two police forces, was still poorly watched over in the first half of the thirteenth century, it was partly because the levy for the commercial patrols was absurdly low.[268] It is not known when this fact began to penetrate royal thinking. Some tentative effort to raise the amount of the levy might very well have been undertaken on the eve of the crusade. Evidence is hard to come by, but there are indications during the regency of Blanche of Castile that merchants were complaining about the rates. It seems improbable that they complained over payments that had not been elevated.[269]

As usual it was after the crusade that more than a merely cursory or formal effort was made to solve the problem of poor policing in Paris. The first indication of this is the fact that a great many more merchants became dissatisfied with the exaction of money for the watch.[270] The payment traditionally had been in the form of a lump sum,[271] which, if the previous argument is correct, must have been increasing in size during the crusade and immediately after. The latest figures we have on the lump sum payment (for 1253) give an

[266] Even when there had been two *prévôts* only the judicial functionary had police authority; Borrelli de Serres, *Recherches*, I, 553.
[267] Discussions of this complex subject start from Brussel, *Usage général des fiefs*, I, especially p. 471. See also Cazelles, *Nouvelle histoire de Paris*, pp. 186-88.
[268] Cf. Lespinasse and Bonnardot, *Livre des métiers*, p. 110n.
[269] Ibid.
[270] Ibid., p. 185 and index entries on *guet*, p. 337.
[271] Borrelli de Serres, *Recherches*, I, 565 n. 3.

assessment of one hundred pounds per term (probably three hundred per year).[272]

Seemingly, negotiations with representatives of the whole community of merchants to get the lump sum increased were not so successful as Louis had hoped. The merchants wanted more protection; they did not want to pay more for it. Consequently, about a year after he returned from crusade Louis decided, no doubt with the consent of the merchants, to modify procedures, and he began negotiations with separate gilds for separate assessments.[273] (In terms of more general trends in record-keeping throughout the administration, this tendency to break things down into their component parts became a common aspect of post-crusade government.) But this method of assessment had negative repercussions. Perhaps the king was too liberal in granting exemptions.[274] During the Ascension term 1255, the royal *prévôt(s)* received only 73 pounds from the levy for the commercial watch. What is more, they claimed expenditures of 107 pounds,[275] a discrepancy that could not help but cry out in favor of further reforms. The royal sergeants (*servientes Castelleti*), on the other hand, had been supported in the same term with 112 pounds.[276] Assuming a rough equality in income per term, about 600 pounds per year were being spent on the Paris police forces, commercial and royal.

A reasonable question, and one which will crop up again, is why the number of merchant police was not simply reduced to coincide with the amount of revenue collected under the term *guet*. I have hinted before at what I think the answer is.[277] It is very likely, as in the twin public works administrations, that the two police forces had somewhat separate responsibilities, the royal police guarding those areas of the city given over to the functions of the central government, the merchant police guarding the commercial sections.[278] Despite the reluctance of the merchants to contribute more money, Louis felt it was his

[272] Lespinasse and Bonnardot, *Livre des métiers*, p. 110n.; it is not necessarily to be supposed that each term yielded equal revenue (Gravier, "Prévôts," p. 572), but the one hundred pound figure is suggestive.
[273] Borrelli de Serres, *Recherches*, I, 565 (nn. 2-3), 568. Cf. *Olim*, I, 584-85 vi.
[274] Lespinasse and Bonnardot, *Livre des métiers*, p. cxlii, also title XI, article 10. See also Fagniez, *Études sur l'industrie*, p. 47; and Cazelles, *Nouvelle histoire de Paris*, p. 186. It has not been possible to determine how many exemptions were owed directly to Saint Louis and how many were already traditional in his day.
[275] The documents are printed in Brussel, *Usage général des fiefs*, I, 471 (they are also available in *HF*, XXII, 742-44).
[276] Ibid.
[277] Cazelles was also struck by the peculiarities of the payment system (*Nouvelle histoire de Paris*, pp. 187-88).
[278] Early fourteenth century evidence, for what it is worth, is equivocal. Cf. Lecaron, "Origines de la municipalité parisienne," pt. 1, p. 115, and Borrelli de Serres, *Recherches*, I, 565 n. 4, 571.

responsibility to see that the commercial sections were adequately protected. His subsidy for the merchant police must be understood in terms of this attitude.

As commercial prosperity increased, that subsidy increased. By All Saints 1261 the commercial police were receiving almost 350 pounds *pro mutuo* from the royal government (the merchants contributed only 55) to support a force of twenty patrolling foot sergeants, an unspecified number of sergeants with stationary posts, and twelve mounted sergeants.[279] In comparison with expenditures in 1255 the commercial police force had grown fourfold. But the legal fiction was preserved. Officials continued to regard the *guet* as the merchants' police even though the brunt of support came from direct royal revenue. To have acquiesced in the elimination of the traditional differentiation of the two police forces would have been to introduce a new custom which would have relieved the commercial sector of a duty which Louis IX thought was rightfully theirs.

Concurrent with the attempt to establish a workable financial system to support the police, Louis began a reorganization of the internal structure of the *guet*. Feeling perhaps that the merchant patrols were too undisciplined and unsupervised, he appointed a professional captain for them, giving him all the appropriate paraphernalia of his new office. The formal title he bore was *Custos* or *Chevalier du Guet*.[280] Although there may have been some sergeant who served as head of the *guet* before Louis's innovation,[281] the importance and dignity of the men chosen for the captaincy beginning in 1260 are good evidence that a fundamental change was envisioned. In order of appointment, the list included Geoffroy de Courferaud (1260), Guillaume de Garennes (1261), Adam d'Ybly (1262), Jean de Rusellières (1265).[282] These men were important administrators in their own right and sometimes scions of administrative families of knightly status. The "de Courferauds," for example, had a member of their family, Arnoul, as *bailli* of Caen in the late 1250s.[283] The connections of Guillaume de Garennes are less certain, but he too may have been a member of a distinguished administrative family.[284] Jean de Rusel-

[279] Brussel, *Usage général des fiefs*, I, 471 (*HF*, XXII, 744-45). We have no figures on the royal sergeants, assuming that they were still being distinguished in the financial records.
[280] Ibid. (and *HF*, XXII, 743 n. 5). See also *HF*, XXIV, "Chronologie," p. 23; and Cazelles, *Nouvelle histoire de Paris*, p. 188 (apparently following Borrelli).
[281] Borrelli de Serres, *Recherches*, I, 565 n. 3.
[282] Brussel, *Usage général des fiefs*, I, 471. See also Borrelli de Serres, *Recherches*, I, 564 n. 4.
[283] Cf. Porée, "Note sur Pèlerin Latinier," p. 62.
[284] It is possible that Guillaume de Garennes was Brussel's rendering into French of the Latin *nomen* "Guillelmus de Crannis" which really should have been put into French

lières served the king in a number of high administrative capacities before his appointment to the captaincy according to the wax tablets of the treasury kept by the chamberlain, Jean Sarrasin.[285]

The king, through Étienne Boileau, and Étienne, through the capable captains of the police, helped change popular perceptions of life in Paris. "There was no malefactor or thief or murderer who dared to remain in Paris who was not forthwith hanged or exterminated. Neither kinship, nor birth, nor gold, nor silver could save him."[286] Of course, the fact that there were more police and that they were more efficiently organized is not the only reason—indeed it may have been the least important reason—that life in Paris improved.[287] If Paris turned around, it was as much due to impersonal causes, such as the ready availability of jobs in a period of commercial prosperity, as to the existence of more and better police. Probably the fundamental factor was that to which we constantly return, the presence of the king, which imparted, in ways still only partly understood, the sense or perception that order should be maintained.

In fact an administration like this in Paris and throughout the kingdom was still quite primitive. At base, it depended largely upon one man who took his personal role as a ruler seriously and on a small group of men who shared with him common assumptions about government—Julien de Péronne, Mathieu de Beaune, Étienne Boileau, the *enquêteurs*, and a few others. The impersonal improvements on which I have laid such stress constituted an elaborate structure of supervision and a kind of code of ethical behavior for everyone from Jews to royal functionaries to municipal officials in Paris. All these so-called impersonal improvements, however, drew most of their vitality from the king. Hence it is no surprise that many of the reforms which illuminated the realm in the middle-thirteenth century, even if the forms persisted, lost much of their luster on the death of their creator. But the *imago* of an ideal kingdom, one that had existed briefly on this earth, endured as a constant theme in royal propaganda and in both popular and learned criticisms of future kings.[288] The memory of Saint Louis hung heavily over the later Capetians. To some of them, no doubt, it was more oppressive than it was worth.

as Guillaume d'Escrennes. If so, Guillaume was part of an administrative family of no mean importance (Griffiths, "New Men," p. 238), one member of which, Gervaise, had been a fellow-crusader with the king and had recrived a royal pension (*Layettes*, III, no. 3986). Two other members, Jean and Galeran, were *sénéchal* of Carcassonne and *bailli* of Étampes, respectively; Appendix One.

[285] *HF*, xx, 359: J. de Rosilère.
[286] Joinville, chap. CXLI.
[287] Cf. Stead, *Police of Paris*, pp. 15-16; and Frégier, *Histoire de la police de Paris*, I, chap. 1, esp. pp. 7, 10-11.
[288] Below chapters 7 (nn. 1-9) and 8 (nn. 24-39).

·7·

THE MOST CHRISTIAN KING

The epithet *most Christian* was not official in Louis IX's reign, but already in his lifetime and soon after his death chroniclers were searching for the perfect phrase to describe him; some, like a liturgist in Aix-en-Provence, did choose *christianissimus*.[1] Matthew Paris, on the other hand, described the living Louis as the pinnacle of the kings of the earth.[2] A provincial chronicler, struck by the king's virtues as a judge, referred to him as *Ludovicus Justus*.[3] And the chronicler of Limoges, unable to come up with a sufficiently striking epithet, contented himself by stating simply that there had never been a better prince than Louis IX.[4]

It was, however, the Italian chronicler Salimbene who hit upon the most appropriate description, "saint." Salimbene, who died in 1288,[5] was using this word long before the king was officially canonized in 1297.[6] *Sanctus*, of course, is ambiguous; it may designate sanctity either in a technical sense or more loosely. It is not entirely unreasonable to suppose that Salimbene meant it technically since the first official requests for Louis's canonization went back to 1275.[7] Moreover, in the popular imagination Louis was considered a true saint from the moment of his death, as the rapid proliferation of his miracles attests.[8] Salimbene was to report some of these miracles in his native Parma.[9]

In this chapter, I want to explore some themes of Louis's rulership which helped justify the attributions of excellence and holiness made by his contemporaries, themes which were developed largely in

---

[1] Marbot, "Deux bréviaires," p. 390. See also Strayer, "France: The Holy Land, the Chosen People, and the Most Christian King," pp. 306-7.

[2] MP, v, 466.

[3] *Chronicon Girardi ab Arvernia*, HF, XXI, 215.

[4] HF, XXI, 777. See also the description of an anonymous chronicler, HF, XXI, 85.

[5] Musetti, *Fra' Salimbene*, p. 47; Doren, *Chronik*, I, xvi; Scalia in Salimbene, *Cronica*, II, 961; Laureilhe, *Routes d'Europe*, p. 148.

[6] Salimbene, *Cronica*, I, 429, 438, 444, 543, 629; II, 659, 661, 686, 707, 761, 802, 808, 821, 862, 865.

[7] GC, XII, "Instrumenta," cc. 78-79 no. CII.

[8] Delaborde, "Fragments de l'enquête," pp. 15, 44, 60, 62 (nos. 172, 254, 262). See also Lecoy de La Marche, SL, *son gouvernement*, p. 341; Carolus-Barré, "Enquêtes," p. 19.

[9] Salimbene, *Cronica*, II, 707, 865.

response to the failure of the king's first crusade and his hopes for success in a future one. Each, in its own way, illuminates not only the inner workings of the king's personality but also his vision of the world in which he lived. The themes, three in number, concern the forms of royal charity and devotion, the crown's attitude toward Christian warfare, and the reform of the royal coinage, a traditional symbol of a monarch's effort to unite his realm.

The twelfth century German mystic Hildegard of Bingen once called charity the most beautiful friend that a king could have.[10] Perhaps by charity she meant the mutual love of a king and his subjects, but such love, at least on the king's part, would reveal itself in traditional philanthropic forms. Now, it is a commonplace of studies of Louis IX to say that he was charitable.[11] Though an accurate reckoning of the amount of money he actually spent on charity would be impossible to make, it was certainly large. Tillemont estimated it very crudely at two hundred thousand pounds.[12] Some chroniclers talk about alms reaching two or three thousand pounds per year, even seven thousand pounds.[13] All the major narrative sources (whose information is frequently verifiable by deeds of gift in the royal archives or in cartularies) list in tedious detail the plethora of donations and endowments which proceeded from the king's hand.[14] Louis's testament is little more than the page of an account book detailing an enormous number of donations to religious institutions (this set a pattern which the later Capetians slavishly followed perhaps to the detriment of their financial solvency).[15]

Granted that Louis's expenditures for religious devotion were enormous, still the manifestations of his charity were limited to a few specific types which help define his character and his concerns. It is not always possible to explain his interest in one type or another—or, more properly, it is possible only to hint at his motives. Thus, one can identify a thread in Louis's charity which seems to have been cathar-

[10] *PL*, cxcvii, c. 180: "pulcherriman amicam regis, videlicet charitatem."
[11] Tillemont, *Vie de SL*, v, 307, cf. iv, 207-8; Wallon, *SL*, ii, 482-89.
[12] *Vie de SL*, v, 307.
[13] Anonymous of Saint-Denis, *HF*, xx, 52; Delaborde, "Une Oeuvre nouvelle," p. 284.
[14] The narrative sources, not yet cited, which have valuable information include the lives of Louis IX by Geoffroy de Beaulieu, *HF*, xx, 11-12; by Guillaume de Nangis, *HF*, xx, 406-7, 650; and by Guillaume de Saint-Pathus, *HF*, xx, 75-77; the chronicle known as *Primat*, *HF*, xxiii, 16; and several anonymous chronicles (*HF*, xxi, 84, 200; xxiii, 353). Other works will be mentioned in the subsequent discussion; and the assertion that documentary material sustains the narrative sources will also be proved.
[15] Louis's testament may be found in *Layettes*, iv, no. 5638. On the later Capetians, see Brown, "Royal Salvation."

tic. Money or goods seized illegally by royal officials, for which no restitutions could be made owing to the death of the injured party and
the absence of heirs of the body, were allocated by the king as alms.
Similarly, confiscations of money and property from usurers needed
to be purified. Except when they could be spent on the crusade, the
king turned over the proceeds of these gains to the charitable
uses of bishops.[16] The episcopal hierarchy, beginning in 1258, gladly
sanctioned these efforts.[17]

Another and not the least important manifestation of Louis's religious devotion was his attraction to the two great orders of friars—the
Franciscans and the Dominicans. This closeness has been dealt with at
some length in preceding chapters;[18] and many scholars have made a
great deal out of it.[19] Louis's "involvement" with the friars puts him
squarely in the center of the aggressive Christianity of the mid-
thirteenth century. Contemporaries criticized it, considered it an
exaggeration.[20] But this did not cause him to forsake his association
with the mendicants. Arguments contrary to this, based mainly on
elitist criticisms of the king and the diminution of the percentage of
mendicant *enquêteurs*, after the crusade, are not convincing.[21]

On the one hand, half of the post-crusade *enquêteurs*, as has been
pointed out before, were mendicants.[22] Moreover, foundations and
endowments of mendicant convents continued uninterruptedly after
the crusade:[23] we have royal records for Normandy of grants to the
Dominicans of Rouen, of permission to build a convent given to the
Franciscans of Rouen, and of the assignment of a building site to the
Franciscans of Falaise, all in the late 1250s.[24] Dufeil has discovered
and edited a royal order of September 1257 exempting the Dominicans from all tolls throughout the realm.[25] And the influence of men-

[16] *Layettes*, III, nos. 4502, 4507, 4510-38, 4541-48, and IV, no. 5091; *GC*, XIV, "Instrumenta," c. 161. See also Tillemont, *Vie de SL*, IV, 207-8.

[17] *Layettes*, III, nos. 4511 (Eudes of Rouen), 4516 (Richard of Avranches), 4517 (Foulques of Lisieux), 4518 (Gui of Bayeux), 45234 (Jean of Coutances), and 4530 (Thomas
of Sées).

[18] Above chapters 3 (nn. 107-8) and 5 (nn. 163-64).

[19] Little, "SL's Involvement" and *Frater Ludovicus*. See also Wyse, "Enquêteurs," and
Callebaut, "Deuxième croisade de SL."

[20] Above chapter 5 n. 163.

[21] Cf. Little, "SL's Involvement" and *Frater Ludovicus*, pp. 148-60, 165-80. Griffiths,
Counselors, pp. 332-33 nn. 224-25, for different but equally persuasive reasons rejects
Little's conclusions.

[22] Above chapter 3 n. 142. See also Wyse, "Enquêteurs," pp. 52-54.

[23] For narrative sources, see Salimbene, *Cronica*, I, 457; Guillaume de Chartres, *HF*,
XX, "Vita sancti Ludovici"; and the canonization sermon of Boniface VIII, *HF*, XXIII,
150. Cf. Laurent, Bloch and Doinel, p. 289; *Layettes*, III, no. 4365. See also Tillemont,
Vie de SL, V, 305.

[24] Delisle, *Cartulaire normand*, nos. 559, 563, 576-77.

[25] *Guillaume de Saint-Amour*, p. 356 no. iv.

dicants on the king's second crusade was immense.[26] On his death even Louis's books were divided between the Dominicans and Franciscans of Paris, and the Dominicans of Compiègne; among regular clergy only the monks of Royaumont, his mother's monastery, got a portion of the bequest.[27]

The friars have traditionally made much of their association with the king, perhaps too much. Dominicans point out with great pride that he once dined with the Angelic Doctor.[28] The Franciscans have gone so far as to claim him as a lay brother on the basis of a very late tradition.[29] Members of both mendicant orders have incorporated Louis's name into the lists of saints proper to them.[30] In fact, however, as the traditional mendicant orders became more staid and sophisticated in the course of the thirteenth century, Louis sought out those offshoots of the great orders which seemed more effectively to be preserving the original fervor of the movement. On the female side these were comprised of Dominican and Franciscan nuns and more loosely organized female religious known as *béguines*; on the male side they included the Pied Friars, Sack Friars, Crutched Friars, Carmelites, Augustinians, and so forth.[31]

Louis's support for mendicant nunneries and *béguinages* was part of a broader program of charity for vulnerable segments of society and for poor women in particular. In Joinville's words,

> . . . the king daily gave countless generous alms to poor religious, to poor hospitals, to poor sick people, to other poor convents, to poor gentlemen and gentlewomen and girls, to fallen women, to poor widows and women in childbed, and to poor craftsmen who from old age or sickness were unable to work or follow their trade.[32]

What is striking about Joinville's description is that his specific examples tally so nicely with the objective evidence. Alms to hospitals, for example, were a distinctive aspect of Louis's charity. Thus he built

[26] Callebaut, "Deuxième croisade de SL.," p. 286 et passim.

[27] Cf. Delaborde, "Bâtiments," p. 161.

[28] The incident is reported in Foster, *Life of Saint Thomas*, p. 45 (from the *Life* by Bernard Gui).

[29] di Pietro, *Vita de san Luigi*, pp. 157-73. Franciscan zealousness to adopt Louis IX as one of their own has been gently upbraided by Bertaux, "Les Saints Louis," pp. 619-20.

[30] Husman, *Tropen*, pp. 100, 155-56.

[31] In general, on the female religious, McDonnell, *Begunes*, p. 224; and Le Grand, "Béguines," p. 305; both McDonnell (pp. 226-28) and Le Grand (p. 342) show that gifts to the *béguines* became a frequently imitated activity by the later Capetians. For a good general introduction to the male orders, see Fontette, "Mendiants supprimés." See also Emery, *Friars*, p. 8.

[32] Joinville, chap. CXLII. I have substituted "craftsmen" (from Shaw's translation, p. 342) for "minstrels," Hague's word, which seems out of place. *Menestriers*, used in the original OF, however, does bear both meanings.

or sustained by his endowments the hospitals at Beauvais, Pontoise, Saint-Cloud, Vernon, Compiègne, Paris, Verneuil, Lorris, and Bellème. Of course, the extent of these endowments varied considerably depending on the particular needs of the hospitals. Louis's satisfaction with the work of the Maison-Dieu of Saint-Jean of Beauvais was expressed in May 1261 both in a confirmation of its traditional privileges and the special grant of the right to take live wood in the forest of Hez.[33] The hospital at Pontoise received a succession of gifts beginning about 1260;[34] the Maison-Dieu of Saint-Cloud was endowed with a perpetual rent of six *sétiers* of grain probably about the same time;[35] and numerous similar gifts were accorded to the hospital at Vernon in Normandy beginning, evidently, in 1256 with the king's general tour of the duchy.[36]

A great deal more royal support, starting in 1257, went into the expansion of Compiègne's Hôtel-Dieu. Louis himself carried the first patient into the rebuilt building in 1259. And his interest in the hospital never diminished after that date.[37] Likewise, the hospital for the blind at Paris, the famous Quinze-Vingts, received generous endowments continuously from perhaps as early as 1254, that is, from the time Louis first began to take seriously the idea of reforming Paris.[38] But even as these major efforts were underway, the king never ignored the isolated plea of an impecunious hospital for support. The period from 1260 until his death saw him endow the hospital at Verneuil with mills and certain agricultural rights;[39] it saw him accord privileges in the royal forests to the Hôtel-Dieu of Lorris;[40] and, as late as 1268 (after, that is, he had commenced in earnest preparations for a new crusade), he assigned similar privileges to the hospital of Bellème.[41]

As Joinville made clear, however, Louis did not confine his alms to institutions. His direct, personal charity to the sick, especially lepers,

[33] Lépinois, "Recherches . . . de Clermont," p. 195 no. cxv[1]; Leblond, *Cartulaire . . . Hôtel-Dieu*, pp. 324-25 no. 277, cf. pp. 612-14 no. 458.

[34] Joinville, chap. cxxxix; Depoin, *Cartulaire de l'Hôtel-Dieu de Pontoise*, pp. 30-32, 34, 44-45, 124-25; cf. 109-10. See also Tillemont, *Vie de SL*, v, 305.

[35] Le Grand, "Maisons-Dieu," p. 200.

[36] Joinville, chap. cxxxix; Delisle, *Cartulaire normand*, no. 634. See also Tillemont, *Vie de SL*, v, 305; and Poulain, *Séjours*, p. 96.

[37] Of the standard sources, see Joinville, chap. cxlii; Morel, *Cartulaire . . . S-Corneille*, ii, 473-74, 480-83. See also Tillemont, *Vie de SL*, v, 305; Ozanne, "Hôpital," pp. 131-36. There is a valuable new synthesis of the available material in Sulpice. *Histoire de l'Hôtel-Dieu*.

[38] Joinville, chap. cxlii; Fontette, "Vie économique," p. 526 no. 30. See also Tillemont, *Vie de SL*, v, 305-6; Le Grand, "Quinze-Vingts"; and Vaughn, "Notice historique," pp. 1-3.

[39] Delisle, *Cartulaire normand*, no. 661.

[40] Bernois, "Lorris," p. 411.   [41] Delisle, *Cartulaire normand*, no. 732.

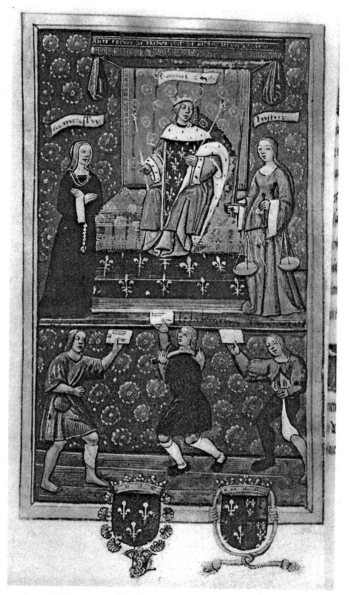

3. Saint Louis Accepting the Petitions of the Sick.

permeate the sources.[42] His concern for poor sick people manifested itself in Languedoc in the return of property confiscated from them for suspected complicity in heresy. According to a rigorous interpretation of the law he could have retained the property, but he did not, owing perhaps to a congeries of motives—compassion, piety, a sense of justice—delicately illustrated in a sixteenth century miniature (see accompanying illustration) showing him flanked by his mother and Justice, receiving the petitions of the sick.[43] Even alms for a poor woman in childbed are recorded in the royal accounts[44] and may owe something to the horrendous experience of Margaret's childbearing, one instance of which Louis witnessed and another of which became almost legendary.[45]

As to fallen women, poor convents, and women religious in general, a useful introduction comes from two paintings commissioned by Louis IX's daughter Blanche for the Franciscan nunnery at Lourcines which represented his founding of nunneries as a prominent element of his religious devotion.[46] Joinville puts into words what the two paintings symbolized.[47]

[42] Besides the evidence in chapter 5 nn. 154-57, the following information should be noted. In 1254 Louis IX confirmed the diploma of Philip II in favor of the leprosarium of Saint-Lazare of Paris, prohibiting anyone from doing violence to the house, and in 1262 he confirmed the knights of Saint-Lazare of Jerusalem in their property at Boigny in the diocese of Orléans and gave them an additional house in Paris (la maladrene du Roule); Boullé, "Maison de Saint-Lazare," pp. 130, 134. The king ordered his foresters on 29 December 1256 to allow the leprosarium of Pontfraud to enjoy certain rights of usage in the forest of Paucourt; Stein, "Recueil . . . Pontfraud," p. 71. And in 1260 he gave a rent "d'un muid de blé à prendre sur le grange royale de Gonesse" to the leprosarium of Fontenay-sous-Bois; Le Grand, "Maisons-Dieu," p. 80.

[43] On his leniency to the sick in Languedoc, see HF, xxiv, 620-21.

[44] The Latin is very problematical here, but twelve shillings were assigned "pro filio cujusdam feminae nutriendo." Unfortunately the record of this payment, except for Joinville's comment, is the only notice of such alms-giving that I have been able to find. It is very early, being in the royal accounts for 1234 (HF, xxii, 566-67), and this suggests that such alms were a traditional form of royal charity. Joinville's emphasis may be evidence that here again, without actually innovating, Louis IX put more stress than was typical on this type of charity, but in the absence of better evidence this hypothesis is at present tentative.

[45] In Louis's presence Margaret collapsed under the strain of pregnancy in a touching scene recorded by Joinville, chap. cxix. An anonymous chronicler (HF, xxi, 81) mentions the long time the queen was childless after marriage (1234-1240) which might be an indication that there were a number of miscarriages since she was only fourteen at the time of her marriage. On the crusade she bore a son, Jean Tristan; he was called Tristan because he was born in triste, sadness. Margaret had been obliged to get up almost immediately after the birth in order to keep the defenders of Damietta from deserting; Joinville, chap. LXXVIII. See also Pernoud, Reine Blanche, pp. 348-49; and Labarge, SL, p. 57.

[46] Longnon, Documents, p. 16 (VI, VII). See also for a variety of gifts to female institutions, "Beati Ludovici vita, partim," HF, xxiii, 170-71; Cartulaire de l'abbaye de Morienval, pp. 41-42, 46, 76 (cf. pp. 57-59, 63); Vanhaeck, "Cartulaire . . . Marquette," I, 178 no. 185.

[47] Joinville, chap. cxlii. For each foundation noticed by Joinville I have tried to indi-

He [Louis] founded the convent of Saint Matthew at Rouen, where he installed Dominican nuns[48] and that at Longchamps for Franciscan nuns, and gave them large endowments for their support.[49]

. . . .

Soon afterwards he built another house outside Paris, on the road to St. Denis, which was called the House of the Daughters of God, and in this hostel he installed a large number of women who through poverty had abandoned themselves to the sins of the flesh, and gave them a revenue of four hundred pounds for their maintenance.[50] In several places in his kingdom he built and endowed houses of Beguines and ordered that in them should be received women who wished to devote themselves to a life of chastity.[51]

What Joinville says in general with regard to the *béguinages* may be made more specific from a variety of documentary sources. An act of *parlement* informs us of a *béguinage* founded by the king in Tours;[52] a bill of sale in the royal archives makes this equally clear for the famous *béguinage* of Paris.[53] All of these varied foundations and endowments date from after the crusade.[54]

Louis's support of the male offshoots of the two great mendicant orders is equally striking. "The king," wrote Joinville,

loved all who devoted themselves to the service of God and wore the religious habit, and none such came to him and failed to find

---

cate where corroborative documentary and supplementary narrative evidence may be found.

[48] This foundation took place at least by 1263, perhaps as early as 1260; see, besides Joinville, *Layettes*, IV, no. 5638; and the contemporary list of Dominican foundations in *HF*, XXIII, 183. See also Sauvage, "Notes . . . des Emmurées," pp. 204, 213, n. 2, 226, and 230-31 (the king sent a thorn of the crown of thorns to the sisters in December 1269, on the eve of his departure for his second crusade).

[49] This was the foundation he carried through for his sister Isabella, discussed above chapter 1 n. 41.

[50] See also "Beati Ludovici e veteri . . . ," *HF*, XXIII, 162; a chronicle of Rouen, *HF*, XXIII, 353. Le Grand, "Maisons-Dieu," pp. 252, 256, has collected some of the most important information on "les Filles-Dieu." Founded probably in the late 1250s, they received many gifts from the king (Le Grand believed that an unimportant house was already in existence when Louis decided to turn it into a major institution). The king assigned it the rent of four hundred pounds *parisis* mentioned by Joinville and two "muids de blé." Later he augmented their buildings. Finally in 1265 he conceded to them "une prise d'eau sur la fontaine de Saint-Ladre." The sisters eventually possessed a relic, a finger, of their benefactor (p. 253).

[51] See also the Anonymous of Saint-Denis, *HF*, XX, 53; a chronicle of Rouen, *HF*, XXIII, 353; "Beati Ludovici e veteri . . . ," *HF*, XXIII, 162. In addition see Le Grand, "Béguines," p. 305; Vaultier, *Histoire . . . de Caen*, p. 108; Colliette, *Vermandois*, II, 610.

[52] Boutaric, *Actes*, I, no. 961 (the act is dated 1265, the *béguines* had been installed about 1258). See also Jordan, "Contrats d'acquisition royaux," n. 11.

[53] Teulet, *Layettes*, IV, no. 4806. See also McDonnell, *Beguines*, pp. 224-25; Le Grand, "Béguines," p. 303 (the foundation is dated circa 1264).

[54] See the dates given in the accompanying notes.

189

what he needed for his support. He provided for the Brothers of Carmel and bought them a place on the Seine near Charenton, built their house and bought them vestments, chalices and such things as are needed for the service of God. Afterwards he provided for the Brothers of St. Augustine, and for these he bought a farm belonging to a citizen of Paris, with all its appurtenances, and built them a church outside the Montmartre gate.

He provided also for the Brothers of the Sacks and gave them a place on the Seine near St. Germain des Pres, where they lived. . . . After the Brothers of the Sacks had been installed, another sort of Friars came, known as the Order of the White Mantles, who asked the king to help them stay in Paris. The king bought them a house to live in with some old outbuildings round it, near the Old Temple Gate in Paris, quite close to the Weavers. . . .

Later arrived another sort of Friars, who called themselves Brothers of the Holy Cross, and wore a cross on their breast. They asked the king for his support. He granted it readily, and lodged them in a street which was then called Temple Crossroads but is now known as Holy Cross Street. Thus the good King surrounded the city of Paris with men of religion.[55]

It is not surprising that the documentary evidence of these foundations dates them all in the post-crusade period.[56]

Outside of Paris the king was just as active in supporting these orders.[57] He established houses for the Friars of the Sack at Rouen sometime between 1257 and 1259,[58] possibly at Orléans around 1265,[59] and at Sens sometime between 1264 and 1266.[60] There is some reason to think that he founded other houses for one or more of these less prestigious orders at Villeneuve-le-Roi in 1258 and at Vaudreuil in 1259.[61] The Trinitarians, who some scholars argue also tried to reform themselves in a mendicant mode briefly in the thirteenth century, received royal endowments for their houses at Fontainebleau in 1259[62] and at Compiègne in 1265.[63]

[55] Joinville, chap. CXLIII.
[56] The standard catalogue is Emery, *Friars*. For these houses, all founded in 1258 or 1259, see p. 109.
[57] Cf. Jordan, "Contrats d'acquisition royaux," nn. 12-13. See also *Formulaires*, no. 6, items 62, 131.
[58] *Layettes*, III, no. 4343; Emery, *Friars*, p. 112.
[59] Emery, *Friars*, p. 84. Cf. *Layettes*, IV, no. 4769.
[60] *Layettes*, IV, no. 4931; Emery, *Friars*, p. 123.
[61] See the argument advanced in Jordan, "Contrats d'acquisition royaux," nn. 12-13.
[62] *GC*, XII, "Instrumenta," cc. 74-76 no. xcix; Emery, *Friars*, p. 110. See also Tillemont, *Vie de SL*, IV, 206.
[63] Emery, *Friars*, p. 99. See also Sulpice, *Histoire de l'Hôtel-Dieu*, pp. 13, 56. On the argument that at this time the Trinitarians should be regarded as mendicants, see Emery, p. 13.

In addition to the protection and sustenance he offered the satellite mendicant orders, concern for the dead—or for a type of religious devotion which commemorated victory over death—constituted another pronounced aspect of Louis's piety in the latter half of his reign. I do not mean his obsession with the memory of his brother Robert and his mother Blanche, as suggested by his endowment of thousands of masses in their honor.[64] The type of religious devotion I have in mind is that which commemorated death as a release (as in the martyrdom of the saints) or as the necessary pathway to salvation (as in the sacrifice of Jesus); this became an important motif in the king's mature piety.

We have the extraordinary data, accumulated by Carolus-Barré, on Louis's attendance at *translationes* of the relics of saints' bodies. Only one of these took place before the crusade, indeed on the eve of the crusade (in 1247); it blended together the idea of the French crown as the protector of the saints in their travail on earth and the crusade as a further manifestation of the holiness of the French monarchy. The saint honored in 1247 was Archbishop Edmund of Canterbury whose body was at Pontigny. According to widespread belief, in 1240 Saint Edmund, like Becket and Anselm before him, had chosen voluntary exile in France in preference to humiliation in England at the hands of Louis's traditional enemy King Henry III.[65]

The French king had first gone to Auxerre, whence, with the bishop of Auxerre and the royal entourage, he set out for the monastery at Pontigny. The festivities at Pontigny, which began with the lighting of one thousand candles and continued—as Carolus-Barré has written—with a vigil-fast and prayers, culminated in the exposition and veneration of the uncorrupted body of Saint Edmund. Throughout, the king of the Franks took an active and public part in the proceedings. Important negotiations regarding the planned crusade were carried on after the public festivities were completed.[66]

The king found these *translationes* morally uplifting, and what had been a unique occurrence before the crusade was repeated with characteristic frequency after it. He attended at least nine others (from

[64] Wallon, *SL*, ii, 487. The king did not always pay directly for these masses. For example, in March 1258 he simply remitted certain customary annual gifts rendered to the crown by the nunnery of Morienval in return for the nuns' promise to celebrate his mother's memory on her anniversary in perpetuity; *Cartulaire de l'abbaye de Morienval*, p. 46.

[65] Carolus-Barré, "SL et la translation des corps saints," pp. 1089-91. Cf. *New Catholic Encyclopedia*, v, s.v. "Edmund of Abingdon, St.," p. 109. The declamation of Blanche of Castile on this occasion (reported by Matthew Paris, iv, 631; see also vi, 128 no. 68) was a minor masterpiece of French propaganda.

[66] Carolus-Barré, "SL et la translation des corps saints," pp. 1089-91. See also Chardon, *Auxerre*, i, 192; and Massé, *Vie de saint Edme*, pp. 356-57.

TABLE 9 ● Donations of Relics of the Passion

Date	Recipient
1239	Cathedral of Sens[a]
12 August 1239	Bishop of Le Puy[b]
May 1248	Cathedral of Toledo[c]
1251	Roger of Provins, canon of Saint-Quentin and royal physician[d]
March 1256	Bishop of Valence[e]
24 August 1258	Mansueto de Castiglioni Fiorentino O.F.M., papal chaplain[f]
1 October 1259	Franciscans of Sées[g]
11 December 1259	Bishop of Vicenza[h]
May 1260	Trinitarians of Paris[i]
17 September 1261	Priory of Mont Saint-Éloy[j]
1261?	Abbey of Saint-Lucien of Beauvais[k]
1261?	Cathedral of Cologne[l]
February 1262	Abbey of Saint-Maurice d'Agaune[m]
1262	Dominicans of Barcelona[n]
1264?	Abbey of Saint-Maurice d'Agaune[o]
September 1267	Dominicans of Liège[p]
1267	Abbey of Vézelay[q]
December 1269	Bishop of Clermont[r]
December 1269	Dominican Sisters of Rouen[s]
March 1270	Convent of Bourmoyen of Blois[t]
?	Cathedral of Notre-Dame of Paris[u]
?	Dominicans of Paris[v]
?	Franciscans of Paris[w]
?	Abbey of Vaucelles[x]

NOTES:

[a] Riant, *Exuviae*, II, 123; *SL*, Exposition, p. 108 no. 229.

[b] Riant, *Exuviae*, II, 125.

[c] Ibid., pp. 137-38; Lemaître, *Reliquaire*, p. 7.

[d] Colliette, *Vermandois*, II, 639; Riant, *Exuviae*, II, 139; Lemaître, *Reliquaire*, p. 7.

[e] Riant, *Exuviae*, II, 140; Lemaître, *Reliquaire*, p. 7.

[f] Riant, *Exuviae*, II, 275; Lemaître, *Reliquaire*, p. 8; see also S., Review of Callebaut's *Provinciaux*, p. 362.

[g] Riant, *Exuviae*, II, 240; Delisle, *Cartulaire normand*, no. 633; Lemaître, *Reliquaire*, p. 7. According to the records of the Sainte-Chapelle the donation may not have been finalized until 13 January 1260; Vidier, "Trésor," pt. 3, p. 262.

[h] Riant, *Exuviae*, II, 141, 154, 159; Lemaître, *Reliquaire*, p. 7.

[i] Vidier, "Trésor," pt. 3, p. 262.

[j] Riant, *Exuviae*, II, 143-44; Lemaître, *Reliquaire*, p. 7.

[k] Carolus-Barré, "SL et la translation," p. 1098 (and n. 61).

[l] This donation is hypothetical; for Carolus-Barré's arguments, ibid., p. 1100 (cf. n. 71).

m Riant, *Exuviae*, II, 143; *SL*, Exposition, pp. 106-7 no. 224; Aubert, *Trésor*, I, 57, 170-71, and II, "pièces justificatives," p. 228 no. 24; Lemaître, *Reliquaire*, p. 7.

n Riant, *Exuviae*, II, 145; Lemaître, *Reliquaire*, p. 7.

o Aubert, *Trésor*, I, 177, gives his argument in support of the reality of this donation. It is doubted in *SL*, Exposition, no. 232.

p Riant, *Exuviae*, II, 156-57; Lemaître, *Reliquaire*, p. 7. Whether the Louvre crown is the reliquary for the original gift is in dispute; cf. Eydoux, *SL*, headnotes to illustration between pages 32 and 33.

q Riant, *Exuviae*, II, 154-55; Lemaître, *Reliquaire*, p. 7.

r Riant, *Exuviae*, II, 159; Lemaître, *Reliquaire*, p. 7.

s Vidier, "Trésor," pt. 3, p. 267; Sauvage, "Notes . . . des Emmurées," p. 230-31.

t Riant, *Exuviae*, II, 158-59; Lemaître, *Reliquaire*, p. 7.

u Lemaître, *Reliquaire*, p. 8, but the evidence is very thin on this donation.

v Ibid., pp. 6-9.

w Ibid., p. 9. The argument of Lemaître has logic but little evidence in its support. Cf. *SL*, Exposition, p. 109 no. 230.

x AD: Nord 28 H 9 as noted in Bruchet, *Répertoire*, p. 302.

1256 to 1267) in the concluding period of his reign.[67] At each he performed the symbolic *gestes* that put him into spiritual communion with the martyrs and confessors: he would lie supine on the ground as an act of humiliation;[68] he would accept small portions of the saints' relics.[69] Although Louis did not create a completely new form of royal piety (for some of his predecessors had been known to attend *translationes*), he gave this form of religious devotion a new and, as it happened, permanent emphasis.[70]

The supreme manifestation of victory over death was Christ's sacrifice and resurrection, and it is with one aspect of Louis's devotion to this symbol that I want to close my discussion of his piety. I mean of course his donations of relics of the Passion. The cache of relics, purchased in the late 1230s from the emperor of Constantinople,[71] was barely touched before the crusade. Two gifts (the most common types were a thorn from the crown of thorns or a piece of the true cross)[72] were given at the occasion of the reception of the relics in France in 1239 (table nine). But no other donation was made until May 1248 when Spanish representatives of the cathedral of Toledo received a

[67] Carolus-Barré, "SL et la translation des corps saints," pp. 1091-1110.

[68] Ibid., p. 1093.

[69] He did not do this at Pontigny in 1247 because Edmund's body was uncorrupted, and it would have been presumptuous to "dismember what God Himself had left intact" (ibid., p. 1090); but he accepted portions of the saints' bodies at the translation of Saint Aignan at Orléans in 1259, of Saint Lucien at Beauvais in 1261, and of Saint Mary Magdalene at Vézelay in 1267 (ibid., pp. 1093, 1098, 1108).

[70] Ibid., p. 1112: "Saint Louis n'innova point en ce domaine, sinon par le nombre de translations auxquelles il prit part."

[71] Above chapter 5 n. 14.

[72] Thorns could be given away without detriment to the integrity of the crown because any thorn once touched to the relic in a sufficiently sacred way absorbed part of the potency of the original; Labarge, *SL*, p. 63n. (citing Cabrol and Leclerq).

portion of the relics, probably on the occasion of their exposition to the faithful at the Sainte-Chapelle during the solemnities attending the royal departure for the crusade.[73] Thereafter it was a different story.

In 1251, after his release from captivity in Egypt, Louis gave his physician and adviser, Roger of Provins, a portion of the relics. Coinciding, as this gift does, with the cultural productions of the small band of crusaders who took up the struggle in the Holy Land with the king,[74] the gift was probably not only a thank-offering to the skilled physician but, more profoundly, a mutual affirmation by giver and recipient in the face of defeat. When Louis returned to France, he continued this sort of giving. Everybody wanted relics from the vast hoard. In later years, fancy caused several monastic institutions to cherish pious but illusory traditions that they received them. Nonetheless, it is possible to separate the wheat from the chaff in most instances, and it can be shown that from 1256 to 1270 the king made approximately fifteen of these precious gifts.

They were sent in reliquaries cast in gold and decorated with precious stones.[75] Many of these have disappeared in the passage of time but three remain: a gold and jeweled crown in the Louvre,[76] an ornamental stand in the *trésor* of the abbey of Saint-Maurice-d'Agaune, and a decorative cross in the same abbey. The last two are interesting iconographically. The stand is very simple.[77] Its base is surmounted by a single upward extension which culminates in an almost circular summit with a rather long and thin internal ray (see accompanying illustration). Not surprisingly, this upper part is a direct symbolization of a single thorn proceeding out of the base of the crown of thorns in the direction of Christ's brow. In a hymn in honor of the crown of

---

[73] Above chapters 2 (n. 103) and 5 (nn. 19-20).

[74] Above chapter 5 nn. 170-82.

[75] As is confided to us by the documents recording these donations collected by Riant (see, for example, *Exuviae*, II, 154, 245).

[76] I am not discussing this artifact in the text because Eydoux, *SL*, headnotes between pp. 32 and 33, calls the attribution into question, and the Louvre, which used to assign the crown to the Dominicans of Liège (*Louvre: General Guide*, p. 121—misdated 1257 instead of 1267), has now removed this labeling. Although it would be hard to prove the case that this particular crown was the reliquary of the Dominicans of Liège for the piece of the true cross they received from the king in 1267, the belief that the crown served as a repository for one of Louis's gifts is not unreasonable. For one thing, this crown was once decorated with cameos (cf. the eighteenth-century drawing in Montfaucon, *Monumens*, II, pl. xxvi no. 1), and cameos were included in the cache of relics purchased by Louis in 1238. Moreover, reliquaries in crown-form were not rare at any time; Schramm, *Herrschaftszeichen*, III, 869-83. For Schramm's important discussion of the Louvre crown, see pp. 870-71.

[77] Aubert, *Trésor*, I, 57, 170-71; II, p. xxxiii; II, "pièces justificatives," no. 24, p. 228. See also *SL*, Exposition, pp. 106-7 no. 224.

thorns, written about 1239, we find the passage that may have inspired the design: "the sting of death is the thorn, but the circle of the crown is victory over death."[78] The ornamental cross, also at Saint-Maurice, bears a similar message.[79] Designed as a repository for a piece of the true cross, the reliquary is supremely remarkable for the symbolic affirmation at the vertex of its crossing beams, the Lamb of God Triumphant (see accompanying illustration).

A final feature of the king's gifts should also be mentioned. He expected the institutions given relics of the Passion to commemorate the donations in some way (stained glass, new altar, altar cloth). Few recipients could go so far as the bishop of Vicenza who built a church for the Dominicans as a testimony of his jubilation for the relic which Louis had given him in 1259.[80] But nearly all could produce something, if only a special service that recalled the king's generosity.[81]

Taken together, the types of charity and religious devotion practiced by Louis IX with vigor after the crusade formed a recognizable pattern. Like the quality of his rulership in general, this pattern was penitential. He sought to purify himself of any imputation of avarice or base motivations. He favored with his alms those militantly ascetic expressions of Christian piety (like radical mendicancy) that stripped the individual of worldly concerns. These commitments were, in a sense, preparation for his own ultimate purification, the joy of Christian martyrdom. This explains (or helps to explain) the confessional quality that attended his participation in the *translationes sanctorum* and the constant celebration—through the donations of the relics of the Passion—of the ultimate sacrifice of his Lord. Is it any wonder that Matthew Paris found *piissimus* to be a thoroughly appropriate word to describe the king of the Franks.[82]

As important as they were, however, it was neither the quality nor the quantity of Louis's religious devotions that excited in his own lifetime the most praise. More significant, at least to contemporaries, seems to have been his attitude toward Christian warfare. To say he

---

[78] *Antiphonale*, pp. 75-77: *Spina mortis stimulus / Sed coronae circulus / Mortis est victoria.*

[79] The dating of this artifact is not precise (*SL*, Exposition, no. 232), but Saint-Maurice became of royal interest only about 1259 when Louis began the process of establishing a permanent foundation; see Aubert, *Trésor*, II, 228-31 no. 25; Rendu and Coüard-Luys, *Inventaire-sommaire . . . Oise . . . H*, I, 220-22; *Layettes*, IV, nos. 4756, 4796, 4816; *GC*, x, "Instrumenta," cc. 462-63 no. cxvi. See also Tillemont, *Vie de SL*, IV, 255. Art criticism assigns the cross to Louis's reign and tradition attributes it to his gift; Aubert, *Trésor*, I, 177; II, pl. xxxvi.

[80] Riant, *Exuviae*, II, 142.

[81] Ibid., pp. 137, 140-41, 143, 145, 154, 156, 158-59.

[82] Matthew Paris uses this word in passing to describe Louis after the crusade; v, 466. See also MP, IV, 638-39, where he regards the king's commission of friar-*enquêteurs* as an additional proof that Louis was *piissimus*.

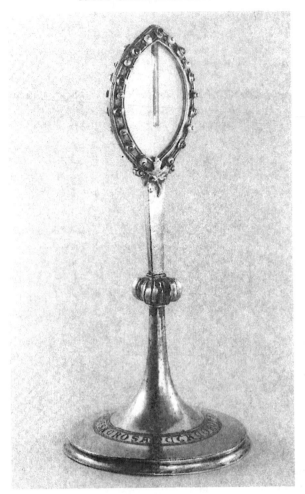

4. Reliquary of a Thorn of the Crown of Thorns.

was against it is true but banal.[83] One of the most telling factors in his failure on the crusade had been his inability to get Christendom behind him because of the internal struggles which characterized politics in the pre-crusade period. He did everything in his power to prevent this from happening again. He became, in Kienast's words, the "Arbiter of Europe" and the "uncrowned Emperor of the West."[84] He

[83] Joinville, chap. CXXXVII, has a poignant description of the king's love for peace, but for all its poignancy, the proposition applied to Christians only, not to the affairs of Christians and the "enemies of the faith."
[84] *Deutschland und Frankreich*, III, 634, 643-50.

5. Reliquary of a Piece of the True Cross.

began the process which earned him these epithets by bringing to solution the lingering struggles in which he himself was involved.

England came first. Louis initiated discussions with Henry III almost immediately on his return from the Holy Land, discussions
which had as their goal the elimination of the technical state of war
that had existed between their two kingdoms since 1202.[85] These dis-

---

[85] The records of the negotiations, interim agreements and proposals, may be found
in *Layettes*, III, nos. 4105, 4178, 4413, 4415-18, 4420, 4423, 4426, 4461-63, 4466, 4500-
501; V, 652, 687. The best narrative source on the discussions is Matthew Paris's chronicle, V, 475-83, 489, 585, 611, 620, 650, 659, 720-71.

cussions culminated in the Treaty of Paris of 1259 by which the conflicting claims of the two monarchs in Poitou, Anjou, Maine, Normandy, and the upper reaches of Aquitaine were formally resolved.[86]

The negotiations were far from easy. Both sides had to yield on important issues. Henry III had to face up to the fact that the historic patrimony of the Angevin house had been lost; Louis indemnified him with the resources to support five hundred knights for two years, an investment that would cost over one hundred thousand pounds *tournois*.[87] But the French towns that were forced to pay this indemnity balked at what they regarded as an unwarranted attack on their financial livelihood. They had already supported the king's crusade and Charles of Anjou's expedition in Hainaut. They could hardly do more.[88] Louis finally had to compromise with them, reschedule levies, and do much more to mollify their distress.[89]

The French king also gave up border areas in Périgord, Quercy, and the Limousin to Henry III even though his claims were as strong. It may be significant in this respect that the peripatetic king of the Franks never attempted to visit these regions after the crusade; he made no attempt, that is, to capture their loyalties. This raises an interesting but unanswerable question. Had he intended from the moment he returned from the Levant to return these provinces to Henry III, to a man who, for all his personal piety, had threatened the territorial integrity of France until 1254?

Louis IX's leniency with Henry provoked the stern but ineffective opposition of his counselors.

> We are astonished that you should have decided to surrender so large a part of your territory which you and your predecessors obtained from him by your conquest and his forfeiture. Our opinion of the matter is that if you do not think that you have a right to the territory you are not making proper restitution to the King of England unless you surrender all your predecessors' conquests; but if you do believe that you have a right to them, then we think that you

[86] *Layettes*, III, nos. 4554-55; MP, v, 737; Guillaume de Nangis, *HF*, xx, 410-13. There are two studies of the treaty, a rather specialized article by Chaplais, "Making of the Treaty of Paris (1259) and the Royal Style," and Gavrilovitch, *Étude sur le Traité de Paris*.

[87] Gavrilovitch, *Étude sur le Traité de Paris*, p. 120 no. iv; Powicke, *Thirteenth Century*, pp. 127-28.

[88] I have made reference to the municipal accounts in which the records of the towns' problems are preserved (above chapter 6 n. 98). See also Borrelli de Serres, *Recherches*, I, 104-5; Stephenson, "Aides," p. 44.

[89] There is as yet no thorough study of this question; I hope to deal with it at some length very soon. But the references in the preceding note are helpful. See also Powicke, *Thirteenth Century*, pp. 127-28.

are simply throwing away all the territory which you are ceding to him.[90]

The king replied, in the same passage, that he knew he was not obliged to return the regions in question but that he was motivated by familial love. He and Henry were brothers-in-law. Their children and successors were cousins. Additionally, he argued, he was receiving an important concession from Henry as a result of the return of the march between Aquitaine and Poitou, namely, that Henry acknowledged his feudal subservience to Louis in France, not for the march itself (which would have been ridiculous) but for Aquitaine which had always had a rather peculiar status.[91]

It was not only the opposition of his counselors, however, which complicated Louis's search for peace. The personal idiosyncracies of Henry III did not make matters go smoothly either. His piety, which made him stop to hear mass at every church on the route to the negotiations, exasperated the French king who was eventually constrained to order his men to lock the doors of those churches that Henry had to pass. More importantly, Henry's incompetence at home, which precipitated the baronial crisis of 1258, was also to affect the outcome of negotiations between France and England. Right up to the last moment Henry was reluctant to give up his claims to the historic lands of his fathers. It was, in fact, the barons who, having become completely disgusted in their king, ultimately compelled him to bring the treaty to fruition.[92]

Less difficult, evidently, were the negotiations that Louis IX opened with the Aragonese to resolve the jurisdictional tangle that characterized the "border" of French Languedoc and Aragon. Earlier, in my discussion of "foreign" policy on the eve of the crusade, I suggested that before he left France, Louis made it clear to King James I that an arrangement should be worked out since active heresy and rebellion (and with them the role of Aragon as a sanctuary for Louis's enemies) had ceased to be a problem. Unfortunately, we know little of the details of the negotiations that led to the Treaty of Corbeil in 1258, but the agreement did effectively draw the boundary between the two countries at the Pyrenees, the natural frontier.[93] The one major ex-

[90] Joinville, chap. cxxxvii.

[91] Chaplais, "Le Traité de Paris . . . et l'inféodation de Gascogne."

[92] On the negotiations with Henry and the role of the barons, see Treharne, *Baronial Plan of Reform*, p. 141; Sayles, *Medieval Foundations*, p. 425; and Powicke, *Thirteenth Century*, pp. 126-27.

[93] Indications of discussions by letter between the two monarchs, even while Louis was on crusade, are noticed in Burns, *Moors and Crusaders*, essay IV, p. 14 n. 8. Relevant

ception was Montpellier, the native city of the Aragonese royal house, in which James maintained his interests.

The anomaly of Montpellier caused future problems which only the outright annexation of the city by Philip IV finally solved. The reason for the troubles lay mainly in the relations of the Aragonese crown with the *bourgeois* of Montpellier who wanted to be free of the Aragonese king's overlordship. War often threatened, but Louis refused to let his subjects, even voluntarily, help either side. He also prohibited the passage through his land of Aragonese troops who intended to attack the city and bring it into line. The role he played was a precarious one. He did not want to be in a hostile posture with Aragon especially as his second crusade approached, but the only alternative, besides working out a peace between the two sides (which never came about), would have been to let Aragonese troops march through his territories to attack other Christians. Not only would the granting of such permission have been harmful to Louis's relations with the *bourgeois* of Montpellier, it was repugnant to the king's sensibilities. Thus the tension persisted.[94]

Nonetheless, the very desire for peace which animated all of Louis IX's actions and the feeling that began to grow in Christendom that the French king was above petty politics combined to elevate him in the European imagination to the level of supreme arbiter of "international" disputes.[95] This is no exaggeration. When the count of Brittany and the count of Champagne (who was also king of Navarre) quarreled in 1254, they turned to Louis to settle their grievances.[96] When the count of Champagne found himself embroiled in disputes with the Burgundian nobility around 1255, with the abbey of Saint-Denis in 1260, and with the count of Bar in 1268, he again turned to the French king to arbitrate.[97] Arguing among themselves, Burgun-

---

documents on the negotiations for the Treaty of Corbeil and the final instrument may be found in *Layettes*, III, nos. 4399-4400, 4411-12, 4433-35; *HGL*, VIII, cc. 1429-30; (Berthelé) *Archives . . . cartulaires*, p. 100 no. 696; and Berthelé, *Archives . . . Montpellier*, I, 2d fasc. (individual pagination): *Grand Chartrier*, p. 15 no. 121. See also Shneidman, *Rise of the Aragonese-Catalan Empire*, II, 300; and Hillgarth, *Problem of a Catalan Mediterranean Empire*, p. 14.

[94] The records touching upon these matters are collected in *HGL*, VIII, cc. 1362-63, 1365-66 (cxxx), 1393-95, 1411-12, 1519-26. See also Boutaric, *Actes*, I, no. 1265.

[95] A good rundown of the disputes is given in Joinville, chap. cxxxvii. Cf. *MP*, V, 720-21. See also Kienast, *Deutschland und Frankreich*, III, 643-50; Wallon, *SL*, II, 412-14; and the material scattered throughout vols. IV and V of Tillemont, *Vie de SL*.

[96] *Layettes*, III, no. 4132. See also Arbois de Jubainville, *Histoire . . . de Champagne*, IV, 354-57.

[97] On Thibaut's disputes with the Burgundians (the count of Châlon and duke of Burgundy), see Joinville, chap. cxxxvii. See also Tillemont, *Vie de SL*, V, 411. On his

dian nobles looked to Louis for a decision in 1254;[98] Rhineland barons sought him out at least twice in the post-crusade period.[99] Lyonnais notables asked for his mediation in 1269,[100] and Savoyards also in 1269.[101] The implications of this sort of involvement were profound. Writing lyrically of these arbitrations, Joinville asserts that the noblemen the king reconciled "loved and obeyed him, so much that I have seen them appear before him, at the royal court at Rheims and Paris and Orleans. . . ."[102] Louis's justice was simply the best justice to be had. Louis the arbiter was Solomon returned.[103]

Closer to home, the university of Paris, agonizing under internecine strife in the middle and late 1250s, made use of the king's good offices as well. Here Louis was brought into the disputes personally because the secular party at the university, led by Guillaume de Saint-Amour, attacked not only the mendicant teachers but the king's attraction for the mendicants. Guillaume considered Louis's religious devotions unnecessary and exaggerated. The king would have none of it. To him the mendicant mode of piety was the most excellent; and although he could endure personal criticism of his own life style, he did not tolerate the aspersions which Guillaume cast upon the crown. Acting with the consent of the papacy, which condemned Guillaume's writings, he had the master exiled from Paris, and a modicum of peace was restored to the faculty of theology.[104]

Louis's brothers also found him, or perhaps felt constrained by family loyalty to find him, the perfect arbiter of their disputes as well. Saint Louis arbitrated the problems Charles faced with the lord of the Dauphiné in 1256 and with Beatrice, the countess-dowager of

---

disagreements with the abbey of Saint-Denis, *Layettes*, III, no. 4646. And on his strained relations with the count of Bar, see *Layettes*, IV, nos. 5366-70, and V, nos. 835, 838.

[98] On the role of Louis in settling the war between the count of Châlon and the duke of Burgundy, see Joinville, chap. CXXXVII.

[99] The king arbitrated the dispute between the counts of Bar and Luxembourg in 1267 (Joinville, chap. CXXXVII; cf. *HF*, XX, 88. See also *Layettes*, IV, nos. 5357-65, and V, no. 835). Around 1268 he seems to have tried to work out a settlement of outstanding disputes between the count of Bar and the lord of Choiseul (*Layettes*, IV, nos. 5471-80).

[100] The dispute involved the *bourgeois* of Lyon and the cathedral chapter; Charmasse, *Cartulaire de l'évêché d'Autun*, pp. 231-32 no. ccxii. See also Fournier, *Royaume d'Arles*, p. 213.

[101] Fournier, *Royaume d'Arles*, p. 213; the lord of the Dauphiné was at odds with Philip, the count of Savoy.

[102] Chap. CXXXVIII; Joinville is specifically referring to "Burgundians and Lorrainers." See also Wallon, *SL*, II, 510-11.

[103] Folz, "Sainteté," p. 33; Buisson, *König Ludwig IX und das Recht*, p. 247.

[104] The old study by Douie, *Conflict between the Seculars and the Mendicants*, is still quite useful if only for its lucid brevity, and the remarks of Tillemont, *Vie de SL*, VI, 182-85, are to the point. Dufeil, *Guillaume de Saint-Amour*, has recently dealt with the quarrel in detail; see also idem, "Le Roi Louis dans la querelle des mendiants et des séculiers," pp. 280-89.

Provence, in the same year.[105] Alfonse called upon his brother's mediation in 1257 in a dispute with the countess of Boulogne.[106]

But by far the most important arbitration was that between the English king and his barons; it is preserved in the Mise of Amiens of 1264.[107] Like others who sometimes asked for his mediation, the English barons were not pleased with Louis's decision and fought a civil war to set it aside. Yet, as Wood has shown,[108] the Mise, in its own right, is an important document, for it expresses at base Louis's ideal of monarchy, an ideal, unfortunately for the English barons, in which rebellion had no proper place.[109] But it expressed more than that. A king was the center of government; he was obliged by God to rule. There was even a kind of absolutism in the Frankish king's pretensions.[110] But as Professor Gaines Post might say, Louis did not feel arbitrarily absolute. He ruled, and he believed every king should rule, with good counsel, in the spirit of the divine, as an upholder of law and good custom; and even the nascent ideas of sovereignty which attached themselves to the court circle expressed indeed a very limited, a very medieval view of sovereignty.[111] The authority of a Christian king, at its best, was a moral authority, a point stressed by Gilbert de Tournai in a treatise on the duties of a prince which the saint-king commissioned.[112]

This role of peacemaker and moral conscience was not always comfortable. The king's advisers, many of whom could not quite live up to

---

[105] *Layettes*, III, nos. 4300, 4336. See also Fournier, *Royaume d'Arles*, pp. 212-13. Charles imitated his brother, offering his services as arbiter to the cities of Montpellier and Marseilles which were in dispute over commercial matters in 1257; *HGL*, VIII, cc. 1413-19.

[106] *Layettes*, III, no. 4326.

[107] The records of the negotiations are preserved in *Layettes*, IV, nos. 4884-86, 4888, 4898. A partial English translation of the Mise is readily available in Stephenson and Marcham, I, 148-49. The full Latin text, with English facing, and an impressive critical apparatus may be found in Treharne and Sanders, *Baronial Movement*, pp. 280-91.

[108] Wood, "Mise of Amiens and SL's Theory of Kingship."

[109] "Louis was a King who held a high ideal of the dignity and authority of his office, and to him the constitutional checks which Simon [de Montfort] desired to impose upon the royal authority must have seemed such an invasion of royal rights and duties as to be almost sinful, impious, and sacrilegious"; Treharne, *Baronial Plan of Reform*, p. 337 (also, more generally, pp. 333-34, 337-40).

[110] Besides Wood's article, "Mise of Amiens and SL's Theory of Kingship," one should consult the brief but effective study by Petit-Dutaillis, "L'Établissement pour le commun profit au temps de SL," pp. 199, 201-2. Petit-Dutaillis stresses Louis IX's appreciation after the crusade of the fact that to carry through the reforms he intended in society, government had to become more theocratic and, within reason, more authoritarian.

[111] The most radical view of royal sovereignty was taken on the issue of the coinage reform, on which see below n. 158.

[112] Congar, "Église et l'état sous SL," p. 259, has characterized the treatise as "un exposé purement moral."

his vision of the Christian world, would have been quite happy to see rival princes spend themselves in useless slaughter. The king had two answers for their doubts, one a little fantastic, the other genuinely sublime. Perhaps, he said, in the heat of his first reaction to their criticisms, these princes "might put their heads together and say, 'It is from malice that the King is leaving us to fight one another'; thus the ill will they bore me might lead them to attack me, and I might well be beaten." But then he added more reflectively, to ignore the wars that Christians fought among themselves would be to bring down on him "the hatred of God, who says, 'Blessed are the peacemakers'."[113]

Scholars have tended to sympathize with the king and have usually acknowledged the altruistic motives behind his role as arbiter. From time to time, of course, revisionists muddle the picture. For example, one historian, in the grip of nineteenth century patriotism, once tried to show that the king's "interference" in the Rhineland was a precocious and deliberate striving after France's natural boundaries;[114] but assertions such as this have no evidentiary basis. The king was simply a peacemaker, and the earliest reference to his virtues in the liturgy of the Roman Church, a reference which, according to Kantorowicz, dates from his own lifetime, identifies him without further elaboration as the *rex pacificus*.[115] The metaphor became proper to Louis IX. In his announcement of his father's death, Louis's son and successor referred to the dead king as *rex pius, rex pacificus*.[116] The Latin oration that heralded the reception of the news in France that the king had been canonized identified the *lilium Franciae* as the symbol of the peace-loving king.[117] And the author of the office proper to the saint-king's feast day overwhelmed his texts with allusions to Louis's search for Christian peace.[118]

For a man who inspired this sort of enthusiasm, nothing could have been more difficult than to fight his fellow Christians or to permit them, if he could help it, to fight each other. This is the true meaning

---

[113] Joinville, chap. CXXXVII.　　　　　[114] Abel, "Louis IX," pp. 128, 149-68.

[115] The metaphor is Christocentric (cf. John 16:33, Romans 15:33, Philippians 4:7, Hebrews 7:2, also Psalms 85:8) and had been applied to earlier French kings (see the royal *laudes*, Paris, BN, MS Latin 778 fol. 218—twelfth-century office of Narbonne). The reference noted in the text is in a thirteenth-century liturgical manuscript written at Reims (it is now in Italy, Assisi, Biblioteca comunale MS 695—sometimes known as As695) dated conjecturally by musicologists 1225-1250. Seay, "Manuscrit 695," p. 22, actually prefers but does not insist upon a more narrow dating to 1228-1234. There are clear references to the existence of the manuscript in the 1270s (cf. Reaney, *Manuscripts of Polyphonic Music*, pp. 606-7). Kantorowicz, *Laudes regiae*, p. 18 n. 14, dated the manuscript 1257-1259, and he identified the *rex pacificus* in the *laudes regiae*, the chants in praise of the king, with a special liturgical addition in honor of Louis IX (p. 236).

[116] "Epistola publicata super obitu Ludovici noni regis," p. 441.

[117] "Religiosissimi . . . oratio," Duchesne, *Historiae*, v, 495-97.

[118] Longnon, *Documents*, pp. 53-55, 58. Folz, "Sainteté," pp. 41-42 nn. 70-71.

of the record of his arbitrations and also, for that matter, of his attempts to limit trial by combat. Because the evidence is sparse and the applicability of *ordonnances* sometimes very restricted in France, it is not always possible to be sure of the details of his actions in the latter sphere.[119] Some scholars believe that the king limited trial by battle in "civil" cases as early as 1254 and in "criminal" cases around 1258.[120] The workings of the appellate structure by which the traditional procedure would have had to be circumvented are not precisely understood.[121] But the ban on judicial combat, however and wherever it applied, was strict and probably became relatively more encompassing as time passed. In 1258 the king outlawed private war outright, although the generality of this prohibition has been challenged.[122] Whatever the case, Rutebeuf found this and similar restrictions on baronial privileges distasteful to his aristocratic sensibilities.[123] In 1260 Louis also circumscribed the aristocratic pastime of tournaments, the seedbed of many a private war;[124] and in 1265 he may even have prohibited the carrying of arms.[125]

Recognizing his antipathy toward Christian combat, one is somewhat sobered to see the French king authorize a war between Christians; yet, it was Louis IX who approved the violent suppression of the Hohenstaufen by Charles of Anjou. To begin with, Louis had never

[119] For the relevant documents, see Delisle, *Jugements de l'Echiquier*, no. 803; *Ordonnances*, I, 86; Boutaric, *Actes*, I, no. 523.

[120] The views of Guilhiermoz on civil cases may be found in his "SL, les gages de bataille"; Tardif's views on criminal matters in his study, "Date et le caractère de l'ordonnance de SL sur le duel judiciaire," especially pp. 171-74. A comparison of their opinions has been undertaken by Fontaine, "Revue," p. 267. See also Olivier-Martin, "Roi," p. 118, Griffiths, "New Men," pp. 256, 267; Carbasse, "Duel judiciaire," pp. 385, 390-91.

[121] The best discussion on this point is Mortet, "Constitucions," pp. 15, 22, 28-31. He argues that when Louis limited trial by battle he did not do so in baronial courts. However, in royal courts, by the oath *de calumnia*, the judicial duel could be set aside and judgment then made according to inquest. Cf. Lot and Fawtier, *Histoire*, II, 426; Cazelles, "Réglementation de la guerre privée," p. 541.

[122] Lot and Fawtier, *Histoire*, II, 425-26, on insufficient grounds it seems to me, see the restriction, urged by the former *enquêteur* Gui Foucois, as limited to the diocese of Le Puy where Gui was bishop-elect at the time. Cazelles, "Réglementation de la guerre privée," p. 539, supports this view, but also seems to think (p. 541) that the prohibition influenced the whole realm informally. See also the discussions in Tillemont, *Vie de SL*, IV, 122-23; Olivier-Martin, "Roi," p. 117; Du Cange, "On Private Wars," in Johnes, *Memoirs*, II, 209-22. Cf. *Formulaires*, no. 6, items 322, 333.

[123] Bastin and Faral, *Onze poèmes*, pp. 33-34 and notes; Petit-Dutaillis, "Établissement pour le commun profit," p. 201. See also Carbasse, "Duel judiciaire," pp. 390, 396 n. 51; Gaudemet, "Ordalies," pp. 130-31; and Boulet-Sautel, "Aperçu sur les systèmes des preuves," pp. 300-301.

[124] He encouraged those who still wanted to fight to try their hand in the East. Cf. Du Cange, "On the Origins and Usage of Tournaments" in Johnes, *Memoirs*, II, 87, 90.

[125] Boutaric, *Actes*, I, no. 980 n. 1: "cette ordonnance est perdue."

forgotten that peace between the empire and the papacy was necessary for a successful crusade. By the time he unleashed Charles this
realization was of great importance because he was on the verge of
setting a definite date for a new crusade.[126] Since the English king,
owing to his domestic problems, was in no position to give the papacy
any aid against the heirs of Frederick II after the 1250s, the problem
was a pressing one: Louis did not approve of the traditional obstinacy
of the papacy;[127] he may not even have trusted most of the mid-
century popes with the exception of Clement IV (1265-1268), his
friend and former *enquêteur*, Gui Foucois. But the papacy was the
head of Christian Europe. The pope too should take counsel, but he
should act in the spirit of the divine, for ultimately his authority was a
moral authority, a supreme moral authority on earth. Louis accepted
that fact. He tried first to reconcile the parties—he was an arbiter to
the last[128]—but when arbitration failed he felt it was his duty to send
his brother, eager for the opportunity, off to war. No one blamed
him.[129]

Out of this decision the king got very little. Charles's conquest,
which made Sicily available to Louis if he had wanted it in his final
crusade, made little difference. If the king thought that what he had
done, despite his hesitation and soul-searching, was necessary for the
survival of a healthy Christendom and for the success of the crusade
against the Infidel, he labored under two illusions. In the first place,
Charles manipulated the crusade itself into an aggrandizing escapade
at a time when Louis was too sick to comprehend and resist the de-
signs of his false-hearted brother.[130] In the second place, the king of
the Franks, by permitting his brother to become involved in papal
politics, had set in motion the train of events that was to make his vision of the world impossible ever to be fulfilled.[131] Perhaps Louis
eventually realized his error, for at the end of his life, in the lessons he

---

[126] He swore the crusader's vow in 1267; cf. Wallon, *SL*, II, 490.

[127] Huillard-Bréholles, *Historia diplomatica Friderici Secundi*, VI, pt. 2, p. 641.

[128] Cf. Labarge, *SL*, pp. 222-24.

[129] Fournier, *Royaume d'Arles*, pp. 188-89, has nothing but respect and praise for the
way Louis agonized over his decision.

[130] This is my interpretation of the use Charles finally made of the crusade—he
created himself overlord of Tunisia. See also below chapter 8 n. 4, and P.G.G., "Documents," pp. 249-50. A case can be made about the strategic wisdom of a North African
invasion in 1270; cf. Strayer, "Crusades of Louis IX," pp. 185-88. Recently, Longnon,
"Vues de Charles d'Anjou," has taken vigorous exception to the culpability of Charles.

[131] This is a rather rhetorical statement and yet the interesting article by Strayer,
"Crusade against Aragon" ends with the proposition that the humiliation of the papacy
in the later Middle Ages at the hands of the French crown can be traced to the unfortunate involvement of the French in Sicilian affairs, involvement which Louis IX had first
approved around 1260.

transmitted to his heir on the ideals of Christian rulership, he spent more time on the issue of not harming another Christian in war than upon any other single proposition.[132]

The third and final major aspect of Louis's rulership that I want to discuss concerns his reform of royal coinage in the latter half of the reign. Strange as it may seem to modern sensibilities, it was actually on the issue of coinage that many aspects of Louis's vision of the Christian world took their most dramatic and even radical shape. Fundamentally, in his reform of the coinage the king found a way to link the moral lessons of the past, particularly the failure of the crusade, with the values most important to him in the twilight of his life.

Louis was constantly interested in coinage as any medieval prince had to be.[133] He had issued regulations on the eve of the crusade concerning his money in an attempt to assure that the currency remained sound during his absence abroad.[134] He was always very much aware of the regalian powers traditionally attached to coinage, especially the notion that a suzerain had to supervise the use and exchange of different currencies in his principality.[135] However, it was during the crusade itself that Louis first showed how truly fascinated he was with the question of coinage.

He issued his first gold coin in 1251 when he re-minted the crusaders' *sarrazinas* hitherto engraved, for commercial purposes, with legends favorable to Mohammed.[136] Around 1253 the king's friend, Prince Bohemond of Antioch, also issued a gold coin, probably with Louis's encouragement, bearing the Lamb of God Triumphant and

[132] Composed in late 1267 or early 1268 according to O'Connell, *Propos de SL*, p. 185, the remarks on war occupy nos. 24 and 25 of his edition (pp. 189-90).

[133] Besides the information accumulated in this and subsequent paragraphs sustaining Louis's interest, it should be noticed that the royal archives were full of the most varied information on the question of coinage; *Formulaires*, no. 6, items 107, 325-31, 335, 377, 382. Courtenay's suggestion ("Token Coinage," p. 284) should also be noticed, namely that it was Saint Louis who first allowed token coins to circulate in the household administration of Blanche of Castile and Margaret of Provence. Courtenay also suggests, but without evidence, that the king might have used token coins as Maundy Thursday offerings to the poor. For a good general discussion of coinage in Louis's reign, see Bisson, "Consultative Functions," pp. 360-63; see also Babelon, "Monnaie de SL." A work by Yvon on Louis's monetary policies, presented to the Colloquy of Royaumont in 1970 (*Septième centenaire de la mort de SL*, p. viii) unfortunately has not been published.

[134] MP, IV, 608, 632; *HGL*, VIII, c. 1195. See also Guilhiermoz, "Sources manuscrites de l'histoire monétaire de SL," p. 99; and Bisson, "Coinage," pp. 454-57, on the pre-crusade mints. Cf. the activities of Alfonse of Poitiers in 1253; *Layettes*, III, nos. 4048-49, 4051, 4064.

[135] Cf. the royal controls exercised over the use of *nantois* and *nimois* currency before the crusade; *HF*, XXIV, 174 no. 887, 494 no. 184. See also Froger, "Enquêtes . . . à La Flèche," p. 15; and Bisson, "Coinage."

[136] Blancard, *Bésant*, p. 24.

the legend, *Christus Vincit, Christus Regnat, Christus Imperat*.[137] Inspired by these two examples of gold coinage (we shall have the opportunity to consider their influence at greater length later) and perhaps also by the issuance of the gold florin in 1252,[138] Louis IX decided to strike a gold coin in France when he returned to his own kingdom.[139]

Before he did so, however, a great deal of time was to intervene. Initial delays may have been caused by the shortage of specie in France after the crusade.[140] More generally, the European mainland endemically suffered from shortages of gold bullion even after the major commercial centers, like Florence, began to reissue gold coins.[141]

A second cause for the delay was the fact that Louis felt obliged to try to get control of bad local currencies before he began a major reform. The process was slow. The king could not abrogate long-standing feudal privileges; and the baronial right to mint coins went back as far as the breakup of the Carolingian Empire and was distributed chaotically among nobles and prelates.[142] But we find evidence of tentative royal orders tightening up or modifying the monetary system in 1263 and 1264.[143] Also in 1263 the king ordered the *bailli* of Vermandois to observe carefully the minting of money by his brothers, the counts of Poitou and Anjou.[144] By 1265 all preliminary efforts were completed.

In that year Louis reiterated his view that his money should run throughout France as a regalian right while barons' money should run only in their own domains.[145] To simplify the exchange of feudal coins for royal coins, he required that baronial coinage be as high in quality as his own.[146] He forbade mismanagement of baronial coin-

[137] See the argument advanced in chapter 5 nn. 178-80.

[138] Kantorowicz, *Laudes regiae*, Appendix II, pp. 222-23.

[139] *SL*, Exposition, p. 65 no. 107; Labarge, *SL*, pp. 217-19. Cf. Balog and Yvon, "Monnaies," pp. 138-39.

[140] Cf. Hénocque, *Saint-Riquier*, I, 513 n. 2. See also Barthélemy, "Essai sur la monnaie parisis," p. 155.

[141] Pirenne, *Economic and Social History*, pp. 114-15.

[142] Ibid., pp. 111-12; Boutaric, *SL et Alfonse*, pp. 216-17; Wolff, "Significance of the 'Feudal Period' in the Monetary History of Europe." Despite Louis's partial successes in inducing some barons to concede their minting privileges, the problem of competing baronial coinages remained important down to the reign of Philip V; cf. Henneman, *Royal Taxation*, p. 34.

[143] Bisson, "Coinage." Idem, "Registre municipal." Besides the royal directives mentioned in the text Bisson identifies an interpretative order of the *sénéchal* of Carcassonne-Béziers of 1264.

[144] Thillois, "Cartulaires du diocèse de Laon," p. 209.

[145] *Ordonnances*, I, 94-95; Mouynes, *Ville de Narbonne, Inventaire, Annexes de la série AA* (separate pagination), pp. 91-92. See also Bisson, "Coinage," pp. 457-62. Cf. Bardon, *Alais*, pp. 145-46.

[146] *Ordonnances*, I, 94-95. See also Labarge, *SL*, pp. 218-19. Cf. O'Connell, *Teachings*, pp. 59-60 n. 30.

age[147] and established, by ordinance at All Saints 1265, internal exchange rates for money from Laon, Nantes, Anjou, Mantes, and the English-dominated southwest (the sterling regions).[148]

The barons, needless to say, were outraged at this systemization of the monetary system, for the king used their failure to live up to his new prescriptions as the justification for seizing ("usurping" as one chronicler wrote) the coinage rights of his feudatories.[149] The bishop of Mende went so far as to claim palatine rights and, by doing so, tried unsuccessfully to protect his currency by forbidding the circulation of the king's in his domains.[150]

Before the issuance of the regulations the king had already begun experimenting with a new standard form of royal coinage; the final product, the famous *gros tournois*, a silver coin, not only circulated throughout the realm, but, owing to Louis's absolute refusal to debase it for temporary gain, was much sought after by merchants in preference to competing baronial currencies.[151] It linked itself to the royal crusader's past, it has been argued, by borrowing the iconography of the *sarrazinas* of 1251.[152] Yet it remained iconographically unique in France because the king's directives forbade the visual imitation of his coins.[153]

The last point was well worth remembering. Failure to observe this proviso was probably equivalent to counterfeiting,[154] and, as antiquaries so often like to point out with evident glee, one boiled false-moneyers or buried them alive.[155] Not long before the ordinances on coinage, Louis IX had shown in the affair of Enguerran de Coucy, where different but equally important issues were at stake,

[147] *Olim*, II, 172 no. iii. See also Bisson, "Coinage," pp. 468, 469 n. 1.
[148] Wallon, *SL*, II, 110-11; Bisson, "Coinage," pp. 462-65.
[149] The chronicler of Nevers wrote, "Habebat enim eo tempore [1262] comes Nivernensis jus cudendi monetam; sed regia auctoritas ea omnia usurpavit"; (Lespinasse) "Chronique . . . de Nevers," p. 62 (also p. 23). See also Lebeuf, *Auxerre*, I, 385-86, and the references above n. 147.
[150] Michel, *Beaucaire*, Appendix III, "La Monnaie," p. 327.
[151] *SL*, Exposition, p. 65 no. 108; Favier, "Finances de SL," p. 135; Pirenne, *Economic and Social History*, pp. 113-14.
[152] Blancard, *Gros tournois*, p. 2 n. 1. Cf. Grierson, "Rare Crusader Besant," p. 177 and especially n. 21.
[153] *Ordonnances*, I, 94-95; Natalis de Wailly, "Recherches sur le système monétaire de SL," pp. 137-39, citing BN Cartul. 210. See also Guilhiermoz, "Sources manuscrites de l'histoire monétaire de SL," p. 99.
[154] Dieudonné, "Théorie de la monnaie," p. 100, believed that the prohibition against imitation of royal money only applied to those baronial currencies which did not match Louis's in the content of precious metal. In other words, to stamp baronial coins with the royal image might have been counterfeit, but more general similarities would have been tolerated *if* the baronial currency was good. Bisson, "Coinage," pp. 458-60, seems to disagree.
[155] Le Fils, *Montreuil-sur-Mer*, p. 116; Fauqueux, *Beauvais*, pp. 38-39.

that not even barons would be allowed to escape the power of the law. They could extrapolate from this fact what was to be expected if they disregarded the regulations on coinage.[156]

Perhaps because the consequences of disobeying the directives could have been so severe, questions about coinage reform seem to have stimulated debate at the university of Paris. More probably the reason that the university took up the matter is that it raised interesting questions about the limits of royal power.[157] The general opinion among the Paris faculty, as expressed by Gérard d'Abbeville, was that coinage remained residually a regalian monopoly. Consequently, anything the king did to improve the coinage was acceptable for the common good and, to a certain extent, consistent with traditional proprieties.[158] Thus issues about coinage were raised to a high matter of the common welfare and became the foundation for the most powerful assertions of sovereignty in Louis's reign.[159]

Just how far Louis subscribed to these views is not at all clear. Certainly he would exercise suzerain rights over disputed privileges of coinage.[160] Certainly he would inquire into the warrant of particular barons to strike coins.[161] Did he mean to go further? His *baillis*, almost too enthusiastic, seem to have thought so. The episcopal right to mint coins in the see of Cahors appears to have been challenged in November 1265; the viscomital right in Narbonne in December of the same year.[162] Meanwhile the *sénéchal* of Beaucaire-Nîmes prohibited the

---

[156] Around 1259 Lord Enguerran IV de Coucy had seized three young boys for poaching and, without according them due process, had had them hanged. Although many people recognized that the baron's actions were ill-conceived, they were shocked by Saint Louis's reaction. Because of the abuse of his judicial privileges, Enguerran was stripped of high justice, fined ten thousand pounds *parisis*, ordered to erect a memorial chapel in honor of the three boys suitably endowed for perpetual masses in their honor, and, finally, commanded to go on crusade to the Holy Land as purification (he was allowed to redeem this vow for twelve thousand pounds *parisis*). On the case, which is not reported in the *Olim* but is mentioned in chronicles and in the crown's financial records, and on the hostile aristocratic reaction to Louis's judgment, see Faral, "Procès d'Enguerran de Coucy," passim but especially pp. 232-46 and 248-55; Bastin and Faral, *Onze poèmes*, pp. 33-34 with notes. On the important place occupied by the Coucy family in French politics and society and on the life of Enguerran IV, see Tardif, "Procès d'Enguerran de Coucy," pts. 1 and 2. Cf. Griffiths, "New Men," p. 240.

[157] Michaud-Quantin, "Politique monétaire," p. 149 (I owe this reference to the kind help of Professor Gaines Post).

[158] Ibid., passim but especially pp. 150-51.

[159] Cf. Griffiths, "New Men," p. 271; he does not believe that the directives on reform of the coinage had a generalized, almost legislative, aspect.

[160] On the bishop of Auxerre and the count of Nevers at odds on this issue, see GC, XII, "Instrumenta," c. 350 no. lxii. See also Natalis de Wailly, "Recherches sur le système monétaire de SL," pp. 137-38; and above n. 149.

[161] Wallon, SL, II, 106; Pirenne, *Economic and Social History*, p. 112.

[162] These public inquests in Cahors and Narbonne were local affairs, but the coincidence of their occurrence in November and December 1265, immediately after the

bishop of Mende from minting silver coins, a judgment that was reversed by the scrupulously honest king in 1266. Yet, as we have seen
in other contexts, royal officials at this level of the administrative
hierarchy had almost a missionary zeal about defending royal prerogatives. The bishop was still complaining about the *sénéchal*'s challenges to his rights of minting in 1269.[163]

It was not until 1266 that Louis issued the long-planned gold coin
for France, the *écu*, which bore the legend *Christus Vincit, Christus
Regnat, Christus Imperat* (see accompanying illustration).[164] The emblem, the shield of the militant pilgrim, and the legend were both
links to the crusader's past. The legend, in particular, recalled the
gold coin that Louis's friend, the prince of Antioch, had struck in
1253.

> Like the royal miracle of healing scrofula by touch [wrote Kan-
> torowicz], like the Holy Vial containing celestial balm for anointing
> the king, like the Oriflamme, or the Golden Lilies, the three clauses
> [*Christus Vincit, Christus Regnat, Christus Imperat*] . . . [became] a sym-
> bol of the crown of France. . . .
>
> . . . The adoption of the new legend fits perfectly with all the
> other achievements of this royal crusader and saint whose reign
> marks the high tide of the French cult of kings, the "Religion of
> Rheims and St.-Denis." It was St. Louis, who in every respect en-
> riched that treasure of grace on which all his successors would
> thrive. It was he whose kingship was elevated to transcendancy by
> the Spiritualists and Symbolists of his age and who, in turn, be-
> stowed the thin and light air of the angelic kingdoms upon his
> country. . . . In putting the three clauses as his device on his gold
> coins, he had, as it were, commended his government to Christ the
> victorious, the royal, the imperial, whom he himself represented on
> earth more perfectly, perhaps, than any other king ever did.[165]

In later Capetian propaganda invocation of the legend *Christus Vincit* would be synonymous with invocation of the saint-king's guidance.
Guillaume de Nogaret, for example, employed the legend in his
opening harangue against the Templars in 1308—appealing, by his

king's reforms of All Saints, is certainly suggestive. The inquests are reported in Bisson, *Assemblies*, Appendix II nos. 3, 4.
[163] Michel, *Beaucaire*, Appendix III, "Monnaie," p. 329, and "pièces justificatives," p. 455 no. 49.
[164] Lafaurie has shown (*Monnaies*, pp. 23, 29) that no other gold coin was issued in France except the *écu*. Earlier opinions that, besides the *écu*, an *agnel d'or* was also struck by the saint-king (*Trésor de numismatique*, V: *Histoire de l'art monétaire*, p. 3 nos. 7-9) are the result of a misreading of the original texts.
[165] Kantorowicz, *Laudes regiae*, pp. 3-4. See also *SL*, Exposition, p. 65 no. 107; Grier-son, "Rare Crusader Besant," pp. 176-77.

6. The *Ecu d'Or* of Saint Louis, Obverse and Reverse.

usage, to the memory and approbation of Saint Louis.[166] The publicists of Charles V argued, rather more elaborately, that Louis had chosen the legend for his *écu* in order to intensify perceptions that it was Christ Himself Who worked through the French kings when they healed scrofula by touch. The link between the two entities—the legend and scrofula—was furnished by the fact that an *écu* was sometimes given to poor recipients of the royal touch.[167] Like the image of the *rex pacificus*,[168] the legend *Christus Vincit* also had wide ramifications on the liturgical "remembrance" of the saint-king. When Philip III visited the Narbonnais in 1273, the *Christus Vincit* acclamations were sung on 25 August for the anniversary mass of his father's death; they were normally sung at Easter and coronations only.[169] As

[166] Kantorowicz, *Laudes regiae*, p. 4.   [167] *Ibid.*, p. 5 n. 13; Bloch, *Royal Touch*, p. 282.
[168] Above nn. 115-18.
[169] A twelfth century manuscript of the mass celebrated at Narbonne (Paris, BN, MS latin 778) has interlinear additions in a later hand (fols. 217 verso, 218) identifying the pope, archbishop, and king whose *laudes* were sung together on one occasion. These additions—*Gregorius, Petrus,* and *Philypus*—suffice to date the interpolation 1272-1276. I presume the manuscript was glossed in this way as an aid in singing, not generally but for a particular time. In favor of this interpretation is the fact that other marginal additions in the same hand give instructions on singing the *laudes* (fol. 217 verso; Kantorowicz, *Laudes regiae*, pp. 243-44 n. 4). Within the period 1272-1276, the year 1273 is the most likely date for the glosses. In the late summer of that year Philip III, the king who must be referred to in the interlinear addition, made an extended trip to Languedoc and was in the Narbonnais on 25 August; "Regum mansiones et itinera," *HF*, XXI, 425. I assume that a mass in honor of Louis IX was celebrated in the new king's presence on the twenty-fifth, the anniversary of Louis's death (the obit of the former king had been celebrated annually at the cathedral of Narbonne since 1271; *HGL*, VIII, c. 252). In Europe *laudes regiae* were usually sung at coronations (Eisenhofer and Lechner, *Liturgy*, p. 283); in France, however, they were sung during the great festivals (Kantorowicz, p. 100). At Narbonne, according to this manuscript, they were sung at Easter (fol. 217 verso). I believe, however, that an exception was made on the occasion of the visit of Philip III, not only because he was a king and entitled to the *laudes regiae* but also because the acclamation *Christus Vincit*, the text of the Narbonne *laudes*, had been special to Louis IX. (The idea that the *laudes regiae* could be used in an inappropriate liturgical context, as argued here, is not very radical; they were sometimes chanted in completely nonliturgical contexts; cf. Guenée and Lehoux, *Entrées royales*, p. 143.)

a general principle, the canonization of Louis IX in 1297 prepared the way for the substitution (or addition) of his name for (or to) that of Saint Michael in the *Christus Vincit* orations of the French mass.[170]

Leaving the symbolism aside, what practical use did Louis have in mind for the *écu*? This question is not easy to answer. Prestige may have played a part. Why should France lack a gold coin at a time when the minting of gold looked like the wave of the future? Moreover, foreign coins, by the coinage reform, could not run in France.[171] To facilitate exchange, then, a French gold coin would have been very valuable to the crown if it could serve as a kind of money of account directly exchangeable with another major currency outside of France. If the *écu* was intended to play this role, however, it was badly designed. It had no direct or simple weight or value relationship with any other European coin.[172]

This very lack of affinity with other coins is one factor which suggests that the *écu* had a quite different purpose. That purpose is strongly hinted at in a fifteenth century record describing a meeting in Paris of sovereign princes, arranged by Saint Louis about the middle of the thirteenth century. The princes, from both sides of the Alps, discussed a "European" coinage regulated by weight.[173] Perhaps no meeting of this sort took place on the scale suggested by the author of the receipt, but the possibility that the document preserves a kernel of truth should not be ignored. Meetings of the curia, referred to by contemporary sources, are often not mentioned in the official records, the *Olim* (the case of Enguerran de Coucy is classic).[174] It is not unreasonable to think that at one of the sessions of the curia, a few "border" princes who did not normally attend the king's court were present for discussions about the many coinage reforms which Louis planned and which might affect them. Perhaps he even invited them to come, out of a desire on his part to assure them that he was not encroaching un-

[170] David, "Acclamations *Christus vincit*," p. 2 no. 1; *Antiphonale*, pp. 33*-36* second set.

[171] See the references above nn. 145, 148.

[172] Lafaurie, *Monnaies*, pp. 23, 29, 24. Favier, "Finances de SL," p. 135, calls the success of the introduction of the *écu* "plutôt limité." Later, especially in the fourteenth century, however, the *écu*, because of its soundness, was "adopted," informally as it were, as a fictitious international money of account; de Roover, *Evolution de la lettre de change*, pp. 15-16 n. 20; Einzig, *History of Foreign Exchange*, pp. 71-74, 105-6. Partly because of its association with Saint Louis, it became iconographically a "European standard coin . . . which was to be repeatedly copied or imitated"; Kantorowicz, *Laudes regiae*, Appendix II, "Notes on the Diffusion of the Christus vincit Legend on Coins," esp. pp. 222-23; cf. Saint-Amans, "Observations sur quelques monnaies," pp. 213-14.

[173] Kantorowicz, *Laudes regiae*, Appendix II, p. 228 n. 31, cites the document. It refers to the meeting as having occurred in 1250 in Paris, but this dating could only be approximate since Louis was on crusade in that year.

[174] Above n. 156.

justly on the rights of others. In the course of the discussions the idea of a universal Christian coinage might well have been suggested. In this scheme, which, if it existed at all, came to nothing, the gold *écu* bearing the inscription *Christus Vincit* and having no affinities with any other coins may have had the most important role to play.

In the absence of better evidence, of course, we have to continue to regard the minting of the *écu* as symbolic only, Louis's way of affirming a link to his past as a crusader and, with its powerful legend, the glory of the future. It was a timely symbol, but, as it turned out, one that failed of expectation. The crusader principalities under the suzerainty of Bohemond of Antioch, to which the legend of the coin made reference, were in desperate trouble in 1266. They struggled on for a while but collapsed irretrievably in 1268, two years before Louis could mount his own ill-fated expedition to draw off the forces that besieged them.

What lay behind the achievements and the failures of Louis IX in establishing a popular ascetic style of religious devotion, in bringing peace to Europe, and in giving his realm a coinage which symbolized its willing submission to all that he thought was best in Christian life? What motivated him to attempt such a purification? There should be no doubt that behind it all—if such a phrase does not do too much injustice to the organic unity of his actions and motives—was his seeking after personal salvation. But, as has been stressed repeatedly in these pages, personal salvation, for a Christian king in the Middle Ages, insofar as human will had anything to do with it, was only partly a consequence of personal morality narrowly defined. A ruler had to rule well; it was his Christian duty to do so. But ruling well was not simply ruling efficiently or even ruling according to legal forms. Ruling well meant putting active principles of religion into every policy and program and generally making the practice of the Christian religion profounder in the realm than the ruler had found it.

The ruler, at his best, was example and guide, stern teacher and gentle master. For Louis the ultimate demonstration of this fact was his commitment to the crusade, to an enterprise which he believed summed up the potential unity and profound holiness both of Christian society as a whole and of that part which he ruled. Modern sensibilities sometimes rebel at such sentiments, but historians must try, as Frederick William Maitland was fond of reminding the scholars of his generation, to think the thoughts of medieval men as they thought them. For Louis IX all that went before was merely discipline and preparation for the final purification, the purification of Holy War, the ultimate and perfect test of the quality of his rulership.

• 8 •

CONCLUSION:
A NEW CRUSADE

The worsening situation in the Levant was the immediate stimulus for Louis's last major effort to help the crusader states.[1] Until about 1266 he was not in a position to commit himself actively to a crusade, but he had done all he could in a piecemeal way to help the embattled Christians. When he finally set about preparing a new expedition in 1267, he encountered a world which, despite his example, was still lacking in enthusiasm. He was physically in less of a position to inspire it. He was weak and growing weaker, if Joinville's description can be trusted, though his friend may perhaps be exaggerating in order to insulate himself from criticism that he too refused to join the king on the last expedition.[2]

Louis, however, was just as careful if not more careful in making his preparations than he had been before.[3] He sought out the same sort of help from foreign states. His brother, Charles, now king of Sicily, was persuaded to join the expedition, perhaps by the opportunity of invading Tunisia.[4] He knew that if he could establish his influence in North Africa, he would have a virtual monopoly of authority in the central Mediterranean. Alfonse did not have to be persuaded; he had decided to go on crusade, as far as can be determined, largely for reasons of salvation. He died shortly after the expedition dissolved.[5] England under Lord Edward, the heir presumptive who much admired the French king, made more of a contribution than it had to Louis's original expedition. Edward, as Louis had done before him, induced erstwhile rebellious barons to accompany him on crusade.[6] In Ed-

[1] Many of the issues relevant to Louis's second crusade have already been mentioned; there is a good summing up of both the material side of his preparations for this expedition and the very brief military actions that took place in Strayer, "Crusades of Louis IX," pp. 181-92 (for the events recalled in this paragraph, see especially pp. 181-83).

[2] Joinville, chap. CXLIV.

[3] Strayer, "Crusades of Louis IX," pp. 183-84.

[4] *Layettes*, IV, no. 5286 *bis*. See also Strayer, "Crusades of Louis IX," pp. 185-88; and Delaborde, "Revue." Cf. above chapter 7 n. 130.

[5] On the ascending thrust of Alfonse's charity before this crusade, see *Layettes*, IV, p. lxi; and the analysis of his will in Little, *Frater Ludovicus*, pp. 40-42. His itinerary in his last days (he died on 21 August 1271) is published in Fournier and Guébin, *Enquêtes administratives*, p. xxi.

[6] Beebe, "English Baronage."

ward's case and in the case of numerous other nobles, the first gestures of support were quickly followed by pleas for financial help. History repeated itself when Louis generously complied.[7]

As with the first expedition, an array of financial expedients were used to finance the crusade.[8] The tenths were levied (for three years) and apportioned according to Louis's wishes. Even certain monasteries which were exempt from taxation for the crusades gave gracious grants to the king without prejudicing their privileges.[9] A levy for the knighting of Louis's son was modified, after counsel and consent, into a levy for the Holy War.[10] Still another search was made for usurers in order to seize their illegal profits.[11] Negotiations were also completed with southern towns that had not given to the first expedition; they acknowledged their obligations to the crown and contributed.[12] Altogether, however, Louis seems to have been more scrupulous, less hasty and exacting, than before his first crusade. Perhaps for this reason the size of the army was only about two-thirds that of 1248.[13]

It is true that historians know a great deal less about the king's second crusade than about his first. Part of the explanation for this is that the expedition turned out to be of no military importance in salvaging Christian conquests in the Levant.[14] Another reason, alluded to before, is that preparations at home did not spark violent controversies. Of course, "jongleurs and troubadours . . . criticized the whole crusading idea,"[15] but the officials who carried out Louis's orders behaved better in the late 1260s. They were responding to the moods and enthusiasms of a mature saint, who had carefully schooled them in the

---

[7] Strayer, "Crusades of Louis IX," pp. 183-84.

[8] Besides the evidence adduced in subsequent notes with respect to the financial policies of Louis IX, see Favier, "Finances de SL," p. 135. Dossat has called attention to Alfonse of Poitier's financial efforts as well, especially his sale of forest properties to raise money for his expedition; Dossat, "Alfonse de Poitiers et la préparation de la croisade de Tunis: Les Ventes de forêts." See also Bisson, "Negotiations for Taxes"; and Jusselin, "Documents financières."

[9] On the tenths, see Strayer, "Crusades of Louis IX," pp. 184-85. On the gracious grants, see above chapter 4 n. 109.

[10] Strayer, "Crusades of Louis IX," p. 184.

[11] Ordonnances, I, 96 (year 1268); Layettes, v, no. 849; Arbois de Jubainville, Histoire . . . de Champagne, VI, nos. 3531-32; Boutaric, Actes, I, nos. 1462, 1465, 1522, 1531. See also Lépinois, Histoire de Chartres, I, 149.

[12] Boutaric, Actes, I, no. 1504; HGL, VIII, cc. 1668-71; and Mouynes, Ville de Narbonne, "Annexes de la série AA," p. 96 no. lxi-lxii. On the successful review and organization of southern records in the royal archives which must have strengthened the crown's hand considerably in the negotiations, cf. above chapter 4, nn. 165, 200.

[13] Strayer, "Crusades of Louis IX," p. 189, estimates the full army at ten thousand.

[14] Part of the forces, a very small part under Lord Edward, actually got to the Holy Land, but little was accomplished; ibid., pp. 191-92.

[15] Ibid., p. 183.

CONCLUSION

proprieties of government, rather than to the exuberance of a late-blooming adolescent. No one could have accused the king, as they had in the 1240s and early 1250s, of being a ruthless exploiter; and no one did.

On the eve of his departure Louis made arrangements for the transmission of his authority to a group of regents. Margaret of Provence was not to accompany the king although Alfonse's wife, Jeanne, and Louis's eldest living son's wife, Isabella, accompanied their husbands.[16] This seems to suggest that the king's marriage no longer had much vitality. Though the queen remained in France, the regency was denied her. It went to a knight and cleric (both of whom had alternates should anything happen to them). Certain duties were distributed outside this small circle, but no special powers were given to Margaret.[17]

The ceremonial events which marked Louis's preparations for departure were similar to those of 1248. In December of 1269 he offered the bishop of Clermont a gift from the relics of the Passion in the Sainte-Chapelle. Nothing could have been more appropriate than this implicit joining of the spirit of the first crusade, which had been declared at Clermont, with the hopes Louis took with him on his last expedition. It is unlikely, however, that he regarded his final enterprise as the true culmination of the crusading movement. The gift was only, if I am correct, a symbol of affirmation.[18]

Following the completion of a ritual *tournée* of the domain,[19] the king departed from Paris "not afraid to bear the burdens and expenses of another crusade."[20] He went south to Aigues-Mortes for the last time in early 1270 and set sail for Sardinia, the final rendezvous, on 2 July.[21] By 18 July the army had landed in Tunisia, there having been no long period of additional preparations as on Cyprus in 1249.

[16] Jeanne of Toulouse died a few days after her husband Alfonse on the return trip; Fournier and Guébin, *Enquêtes administratives*, p. xxi n. 1. Philip III's wife died in childbirth on the return trip; Strayer, "Crusades of Louis IX," p. 191.
[17] *Layettes*, IV, nos. 5662-64. The alternates chosen for the knight and cleric in 1270 were selected from the same orders; *Ordonnances*, XI, 346; Le Sueur, "Histoire . . . de Ponthieu . . . par Du Cange," pp. 173-74. The bishop of Paris was granted the power to make appointments to royal benefices; *GC*, VII, "Instrumenta," cc. 115-16 no. cliv. See also Strayer, *Royal Domain*, p. 6, on advisory roles assigned to royal administrators like Julien de Péronne.
[18] References to the gift may be found above chapter 7 figure ten.
[19] Above chapter 6 text following n. 75.
[20] The clause quoted is an amalgam of various similar clauses found in several of the major chroniclers of the reign: Anonymous of Saint-Denis, *HF*, XX, 54-56; Guillaume de Nangis, *HF*, XX, 562; Gerardus de Fracheto, *HF*, XXI, 5; Bernardus Guido, *HF*, XXI, 701, and XXIII, 177; an anonymous chronicler of Caux, *HF*, XXII, 23; Salimbene, *Cronica*, II, 702.
[21] Strayer, "Crusades of Louis IX," pp. 188-90.

After a few indecisive skirmishes the two sides settled down to glare at each other—the Moslems from posts safe within the walls of Tunis, the Christians from their camps not far away. A month later, daily expecting the additional forces that Charles of Anjou would bring for a great attack, Louis watched his son Jean Tristan, born on his first crusade, fall ill and die on his second. A few days later the king of France joined his son. As far as Louis IX was concerned, command of the crusade passed to his heir and a new generation. He could not have known that with his death the "age of the great crusades, led by the kings of the West, had ended."[22]

The king's death on crusade was the appropriate culmination of a life led earnestly in pursuit of one ideal. Yet he did not die the perfect death because he fell neither in battle nor under torture. Consequently, the Roman Church could not elevate him to the rank of martyr, for a martyr, by definition, had to have met his end as a direct result of his faith. The less exalted rank of confessor, which was conferred on Louis, implied a man's deep commitment to the faith but not his ultimate sacrifice for it. Joinville found the legalism distasteful:

> I cannot but think that it was an injustice to him not to include him in the roll of the martyrs, when you consider the great hardships he suffered as a pilgrim and Crusader during the six years that I served with him; in particular because it was even to the Cross that he followed Our Lord—for if God died on the Cross, so did St. Louis; for when he died at Tunis it was the Cross of the Crusade that he bore.[23]

Louis's influence and importance as a model of Christian rulership did not die with him. Indeed, to a degree, his admirers—especially the modern ones—have exaggerated his achievements to the detriment of the earlier Capetians. Yet even when we pay due regard to the impressive accomplishments of the saint-king's predecessors, it may still be said, and quite truthfully, that it was Louis IX who was chiefly responsible for giving substance to the hitherto vague sense of identity, purpose, and destiny of the kingdom of France.[24] This was felt to be so by near contemporaries. Among them, preoccupation with Louis's reign as an all-too-brief encounter with terrestrial Paradise touched all aspects of French culture.[25] One elegist, perhaps in-

[22] Ibid., pp. 190-92.

[23] Joinville, chap. 1. See also Folz, "Sainteté," p. 43.

[24] See Spiegel, "Cult of Saint-Denis," pp. 62-65, and Giesey, *Juristic Basis*, p. 37, who both, while recognizing the contributions of earlier kings to the elaborate edifice of mystical kingship in France, put their major emphasis squarely on the role of the saint-king.

[25] See the references below nn. 32, 35-36.

fluenced by the terrifying descriptions of the last days in current apocalyptical texts, went so far as to assert that the king's death had brought an end to charity and compassion.

> I say that justice is dead and loyalty extinct
> Since the good king, the holy creature, died
> Who did justice to each upon his complaint . . .
> To whom can the poor people now cry
> Since the good king is dead.[26]

Certain future kings, notably Philip the Fair, suffered emotionally from constant comparison with Louis IX.[27] Joinville, for example, used his book to upbraid and threaten his friend's grandson.

> Great [will be] the reproach . . . to those of his house who seek to do ill, for fingers will be pointed at them and it will be said that the holy King from whom they are sprung would have scorned to do such wrong.[28]

Although Louis's successors should have "derive[d] profit" from the example of his life,[29] the condition of the kingdom which he passed on to them was becoming, according to Joinville, "constantly worse."[30] Yet the truth is that Louis's successors faced far more difficult problems—natural and man-made—than he had ever faced;[31] it was unfair or at least grossly insensitive of their efforts that they should have got so little sympathy when they failed.

However, the majority of Louis's successors successfully manipulated remembrance of the saint-king to their advantage. Without forgetting that they stood in a long line of illustrious rulers (or so they would have it) they ordinarily stressed the historical existence of Saint Louis as the fundamental proof of their distinction. It was by using him as an image that French publicists began to call themselves and their compatriots the Chosen People and their king the Most Christian King. France was a Holy Land largely because an Ideal Crusader, Louis IX, had sanctified it by his sojourn upon earth and because his blood coursed through the veins of his royal descendants.[32]

[26] Jean de Pange, *Roi très chrétien* (cited and translated in Labarge, *SL*, p. 250).
[27] Strayer, "Philip the Fair, A Constitutional King," pp. 208-9.
[28] Joinville, chap. CXLVII. [29] Ibid., chap. XV.
[30] Ibid., chap. CXLIV; cf. also chap. III.
[31] On secular changes in weather, see Eddy, "Maunder Minimum," p. 1199, but cf. Herlihy, "Ecological Conditions," p. 13. For other aspects of late medieval crises relevant to the point in the text, see the two important articles by Strayer, "Fourth and Fourteenth Centuries" and "Economic Conditions."
[32] See the references above n. 24. See also Leclercq, "Un Sermon"; Kantorowicz, *Laudes regiae*, pp. 3-4; Fustel de Coulanges, *SL et le prestige de la royauté*. Cf., of course, Strayer, "France: The Holy Land, the Chosen People, and the Most Christian King."

All these claims—no matter how farfetched—owed much of their persuasive character to those practical accomplishments of Louis's rule which made his reputation in his own time. It is appropriate, in closing, that some attempt be made to review and summarize these accomplishments if only to appreciate the range and inclusiveness of his achievement.

In regional politics he had succeeded, with the help of his mother, in bringing the unruly baronage to heel, and he had made both nobles and prelates recognize and respect the legitimate prerogatives of the crown. As a result, from 1243 until 1314 there were no serious challenges to monarchical authority in France. In contrast, England and Germany, in the same period, were wracked with internal strife and civil war. The king had also succeeded in securing the allegiance of Languedoc to the crown. Despite some residual anti-French feeling in the deep south, the rapid assimilation of this region must be accounted one of the most extraordinary accomplishments of medieval political history.[33]

If we turn to international affairs, we find that the reputation of Louis IX and, therefore, of France was unexcelled. In the twelfth century English justice stood in such high repute that two sovereign princes, the kings of Castile and Navarre, had submitted disputes between them to Henry II.[34] In the thirteenth century Louis IX played the role of international arbiter almost a dozen times. This role of peacemaker came naturally to him. Except for the crusades themselves, France engaged in no major war with any other power in the reign of the saint-king, and even the occasional skirmishes that had characterized relations between Henry III and the young Louis IX essentially came to an end in 1243. The thirteenth century was a century of peace fundamentally because Louis IX was a man of peace. The imperial-papal confrontation would certainly have been even more terrible and more demeaning without the careful considerations given the matter by Louis IX.

In administrative affairs, Saint Louis gave a tone to government which it is hard to overpraise. By the time of his death arbitrary power had been more successfully restrained than at any prior time. It was always to the saint-king that men made allusion in their desire for

---

Apropos of this last article I am not saying that Louis IX articulated these theories (that was the job, as Strayer shows, of the publicists of Philip IV among others) but these theories found "validity" because Louis IX had lived.

[33] Guiraud, *Histoire de l'Inquisition*, II, 236: ". . . par sa politique de bienveillance et de justice envers les vaincus et ses adversaires de la veille, saint Louis transforma ces sentiments en fidelité, puisque, non contents de le servir, certains de ses seigneurs lui temoignèrent, à la Croisade et jusqu'à la fin de leur vie, un inalterable attachement."

[34] Cf. Pollock and Maitland, *History of English Law*, I, 160.

good government:[35] "l'imagination populaire ne pensait qu'à saint Louis."[36] His successors, whom popular imagination often condemned, slavishly claimed to or tried to imitate his style of governance.[37] Usually they maintained the forms while forsaking the spirit. Thus, for example, the *enquêteurs* continued as a permanent feature of French administration, but the mendicant element or "cast of mind," which had given the office its luster under Saint Louis, was eliminated.[38] The former high reputation of the officials went down considerably.[39]

The king gave his poorer subjects generous alms, his vulnerable subjects necessary support. Toward the end of his life he bestowed on the realm an important symbol of unity in his excellent coinage.[40] Louis's only real failure—or so the story goes—was the crusades, but I would argue that even here, in the personal and spiritual terms that mattered most to him, at least some slight modification can be made in this judgment. Of course, he was defeated on his first crusade, and this memory oppressed him the remainder of his life. Of course, the fact that he could not participate fully in the last crusade clouded his final days. However, in the sense that the original crusade inspired him to be a ruler and eventually to be more conscientious in his rulership and that the second crusade provided him with the setting most appropriate for his death, his expeditions were the beginning, the end, and the meaning of his life.

Well may we, and with piety, mourn the death of this holy Prince, who held his Kingdom with such sanctity and truth. . . .[41]

[35] Cf. the complaints of the baronial party against Philip the Fair in 1314-1315, summed up in Artonne, *Mouvement de 1314*, p. 31. See also Denisova-Khachaturian, "Sotsial'no-politicheskie aspekty," p. 170.

[36] Bessot de Lamothe and Bligny-Bondurand, *Inventaire-sommaire, Gard*, 1: *Arrondissements*, p. 267

[37] Cf. Artonne, *Mouvement de 1314*, pp. 166-67; and (Berthelé) *Archives . . . Montpellier*, 1, 2d fasc. (individual pagination): *Grand Chartrier*, no. 2, for examples of King Louis X and King Charles V ordering their administrators to do their work as Saint Louis had ordered. On his deathbed Philip the Fair instructed his son to govern the kingdom like Saint Louis: "teneretque regnum Francie in bonu statu, prout ipsum tenuit beatus Ludovicus" (Baudon de Mony, "Mort . . . de Philippe le Bel," p. 12).

[38] Glennison, *Enquêteurs-Réformateurs*, appendixes.

[39] Cf. Henneman, "Enquêteurs-Réformateurs."

[40] Cf. the remarks of Wolff on the longings for the good money of Saint Louis in the fourteenth century; "Significance of the Feudal Period," p. 78.

[41] Joinville, chap. CXLVI.

APPENDIX ONE

BAILLIS, SÉNÉCHAUX, and PRÉVÔTS of Paris

The basic data, provided in Delisle's "Chronologie," *HF*, xxiv, have been updated and adjusted according to the results of supplementary research as indicated in the notes.

Rouen

Guillaume Poucin	1204-1207
Guillaume Escuacol	1208-1217
Jean de La Porte	1219-1228
Jean des Vignes	1228-1244
Étienne de La Porte	1247-1253[1]
Guillaume de Voisons	1255-1260

Caen

Pierre du Thillai	1205-1224
Renaud de Ville-Thierri[2]	1222-1227
Jean des Vignes	1226?-1239
Jean de La Porte	1227
Girard de La Boiste	1239-1246?
Jean Le Jeune	1247-1249
Robert de Pontoise[3]	1251-1254, 1256
Arnoul de Courferaud[4]	1256-1263

[1] Relieved in 1253, he reentered royal service after the king's return from crusade. *HF*, xxiv, "Chronologie," p. 103; Griffiths, "New Men," p. 243 n. 47 (Étienne was probably not a Norman).

[2] Stein, "Recherches," *ASHGâtinais*, xx, 199 (origin, "du Gâtinais"; the date of administration given by Stein is superseded by the date in *HF*).

[3] When Delisle compiled his chronology of *baillis*, it was clear that Robert de Pontoise was *bailli* of Caen from 1251 through 1253 or early 1254 (n.s.) but only one record, a document of the Exchequer of Falaise, bore his name in 1256. Delisle did not definitely conclude from this that Robert was *bailli* of Caen continually from 1251 through 1256, and, thus, dated Robert's administration "1251-1256?." Strayer eliminated the question mark when he discovered additional published evidence relating to the administration of Robert for the year 1256; Strayer, *Administration*, Appendix I, p. 112. But even with this and certain other evidence, it is not absolutely certain that Robert was *bailli* of Caen from 1251 through 1256 without interruption. It is interesting that the wax tablets of Jean Sarrasin mention another *bailli*—not included by Delisle—in 1256. I would suggest that this man, Stephanus de Podio, served from 1254 to 1256, but the case cannot be proved.

[4] Stein, "Recherches," *ASHGâtinais*, xx, 21; xxiv, 90 (origin, "du Gâtinais"—the date given by Stein was later revised in accord with *HF*, xxiv, in *ASHGâtinais*, xxiv); see also Porée, "Note sur Pèlerin Latinier," p. 62; Griffiths, "New Men," p. 245 n. 57.

Caux

Jean de Rouvrai	1204-1210?
Guillaume de La Chapelle	1210
Geoffroy de La Chapelle	1212-1238?
Thibaud de La Chapelle[5]	1224-1245
Barthélemi Chevalier	1248-1253
Gautier de Villers[6]	1256-1270

Gisors

Jean Ascon[7]	1209
Aleaume Hescelin	1209-1217
Hugues de Bouconvilliers	1211
Guillaume de Ville-Thierri[8]	1219-1227
Thibaud dit Macer[9]	1223, 1226
Jean des Vignes	1227-1228[10]
Raoul Arundel	1231-1235[11]
Renaud de Triecoc[12]	1235-1237
Guiard de Seuil	1237-1239
Luc de Villers	1243-1247[13]
Dreu de Montigni[14]	1247-1254
Jean de Sens	May 1254
Ferri d'Autenville	June 1254
Jean de Carreis	1258-1260

Mantes

(Under the administration of Gisors)	? -1256
Bérenger Rabot	1256-1262

[5] *HF*, xxiv, "Chronologie," pp. 110-12; Griffiths, "New Men," pp. 236 and 243; Stein, "Recherches," *ASHGâtinais*, xxxiv, 28-35. Originally of the Gâtinais, the family was of the "petty nobility," that is, knightly.

[6] See Griffiths, "New Men," p. 243 n. 48 (origin, Normandy); Carolus-Barré, "Baillis de Philippe III," p. 239.

[7] Goineau, *Gisors*, p. 127.

[8] Stein, "Recherches," *ASHGâtinais*, xx, 199; xxxiv, 93 (origin, "du Gâtinais"; for the date, *HF*, xxiv).

[9] Goineau, *Gisors*, p. 127.

[10] Ibid., p. 128. [11] Ibid.

[12] See also Griffiths, "New Men," pp. 241 n. 36, 243 n. 49 (origin, the Beauvaisis); he was "lord [petty seigneur] of Triecot."

[13] Goineau, *Gisors*, p. 128.

[14] Dreu was terminated well before the return of Louis IX. There also seems to have been a rapid turnover from May 1254 through 1258. The list here does not include several other doubtful *baillis* from this period. Unfortunately there are no indications of the precise causes of this rapid turnover (cf. ibid. on the rendering of the accounts in 1256). By 1258 the situation stabilized. Jean de Carreis was succeeded in 1260 by Anseau Le Vicomte who was *bailli* until 1271. See ibid., p. 129.

Verneuil

Barthélemi Droon	1211-1227
Fouque Carrel	1212-1214
Berruyer de Bourron[15]	1226-1232
Raoul Arundel	1235
Jean de Maisons	1235
Guerne de Verberie	1237-1244
Jean Le Jeune	1248
Jean de Meulan	1249
Guillaume de Voisons	1249-1254
Julien de Péronne[16]	1256-1258
Jean de Criquebeuf	1258-1273

Le Cotentin

Renaud de Cornillon	1207-1214
Miles de Levis	1215-1223
Baudoin de Danemois[17]	1227
Jean de Fricamps	1227-1231
Geoffroy de Bulli	1234
Jean de Maisons	1237-1246
Luc de Villers	1249-1252
Jean de Maisons	1254
Renaud de Radepont	1258-1267

Pont Audemer[18]

Cadoc	1204-1219
Jean Rapace	1246

Bayeux[19]

Renaud de Ville-Thierri	1206-1226
Eudes de Gisors[20]	1248-1252

[15] Stein, "Recherches," *ASHGâtinais*, xxxiv, 9 (origin, "du Gâtinais").

[16] Strayer, *Royal Domain*; Griffiths, "New Men," p. 244 n. 50 and pp. 259-61 (Julien's original home was probably Vermandois; he was a knight with legal training). See also Carolus-Barré, "Baillis de Philippe III," p. 214.

[17] Stein, "Recherches," *ASHGâtinais*, xx, 192; the date given by Stein is superseded by that in *HF*, xxiv.

[18] From 1226 to the mid-1240s, Pont Audemer, though retaining its individual character, was administered by the *bailli* of Rouen, Jean des Vignes. When Jean Rapace became *bailli* in Pont Audemer in 1246, he was considered Jean des Vignes's replacement.

[19] From 1229 or thereabouts to 1247 the *bailliage* of Bayeux was administered by the *baillis* of the Cotentin.

[20] Eudes de Gisors, relieved after 1252, was back in the king's service by 1259.

Paris

Eudes Popin, Eudes Arrode	1205
Philippe Hamelin	1207
Nicolas Arrode, Philippe Hamelin	1217-1219
Renier Arrode	1220
Nicolas Arrode, Jean Le Roi[21]	1223-1224
Jean des Vignes	1223-1227
Raoul Dessus L'Eau	1231
Guillaume Barbette	1234
Pierre Gentien, Nicolas Barbette, Omond Le Poissonier, Pierre Le Flamande, Jean Blanchot[22]	1238
Simon Barbette, Eudes Popin, Philippe Boucel[23]	1241
Hunold d'Étaples	1243
Eudes Popin, Raoul de Paci	1245
Renaud Le Conte	1246
Gautier Le Maître, Guerne de Verberie, Eudes Popin, Eudes Le Roux[24]	1247
Gautier Le Maître, Nicolas Barbette	1250
Eudes Popin, Eudes Le Roux	1250
Eudes Popin, Hervé d'Hierre	1250
Guerne de Verberie, Gautier Le Maître[25]	1251-1252
Étienne Tastesaveur d'Orléans, Guerne de Verberie	1252-1253[26]
Jean Bique	1253
Eudes Le Roux, Hervé d'Hierre	1256-1258
Jean de Champbaudon, Pierre Gontier	1258-1259
Pierre Gontier	1260-1261
Étienne Boileau[27]	1261-1269

Amiens

Pierre de Béthisi	1196-1211

[21] Vidier, "Municipalité parisienne," pp. 278-79.
[22] Ibid. [23] Ibid. [24] Ibid., for the last two officials.
[25] Ibid.; Bloch, "Blanche de Castille," p. 227 n. 4. Some of the undated references to Guerne de Verberie in *Layettes*, v, no. 885, and Boutaric, *Actes*, I, nos. 1560D, 1560K, I believe refer to the period before 1248.
[26] The date of appointment is given by Vidier, "Municipalité parisienne," pp. 278-79.
[27] Joinville, chap. CXLI; Borrelli de Serres, *Recherches*, I, chapter on the reform of the *prévôté* of Paris; cf. Stein, "Recherches," *ASHGâtinais*, XXXIV, 90 n. 7.

Jean de Fricamps	1225-1227
Geoffroy de Milli[28]	1237-1244[29]
Girard Wideuve	1247-1248
Hugues de Pierrelate	1249
Pierre d'Ernencourt[30]	1252?
André Le Jeune	1253
Jean Colrouge	1254-1255
Dreu de Braie	1256-1263

Sens

Étienne de Hautvillers[31]	1205-1227
Berruyer de Bourron	1222-1224
Nicolas de Hautvillers[32]	1222-1249[33]
Thibaud Clairambaut	1248
Nicolas de Menou	1249-1252
Pierre d'Échantilli	1252?
Étienne Tastesaveur	1253?
Arnoul de Montlhéri	1254?
Étienne Tastesaveur	1255-1271

Orléans

Guillaume de La Chapelle	1198-1214
Roger Le Péager	1217-1218
(Under the administration of the Queen dowager, Ingeborg, d. 1236)	circa 1218-1234
Jean Le Gai	1234-1239
Pierre d'Échantilli	1239-1246
Jean Le Monnoyer[34]	1248-1253
Mathieu de Beaune[35]	1254-1256
Girard de Chevresis	1256-1263

[28] Stein, "Recherches," *ASHGâtinais*, xxxiv, 25 (origin, "du Beauvaisis").

[29] Ibid. (Stein has refined the *HF*, xxiv, entry of 1228-1244).

[30] Cf. Griffiths, "New Men," p. 244 n. 55 (origin, Nogent-sur-Marne).

[31] Stein, "Recherches," *ASHGâtinais*, xxxii, 202 (cf. xxiv, 100), disputed the spelling (and, therefore, the meaning) of the last name. He preferred Auvillers. Étienne was "du Gâtinais."

[32] Ibid.

[33] The chronology of *HF*, xxiv, has been followed above, but Stein ("Recherches," *ASHGâtinais*, xxxii, 202; xxxiv, 100) was undecided, preferring at different times terms of 1222-1240 and 1222-1243.

[34] Cf. Griffiths, "New Men," p. 243 and his list ii (status: "commoner?"). Despite his dismissal in 1253, Jean Le Monnoyer returned to the king's service.

[35] Stein, "Recherches," *ASHGâtinais*, xxi, 354 (cf. xxxiv, 98-99 n. 7); origin, "du Gâtinais." Stein accepted the date of administration given in *HF* in the latter article. Griffiths, "New Men," p. 244 n. 52, prefers a Burgundian or Orléanais origin for Mathieu. See also Bourgin, *Soissons*, p. 51 n. 5 (status, circa 1260?, knight).

Étampes or the Gâtinais[36]

Adam Héron	1204-1226
Galeran d'Escrennes[37]	1224-1234
Adam Le Panetier	1236-1238
Philippe de Remin	1242-1249
(Under the administration of another	
bailliage, perhaps Orléans)	circa 1249-circa 1253?
Philippe de Chenevières[38]	1253
(Administered with Orléans)	1253?-1265?

Senlis

Guillaume Pasté	1202-1217
Gilles de Versailles	1207-1233
Guillaume de Châtelliers	1214-1227
Renaud de Beron[39]	1223-1234
Eudes de Gonesse	1234-1235
(Under the administration of	
Vermandois)	1236-1254
Thibaud d'Escuelles[40]	1254-1256[41]
(Under the administration of	
Vermandois)[42]	1258-1261

Vermandois[43]

André Le Jeune	1236-1246[44]
Simon des Fosses	1246-1251[45]

[36] Although Étampes, seemingly, was given over to Louis's brother Robert from 1237 to 1250, a royal *bailli* continued to function in the Gâtinais. See Loisne, "Catalogue des actes de Robert I," pp. 139-40; cf. *HF*, XXIV, "Chronologie," *sub* "Étampes (ou Gâtinais)."

[37] Stein, "Recherches," *ASHGâtinais*, XX, 11-12 (origin, "du Gâtinais"; the date given by Stein has been superseded by *HF*, XXIV). On the family, see Griffiths, "New Men," p. 238 n. 18.

[38] In this year alone he aided in the administration of the Cotentin; *HF*, XXIV, "Chronologie," p. 53.

[39] Cf. Laurain, "Renaud de Béronne."

[40] Stein, "Recherches," *ASHGâtinais*, XXI, 343 (origin, "du Gâtinais").

[41] Stein, (*ibid.*, XXXIV, 96) suggested that the administration of Thibaud extended through 1261, but this still remains tentative.

[42] For the periods of administration under Vermandois, see Waquet, *Vermandois*, Appendix I; cf. Bourgin, *Soissons*, p. 261 (in 1265, the *bailliage* of Senlis, in Bourgin's words, "se detache du Vermandois"). See also Carolus-Barré, *Chronologie des baillis de Clermont*, p. 9; and the remarks in the preceding note.

[43] Up to 1236 the *baillis* of Vermandois are impossible to distinguish from those of Senlis. Though Delisle did not refer to Essigny's list of *baillis* of Vermandois published in the latter's history of Roye in 1818, he did have access to Colliette's still earlier list which, apparently, was the basis of Essigny's work.

[44] Waquet, *Vermandois*, Appendix I. [45] Ibid.

Pierre de Fontaines[46]	1253
Pierre Angelart	1253-1255[47]
Mathieu de Beaune	1256-1260

Artois
Adam de Milli[48]	1223-1227
Pierre Tristan[49]	1227-1234
Simon de Villers[50]	1236-?[51]
Achard de Villers[52]	1253
(Appanage of the Count of Artois)	1237-1313

Touraine
Guillaume d'Azai	1213
Robert de Crespières	1214-1217
Robert des Loges	1217-1218
Thierri de Gallardon	1219-1227
Guillaume de Fougerei	1230-1232
Pierre Le Ber	1234-1238
Adam Le Panetier	? -1239
Josse de Bonnes[53]	? -1248

[46] See Griffiths, "Pierre de Fontaines," on the early career of Pierre; see also his "New Men," pp. 251-59, especially 244 n. 51 (origin, Vermandois; social status, knight with legal education). Compare, however, his interpretation of Pierre's service in 1253 (p. 252) as a training period.

[47] Waquet, *Vermandois*, Appendix I.

[48] Stein, "Recherches," *ASHGâtinais*, XXXIV, 25 (origin, "du Beauvaisis").

[49] Griffiths, "New Men," p. 243 (bourgeois status, later ennobled): Loisne, "Chronologie des baillis," p. 314, assigns him the status of a knight very early on.

[50] Cf. Griffiths, "New Men," p. 243 n. 48—the Villers family may have been Norman. Loisne, "Chronologie des baillis," pp. 314-15, assigns him the social status of a knight.

[51] Loisne, "Chronologie des baillis," pp. 314-15, dates the termination 1258.

[52] He acted as bailli in 1253 instead of the name of the countess dowager or her minor son. As *petit bailli* of the town of Arras he is listed in ibid., pp. 316-17, for the years 1253-1259. Loisne does not account him a *grand bailli* of Artois. Cf. *HF*, XXIV, "Chronologie," pp. 88-89; "Preuves," no. 138; d'Hérbomez, "Arras," p. 456.

[53] Stein, "Recherches," *ASHGâtinais*, XXXII, 197 (origin, "du Gâtinais"). Josse de Bonnes had both Touraine and Anjou under his administrative supervision in 1245. When Anjou was detached from the royal domain in 1246, he remained in charge of Touraine. Delisle noticed that there were numerous complaints against him brought before the *enquêteurs* by the people of Maine and Anjou. No doubt partly as a result of these complaints he lost his post in Touraine in 1248, but the decisive argument in favor of his dismissal was related to two different factors. First, the period of his separate administration of the Touraine was as bad as the period when he was probably overworked by having the county of Anjou appended (witness the complaints from Touraine presented to the *enquêteurs*). Second, the small size of a crusading grant, 2,000 pounds, which he collected from Tours at Ascension 1248, was probably also influential in bringing about his removal. Even with other revenues of the *bailliage* added in, gross income in the term was 2,592 pounds *tournois*. The *bailli* in 1238, during the same term, had collected more than that in ordinary revenue alone. Even if some of the *bailliage*

Philippe de Saint-Florentin	1249
Geoffroy Bernier	1249-1250
Aimeri "de Gaiis"	1252-1255
Raoul Le Grand	1256-1261

Mâcon[54]

Amauri de Courcelles	1239
Gui Chevrier	?-June 1241[55]
Raoul de Sens[56]	1242-1244
Guillaume de Pian	1245-1248
Guillaume Le Desréé?[57]	1248?
Guillaume de Hus[58]	?
Baudoin de Pian	1249-1253
Henri de Courances	1254-1260

Bourges

Gilbert "de Minpinc"	1217
Colin de La Chapelle	1220-1221
Pierre de Rouci	1221-1234
Raoul de Gandelus	1236-1239
Philippe de Grandchamp	1245
Jodouin d'Alonne	1247-1248
Mathieu Dreu (Droon)	1249-1250
Garnier Olivier	1252
Nicolas de Menou	1253-1257
Guillaume de Chenevières	1258-1262

Limousin

Thibaud de Blaizon	1229
Bernard de Livron?	1236
Pierre des Saux	circa 1240
Gérard de Malemort	1243-1245
Pons de La Ville	1246?

had been lost to the appanage system, as appears to be the case, every indication is that the falloff in income should not have been so enormous. Josse left the king's service permanently in 1248. On these points, see Stein, "Recherches," *ASHGâtinais*, XXXII, 196-97; *HF*, XXI, 280-81; XXIV, "Chronologie," p. 159; and Froger, "Enquêtes . . . à la Flèche," pp. 12, 17.

[54] The chronology is difficult to establish in Mâcon; Fournier, "Origines . . . Mâcon," pp. 477-78 (cf. 473-76).

[55] Ibid., pp. 477-80; he was probably assassinated circa 1244.

[56] Ibid., pp. 477-78; cf. *HF*, XXIV, which lists a royal agent, Raoul, in 1236, before the royal purchase of the county.

[57] He is not in Fournier's list, but is listed in *HF*.

[58] Fournier does not include him, but he is listed by Delisle.

Aimeri de Malemorte	1254
Aimeri Danais	1256-1258

Périgord-Quercy

Gilbert de Maubisson	1233
Gérard de Malemorte	1244-1245
Pons de La Ville	1246
Raoul de Bonnevoie	1252
(Administered with Limousin)	? -1281

Beaucaire-Nîmes

Guillaume de Benne	1226?
Pèlerin Latinier[59]	1226-1238
Jacobin (Latinier)[60]	1239[61]
Pierre Le Feare d'Athies[62]	1239-1241[63]
Pierre d'Ernencourt	1241-1243[64]
Oudard de Villers	1243-1253
Raoul "del Royre"	1251-1252
Guillaume d'Authon[65]	1254-1258
Geoffroy de Roncherolles[66]	1258-1260

Carcassonne-Béziers

Philippe Goloin	1226
Pierre Sanglier	circa 1228
Eudes Le Queux	1228-1235
Jean de Fricamps[67]	1236-1239
Guillaume d'Ormois (des Ormeaux)	1239-1243
Hugues d'Arcis	1243-1246

---

[59] Stein, "Recherches," *ASHGâtinais*, XXXIV, 62 (origin, "du Gâtinais"); Porée, "Note sur Pèlerin Latinier," p. 62.

[60] Stein, "Recherches," *ASHGâtinais*, XXXIV, 62 (origin, "du Gâtinais").

[61] Michel, *Beaucaire*, p. 335. See also Porée, "Note sur Pèlerin Latinier," p. 59 n. 2, who interpreted the data on Jacobin (or Jacobus) to mean that he was lieutenant of the *sénéchal* Pèlerin, and only held office himself as *sénéchal* briefly until a successor was appointed for Pèlerin.

[62] Porée, "Note sur Pèlerin Latinier," p. 62 (Pierre d'Athies was perhaps Norman). But cf. *HF*, XXIV, 713, which seems to suggest he was from Vermandois.

[63] Michel, *Beaucaire*, p. 335.

[64] Ibid.

[65] Porée, "Note sur Pèlerin Latinier," p. 62 (origin of Guillaume d'Authon, near Dourdan); Griffiths, "New Men," p. 245 n. 61.

[66] Porée, "Note sur Pèlerin Latinier," p. 62 (origin of Geoffrey, Vexin or Beauvaisis); Griffiths, "New Men," p. 245 n. 60.

[67] Porée, "Note sur Pèlerin Latinier," p. 63 n. 1 (Jean was originally from the Amienois).

Jean d'Escrennes[68]	1246-1248
Guillaume de Pian[69]	1248-1254
Pierre de Voisons	1254
Pierre d'Auteuil[70]	1254-1263

Auvergne
Béraud de Mercoeur	1227
Amauri de Courcelles	1238-1239
(Appanage of the Count of Poitiers)	1241-1271

Saint-Omer[71]
Nicolas du Castel	1212
Adam de Neuilli	circa 1215
Étienne L'Échenson	1224-1228
Guillaume de Vauhuon	1228
Gui de Marisac	1229?
Pierre Tristan	1231-1234[72]
Simon de Villers[73]	1236
(Appanage of the Count of Artois)	1237-1313

Anjou
Hamelin de Roorte	1211-1221
Pierre Le Ber	1228-1242?
Guillaume de Fougerei	1230
Geoffroy Payes	1239-1241
Josse de Bonnes	1245-1246
(Appanage of the Count of Anjou)	1246-

Poitou
Geoffroy de Bulli	1225
Thibaud de Blaizon	1227-1230

[68] On the family, above chapter 6 n. 284.
[69] There is a misprint in *HF*, xxiv, "Chronologie," p. 249.
[70] Griffiths, "New Men," p. 245 n. 62 (origin, Auteuil in the present *département* of the Oise).
[71] Cf. the remarks of Loisne, "Chronologie des baillis," on the nature of the *bailliages* of Saint Omer and other towns (p. 311).
[72] Ibid., p. 325 (he is assigned only a one-year term here, 1231).
[73] After Saint Omer became part of Robert's appanage, Simon continued as *bailli* there in the count's name until 1247; ibid.

Guillaume de Fougerei	1230
Adam Le Panetier	1230-1234
Hardouin de Maille	1231-1242
(Appanage of the Count of	
Poitiers)	1242-1271

MENDICANT FOUNDATIONS
UNDER LOUIS IX

The purpose of this appendix is to describe the method and tabulate the results of recent investigations into the rate of growth of the two largest mendicant orders, the Dominicans and the Franciscans, in France. This subject is important to the general theme of Louis IX's rulership insofar as there is evidence that the king was a heavy supporter—financial and otherwise—of the mendicant movement[1] and that barons under his influence imitated his largesse: Martin has argued that in Brittany the coming of the crusade of 1248 stimulated local notables to found mendicant houses.[2] I hope to show in this appendix that there was a spurt of foundations before both of Louis's crusades suggesting that the phenomenon described by Martin may be general throughout the realm.

The basic source I have used is the now standard catalogue of Emery, adjusted where necessary by later research.[3] The period I cover is 1226 to 1270 (not including the latter year since Louis left Paris for his second crusade rather early). I have arranged the data in five-year groups so that the eves of both crusades (1245-1249 and 1265-1269) can be seen at a glance.[4] This has necessitated that the tabulation actually begin with a four-year period (1226-1229).

The dating of the foundations of mendicant houses, as Professor Emery has readily acknowledged, is relatively imprecise.[5] Many of the data in his catalogue are given in the form of "−" or "+" and then a date, indicating that the foundation can only be dated "before" or "after" the year given. Although in the runs of data that I have had to use, there were no "+" entries, there were many "−" entries. Despite the obvious skewing that might occur, I have chosen to enter such notations under the year following the sign in making my own tabula-

---

[1] Above chapters 3 (nn. 104-10) and 7 (nn. 23-29).

[2] Martin, *Ordres mendiants en Brétagne*, p. 18.

[3] Emery, *Fnars*; see also Fontette, "Villes médiévales."

[4] Many crusaders did not leave until 1249 on the first crusade which makes the period 1245-1249 a very nice one. On the other hand, almost all the crusaders left in 1270 with the king which makes the five-year span 1265-1269 equally appropriate as the eve of the second crusade.

[5] It is possible that ways could be found to make it more precise; cf. Jordan, "Contrats d'acquisition royaux."

tions, my assumption being that the convent under discussion was founded relatively near the date following the sign.[6]

Professor Emery enumerated the foundations *département* by *département* following modern French administrative divisions. I reformulated the data as best I could to meet thirteenth century political criteria. Since Louis had little political influence in eastern Burgundy, eastern Provence, or in Aquitaine, I have not tabulated data from these regions. Although the limits of English political power expanded beyond Aquitaine after the treaty of Paris in 1259; still, areas like Périgord-Quercy, which were reunited with the Angevin dynasty, remained susceptible to strong French influence. Consequently, I included the data for such areas in my tabulation.

Many areas in which Louis's direct political authority was weak still came under his influence—if only because they were so close to the center of his own power. Such areas included Champagne, Brie, Blois, western Burgundy, and Brittany.[7] The appanages would, in a sense, also be relevant here. In all the appanages Louis and his mother exercised authority before circa 1240, and therefore information relevant to the dates for the foundations of mendicant houses in lands that were to become appanages is included with that of other crown lands before 1240.[8] After that date, however, it seemed more reasonable to separate the data for the appanages. The data on new foundations of mendicant houses in territories that later came under the control of Louis's brothers (Provence for Charles in 1246; Toulouse for Alfonse in 1249) are included after the appropriate dates in the summaries of information for them.

The one exception to the statements in the preceding paragraph concerns the appanage of Robert of Artois. His brief rule of thirteen years, the last two of which were spent on crusade, the difficulty of deciding precisely how much of Artois was under his control, and the fact that, during the minority of his son, Louis's influence in the appanage was paramount—all these factors made it seem advisable not to attempt to isolate the data for Robert's lands.[9]

Organized by *département*, data relevant in Emery's catalogue for Louis IX (the regions around Paris, Normandy, Artois, Mâcon, Beaucaire-Nîmes, Carcassonne-Béziers, Périgord-Quercy, etc.) may

[6] Cf. Emery, *Friars*, p. 29 no. 7, p. 33 no. 3.

[7] On relations with Champagne-Brie, Burgundy, and Brittany see above, chapter three. On Blois, cf. Joinville, chap. xix.

[8] Alfonse received his appanage in 1241, Charles his in 1246; but it is possible that each brother may have taken an interest in his land before the formal investiture.

[9] Above on the problems mentioned here, chapter 3 n. 89 See also *HF*, xxiv, "Chronologie," pp. 87-89.

be found under the following headings: Aisne, Ariège, Aude, Cal-
vados, Cher, Corrèze, Dordogne, Eure, Eure-et-Loir, Gard, Haute-
Vienne, Hérault, Loiret, Lot, Lozère, Manche, Oise, Orne, Pas-
de-Calais, Saône-et-Loire, Seine, Seine-et-Marne, Seine-et-Oise,[10]
Seine-Maritime, Somme.

For Alfonse's territories (Poitou and Auvergne; after 1249,
Toulouse): Allier, Ardèche,[11] Aveyron (after 1249), Cantal, Charente,
Charente-Maritime, Deux-Sèvres, Haute-Garonne (after 1249),
Haute-Loire, Indre, Indre-et-Loire, Puy-de-Dôme, Tarn (after 1249),
Tarn-et-Garonne (after 1249), Vendée, Vienne.

For Charles's territories (Anjou-Maine; after 1246, Provence):

Data on Numbers of Foundations by Territories

	Louis IX	Territories of Alfonse of Poitiers	Charles of Anjou	Champagne, Brie, Blois	Burgundy	Brittany
Franciscans						
1226-1229	3	—	—	1	1	0
1230-1234	19	—	—	5	1	1
1235-1239	5	—	—	1	0	0
1240-1244	2	5	0	0	1	0
1245-1249	9	1	3	1	1	2
1250-1254	4	2	1	1	0	0
1255-1259	4	1	2	1	3	0
1260-1264	4	3	1	0	0	0
1265-1269	7	15	2	0	1	1
Dominicans						
1226-1229	3	—	—	1	0	0
1230-1234	7	—	—	2	1	1
1235-1239	1	—	—	0	1	1
1240-1244	3	1	0	1	0	0
1245-1249	3	0	0	0	0	0
1250-1254	2	2	0	0	0	1
1255-1259	2	1	1	0	0	0
1260-1264	3	0	0	0	0	0
1265-1269	2	1	1	0	0	1

[10] Fontette, "Villes médiévales," p. 402, on the Franciscans of Pontoise, 1248, rather
than "1233."
[11] Largely ecclesiastical lands; cf. Labarge, SL, map, p. 71.

Bouches-du-Rhône (after 1246), Drôme (after 1246), Maine-et-Loire, Sarthe, and Vaucluse (after 1246).[12]

For the other autonomous counties, which I alluded to earlier, I have chosen the obvious modern districts, employing for this purpose various atlases and specialized maps.[13]

---

[12] On Alfonse's interest in the Vaucluse, see Emery, *Friars*, p. 119.

[13] Droysen, *Allgemeiner historischer Handatlas*; Shepherd, *Historical Atlas*; *Times Atlas*; various maps in Labarge, *SL*, in Yver, *Égalité entre héritiers*, and in the series *Dictionnaire topographique de la France*.

THE *ENQUÊTES*:
PETITIONERS AND DECISIONS

In this appendix I shall try to describe the breakdown of petitioners in the surviving *enquêtes* by sex, status, and wealth, and to collate this information with what is known of the *enquêteurs'* decisions. These records have not been subjected to this sort of analysis before[1] although a significant number of the surviving twelve thousand cases (eight thousand of Louis's *enquêteurs*; four thousand of Alfonse's) have recoverable judgments.[2]

VARIATIONS IN THE PATTERN OF PETITIONING

All petitioners were free men or free women.[3] Approximately 70 percent of the surviving cases were introduced by men or sexually mixed groups. Individual women or groups of women comprised about 12 percent of the petitioners, a proportion slightly in excess but roughly comparable to that in the regular courts, either for civil or criminal pleas or on appeal.[4] About 15 percent of all plaintiffs were fictitious persons (towns, gilds, parishes, monasteries, and nunneries). Defective cases make up the residual.

The apparently small proportion of exclusive women petitioners

[1] One can find useful remarks, here and there, in Petit-Dutaillis, *"Queremoniae normannorum"*; in Langlois, "Doléances"; and in Sivery, "Enquête."
[2] Above chapter 3 nn. 88, 90. Henceforth references for the royal *enquêtes* will be abbreviated to title and case number and for the comital *enquêtes* to *pièce* number and case number.
[3] The investigation did not extend to the complaints of the servile population although a few plaintiffs claimed to have had their status questioned unfairly by abusive local agents. *QCen*, no. 151; *QTur*, no. 966; *Q . . . exceptae*, nos. 53, 55; *pièce* 45, no. 45. See also Petit-Dutaillis, *"Queremoniae normannorum,"* p. 113.
[4] This is a difficult comparison to make. The women plaintiffs before the *Parlement* of Paris in the early fourteenth century in cases in which that court had original jurisdiction constituted about 10 percent of the total (the figure is a rough one which Professor Strayer kindly established for me). In appealed cases, this was undoubtedly less. In the *parlement* of Toulouse, Alfonse's major appeal court, for example, my own figures for the year 1270 are 31 of 537 cases or 5.8 percent (this roll is published in Fournier and Guébin, *Enquêtes administratives, pièce* 128). Also an *enquête* of reserved cases, in this instance cases referred to the count from Auvergne, gives evidence of only 2 of 54 (3.7 percent) from women (in Auvergne, the regular *enquêtes* normally show 12 percent or 13 percent female petitioners); see *pièce* 52. As I give figures on numbers of cases in the surviving regional résumés, I should caution the reader that the actual number of cases sometimes far exceeds the apparent totals as numbered in the published résumés because the *enquêteurs* often grouped cases of similar origin together under one number.

reflects the decided preference in customary law for males to petition for females. By and large, the men who acted as petitioners for women or sexually mixed groups were members of the same family; most frequently husbands petitioned for their wives. At the same time, this preference for male petitioners was being undermined in the thirteenth century by the growing sensibility that in a dispute over a married woman's real property both husband and wife should appear at the adjudication of the dispute.[5] Varying from region to region and reflecting this trend, such joint petitions accounted for as many as 6 percent of total petitions in individual *enquêtes*.[6]

This variety in the records was a function of the commissioners' practice of adjudicating cases according to local preference. Such concessions to local custom were required only in the post-crusade commissions, especially those authorized by the king,[7] but there seems to have been a tacit acknowledgment from 1247 onward that in the absence of exceptional elements in a case local law was determinative.

Besides women acting in joint petitions of the sort described above, the custumals ordinarily restricted capacity at private law to *femes soles* (widows and spinsters) and women who were merchants.[8] (Practice also favored the right of women who had borrowed money at interest to appear in their own behalf.)[9] It is these categories of women that made up the bulk of female petitioners. Women might petition in sexually exclusive groups (female bakers, for example), but usually these groups were familial in nature (sisters petitioned jointly; mothers and daughters petitioned jointly; and so forth). Association according to other criteria was severely circumscribed in fact if not in principle. This differed markedly from the evidence of petitions from exclusively male groups.[10]

The outstanding regional exaggeration of the restrictions on female plaintiffs was in the duchy of Normandy. There, a married woman did not become a *feme sole*, according to its written customs, until the death of her husband, father, brothers, sons, and nephews since any of these, if of age, might legitimately present a petition in her behalf. Local usage within Normandy often exceeded this. It showed more hostility to joint petitioning (of husbands and wives)

[5] Brissaud, *History of French Private Law*, pp. 170 n. 4, 172 n. 3, 223-24 n. 6.
[6] Cf., for example, *pièces* 41, 64.   [7] *HF*, XXIV, 620-21.
[8] For two excellent surveys of customs regarding women, see Glasson, *Histoire du droit*, VII, 119-40; and Brissaud, *History of French Private Law*, index s.v. "wife," "women." Bouteiller, *Somme rural*, is also helpful; see index s.v. "Femmes."
[9] Cf. Jordan, "Jews on Top."
[10] About two-thirds of the all male group petitions seem to transcend kinship associations.

than is true in other provinces and cultivated an even firmer preference for males of any family connection (grandfathers, cousins,
brothers-in-law) to represent women otherwise alone.[11] Consequently, the percentage of female petitioners in Normandy was extraordinarily low, only 7 percent.

However, except for Normandy, the legal categories establishing
capacity at law for females usually conformed to standard definitions
and varied little from province to province (though there were bound
to be, of course, some subregional inconsistencies). Substantive differences in custom, which were more profound, such as the variations in
the assessment of the widow's portion in her husband's estate, also do
not appear to have skewed the sex ratio among plaintiffs significantly
(indeed, there is no reason a priori why they should have).[12] But certain extra-legal or extra-procedural factors affected the pattern of
petitioning enormously.

The legacy of war was one of these. Numerous people who came
before the *enquêteurs* complained about actions which occurred during the conquest of Normandy, Anjou, Maine, and Poitou, the conquest of Languedoc, and the rebellions following these conquests. A
large number of the complainants were women;[13] their typical com-
plaint concerned the confiscation of their marriage portions.[14] For
example, 17 percent of the petitioners during the royal *enquête* of the
Carcassonne region in 1247 were women, two-thirds of whom
explicitly tied their grievances to the forfeitures incurred during the
Albigensian Crusades. As another example, in the circuit of 1259 for
Poitou-Saintonge held by Alfonse's *enquêteurs*, over 40 percent of
women's cases and at least one-third of men's arose out of the rebellion of 1242.[15]

---

[11] For the custom, see Tardif, *Coutumiers de Normandie*, ii, cap. xli; see also references
in n. 8 above and others in Brissaud, *History of French Private Law*, pp. 221, 787-93 (this
is the best brief statement I know of the extreme anti-female bias of all aspects of Norman law). For the application of the customs, see *QNor*, nos. 75, 246, 291, 486.

[12] On this subject, see Yver, *Egalité entre héritiers*. Perhaps there was a slight bias upward in the proportion of women petitioners in the so-called areas of written law. I find
it difficult to demonstrate this. Also, despite the fact that the customs of Reims were
supposed to be especially favorable to women (Brissaud, *History of French Private Law*, p.
224 n. 2), I find no indication of this reflected in their status as petitioners in the *Inq. in
rem*.

[13] Even in Normandy those cases going back to the conquest show a high proportion
of female (widow) petitioners. These cases were usually grouped together by the *enquêteurs* there. In the cases so grouped in *QNor*, no. 166, there were eight female petitioners, eighteen males; in no. 170, there were thirteen female petitioners, seventeen
males. See also Petit-Dutaillis, "*Queremoniae normannorum*," p. 108. For war cases in the
extreme north of the kingdom, see Sivery, "Enquête," p. 9.

[14] Cf. Wakefield, *Heresy*, p. 182.

[15] The *QCar* may be consulted in *HF*, xxiv; the Poitevin circuit of 1259 is *pièce* 17.

These women plaintiffs, considered together, produced a moving composite picture of themselves drawn largely from the grandiloquent formulae of the law. They almost unanimously qualified themselves as *dominae* or *nobiles mulieres*, women of the nobility whose husbands had opposed the political domination of the French. Despite their noble status and irreproachable behavior, they claimed to have been exposed to the malice, fraud, and injustice of the conquerors' agents. The conditions which, in their view, ought to compel the king and count to address their problems generously included their widowhood, their great age and physical weakness, and their still greater poverty. Perhaps, on second thought, nothing could help them, but surely the government might do something to rescue their disinherited offspring from the gloom of penury.[16]

It appears that, as the wars receded into memory in the peaceful 1250s and 1260s, the proportion of cases presented to the *enquêteurs* which harked back to the unsettled early years of Louis's reign steadily declined. In the north the issue simply ceased to be important after 1248; in the south—with its longer history of rebellion—the drop-off was less precipitate, but by 1260 there too it was a secondary theme. Only the proportion of women's cases originating from wartime conditions stayed consistently at a high level. In one series of *enquêtes* from a single region, for example, the percentage of "war cases" presented by men, which was still 33 percent in 1259, declined to 18 percent by 1261 and 15 percent by the time of the *enquête* of 1266.[17] By contrast, about one-third of women's cases in each of these *enquêtes* referred back to a dispute occasioned by a war. The explanation for this discrepancy is unknown though it is possible that unattached women were more afraid of reprisals and hung back longer, even after successive waves of the *enquêteurs*' investigations made it clear that the government would guard against reprisals.[18]

The *enquêtes* originating in regions with long legacies of rebellion and heresy show other peculiarities in the profile of petitioners. The first was a tendency to attract nobles and corporations (monasteries and towns especially) to the courts since, in some ways, they were the preferred victims of the French conquest. This distortion, though significant, was less pronounced in the early *enquêtes* than in later ones from the same regions. From the beginning, that is, a few of the high-born and powerful tried to redeem their confiscated real property through the *enquêteurs*' courts. Sometimes and without expecting

[16] I have summarized various cases in the *QCar*, but similar descriptions could be drawn from any relevant *enquête*.
[17] *Pièces* 17, 24, 64.
[18] Cf. above chapter 3, the conclusions following n. 122.

to, they succeeded, which in turn stimulated others of the same social status and wealth to appear before subsequent commissions of the investigators. (They had nothing to lose, for the property was already in someone else's hands.)

A few illustrations will be useful at this point. The records for the comital *enquêtes* of Poitou-Saintonge (for those cases where legal status may be determined with some certainty) show a steady increase in the percentage of nobles and squires among individual petitioners from perhaps 30 percent or 40 percent in 1251 to 70 percent in 1259, 90 percent in 1261 and almost 100 percent in 1266.[19] In the royal *enquêtes* of Languedoc, consistently two-thirds or more of the cases for which status can be determined came from nobles.[20] Similarly the proportion of corporations in the total number of complaints in the Poitevin series of *enquêtes* cited above was 7 percent in 1251, no lower (probably quite a bit higher) than 7.8 percent in 1259, 13.4 percent in 1261 and 36 percent in 1266. The medium-sized and smaller *enquêtes* (mostly fragmentary résumés) from war- and heresy-infested areas reiterate this progression.[21]

Compared to more peaceful regions these developments are unusual. Almost no nobles or no one who can be identified with certainty as a noble used the *enquêteurs'* courts in Normandy and Vermandois. In Touraine, Anjou, Maine, and Auvergne one rarely finds that more than 10 percent of the cases in which status is certain came from nobles and only 5 to 10 percent from corporations. In these regions the bulk of the petitioners appears to have comprised townsmen of middling means and free peasants.

Owing to the irregular quality of the data, it is difficult to be precise on the preceding points, but two or three more detailed illustrations may be helpful. In the résumé of cases from Touraine, Maine, and Anjou, approximately 15 percent of the petitioners of readily identifiable status came from artisan backgrounds, 20 percent had commercial or mercantile connections usually of a very modest sort, and about 10 percent were local administrators (who might now be called *petit bourgeois*) complaining against their superiors. Roughly 10 percent came from knightly backgrounds; 40 percent or slightly more were middling people, most, apparently, free peasants. In an *enquête*

[19] *Pièces* 2, 17, 24, 64.
[20] *QCar; Sententiae*; and elsewhere. Cf. Strayer, "Conscience du roi," p. 731, who has suggested that there might have been a counter trend back to middling people in the very latest royal documents from this region.
[21] The relevant medium-sized and smaller *enquêtes* are *pièces* 35 (1262; Poitou-Toulouse), 59 (1264; Poitou-Saintonge), 70 (1266; Toulouse-Venaissin), 71 (1266; Venaissin). The proportion of corporate plaintiffs in order is 12 (or 18) of 41 (29 percent to 44 percent; the incompleteness of the data makes some of the cases uncertain); 8 (or 9) of 22 (36 percent /41 percent); 18 of 47 (38 percent); 10 of 30 (33 percent).

APPENDIX THREE

of Auvergne, 1263-1264, the majority of petitioners whose status can be ascribed with some precision appear to have been free peasants with a healthy smattering also of artisans, parish priests, and small merchants.[22]

These breakdowns, based only on the rather limited selection of cases where status is mentioned or easily ascertained, need to be supplemented by a content analysis of the petitions, specifically the value assigned to *res et bona* in them. There are problems with this approach, such as the inconsistencies in the type of money used to express valuation[23] and perhaps an inclination on the petitioners' part to exaggerate the value of lost property.[24] But these reservations will not invalidate the fundamental conclusions.

The financial issue at stake in a case ordinarily took the form of an annuity or a one-time payment for damages. It seems to me that a petitioner asking for the restitution of even a small annual payment—a rent or quit-rent of 2 s., for example—would probably be of higher social and perhaps legal status than a petitioner asking for damages (such as 3 s. for his ox which was seized in the war). This would not always be true; at best, it is a rule of thumb. But a large proportion of annuities in one record argues in favor of a large proportion of its petitions orginating in the elite even if the record provides no explicit evidence on the subject. Similarly a low number of annuities suggests the presence of social and legal inferiors in court.

In the first of three comital *enquêtes* from Poitou-Saintonge (this one dating from 1259), about one-half of the cases dealt with annuities, especially rents, but in one case *gîte*. This finding tends to reinforce the earlier conclusion, based on the incomplete data on status in the *enquête*, that as many as 70 percent of the petitioners in Poitou-Saintonge in 1259 may have been noble. In subsequent Poitevin records, the value of the *res et bona* increased sharply from this first *enquête*. Annuities in dispute in 1261 and 1266 were one and one-half times or twice the values given in the résumé of 1259. Requests for damages ceased to be trivial financially. They were four to five times higher than in 1259.[25] Taken together, these increases again em-

[22] It would be tedious to examine every case but for the two examples cited, see *QTur* and *pièce* 45.

[23] Although the royal money of account, *parisis*, and the royal currency, *tournois*, were most common, southerners often gave prices in *melgorienne* and *vienne*. Usually the type of coinage is consistent within an individual résumé of cases. For a full review of coinages in the *enquêtes* and exchange rates, see Fournier and Guébin, *Enquêtes administratives*, pp. 473-75 s.v. *moneta*.

[24] Cf. Hilton, *English Peasantry*, p. 46.

[25] The average amount for damages was 8 l. 4 s. 3 d. in 1259, about 19 l. in 1261, about 54 l. in 1266. For annuities the figures would be 3 l. in 1259 and approximately 10 l. in 1261 and 1266.

phasize the growing proportion of upperclass persons in the litigation in Poitou and, by inference, other parts of the formerly rebellious southwest and south.

As with status, so with valuation of goods and property, the more thoroughly loyal or settled regions were quite different. Disputes over relatively inexpensive goods and property remained the defining quality of the cases in these areas. The *enquêteurs'* courts, except in isolated instances, remained the courts of the poor. It hardly matters what record is considered. Annuities will be in a distinct minority; the value of movable property will be minuscule. This was true for Normandy, Touraine, Anjou, Maine, Vermandois, and Auvergne. In Auvergne, for example, there may be 5 or 10 sure petitions for annuities out of 460 cases. In the other cases, the goods for which damages were requested were valued at one pound or less two-thirds of the time.[26]

It should also be pointed out that values assigned by male petitioners to their claimed property were higher than the values assigned by female petitioners to theirs. Geography, in no instance, erased this discrepancy. If claims of men for annuities or real property were being compared to similar claims of women, the difference might have been anticipated since women often put forward requests arising out of the marriage portion (roughly one-third to one-half of the husband's estate). Married men, who felt that the confiscation of their property had been improper, would petition for the return of all of it. Widows, however, often accepted the justness of the confiscation of their husbands' property (for rebellion, heresy, or felony), but they argued that both their life interest in the marriage portion as well as other of their property in which their husbands only had usufruct ought to be returned since they themselves were not criminals.[27]

More curious and problematical is the difference in the values of movable property or payments of damages. In general, a woman's petition—the region is immaterial—was likely to name goods valued at one-half to two-thirds the valuations given in a man's petition.[28]

[26] Let me give the exact figures for Auvergne. Amount of restitution claimed ranged from 10 d. to 129 l. for men in 321 cases where valuation was given; the average was 4 l. 1 s. 11d.; the median 15 s. For women (in 38 cases where valuation was given), the range was 2 s. 4 d. to 15 l., the average 1 l. 8 s. 10 d., median 10 s. I discuss the items mentioned in these cases above, chapter 3 text following n. 115.

[27] Many could have been lying about their sympathy for the heresy. This would have been difficult to prove, however, unless they had taken an active independent part in the resistance to the northerners. But even as overt an act as hiding one's heretical husband did not technically constitute evidence of criminal complicity on a wife's part. On the attractiveness of the Cathar heresy to women, see Dmitrevsky, "Notes," xxxv-xxxvi (1923-1924), 294-305.

[28] Above n. 26 for the Auvergne example; as another illustration cf. *pièce* 17 (1259;

One reason for this is the fact that women who claimed to have lost an article of bedding or clothing to an abusive local agent were unlikely to request anything more in their petitions, but men who complained of the theft of one item were nearly as probable to complain in the same breath about the theft of another.[29] This pattern suggests that the women who appeared in the *enquêteurs* courts were often extraordinarily poor. Many only had one thing worth stealing. Their very presence in court shows that they were *femes soles* at law; the quality of many of their petitions shows that they were *femes soles* in the ambit of their social relations as well.[30]

DECISIONS

The two brothers, being paupers and orphans, asked that their goods and rights be restored to them by his royal Highness, who has God before his eyes and is moved by pity and mercy.[31]

The noble lady petitioned humbly to his royal Highness, that he, having God before his eyes and moved by pity and mercy, might restore to her the goods and rights of her marriage portion because she had served him faithfully and had persevered in her widowhood faithfully for twenty years and more, and she was blameless and pure.[32]

In an enormous number of cases the petitioners appealed to the commonplace notion that authorities should go out of their way to help widows and orphans. Were these appeals successful? Here a different variable enters the discussion, for, as has been demonstrated, the commissioners were largely (but not exclusively) of the new mendicant persuasion. These friars and others who shared their evangelical cast of mind took a high sense of equity into the courts, but one with two levels or attributes. The first was a kind of frenetic intensity in the way they sought out victims of governmental oppression and dealt with the most vulnerable of those victims, widows and orphans. The second was the distinct hostility they showed at times toward, let us say, overmighty subjects.

Among Louis's pre-crusade *enquêtes* the records of the decisions

---

Poitou-Saintonge). There the average in women's cases for damages was 5 l. 16 s. 9 d.; the average for men 9 l. 1 d. The discrepancy was even more pronounced for the traffic in money where men's illegal payments to usurious moneylenders were three to four times those of women; Jordan, "Jews on Top," p. 45.

[29] I have not quantified this impression for every *enquête*, but it can be verified easily in the very short and explicit *récits* of the Auvergne *queremoniae, pièce* 4.

[30] Cf. Jordan, "Jews on Top," p. 52.

[31] *QCar*, no. 82.   [32] *QCar*, no. 81.

survive only occasionally. However, the procedures followed in those investigations have already been shown to be suggestive of the equitable nature of the *enquêteurs'* justice.[33] After the crusade and almost always in Count Alfonse's *enquêtes* the decisions have survived and are very informative. Consider, for example, the work of a comital panel of *enquêteurs* in Poitou from 1263 through 1266.[34] The two Dominicans and the secular clerk who comprised the panel "made restitution" in one case "*de equitate,* . . . although," they explained, "*de rigore juris* it might seem to others that this case should proceed in a different way."[35] This was not exceptional behavior. In another instance they reaffirmed that the petitioners' failure to prove their case *de rigore juris* should not inhibit further investigation. They justified this sentence *ex quadam equitate.*[36] They went so far on one occasion as to say that "although nothing has been sufficiently proved . . . *de rigore juris*; still, since the plaintiff is a good fellow, and it is not likely that he was making any misrepresentation under oath, and [since] the properties for whose homage he is petitioning do not exceed twenty pounds annual rent, therefore [the lord count ought] . . . to do grace concerning the aforesaid matters."[37]

It is true that this last decision did not please the lord count who point blank refused to be gracious.[38] In general it appears certain that the full expression of equity could not take place in the courts of the *miser* Alfonse of Poitier, as easily as in those of the king. Louis himself ordered (and the order was enforced) that the law be bent as much as possible in favor of the petitioners or, at least, the most vulnerable groups of the petitioners, notably widows, the sick, and orphans.[39]

In fact, the king's emphatic command had a more direct effect on widows than on the sick or orphans. The sick are rarely identified anyway, and underaged orphans were never involved in many cases. Almost universally when petitions were received from the latter they were adjudged favorably by both the king and the count's *enquêteurs.*[40] Widows raise a more difficult problem. For them—according to every *enquête*, comital or royal, where their problems demanded particular attention—decisions when they have survived show a 90 percent rate

---

[33] Cf. above chapter 3 nn. 136-39.
[34] Fournier and Guébin, *Enquêtes administratives*, pp. xxxvi, xli, xlii; for their *enquêtes*, *pièces* 41, 59, 64.
[35] *Pièce* 41, no. 17. [36] *Pièce* 64, no. 46.
[37] *Pièce* 64, no. 75. [38] *Ibid.*
[39] Above n. 7. Cf. *pièce* 9, no. 13 (*pièce* 10, no.13); *pièce* 98 no. 15. Below n. 41 for the relevant *enquêtes*.
[40] *Qbit, pars posterior*, nos. 10, 14; *pièce* 45, nos. 4, 43, 52, 194, 195, 200, 218, and elsewhere.

of favorable adjudication.[41] But owing to the king's insistence that widows be sought out for redress of grievances, many more widows received the benefit of the *enquêteurs'* equity in Louis's lands than in Alfonse's. The overall proportion of women plaintiffs in the post-crusade royal *enquêtes* concerning confiscations of property was enormous: 49 percent (458 petitions) in one résumé; 41 percent (52 petitions) in another.[42]

The other somewhat less consistent feature of the commissioners' equity was a marked hostility to the elite. One can find examples of particular résumés in which corporations (the records of whose cases I shall take as a measure of this hostility) fared relatively well.[43] But the overall average of successful petitioning by them was certainly less than 50 percent. Of course, it was easier to give something back to a widow or an orphan who said that events were unfairly crushing them only because a husband or father had gone astray. It assuaged the conscience to do so. It was also pleasant to treat the broken male victims of the northerners' conquest with compassion. Males successfully petitioned to the *enquêteurs* about half the time.[44] It would have been harder to justify a gracious grant to a powerful monastery or municipal oligarchy. This may explain the low rate of favorable petitioning (in comparison, with widows, orphans, and even individual men) by corporations.

Yet one senses more than this. *Enquêteurs* who were friars or who had the evangelical cast of mind to which I have alluded before probably saw the great institutions as corrupt. They did not trust their protestations of mistreatment. Consider again, for example, the panel of comital *enquêteurs* who worked in Poitou from 1263 through 1266. We have seen how they went out of their way to soften the rigor of the law, how in case after case they invoked equity against the *jus strictum*. Yet if we look more closely into the totality of their work, we will see

[41] For the *enquêtes* relevant to this point with final decisions, see the *Sententiae* as well as *pièces* 24 and 64. See also Strayer, "Conscience du roi."

[42] The two documents are the *Exceptiones* and the *Sententiae*. The first, in that it lists challenges to petitions, has a great deal of internal overlapping of cases, but the point is that about one-half of the petitioners who were challenged were women. Before the crusade the proportion of women petitioners was higher in the south than elsewhere (17 percent in Carcassonne, for example, as opposed to the general figure of about 12 percent), but not nearly so high as it eventually became. On a second manuscript of the *Sententiae*, see Strayer, "Conscience du roi."

[43] Cf., for example, *pièce* 24.

[44] For direct comparisons see the *enquêtes* listed in n. 41. Again I must stress that these rates, no matter how low relatively, could not discourage petitioners from appearing. At best complaints might succeed in redeeming already confiscated property or, in the later more formal *enquêtes*, they might have their cases held over for further review. At worst, a preexisting loss of property was legitimized.

the limits of this invocation of equity. During one of its commissions in Poitou, the panel affirmed the petitions of women (read: widows) in seven instances; partially favorable judgments were given in two others; only one petition was denied. Men's petitions were denied eighteen of thirty-three times. The petitions of corporations were denied at least twelve of twenty-two times; partial restitution was made four times. Holding in abeyance a few cases, one finds that the panel only gave two petitions from corporations completely favorable hearings.[45]

Much more statistical sophistication could be applied to the *enquêtes*. This would probably generate powerful conclusions useful to future explorations of French social and legal history. In this appendix, however, I have merely tried to work out the trends and correlations which were most pertinent to a discussion of the rulership of Louis IX.

[45] *Pièce* 64.

THE *ENQUÊTE* OF SALVANÈS

The text published here for the first time *in extenso* is a seventeenth century copy (BN, MS Languedoc-Doat vol. 151 fols. 237-241 verso) of the records of a case held before royal *enquêteurs* in Nîmes in 1256, including the orders instituting the decision of the *enquêteurs*. Thomson, *Friars in the Cathedral*, p. 75 n. 5, made reference to the text; Verlaguet, *Cartulaire . . . de Silvanès*, pp. 442-445, summarized it. A discussion of its contents may be found above, chapter 6 following note 175. Place names and people identified there are not repeated in the notes to the text. Capitalization has *not* been modernized.

TEXT

fol. 237. Acte par lequel le Juge mage de Carcassonne restitue a Gaillard abé et au Monastere de Salvanès les lieux de Calmramon de Blancsegelar et autres biens qui leur avoient esté usurpés par les gens du Roy suivant les letres du Roy St. Louis et la sentence de Philippe Archeveque d'Aix et de Pons de Sancto Egidio de l'ordre des freres precheurs G. Robert de l'ordre des freres mineurs et Guido Fulcodii Inquisiteurs

Les letres du Roy sainct Louis sont du mardi avant la Magdelene 1259

Et la sentence des Inquisiteurs 3° idus Julii 1256

Et l'acte est 2° idus decembris 1259

Anno Incarnationis Dominicae millesimo ducentesimo quinquagesimo nono. Notum sit cunctis quod dominus P. de/237 v./ Autolio[1] senescallus Carcassonae literas patentes domini Regis recepit sub hac forma. Ludovicus Dei gratia Francorum Rex senescallo Carcassonae salutem. mandamus vobis quatinus possessiones adiudicatas per inquisitores nostros abbati et conventui Salvanensi Ruthenensis diocesis Cisterciensis ordinis, terminari faciatis, et obventiones perceptas exinde per gentes nostras a tempore latae sentenciae eisdem abbati et conventui resarciri, ita quod ad nos super hoc ulterius non refferant quaestionem. Actum apud Vicens anno domini millesimo ducentesimo quinquagesimo nono die martis ante festum Beatae Mariae Magdalenae,[2] et cum dictus senescallus esset in Curia

---

[1] P. de Autolio (Pierre d'Auteuil), *sénéchal* of Carcassonne-Béziers, 1254-1263; Appendix One.

[2] 15 July 1259.

Franciae, tempore quod dicta litera emanavit, mandavit magistro Bartholomeo de Podio[3] Iudici Curiae domini Regis, ut ad silvam de Angelis personaliter accederet, et dictum mandatum domini Regis vice eius adimpleret, quo mandato recepto, praefatus Iudex, ad locum accessit memoratum, die sabbati post festum Beati Laurencii,[4] et cum dictus Iudex et abbas salvaniensis memoratus,/238/et Arnaldus Catussa baiulus de Angelis domini Regis in monte de Petris Albis[5] convenissent ad dictorum locorum terminationem, seu limitationem faciendam, dictus abbas produxit coram dicto iudice instrumentum sentenciae Inquisitorum domini Regis sub hac forma Anno dominicae Incarnationis millesimo ducentesimo quinquagesimo sexto, scilicet tertio idus Julii[6] domino Ludovico Dei gratia Rege francorum regnante. Notum sit universis quod cum nos Philippus Dei gratia Aquensis Archiepiscopus, frater Pontius de sancto Egidio de ordine fratrum praedicatorum frater G. Rotberti de ordine fratrum minorum, et Guido Fulcodii[7] convenissemus Nemausi,[8] vir religiosus Gaillardus[9] abbas salvanensis, Cisterciensis ordinis, instanter a nobis petiit, quod reddi faceremus eidem, nomine monasterii sui et dimiti pacifice possidenda loca subscripta, cum suis pertinentiis, scilicet locum qui dicitur Calmramon,[10] et alium qui dicitur Blancsegelar,[11] et omnia quae pertinent ad Grangiam de Marnesio,[12] quoniam dictum monasterium possidet, et usus pascendi, et ligna colligendi ad opus dicti/238 v./monasterii in foresta domini Regis, quae omnia partim ablata, et partim turbata, sibi, et dicto monasterio fuisse dicebat, per gentes domini Regis, et specialiter per ancellum de Ortolio[13] olim tenentem villam, seu balliviam de Angelis, et super his factam dudum inquisitionem per dominum G. de Piano[14] tunc senescallum Carcassonensem de speciali mandato. Regiae Magestatis

[3] Bartholomeus de Podio, royal judge in Carcassonne, on his activities, see *HF*, XXIV, index, s.v. "Bartholomaeus de Podio."

[4] 9 August 1259.

[5] *Petrae Albae* or simply *Petrae*, local place name otherwise unidentifiable (*département*, Tarn); Verlaguet, *Cartulaire . . . de Silvanès*, index s.v. "Petris."

[6] 13 July 1256.

[7] Philippe, the archbishop of Aix (1251-1256); Pons de Saint-Gilles, OP; Guillaume Robert, OM; and Gui Foucois, the royal counselor destined to become Pope Clement IV (1265-1268) were *enquêteurs* in Languedoc in the 1250s.

[8] Nimes (*département*, Gard).

[9] Gaillardus (de Mirabel) was abbot of Salvanès from 1248 to circa 1276; *GC*, I, c 289.

[10] *Calmramon*, local place name otherwise unidentified (*département*, Tarn); Verlaguet, *Cartulaire . . . de Silvanès*, index s.v. "Calm Ramon."

[11] *Blancsegelar*, local place name otherwise unidentified (*département*, Tarn); see ibid., s.v. "Blanc Segalar."

[12] Margnès (*département*, Tarn).

[13] Ancellus de Ortolio (or de Arcolio), besides having been *bayle* of Anglès, had served in various capacities in the south including *viguier* of Béziers and *bayle* or castellan of Cessenon (*département*, Hérault); *HF*, XXIV, 341, 378.

[14] G. de Piano (Guillaume de Pian), *sénéchal* of Carcassonne-Béziers, 1248-1254; Appendix One.

nobis praesentavit, et reddidit dictus abbas scriptam per manum Bernardi Augerii[15] publici Bitterrensis notarii, et sigillo Bitterrarum consignatam. nos vero datum nobis a domino Rege mandatum super huius expeditione negocii per literas speciales ab eodem abbate nobis redditas, exequi cupientes dictam inquisitionem, aparuimus et ea pro utraque parte ad plenum discussa probatum invenimus, tam pro parte dicti monasterii, quam pro parte domini Regis aliquos usus promiscuos in loco, seu territorio quod dicitur Calmramon. testes tamen, qui pro monasterio deponebant invenimus, numero, dignitate, et auctoritate aliis potiores, et quod possessionem monasterii asserebant et declarabant ad plenum causas scienciae/239/reddentes idoneas, et negotio congruentes in quibus defficiebant, testes pro domino Rege producti, de aliis vero locis scilicet de Blancsegelar, et de pertinentiis Marnesii nihil liquidum pro parte domini Regis videbatur probatum, quamvis testes aliqui sub ambiguo, de praedicta materia loquerentur ne vero ad unam probationis speciem videremur nostros animos alligare, vidimus instrumenta monasterii cum sigillis auctenticis Rogerii[16] quondam vicecomitis Bitterris, et inclitae recordationis domini Simonis[17] quondam vicecomitis Carcassonae, et Bitterris, et domini Montisfortis, per quae siquidem instrumenta iustus titulus monasterii probabatur in omnibus suprapetitis. his igitur rationibus moti, possessionem dictorum locorum, scilicet de Calmramon, et Blancsegelar, et pertinentium ad marnesium, si qua de his dominus Rex tenet, et possidet, et dicto abbati, et per ipsum dicto monasterio salvanensi restituendam esse decrevimus, et per virum nobilem senescallum Carcassonensem restitui volumus, et mandamus, et idem dicimus de possessione usus foreste, de Angelis quantum ad pascua/239 v./et ligna ad opus dicti monasterii. haec autem dicimus salvo iure domini Regis et proprietate omnium praedictorum. si de ipsa liquere poterit, dicto tamen monasterio usque ad sentenciam in possessione mansuro, et salvo iure hominum de Angelis si quod habent, et aliarum omnium personarum. In cuius rei testimonium praesens instrumentum per manum publicam, de mandato nostro confectum, sigillorum nostrorum munimine roboramus. Acta sunt haec apud Nemausum in stari quondam Hugonis La guselli praesentibus testibus fratre Berengario Cabal de ordine fratrum praedicatorum,

[15] Bernardus Augerii, notary public in Béziers, may have been the same person who served Alfonse of Poitiers as *bayle* of Buzet (*département*, Haute-Garonne) in 1270; Fournier and Guébin, *Enquêtes administratives, pièce* 128, no. 339.

[16] Raymond-Roger Trencavel, viscount of Béziers, had been deprived of his seigneurie for his resistance to the Albigensian Crusade. He had a son of the same name who laid claim to the viscounty and revolted against Louis IX in 1240; Strayer, *Albigensian Crusades*, index s.v. "Trencavel"; and above chapter 2 nn. 8, 25.

[17] Simon de Montfort, leader of the Albigensian Crusade and conqueror of Languedoc, passed on his conquests to his son Amaury who eventually ceded them to Louis VIII (1223-1226) of France; Strayer, *Albigensian Crusades*, pp. 123-42.

fratre Bernardino de ordine fratrum minorum, magistro Radulfo capellano domini Aquensis Archiepiscopi, Bermondo Jordano priore Beatae Mariae de sede Aquensi, domino Guillelmo de Condoms iurisperito, magistro Petro de Mandolio notario, et me Raimundo Condomi notario publico,[18] qui mandato dicti domini Aquensis— Archiepiscopi, et collegarum suorum praedictorum hanc cartam scripsi, et signavi post modum dictus abbas nominavit, et praesentavit decem testes/240/et Arnaldus Catussa praedictus alios decem testes, ad hostendendum et docendum limitationes, seu terminationes locorum praedictorum, qui testes iurati in forma recipiendorum testium, in praesentia abbatis et Arnaldi Catussae praedictorum fuerunt inquisiti, per praedictum iudicem seorsim, et singulariter et eorum depositiones in scriptis redactae fideliter per Guillelmum Cerdani publicum notarium de Podionauterio[19] domini Regis, et dictus Iudex rem occulis subiciendo, dicta loca cum singulis dictorum testium circuivit tandem cum de limitationibus dictorum locorum certa, vel plena veritas non posset inveniri controversia finalis terminationum seu limitationum, locorum praedictorum per amicabilem compositionem, seu per transactionem fuit terminata et sopita in hunc modum de voluntate et assensu abbatis pro se et conventu suo, et senescalli praedictorum videlicet quod possessio locorum de Calmramon,[20] et de Blancsegelar,[21] et pertinentiarum[22] ad marnesium limitatur, vel confrontatur, et includitur in hunc modum, ex parte sinistra inferiori, cum rivo de Tuna,[23] ubi miscetur/240 v./ cum rivo de Falcono[24] ad lapidem finalem, et sicut inde recte progreditur ad crosum de moleria, et sicut inde recte itur ad rupes Montis de Petris Albis, et sicut inde descenditur recte ibimus ad viam publicam in ipso Monte ad lapidem finalem, et inde sicut eadem via ascendit de Monte

---

[18] This list of witnesses includes men who consistently seem to have been in the entourage of royal officials in Languedoc: for Berengarius Cabal, *HF*, XXIV, 537, and Michel, *Beaucaire*, p. 415; for Bernardinus, Radulfus, and Bermondus Jordanus, see the same references; for Guillelmus de Condoms (properly Codolis), *HF*, XXIV, index s.v. "Guillelmus de Codolis," Verlaguet, *Cartulaire . . . de Silvanès*, p. 443, Michel, p. 415, and Fawtier, *Comptes royaux*, I, no. 13552; for Petrus de Mandolio, *HF*, XXIV, 531, 537, and Michel, pp. 407-8, 412, 414-15; and for Raimundus Condomi, a notary from Tarascon (*département*, Bouches-du-Rhône), see *HF*, XXIV, 531, 537, and Michel, pp. 412, 414-15. The formal holding of this investigation *in stari* (in the house) *Hugonis La guselli* was not unusual. Homes were often identified by the names of recent owners. The La Guselli (or de La Guselli) family was an important one in Nimes; Michel, pp. 407, 445, 448-49.

[19] Pennautier (*département*, Aude). Guillelmus Cerdani was still working as a royal notary in 1262; *HF*, XXIV, 628.

[20] Verlaguet reads *Calm Ramon* here and subsequently in his excerpts

[21] Verlaguet: *Blanc Segalar*.

[22] Corrected silently by Verlaguet to *pertinentium*.

[23] La Tine, rivulet (*département*, Tarn).

[24] *Falconum*, rivulet, modern name unidentified (*département*, Tarn).

de Petris Albis superius, usque ad introitum cabanillorum de Calmramon ad lapidem finalem et sicut planicies de Calmramon exten-
ditur usque ad oram nemoris silvae[25] de Angelis,[26] quod est inter
rivum Petrosum,[27] et planiciem de Calmramon ad lapidem finalem,
et sicut ora dicti nemoris ascendit superius, ad rupes cruce signatas
qui sunt in summitate de Calmramon prope arenacium ad lapidem
finalem et sicut de dictis rupibus et lapide finali recte descenditur ad
rivum de Tuna ad lapidem finalem possessio totius praedictae terrae a
dictis confrontationibus et a rivo de Tuna inclusae remanet dicto abbati, et monasterio suo iuxta tenorem dictae sentenciae, salvo iure
domini Regis in proprietate, si de ipsa potuerit liquere dicto monasterio, usque ad sentenciam in possessione mansuro, et/241/salvo iure
hominum de Angelis, si quod habent, et aliarum omnium personarum et tota terra quae est a parte inferiori, et a parte dextra as-
cendendo, et a parte superiori usque ad praedictas limitationes, vel
confrontationes, vel terminos est de silva de Angelis domini Regis et
domino Regi remanet pro silva de Angelis, et fines, vel limitationes et
termini silvae de Angelis domini Regis, usque ad dictas confrontationes extenduntur. factae sunt istae confrontationes, et terminationes per transactionem, vel amicabilem compositionem inter
praedictum senescallum pro domino Rege franciae, et praefatum ab-
batem pro se, et conventu suo, de voluntate et assensu mutuo par-
tium, et dictus abbas pro fructibus perceptis, vel qui percipi potuerunt
de dictis locis per senescallum, vel suos, vel firmarios a tempore latae
sentenciae per inquisitores domini Regis usque nunc habuit, et recepit
a dicto senescallo quadraginta[28] libras turonenses, et inde se habuit
pro contento, renuncians exceptioni peccuniae non numeratae, et de
dictis fructibus pro dicta peccunia dominum Regem, et suos, et
firmarios/241 v./in perpetuum absolvit, et quitavit, et pactum de non
petendo fecit. Actum Carcassonae in testimonio magistri Bartholomei
de Podio iudicis curiae Carcassonae domini Regis, Guillelmi Arnaldi
et Petri Marsendis notariorum Stephani de Dardens[29] et aliorum et
mei Guillelmi Cerdani de Podio Nauterii publici notarii, qui rogatus
hanc cartam scripsi, et signavi secundo idus decembris[30] Ludovico
Franciae Rege regnante.

[25] Verlaguet: here and subsequently e for the dipthong ae. The seventeenth century
copyist of the Doat manuscript probably added the dipthongs.
[26] Verlaguet: Angules here and subsequently.
[27] Petrosum, rivulet, modern name unidentified (département, Tarn).
[28] Verlaguet: XL.
[29] For further information on the work of these men, see the following: for Bartholomeus de Podi, above n. 3; for Petrus Marsendis, HF, xxiv, 628, 651; for
Stephanus de Dardens, HF, xxiv, 637; for Guillelmus Arnaldi, an all-too common
name, cf. Fournier and Guébin, Enquêtes administratives, pièces 6 (no. 2), 77 (no. 4), 91
(no. 4), and 128 (no. 336).
[30] 12 December 1259.

BIBLIOGRAPHY

The bibliography is divided into four sections. The traditional division between primary and secondary materials has been retained with some qualms since many works usually categorized as secondary print useful documents often as notes or appendixes. A few works, moreover, normally categorized as primary, have been used chiefly for their editorial remarks. I have made special divisions for two types of works: (1) inventories of archives (and similar works); and (2) secondary works published before 1800, that is, those whose authors may have had access to records now lost. In general I have not employed subdivisions in the various sections of the bibliography, except for the traditional separation of printed from manuscript sources, since such subdivisions tend to hinder one's ability to find publication data. In a few cases (notably the works of Blancard) the publication data refer the reader to reprinted articles catalogued as books by the Bibliothèque nationale. Since the reprints were what I used and since they seemed to be readily available in that form, only these are cited in the bibliography. Finally, page numbers for articles have been eliminated as unnecessary.

Specific bibliographic information on the hundreds of primary sources in the great compendium known as *HF* along with evaluations of these sources will be found in the body of the book or in the notes. (Secondary sources in *HF* are cited directly in the bibliography.) In addition, it is only in the notes that I have made specific references to the individual manuscripts which are in the large bundles of documents in the *archives départementales* (the bundles alone are listed in the bibliography). In each case I have tried to describe the markings of the individual manuscript as carefully as possible in order to facilitate the work of subsequent researchers.

Primary Sources

Manuscripts

France, AD: Gard (bundles): H 106; oo 91 Nîmes; SS 17 Nîmes
    AD: Hérault (bundles): B 23; G 1302; G 1475; G 1477; G 4426
    AM: Lunel AA 1, 1639 (*Le Livre Blanc*)
    AN: J 1028ᴬ no. 24 (*enquête*)
    BN: fr. 2813 (*vie de saint Louis*, with illuminations)
         fr. 5716 (*vie de saint Louis*, with illuminations)

Languedoc-Doat vol. 151 fols. 237-41 verso (*enquête*)
lat. 778 (liturgical office of Narbonne)
Great Britain, British Library: Cotton Titus A XVII (*vita sancti Ludovici*, with illuminations)
Royal 16 G VI (*vita sancti Ludovici*, with illuminations)
Italy, Biblioteca comunale: Assisi 695 (liturgical MS of Reims, 13th century)
Netherlands, Library of the University of Leiden: BPL 76 A (psalter of Louis IX and Blanche)
United States, Pierpont Morgan Library: 240 (moralized Bible, Acre circa 1250)

Printed Matter

L'Abrégé de la vie et miracle fait à l'abbaye de Long-Champ sur le tombeau de la bienheureuse Isabel de France. Longchamp: 1637.

Archery, Luc d' (ed.). *Spicilegium sive collectio veterum aliquot scriptorum*, 3 vols. Paris: 1723.

Agnès de Harcourt. *Vita* of Isabella of France. *Acta Sanctorum*, VI August.

Andrieux, J. (comp.). *Cartulaire de l'abbaye royale de Notre-Dame de Bonport.* Evreux: 1862.

Annals of Burton. (Rolls Series, no. 36, vol. 1; ed. H. Luard).

Antiphonale sacrosanctae Romanae ecclesiae pro diurnis horis. Paris: 1924.

Berger, E. and Delaborde, H.-F. (comps.). *Recueil des actes de Philippe-Auguste*, I. Paris: 1916.

Beugnot, A. (ed.). *Les Olim ou Registres des arrêts rendus par la cour du roi.* Paris: 1839.

Bouquet, M. et al. (eds.). *Recueil des historiens des Gaules et de la France*, 24 vols. Paris: 1738-1904.

Boutaric, E. (ed.). *Actes du Parlement de Paris*, 2 vols. Paris: 1863.

Bugnini, A. "Il Messale della Sainte-Chapelle." *Ephemerides liturgicae*, LXII (1948)/LXIII (1949).

Cartulaire de l'abbaye de Morienval. N.p.: n.d.

Cartulaire . . . de la cathédrale d'Amiens, II. Amiens: 1905.

Champollion-Figeac, A. (ed.). *Documents historiques inédits*, 2 vols. Paris: 1841-1843.

Charmasse, A. de (ed.). *Cartulaire de l'évêché d'Autun . . . cartulaire rouge.* Autun and Paris: 1880.

Une Charte de Nolis de s. Louis, publiée par L. T. Belgrano. N.p.: n.d.

Chronique du Bec (Société de l'histoire de Normandie, XIV [1883]).

Coulton, G. (comp.). *From St. Francis to Dante.* 2d ed. London: 1907.

Credo de Joinville, in Joinville, *Histoire*, ed. Natalis de Wailly (English text in Hague translation of Joinville, and Friedman, *Text*).

Delaborde, H.-F. "Fragments de l'enquête en vue de la canonisation de saint Louis." *MHP*, XXIII (1896).

———. "Une Oeuvre nouvelle de Guillaume de Saint-Pathus." *BEC*, LXIII (1902).

Delisle, L. (comp.). *Cartulaire normand de Philippe-Auguste, Louis VIII, Saint-Louis, et Philippe le Hardi.* Caen: 1852.

——— (comp.). *Catalogue des actes de Philippe-Auguste.* Paris: 1856.

———. "Fragments de l'histoire de Gonesse." *BEC*, XX (1859).

———. "Fragments d'un registre des enquêteurs de saint Louis." *Journal des Savants*, 1909.

——— (comp.). *Recueil de jugements de l'Echiquier de Normandie.* Paris: 1864.

———. "Testament de Blanche de Navarre, reine de France." *MHP*, XII (1885).

Denifle, H. (comp.). *Chartularium universitatis parisiensis,* I. Paris: 1889.

Depoin, J. (ed.). *Cartulaire de l'Hôtel-Dieu de Pontoise.* Pontoise: 1886.

Duchesne, F. (ed.). *Historiae francorum scriptores,* V. Paris: 1649.

Duraffour, A. et al. (eds.). *Les Oeuvres de Margurite d'Oingt.* Paris: 1965.

"Epistola publicata super obitu Ludovici noni regis," ed. Duchesne, *Historiae*, V.

"Epistola sancti Ludovici regis de captione et liberatione sua," ed. Duchesne, *Historiae*, V (in French, "Lettre à ses sujets," O'Connell, *Propos*; in English, "St. Louis' Letter," Jean de Joinville, trans. R. Hague).

Epitaph of Bl. Isabella of France. *Acta Sanctorum*, VI August.

Falgairolle, P. "Les Chartes et les transactions des seigneurs de Vauvert et de ses habitants." *Mémoires de l'académie de Nîmes*, 1908.

Fawtier, R. (ed.). *Comptes royaux*, 3 vols. Paris: 1953-1956.

Fleury, G. (ed.). *Cartulaire de l'abbaye cistercienne de Perseigne.* Mamers: 1880.

Formulaires. See Langlois, *Formules.*

Foster, K. (comp.). *Life of Saint Thomas Aquinas.* London: 1959.

Fournier, P.-F., and Guébin, P. (eds.). *Enquêtes administratives d'Alfonse de Poitiers.* Paris: 1959.

Gallia christiana in provincias ecclesiasticas distributa, 16 vols. Paris: 1715-1865.

Giry, A. (comp.). *Documents sur les relations de la royauté avec les villes en France de 1180 à 1314.* Paris: 1885.

Grandmaison, L. de (ed.). *Cartulaire de l'archevêché de Tours*, 2 vols. (*SATouraine: Mémoires*, XXXVII [1892]; XXXVIII [1894]).

Guenée, B. and Lehoux, F. (comps.). *Les Entrées royales françaises de 1328 à 1515.* Paris: 1968.

Guillaume de Tyr, *Continuation de la chronique de. Recueil des historiens des croisades: Historiens occidentaux*, II. Paris: 1859.

Guiraud, J. (ed.). *Cartulaire de Notre-Dame de Prouille*. Paris: 1907.

Héron, A. (ed.). *Deux chroniques de Rouen*. Rouen and Paris: 1900.

Hildegard of Bingen. Letter to Bishop Henry of Bevez. *PL*, CXCVII, c. 180.

The Hours of Jeanne d'Evreux. New York: 1957.

Huchet, A. (ed.). *Le Chartrier ancien de Fontmorigny, abbaye de l'ordre de Cîteaux*. Bourges: 1936.

Huillard-Bréholles, J.-L.-A. (comp.). *Historia diplomatica Friderici secundi*, VI. Paris: 1860-1861.

Husmann, H. (ed.). *Tropen—Und Sequenzenhandschriften*. Munich: 1964.

Jean de Joinville. *Histoire de saint Louis*. Ed. J. Natalis de Wailly. Paris: 1872.

————. *The Life of Saint Louis*. Trans. M. Shaw. London: 1963.

————. *The Life of St. Louis*. Trans. R. Hague. London: 1955.

Johnes, T. (comp.). *Memoirs of John Lord de Joinville* (after Du Cange), II. N.p. (probably London): 1807.

Julliot, G. (ed.). *Chronique de l'abbaye de Saint-Pierre-le-Vif de Sens rédigée vers la fin du XIIIe siècle par Geoffroy de Courlon*. Sens: 1876.

Lachiver, M. (comp.). *Histoire de Mantes et du Mantois*. Meulan: 1971.

Langlois, C.-V. (ed.). *Formules des lettres* (six articles). Paris: 1890-1897.

Laurière, E.-J. et al. (eds.). *Ordonnances des rois de France de la troisième race*, 21 vols. Paris: 1723-1849.

Layettes. See Teulet, *Layettes*.

Leblond, V. (ed.). *Cartulaire de l'Hôtel-Dieu de Beauvais*. Paris: 1919.

Leclercq, J. "Un Sermon prononcé pendant la guerre de Flandre sous Philippe le Bel." *Revue du moyen âge latin*, I (1945).

Lépinois, E. de and Merlet, L. (eds.). *Cartulaire de Notre-Dame de Chartres*, 3 vols. Chartres: 1862-1865.

(Lespinasse, R. de.) "Chronique ou histoire abrégée des évêques et des comtes de Nevers." *Bulletin de la Société nivernaise*, VIII (1872).

Lespinasse, R. de and Bonnardot, F. (eds.). *Le Livre des métiers d'Étienne Boileau*. Paris: 1879.

"The Letter of John Sarrasin." See Jean de Joinville. Trans. R. Hague.

"Lettre à ses sujets." See *Epistola sancti Ludovici*.

"A List of the Knights Who Accompanied Saint Louis in His Expedition to Palestine." Ed. Johnes, *Memoirs*, II.

Loisne, Le Comte de. "Catalogue des actes de Robert Ier, comte d'Artois (1237-1250)." *Bulletin philologique et historique*, 1919.

Longnon, A. (comp.). *Documents parisiens sur l'iconographie de saint Louis*. Paris: 1882.

Massé, L.-F. (ed.). *Vie de saint Edme*. Auxerre: 1858.

Massignon, G. (comp.). *Folktales of France*. Trans. J. Hyland. Chicago and London: 1968.

Matthew Paris. *Chronica majora*, 7 vols. Ed. H. Luard. London: 1872-1883.

Métais, C. (ed.). *Marmoutier, cartulaire blésois*. Blois: 1889-1891.

Migne, J.-P. (ed.). *Patrilogiae cursus completus, series latina*. Paris: 1844-1864.

Minstrel of Reims. "The Chronicle of Reims." Trans. E. Stone, *Washington University Publications in Social Sciences*, x (1939).

Molinier, A. (comp.). *Correspondance administrative d'Alfonse de Poitiers*. Paris: 1894-1900.

———. *Obituaires de la Province de Sens*, 4 vols. Paris: 1902-1923.

Morel, E. (ed.). *Cartulaire de l'abbaye de Saint-Corneille de Compiègne*, 2 vols. Montdidier and Paris: 1904-1909.

O'Connell, D. (comp.). *Les Propos de saint Louis*. Paris: 1974.

———. *The Teachings of Saint Louis: A Critical Text*. Chapel Hill: 1972.

Ordonnances. See Laurière, *Ordonnances*.

Pélicier, P. "Deux lettres relatives à Louis IX." *Bulletin philologique et historique*, 1892.

Potthast, A. (comp.). *Regesta pontificum romanorum*, II. Berlin: 1875.

Pushkin, A. *Sobranie sochineniĭ*, 6 vols. Moscow: 1969.

Reaney, G. (ed.). *Manuscripts of Polyphonic Music, 11th-Early 14th Century*. Munich: 1966.

The Register of Eudes of Rouen. Trans. S. Brown and J. O'Sullivan. New York and London: 1964.

Religiosissimi viri patris Ioannes Ravlin, artium, et theologiae professoris scientissimi oratio ad laudem divi Ludovici Francorum regis. Ed. Duchesne, *Historiae*, v.

Riant, Count P.-É.-D. (comp.). *Exuviae sacrae constantinopolitanae*, 2 vols. Geneva: 1877-1878.

Rouchon, U. "Les Chartes de coutumes du Velay et du Brivadois. La Charte d'Artias (1265)." *Bulletin philologique et historique*, 1906.

Rouillard. Life of Isabella, 1619 (excerpts). *Acta Sanctorum*, VI August.

Rouquette, J. and Villemagne, A. (eds.). *Cartulaire de Maguelonne*, I-III. Montpellier and elsewhere: 1912-1921.

Roze, l'Abbé (ed.). "Nécrologe de l'église d'Amiens." *SAPicardie: Mémoires*, 3d series, VIII (1885).

"St. Louis Letter." See *Epistola sancti Ludovici*.

Salimbene de Adam. *Cronica*, 2 vols. Ed. G. de Scalia. Bari: 1966.

Schlumberger, G. *Numismatique de l'Orient latin*. Paris: 1878.

Stein, H. "Recueil des chartes de la maladerie de Pontfraud près Château-Landon." *ASHGâtinais*, XXVI (1908)

Stephenson, C. and Marcham, F. (comps.). *Sources of English Constitutional History*, I. Rev. ed. New York and elsewhere: 1972.

Strayer, J. (ed.). *The Royal Domain in the Bailliage of Rouen*. Princeton: 1936 (repr. 1976).

Tardif, E.-J. *Coutumiers de Normandie*, 2 vols. Rouen and Paris: 1896.

Teulet, A. et al. (eds.). *Layettes du Trésor des chartes*, 5 vols. Paris: 1863-1909.

Thillois. "Les Cartulaires du diocèse de Laon." *SALaon: Bulletin*, II (1853).

Treharne, R. and Sanders, I. (comps.). *Documents of the Baronial Movement of Reform and Rebellion, 1258-1267*. Oxford: 1973.

Trésor de numismatique et de glyptique, V: *Histoire de l'art monétaire*. Paris: 1858.

Vaissète, J. and Devic, C. (eds.). *Histoire générale du Languedoc*, 16 vols. 2d ed. (Ed. A. Molinier). Toulouse: 1872-1904.

Vanhaeck, M. (ed.). "Cartulaire de l'abbaye de Marquette," 3 parts. *Société d'études de la province de Cambrai: Recueil*, XLVI (1937), XLVII (1938), L (1940).

Van Langeraad, A. and Vidier, A. "Description de Paris par Arnold Van Buchel." *MHP*, XXVI (1899).

Varin, P. (comp.). *Archives . . . de Reims* (incl. *Archives administratives, Archives législatives*, etc.). Paris: 1839-1853.

Walafrid Strabo. *Glossa ordinaria. PL*, CXIV.

INVENTORIES AND RELATED WORKS

Bellée, A. and Duchemin, V. *Inventaire-sommaire des AD: Sarthe*, III. Le Mans: 1881.

Berthelé, J. *Archives de la ville de Montpellier*, I, 2d fasc. (individual pagination): *Inventaire du "Grand Chartrier."* Montpellier: 1896.

——. *Archives de la ville de Montpellier*, III: *Inventaire des cartulaires de Montpellier (980-1789), . . .* Montpellier: 1901-1907.

——. *Répertoire numérique des AC de l'Hérault (AD, série E supplément)*, I. Montpellier: 1924.

Bessot de Lamothe, A. *Inventaire-sommaire des AC de Nîmes*, II. Avignon: 1879.

——. *Inventaire-sommaire des AD, Gard, archives ecclésiastiques—série H*. Mende: 1877.

—— and Bligny-Bondurand, E. *Inventaire-sommaire des AD, Gard, série E. supplément*, I: *Arrondissements de Nîmes, Aiguesmortes, Aiguesvives, Aimargues, Aramon*. Nîmes: 1888.

Bligny-Bondurand, E. *Inventaire-sommaire des AD antérieurs à 1790: Gard, Archives civiles—supplément à la série C—série D—Archives*

réligieuses—supplément aux séries G et H (no continuous pagination).
Nîmes: 1916.

Bruchet, M. *Répertoire numerique: Série H.* Lille: 1928.

Dainville, O. de. *Archives de la ville de Montpellier,* II: *Documents omis dans l'inventaire du Grand Chartrier.* Montpellier: 1955.

Delisle, L. *Le Cabinet des manuscrits de la Bibliothèque Impériale,* I-II. (*Histoire générale de Paris*) Paris: 1868-1874.

———. "Notes sur quelques manuscrits." *MHP,* IV (1877).

Deville, É. *Les Manuscrits de l'ancienne bibliothèque de l'abbaye de Bonport.* Paris: 1909.

Durand, G. *Inventaire-sommaire . . . ; AD, Somme, V: série G.* Amiens: 1902.

Gandilhon, A. *Inventaire-sommaire des AD: Cher, Archives ecclésiastiques—série G, I: Archevêché de Bourges.* Bourges: 1931.

Gouron, M. *Répertoire numérique des AD: Hérault, série G.* Montpellier: 1970.

Inventaire analytique et chronologique des archives de la chambre des comptes, à Lille, 2 parts. Paris and Lille: 1865.

Mouynès, G. *Ville de Narbonne: Inventaire des AC, série AA.* Narbonne: 1877.

Muller, E. *Analyse du cartulaire des statuts, . . . de Notre-Dame de Senlis, 1041-1395.* Senlis: n.d.

Rendu, A. and Coüard-Luys. *Inventaire-sommaire . . . ; AD Oise . . . , série H,* I. Beauvais: 1888.

Saint Louis, Exposition organisée par la Direction Générale des Archives de France, 1960.

Trouillard, G. *Inventaire-sommaire des AD: Loir-et-Cher—Clergé régulier, série H,* I. Blois: 1936.

Secondary Sources

Works Written before 1800

Béziers, M. *Histoire sommaire de la ville de Bayeux.* Caen: 1773.

Bruel, A. (ed.). "Notes de Vyon d'Hérouval sur les baptisés et les convers et sur les enquêteurs royaux au temps de saint Louis et de ses successeurs (1234-1334)." *BEC,* XXVIII (1867).

Brussel, N. *Nouvel examen de l'usage général des fiefs en France,* 2 vols. Paris: 1727.

Charpentier, A. *Le Séjour royal de Compiègne.* Paris: 1647 (repr. 1890).

Chevalier, C. (ed.). *Histoire de l'abbaye de Marmoutier par Dom Edmond Martène,* 2 vols. (*SATouraine: Mémoires,* XXIV 1874, XXV 1875).

Colliette, L.-P. *Mémoires pour servir à l'histoire ecclésiastique . . . du Vermandois,* 3 vols. Cambrai: 1771-1773.

Du Cange (Charles du Fresne, sire). "On the Granting of Armorial Bearings to Families and Respecting Such as Have Been Granted by Princes to various Persons. . . ." Trans. Johnes, *Memoirs*, II.

———. "On the Origin and Usage of Tournaments." Trans. Johnes, *Memoirs*, II.

———. "On Private Wars and on the Right of Customary Warfare." Trans. Johnes, *Memoirs*, II.

———. "On the Torture of the Bernicles and of the Cippus of the Ancients." Trans. Johnes, *Memoirs*, II.

Hénocque, J. *Histoire de l'abbaye et de la ville de Saint-Riquier*, 3 vols. Amiens: 1880-1888.

Lebeuf, J. *Mémoires concernant l'histoire ecclésiastique et civile d'Auxerre*, 2 vols. Paris: 1743.

Le Seuer, A. (ed.). "Histoire des comtes de Ponthieu et de Montreuil par Du Cange." *Société d'émulation d'Abbeville, Mémoires*, XXIV (1917).

Ménard, L. *Histoire de ville de Nismes*, I. Paris: 1750.

Montfaucon, B. de. *Les Monumens de la monarchie françoise*, II. Paris: 1730.

Tillemont, L. de. *Vie de saint Louis*, 6 vols. Ed. J. de Gaulle. Paris: 1849.

1800 to the Present

Abel, C. "Louis IX et le Luxembourg." *Mémoires lus à la Sorbonne*, 1868.

Albaric, A. *Aigues-Mortes*. Château-de-Valence: 1967.

Alef, G. "The Origin and Early Development of the Muscovite Postal Service." *Jahrbücher für Geschichte Osteuropas*, XV (1967).

Andrieu-Guitrancourt, P. *L'Archevêque Eudes Rigaud et la vie de l'église au XIIIᵉ siècle d'après de "Regestrum visitationum."* Paris: 1938.

Arbois de Jubainville, M. d'. *Histoire des ducs et comtes de Champagne*, 6 vols. in 7 parts. Paris: 1865.

Arcq. See Douët d'Arcq.

Artonne, A. *Le Mouvement de 1314 et les chartes provinciales de 1315*. Paris: 1912.

Aubert, E. *Trésor de l'abbaye de Saint-Maurice d'Agaune*, 2 vols. Paris: 1872.

Aubert, F. "Les Huissiers du Parlement de Paris." *BEC*, XLVII (1886).

———. "Nouvelles recherches sur le Parlement de Paris" (part 1). *Nouvelle revue historique de droit français et étranger*, XXXIX (1916).

Auzas, P.-M. "Essai d'un répertoire iconographique de saint Louis." In *Septième centenaire*. Paris: 1976.

Babelon, J. "La Monnaie de saint Louis." In *Siècle de saint Louis*. Paris: 1970.

Bailly, A. *Saint Louis*. Paris: 1949.

Balog, P. and Yvon, J. "Monnaies à légendes arabes de l'orient latin." *Revue numismatique*, 6th series, I (1958).

Bardon, A. *Histoire de la ville d'Alais de 1250 à 1340*. Nîmes: 1894.

Barker, E. and Smail, R. "Crusades." *Encyclopaedia Britannica*, VI. Chicago: 1960.

Barraclough, G. *The Crucible of Europe: The Ninth and Tenth Centuries in European History*. London: 1976.

Barthélemy, A. "Essai sur la monnaie parisis." *MHP*, II (1875).

Bastin, J. and Faral, E. *Onze poèmes de Rutebeuf*. Paris: 1946.

Baudon de Mony, C. "La Mort et les funérailles de Philippe le Bel d'après un compte rendu à la cour de Majorque." *BEC*, LVIII (1897).

Beaune, H. *Introduction à l'étude historique du droit coutumier français*. Lyon and Paris: 1880.

Beaurepaire, J.-C. de. *Saint-Germain-en-Laye*. Paris: 1826.

Beauvillé, V. de. *Histoire de la ville de Montdidier*, I. Paris: 1857.

Beebe, B. "The English Baronage and the Crusade of 1270." *Bulletin of the Institute of Historical Research*, XLVIII (1975).

Bellamy, J. *Crime and Public Order in England in the Later Middle Ages*. London and Toronto: 1973.

Bémont, C. "La Campagne de Poitou, 1242-1243." *Annales du Midi*, V (1893).

Ben-Ami, A. *Social Change in a Hostile Environment*. Princeton: 1969.

Benson, R. *The Bishop-Elect: A Study in Medieval Ecclesiastical Office*. Princeton: 1968.

Benton, J. "The Revenue of Louis VII." *Speculum*, XLIII (1967).

Berger, A. *Encyclopedic Dictionary of Roman Law*. Philadelphia: 1953.

Berger, E. *Histoire de Blanche de Castille*. Paris: 1895.

―――. *Saint Louis et Innocent IV*. Paris: 1893.

Bernois, C. "Histoire de Lorris" (final part). *ASHGâtinais*, XXXI (1913).

Bertaux, E. "Les Saints Louis dans l'art italien." *Revue des deux mondes*, 1900.

Beugnot, A. *Essai sur les institutions de saint Louis*. Paris: 1821.

Bezzola, G. *Die Mongolen in Abenländischer Sicht*. Bern and Munich: 1974.

Billington, J. *The Icon and the Axe*. New York: 1966.

Biollay, L. "Les Anciennes halles de Paris." *MHP*, III (1876).

Bisson, T. "A Propos d'un registre municipal de Narbonne: Notes sur la chronologie des ordonnances monétaires de Louis IX (1263-1265)." Trans. P. Wolff, *Annales du Midi*, 1960.

―――. *Assemblies and Representation in Languedoc in the Thirteenth Century*. Princeton: 1964.

Bisson, T. "Coinage and Royal Monetary Policy in Languedoc during the Reign of Saint Louis." *Speculum*, XXXII (1957).

―――. "Consultative Functions in the King's Parlements (1250-1314)." *Speculum*, XLIV (1969).

―――. "Negotiations for Taxes under Alfonse of Poitiers." *Studies Presented to the International Commission for the History of Representative and Parliamentary Institutions.* Vienna: 1965.

―――. "The Organized Peace in Southern France and Catalonia." *American Historical Review*, LXXXII (1977).

Bisson de Barthélemy, P. *Histoire de Beaumont-sur-Oise.* Persan: 1958.

Blancard, L. *Le Bésant d'or sarrazinas pendant les croisades: Étude comparée sur les monnaies d'or, arabes et d'imitation arabe, frappées en Egypte et en Syrie, aux XIIme et XIIIme siècles.* Marseilles: 1880.

―――. *Essai sur les monnaies de Charles Ier.* Paris: 1868.

―――. *Le Gros tournois est imité du sarrazinas chrétien d'Acre: Lettre à M. Anatole de Barthélemy.* Marseilles: 1882.

―――. *"Le Millarès": Étude sur une monnaie du XIIIme siècle imitée de l'arabe par les chrétiens.* Marseilles: 1876.

―――. *La Reforme monétaire de saint Louis.* Marseilles: n.d.

―――. *Sur l'Agnel d'or imité du sarrazinas chrétien d'Acre.* Marseilles: 1896.

Bloch, M. "Blanche de Castille et les serfs du Chapitre de Paris." *MHP*, XXXVIII (1911).

―――. *Feudal Society*, 2 vols. Trans. L. Manyon. Chicago: 1964.

―――. *The Ile-de-France.* Trans. J. Anderson. Ithaca: 1971.

―――. *The Royal Touch.* Trans. J. Anderson. London: 1973.

Blumenkranz, B. "Louis IX ou Saint Louis et les juifs." *Archives juives*, X (1973-1974).

Boisson, C.-F. *De la Ville de Sommières (Gard), depuis son origine jusqu'à la Révolution de 1789.* Lunel: 1849.

Borrelli de Serres, L. "Compte d'une mission de prédication pour secours à la terre sainte." *MHP*, XXX (1903).

―――. *Recherches sur divers services publics du XIIIe au XVIIe siècles*, 3 vols. Paris: 1895-1901.

Boüard, A. de. *Études de diplomatique sur les actes des notaires du Châtelet de Paris.* Paris: 1910.

Bougerol, G. "Théologie et spiritualité franciscaine au temps de saint Louis." In *Septième centenaire.* Paris: 1976.

Boulenger, J. *La Vie de saint Louis.* Paris: 1929.

Boulet-Sautel, M. "Aperçu sur les systèmes des preuves dans la France coutumière du moyen âge." *Recueils de la Société Jean Bodin*, XVII (1965).

Boullé, J. "La Maison de Saint-Lazare de Paris." *MHP*, III (1876).

Bourgin, G. *La Commune de Soissons et le groupe communal soissonais.* Paris: 1908.

Boutaric, E. "Marguerite de Provence: Son caractère, son role politique." *Revue des questions historiques,* III (1867).

——. *Saint Louis et Alfonse de Poitiers.* Paris: 1870.

Branner, R. *Manuscript Painting in Paris during the Reign of Saint Louis: A Study of Styles.* Berkeley and elsewhere: 1977.

——. *The Painted Medallions in the Sainte-Chapelle in Paris (Transactions of the American Philosophical Society,* new series, LVIII, part 2, 1968).

——. *St. Louis and the Court Style in Gothic Architecture.* London: 1965.

——. "Saint Louis et l'enluminure parisienne au XIIIe siècle." In *Septième centenaire.* Paris: 1976.

Brissaud, J. *A History of French Private Law.* Trans. R. Howell. Boston: 1912.

Brown, E. "Royal Salvation and Needs of State in Late Capetian France." In Jordan et al. (eds.), *Order and Innovation.*

Brühl, C. *Fodrum, gistum, servitium regis,* 2 vols. Cologne: 1968.

Brundage, J. *Medieval Canon Law and the Crusader.* Madison and elsewhere: 1969.

Buche, H. "Essai sur l'ancienne coutume de Paris aux XIIIe et XIVe siècles." *Revue historique de droit français et étranger,* 1884.

Buchtal, H. *Miniature Painting in the Latin Kingdom of Jerusalem.* Oxford: 1957.

Buisson, L. *König Ludwig IX., der Heilige und das Recht: Studie zur Gestaltung der Lebensordnung Frankreichs im hohen Mittelalter.* Freiburg: 1954.

Bünger, F. *Die Beziehungen Ludwigs IX von Frankreich zur Curie in den Jahren, 1254-1264.* Berlin: 1896.

Burns, R. *Moors and Crusaders in Mediterranean Spain.* London: 1978.

Callebaut, A. "La Deuxième croisade de saint Louis et les franciscains." *La France franciscaine,* V (1922).

Campbell, G. "The Attitude of the Monarchy toward the Use of Ecclesiastical Censures in the Reign of Saint Louis." *Speculum,* XXXV (1960).

——. "The Protest of Saint Louis." *Traditio,* XV (1959).

——. "Saint Louis's Ecclesiastical Policy in France." Ph.D. dissertation, Princeton University, 1957.

——. "Temporal and Spiritual Regalia during the Reigns of St. Louis and Philip III." *Traditio,* XX (1964).

Carbasse, J.-M. "Le Duel judiciaire dans les coutumes méridionales." *Annales du Midi,* LXXXVII (1975).

Carolus-Barré, L. "L'Apparition de la langue française dans les actes de l'administration royale." *Académie des Inscriptions et Belles-Lettres: Comptes rendus*, 1976.

————. "L'Apport historique de l'année saint-Louis." In *Septième centenaire*. Paris: 1976.

————. "Les Baillis de Philippe III le Hardi." *Annuaire-Bulletin de la Société de l'histoire de France*, 1966-1967.

————. *Chronologie des baillis de Clermont-en-Beauvaisis, 1202-1532*. Senlis: 1944.

————. "Les Enquêtes pour la canonisation de saint Louis." *Revue d'histoire de l'église de France*, LVII (1971).

————. "Le Gouvernement communal d'après le 'Livre de jostice et de plet.'" *Revue historique de droit français et étranger*, 1940-1941.

————. "La Grande Ordonnance de 1254 sur la réforme de l'administration et la police du royaume." In *Septième centenaire*. Paris: 1976.

————. "La Grande Ordonnance de réformation de 1254." *Académie des Inscriptions et Belles-Lettres: Comptes rendus*, 1973.

————. "La Juridiction gracieuse à Paris dans le dernier tiers du XIIIe siècle: l'Officialité et le Châtelet." *Le Moyen âge*, 1963.

————. Note in *Bulletin de la Société nationale des antiquaires*, 1963.

————. "Le Prince héritier Louis (1244-1260) et l'interim du pouvoir royal de la mort de Blanche de Castille (novembre 1252) au retour de saint Louis en France (juillet 1254)." *Académie des Inscriptions et Belles-Lettres: Comptes rendus*, 1970.

————. "Richart Laban, sergent du roi en la forêt de Retz et le XVIIIe miracle de saint Louis." *Le Moyen âge*, 1934.

————. "Saint Louis dans l'histoire et dans la légende." *Annuaire-Bulletin de la Société de l'histoire de France*, 1970-1971.

————. "Saint Louis et la translation des corps saints." *Études d'histoire du droit canonique (dédiées à Gabriel Le Bras)*, II. Paris: 1965.

Cartier, E. "Remarques." *Revue numismatique*, XII (1847).

Cazelles, R. *Nouvelle histoire de Paris*. Paris: 1972.

————. "Le Parisien au temps de saint Louis." In *Septième centenaire*. Paris: 1976.

————. "La Réglementation royale de la guerre privée de saint Louis à Charles V et la précarité des ordonnances." *Revue historique de droit français et étranger*, 1960.

Chaillou des Barres, C. "Saint Louis à Sens." *Bulletin de la Société des sciences historiques et naturelles de l'Yonne*, VI (1852).

Chaplais, P. "The Making of the Treaty of Paris (1259) and the Royal Style." *English Historical Review*, LXVII (1952).

————. "Le Traité de Paris de 1259 et l'inféodation de la Gascogne allodiale." *Le Moyen âge*, 1955.

Chardon. *Histoire de la ville d'Auxerre*, 2 vols. Auxerre: 1834-1835.

Charpillon. *Gisors*. Les Andelys: 1867.

Chazan, R. "Archbishop Guy Fulcodi of Narbonne and His Jews." *Revue des études juives*, CXXXII (1973).

――――. "The Barcelona 'Disputation' of 1263: Christian Missionizing and Jewish Response." *Speculum*, LII (1977).

――――. *Medieval Jewry in Northern France: A Political and Social History.* Baltimore and London: 1973.

Chénon, E. "L'Hérésie à La Charité-sur-Loire et les débuts de l'Inquisition monastique dans la France du nord au XIIIe siècle." *Nouvelle revue historique de droit français et étranger*, XLI (1917).

Cheyney, C. *Handbook of Dates for Students of English History.* London: 1945.

Cheyney, E. *The Dawn of a New Era.* New York: 1936.

Coët, E. *Histoire de la ville de Roye*, 2 vols. Paris: 1880.

Congar, Y. "L'Église et l'état sous le règne de saint Louis." In *Septième centenaire*. Paris: 1976.

Contamine, P. *Guerre, état, et société à la fin du moyen âge.* Paris and elsewhere: 1972.

Courtenay, W. "Token Coinage and the Administration of Poor Relief during the Late Middle Ages." *Journal of Interdisciplinary History*, III (1972-1973).

Darlington, O. *The Travels of Odo Rigaud, Archbishop of Rouen (1248-1275).* Philadelphia: 1940.

Daumet, G. "Une Femme-médecin au XIIIe siècle." *Revue des études historiques.* 1918.

David, L. "Les Acclamations: *Christus vincit.*" *Revue du chant grégorien*, XXVI (1922), no. 1.

Declareuil, J. *Histoire générale du droit français des origines à 1789.* Paris: 1925.

Decq, E. "L'Administration des eaux et forêts dans le domaine royal en France aux XIVe et XVe siècles," parts 1 and 2. *BEC*, LXXXIII (1922).

Delaborde, H.-F. "Les Bâtiments occupés par le Trésor des Chartes." *MHP*, XXIX (1902).

――――. "Les Classements du Trésor des chartes antérieurs à la mort de saint Louis." *BEC*, LXII (1901).

――――. Review of Sternfeld, *Ludwigs des Heiligen Kreuzzug nach Tunis. Revue de l'orient latin*, IV (1896).

Delalande, J. *Les Extraordinaires croisades d'enfants et de pastoureaux au moyen âge.* Paris: 1961.

Delaporte, Le P.-V. *Saint Louis 1242, drame historique.* No pub. data.

Delaruelle, É. "Saint Louis devant les Cathares." In *Septième centenaire*. Paris: 1976.

Delcambre, É. "Le Paréage du Puy." *BEC*, xcii (1931).

Delisle, L. "Chronologie des baillis et des sénéchaux." *HF*, xxiv.

——. "Les Opérations financières des Templiers." *Mémoires de l'Académie des Inscriptions et Belles-Lettres*, xxxiii (1889).

——. "Préface." *HF*, xxiv.

——. "Visites pastorales de maître Henri de Vézelai." *BEC*, liv (1893).

Demay, G. Communication to the *Bulletin de la Société nationale des Antiquaires*, 1874.

Denisova-Khachaturian, N. "Sotsial'no-politicheskie aspekty nachal'noi istorii general'nikh shtatov vo Frantsii" (Social-political Aspects of the Early History of the Estates-general in France; in Russian). *Evropa v srednie veka*. Moscow: 1972.

Deslandres, Y. "Le Costume du roi saint Louis, étude iconographique et technique," In *Septième centenaire*. Paris: 1976.

Dictionnaire de l'Académie française, i: *A-G*. 8th ed. Paris: 1932.

Dictionnaire du droit canonique, 7 vols. Paris: 1935-1965.

Dictionnaire topographique de la France: Gard. Paris: 1868.

Dictionnaire topographique de la France: Hérault. Paris: 1865.

Dieudonné, A. "La Théorie de la monnaie à l'epoque féodale et royale d'après deux livres nouveaux." *Revue numismatique*, 4th series, xiii (1909).

Dimier, M.-A. *Saint Louis et Cîteaux*. Paris: 1954.

"Dissertations sur les depenses et les recettes ordinaires de s. Louis." *HF*, xxi.

Dmitrevsky, M. "Notes sur le catharisme et l'Inquisition dans le Midi de la France." *Annales du Midi*, xxxv-xxxviii (1923-1926).

Doren, A. (ed.). *Die Chronik des Salimbene von Parma*. Leipzig: 1914. (Consulted for editorial material.)

Dossat, Y. "Alfonse de Poitiers et les clercs." *Les Évêques, les clercs, et le roi* (Cahiers de Fanjeaux 7, 1972).

——. "Alfonse de Poitiers et la préparation financière de la croisade de Tunis: Les Ventes de forêts (1268-1270)." In *Septième centenaire*. Paris: 1976.

——. *Les Crises de l'Inquisition toulousaine au XIIIᵉ siècle*. Bordeaux: 1959.

——. "L'Établissement de l'Inquisition." In *Siècle de saint Louis*. Paris: 1970.

——. "Gui Foucois, enquêteur-réformateur, archevêque et pape (Clement IV)." *Les Évêques, les clercs, et le roi* (Cahiers de Fanjeaux 7, 1972).

————. "Inquisiteurs ou enquêteurs? à propos d'un texte d'Humbert de Romans." *Bulletin philologique et historique*, 1957.

————. "Opposition des anciens ordres à l'installation des mendiants." *Les Mendiants en pays d'oc au XIIIe siècle* (Cahiers de Fanjeaux 8, 1973).

————. "Patriotisme méridional du clergé au XIIIe siècle." *Les Évêques, les clercs, et le roi* (Cahiers de Fanjeaux 7, 1972).

————. "Une Tentative de réforme administrative dans la sénéchaussée de Toulouse en 1271." *Bulletin philologique et historique*, 1964.

Douais, C. "Les Sources de l'histoire de l'Inquisition." *Revue des questions historiques*, XXX (1881).

Douët-D'Arcq, L. *Recherches historiques et critiques sur les anciens comtes de Beaumont-sur-Oise, du XIe au XIIIe siècle*. Amiens: 1855.

Douie, D. *The Conflict between the Seculars and the Mendicants at the University of Paris in the Thirteenth Century*. London: 1954.

Droysen, G. *Allgemeiner historischer Handatlas*. Bielefeld and Leipzig: 1886.

Duchaussoy, J. *Beauquesne, sa commune, son château-fort, sa prévôté royale: Étude historique*. Abbeville: 1898.

Dufeil, M.-M. *Guillaume de Saint-Amour et la polémique universitaire parisienne, 1250-1259*. Paris: 1972.

————. "Le Roi Louis dans la querelle des mendiants et des séculiers (Université de Paris, 1254-1270)." In *Septième centenaire*. Paris: 1976.

Dufour, C. "Situation financière des villes de Picardie, sous saint Louis." *SAPicardie: Mémoires*, series 2, V (1857).

Duplès-Agier, H. "Notice sur une pièce trouvée au Trésor des chartes et concernant la ville de Sens au XIIIe siècle." *Bulletin de la Société archéologique de Sens*, 1851.

Dupont-Ferrier, G. "Histoire et signification du mot 'aides' dans les institutions financières de la France, specialement aux XIVe et XVe siècles." *BEC*, LXXXIX (1928).

————. "Ignorances et distractions administratives en France aux XIVe et XVe siècles." *BEC*, C (1939).

Dupuis, *Senlis*. See Vatin, *Senlis*.

Durand, A. "Beaucaire sous saint Louis," 2 parts. *Revue du Midi*, 1904-1905.

Durrieu, P. "Siècle de la miniature parisienne à partir du règne de saint Louis." *Journal des savants*, 1909.

Duvivier, C. *La Querelle des d'Avesnes et des Dampierres jusqu'à la mort de Jean d'Avesnes (1257)*, I. Brussels and Paris: 1894.

Eddy, J. "The Maunder Minimum." *Science*, CXCII (1976).

"Edmund of Abingdon, St." *New Catholic Encyclopedia*, V.

Einzig, P. *The History of Foreign Exchange.* New York: 1962.

Eisenhofer, L. and Lechner, J. *The Liturgy of the Roman Rite.* Trans. A. and E. Peeler. Ed. H. Winstone. New York: 1961.

Emery, R. *The Friars in Medieval France: A Catalogue of French Mendicant Convents, 1200-1550.* New York and London: 1962.

―――. *Heresy and Inquisition in Narbonne.* New York: 1941.

Erikson, E. *Identity: Youth and Crisis.* New York: 1968.

Essigny, L.-A.-J. *Histoire de la ville de Roye.* Noyon: 1818.

Evergates, T. *Feudal Society in the Bailliage of Troyes.* Baltimore: 1975.

Evropa v srednie veka (Europe in the Middle Ages; in Russian) Moscow: 1972.

Eydoux, H.-P. *Saint Louis et son temps.* Paris: 1971.

Eyssette, A. *Études historiques sur le consulat et les institutions municipales de la ville de Beaucaire.* Paris: 1860.

―――. *Histoire administrative de Beaucaire*, 2 vols. Beaucaire: 1884-1888.

Fagniez, G. *Études sur l'industrie et la classe industrielle à Paris au XIIIe et au XIVe siècle.* Paris: 1877.

Faivre d'Arcier, S. *Gournay et le pays de Bray.* Gournay-en-Bray: 1950.

Faral, E. "Le Procès d'Enguerran IV de Coucy." *Revue historique de droit français et étranger*, series 4, XXVI (1948).

Fauqueux, C. *Beauvais, son histoire.* Beauvais: 1938.

Favier, J. "Les Finances de saint Louis." In *Septième centenaire.* Paris: 1976.

Fawtier, R. *The Capetian Kings of France.* Trans. L. Butler and R. Adam. London: 1960.

Fédou, R. "Les Sergents à Lyon aux XIVe et XVe siècles. Une Institution—un type social." *Bulletin philologique et historique*, 1964.

Fesler, J. "French Field Administration: The Beginnings." *Comparative Studies in Society and History*, V (1962-1963).

Fietier, R. "Le Choix des baillis et sénéchaux aux XIIIe et XIVe siècles (1250-1350)." *Mémoires de la Société pour l'histoire du droit* (Dijon), 29e fasc., 1968-1969.

Flammermont, J. *Histoire des institutions municipales de Senlis.* Paris: 1881.

Fleury, G. *Guide illustré pour Mamers.* Mamers: 1901.

Fleury, L. de. *La Collégiale de Saint-Thomas-le-Martyr-les-Crespy.* Senlis: 1884.

Fliche, A. *Aigues-Mortes et Saint-Gilles.* 2d ed. Paris: 1950.

Folz, R. "La Sainteté de Louis IX, d'après les textes liturgiques de sa fête." *Revue d'histoire de l'église de France*, LVII (1971).

Fontaine, F. de. "Revue des recueils périodiques." *Revue des questions historiques*, XLII (1887).

Fontette, F. de. "Vie économique de la région parisienne d'après des actes de vente immobilière du XIIIe siècle." *Revue historique de droit français et étranger*, 1959.

Fontette, M. de. "Les Mendiants supprimés au 2me Concile de Lyon (1274)." *Les Mendiants en pays d'oc au XIIIe siècle*. (Cahiers de Fanjeaux 8, 1973.)

———. "Villes médiévales et ordres mendiants." *Revue historique de droit français et étranger*, 1970.

Fournier, P. "Les Conflits de juridiction entre l'église et le pouvoir séculier de 1180 à 1328." *Revue des questions historiques*, XXVII (1880).

———. *Le Royaume d'Arles et de Vienne (1138-1378)*. Paris: 1891.

Fournier, P.-F. "Origines des baillis de Mâcon." *Bulletin philologique et historique*, 1959.

Franchet, C. *Saint Louis des lys de France*. Lyon: 1962.

François, M. "Les Bonnes Villes." *Académie des Inscriptions et Belles-Lettres: Comptes rendus*, 1975.

———. "Initiatives de saint Louis en matière administrative: Les Enquêtes royales." In *Siècle de saint Louis*. Paris: 1970.

Frankl, P. *Gothic Architecture*. Baltimore: 1962.

Frégier, M. *Histoire de la police de Paris*, I. Paris: 1850.

Friedman, L. *Text and Iconography for Joinville's "Credo."* Cambridge: 1958.

Froger, L. "Des Enquêtes faites à La Flèche et dans les environs en 1247." *Les Annales fléchoises et de la vallée du Loir*, X (1909).

Fustel de Coulanges, N. S. *Louis et le prestige de la royauté*. Colombes: 1970.

Gabriel, A. *The Educational Ideas of Vincent of Beauvais*. Notre-Dame: 1956.

Galavaris, G. *Bread and the Liturgy*. Madison and elsewhere: 1970.

Ganshof, F. *The Carolingians and the Frankish Monarchy*. Trans. J. Sonderheim. Ithaca: 1971.

Garreau, A. *La Bienheureuse Isabelle de France*. Paris: 1955.

Gastine, L. *Le Roi des rois (saint Louis)*. Paris: 1913.

Gaudemet, J. *La Collation par le roi de France des bénéfices vacants en régale*. Paris: 1935.

———. "Les Ordalies au moyen âge: Doctrine, législation et pratique canoniques." *Recueils de la Société Jean Bodin*, XVII (1965).

Gavrilovitch, M. *Étude sur le Traité de Paris*. Paris: 1899.

Gébelin, F. *La Sainte-Chapelle et la Conciergerie*. 3d ed. Paris: n.d.

Geremek, B. *Le Salariat dans l'artisanat parisien aux XIIIe-XVe siècles*. Trans. A. Posner and C. Klapisch-Zuber. Paris and The Hague: 1968.

Germain, A. *Histoire du commerce de Montpellier*, 2 vols. Montpellier: 1861.

———. *Histoire de la commune de Montpellier*, 3 vols. Montpellier: 1851.

———. "De la Monnaie mahométane attribuée à un évêque de Maguelone." *SAMontpellier: Mémoires*, III (1850-1854).

———. "Notice sur un cartulaire seigneurial inédit." *SAMontpellier: Mémoires*, IV (1855-1859).

Germain, J. *Sauve, antique et curieuse cité*. Montpellier: 1952.

Giesey, R. *The Juristic Basis of Dynastic Right to the French Throne* (*Transactions of the American Philosophical Society*, new series, LI, part 5, 1961).

Giry, A. *Manuel de diplomatique*. Paris: 1894.

Gjerset, K. *History of the Norwegian People*, I. New York: 1915.

Glasson, E. *Histoire du droit et des institutions de la France*. Paris: 1896.

Glenisson, J. "Les Enquêteurs-Réformateurs de 1270 à 1328." *Thèse*, Université de Paris, 1946.

Goineau, F. *Gisors*. Pontoise: 1937.

Gravier, H. "Essai sur les prévôts royaux du XIe au XIVe siècle." *Nouvelle revue historique de droit français et étranger*, XXVII (1903).

Grayzel, S. *The Church and the Jews in the XIIIth Century*. Philadelphia: 1933.

Grierson, P. "A Rare Crusader Bezant with the *Christus Vincit* Legend." *American Numismatic Society Museum Notes*, VI (1954).

Griffiths, Q. "The Counselors of Louis IX." Ph.D. dissertation, University of California, Berkeley, 1964.

———. "New Men among the Lay Counselors of Saint Louis." *Medieval Studies*, XXXII (1970).

———. "Les Origines et la carrière de Pierre de Fontaines, jurisconsulte de saint Louis." *Revue historique de droit français et étranger*, 1970.

Grigulevich, I. *Istoriia inkvizitsii (XIII-XX vv.)* (History of the Inquisition [13th-20th centuries]; in Russian). Moscow: 1970.

Grunwald, K. "Lombards, Cahorsins and Jews." *Journal of European Economic History*, IV (1975).

Guilhiermoz, P. "Saint Louis, les gages de bataille et la procédure civile." *BEC*, XLVIII (1887).

———. "Les Sources manuscrits de l'histoire monétaire de saint Louis et des premières années de Philippe III." *Le Moyen âge*, XXXIV (1923).

Guillain de Bénouville, P. *Saint Louis ou le printemps de la France*. Paris: 1970.

"Guillaume de Chartres." Didot and Didot, *Nouvelle biographie générale*, XXII. Paris: 18.

Guillemot, E. "Les Forêts de Senlis." *MHP*, XXXII (1905).

Guiraud, J. *Histoire de l'Inquisition au moyen âge*, 2 vols. Paris: 1935-1938.

Guth, P. "Qui est saint Louis?" In *Siècle de saint Louis*. Paris: 1970.

———. *Saint Louis, roi de France*. Paris: 1961.

———. *Le Séraphin couronné*. Nancy: 1961.

Gutnova, E. "Sintez v oblasti istorii prava i gosudarstva vo frantsuzskoĭ medievistike vtoroĭ poloviny XIX v." (Synthetic treatment of the history of law and government in French medieval studies of the second half of the 19th century; in Russian). *Evropa v srednie veka*. Moscow: 1972.

Ham, E. *Rutebeuf and Louis IX*. Chapel Hill: 1962.

Harriss, G. *King, Parliament, and Public Finance in Medieval England to 1369*. London: 1975.

Haskins, C. "Robert le Bougre and the Beginnings of the Inquisition in Northern France." *Studies in Medieval Culture*. Oxford: 1929.

Hemmeon, M. *Burgage Tenure in Medieval England*. Cambridge, Mass.: 1914.

Henneman, J. "*Enquêteurs-Réformateurs* and Fiscal Officers in Fourteenth Century France." *Traditio*, XXIV (1968).

———. *Royal Taxation in Fourteenth Century France*. Princeton: 1971.

Hérbomez, A. d'. "A Propos des baillis d'Arras sous le règne de saint Louis." *BEC*, LXVII (1906).

Herlihy, D. "Ecological Conditions and Demographic Change." *One Thousand Years*, ed. R. DeMolen. Boston: 1974.

Hillgarth, J. *The Problem of a Catalan Mediterranean Empire 1229-1327* (*English Historical Review*, Supplement 8, 1975).

Hilton, R. *Bond Men Made Free: Medieval Peasant Movements and the English Rising of 1381*. London: 1973.

———. *The English Peasantry in the Later Middle Ages*. Oxford: 1975.

Histoire d'Aiguesmortes. Millau: 1903.

Histoire de la ville de Mâcon. Mâcon: 1857.

Hughes, A. (ed.). *The Oxford History of Music*, II: *Early Medieval Music up to 1300*. London: 1954.

Huré, E. "Étude sur les origines du notariat." *Société d'émulation d'Abbeville: Bulletin*, 1906-1908.

"Isabella of France, Bl." *New Catholic Encyclopedia*, VII.

Jordan, W. "On Bracton and *Deus Ultor*." *Law Quarterly Review*, LXXXVIII (1972).

———. "Les Contrats d'acquisition royaux." *Études franciscaines* (to appear).

———. "Jews on Top: Women and the Availability of Consumption Loans in Northern France in the Mid-Thirteenth Century." *Journal of Jewish Studies*, XXIX (1978).

———. "The Lamb Triumphant and the Municipal Seals of Western

Languedoc in the Early Thirteenth Century." *Revue belge de numismatique et de sigillographie*, CXXIII (1977).

————. "Problems of the Meat Market of Béziers, 1240-1247—A Question of Anti-Semitism." *Revue des études juives*, CXXXV (1976).

————. "Supplying Aigues-Mortes for the Crusade of 1248: The Problem of Restructuring Trade." In Jordan et al., *Order and Innovation*. Princeton: 1976.

————, McNab, B., and Ruiz, T. (eds.). *Order and Innovation in the Middle Ages: Essays in Honor of Joseph R. Strayer*. Princeton: 1976.

Julia, H. *Histoire de Béziers*. Paris: 1845.

Jusselin, M. "Documents financières concernant les mésures prises par Alphonse de Poitiers contre les juifs (1268-1269)." *BEC*, LXVIII (1907).

Kahn, S. "Les Juifs de Posquières et de Saint-Gilles au moyen-âge." *Mémoires de l'Académie de Nîmes*, part 3, 1912.

Kantorowicz, E. *Kaiser Friedrich der Zweite*, 2 vols. Berlin: 1931.

————. *The King's Two Bodies: A Study in Medieval Political Theology*. Princeton: 1957.

————. *Laudes regiae: A Study in Liturgical Acclamations and Medieval Ruler Worship*. Berkeley: 1958.

Kerov, V. "Vosstanie 'pastushkov' v iuzhnikh Niderlandakh i vo Frantsii v 1251 godu" (The Uprising of the *Pastoureaux* in the Southern Netherlands and in France in 1251; in Russian). *Voprosy istorii*, no. 6, 1956.

Kienast, W. *Deutschland und Frankreich in der Kaiserzeit (900-1270)*, 3 vols. 2d ed. Stuttgart: 1974-1975.

Kimball, E. *Serjeanty Tenure in Medieval England*. New Haven and London: 1936.

Kleimola, A. *Justice in Medieval Russia (Transactions of the American Philosophical Society*, new series, LXV, part 6, 1975).

Klein, C. *Saint Louis, un roi aux pieds du pauvre*. Paris: 1970.

Knowles, D. *The Monastic Order in England*. 2d ed. Cambridge: 1963.

———— and Haddock, R. *Medieval Religious Houses: England and Wales*. 2d ed. London: 1971.

Labal, P. Introduction. *Siècle de saint Louis*. Paris: 1970.

Labande, E. "Saint Louis pèlerin." *Revue d'histoire de l'église de France*, LVII (1971).

Labande, L.-H. *Histoire de Beauvais et de ses institutions communales*. Paris: 1892.

Labarge, M. *Saint Louis*. Boston: 1968.

————. "Saint Louis et les juifs." In *Siècle de saint Louis*. Paris: 1970.

Lacger, L. de. "L'Albigeois au siècle de saint Louis: Les Évêques Durand de Beaucaire et Bernard de Combret, 1228-1271." *Revue d'histoire ecclésiastique*, LII (1957).

Lafaurie, J. *Les Monnaies des rois de France*. Mâcon: 1951.

Langlois, C.-V. "Doléances recueillies par les enquêteurs de saint Louis et des derniers Capétiens directs." *Revue historique*, XXII (1906).

———. "Les Origines du Parlement de Paris." *Revue historique*, XLII (1890).

Langmuir, G. "L'Absence d'accusation de meurtre ritual à l'ouest du Rhône." *Juifs et judaïsme de Languedoc, XIIIᵉ siècle-début XIVᵉ siècle*. Ed. M.-H. Vicaire and B. Blumenkranz. Toulouse: 1977.

———. "*Judaei nostri* and Capetian Legislation." *Traditio*, XVI (1960).

Larcena, J. *Saint Louis de France*. Paris: 1964.

La Serve, F. "Les Juifs à Lyon." *Revue du Lyonnais*, VII (1838).

Lasserre, N. *Histoire populaire d'Aigues-Mortes*. Nîmes: 1937.

Laurain, E. "Renaud de Béronne, bailli de Senlis." *BEC*, LXVII (1906).

Laureilhe, M.-T. *Sur les routes d'Europe au XIIIᵉ siècle: Chroniques*. Paris: 1959?

Laurent, J. "Le Bailliage de Sens du XIIIᵉ au XVIIIᵉ s." *Revue des questions historiques*, CXIII (1930).

Lazard, L. "Les Revenues tirés des juifs de France dans le domaine royal (XIIIᵉ siècle)." *Revue des études juives*, XV (1887).

Lecaron, F. "Les Origines de la municipalité parisienne." Part 1, *MHP*, VII (1880); part 2, *MHP*, VIII (1881).

———. "Les Travaux publics de Paris." *MHP*, III (1876).

Lecocq, G. *Histoire de la ville de Saint-Quentin*. Saint-Quentin: 1875.

Lecotté, R. and Marguet, G. *La Fête du Bois Hourdy*. Persan: 1947.

Lecoy de La Marche, A. "Coutumes et péages de Sens." *BEC*, XXVII (1866).

———. *La France sous saint Louis et Philippe le Hardi*. Paris: 1893.

———. *Saint Louis, son gouvernement et sa politique*. 5th ed. Tours: 1894.

———. *La Société au XIIIᵉ siècle*. Paris: 1880.

Lefils, F. *Histoire de Montreuil-sur-Mer et de son château*. Abbeville: 1860.

Le Goff, J. "France du Nord et France du Midi dans l'implantation des ordres mendiants au XIIIᵉ siècle." *Les Mendiants en pays d'oc au XIIIᵉ siècle* (Cahiers de Fanjeaux 8, 1973).

Le Grand, L. "Les Béguines de Paris." *MHP*, XX (1893).

———. "Les Maisons-Dieu et léproseries du diocèse de Paris au milieu du XIVᵉ siècle, d'après le régistre de visites du délégué de l'évêque (1351-1369)." *MHP*, XXIV (1897).

———. "Les Quinze-Vingts depuis leur fondation jusqu'à leur translation au faubourg Saint-Antoine (XIIIᵉ-XVIIIᵉ siècles)." *MHP*, XIII (1886).

Lehmann, A. *Le Rôle de la femme dans l'histoire de France au moyen âge*. Paris: 1952.

Lemaître, H. *Reliquaire de la Sainte-Croix donné par saint Louis au grand couvent des Cordeliers de Paris.* Paris: 1921.

Lemaître, P. *Une Gloire normande: Le Bienheureux Thomas Hélye de Biville.* Torigni-sur-Vire: 1939.

Le Patourel, J. *The Norman Empire.* Oxford: 1976.

Lépinois, E. de. *Histoire de Chartres,* 2 vols. Chartres: 1854-1858.

———. "Recherches historiques et critiques sur l'ancien comté et les comtes de Clermont en Beauvoisis, du XIe au XIIIe siècle." *SAOise: Mémoires,* x (1877-1879).

Lerner, R. "The Uses of Heterodoxy: The French Monarchy and Unbelief in the Thirteenth Century." *French Historical Studies,* IV (1965).

Le Roy Ladurie, E. *Montaillou, village occitan, de 1294 à 1324.* Paris: 1976.

Levillain, L. "La Vie de saint Louis par Guillaume de Saint-Pathus." *Le Moyen âge,* XVI (1903).

Lévis Mirepoix, le Duc de. *Saint Louis, roi de France.* Paris: 1970.

Levron, J. *Saint Louis ou l'apogée du moyen âge.* Paris: 1969.

Lewis, A. "The Capetian Apanages and the Nature of the French Kingdom." *Journal of Medieval History,* II (1976).

Little, L. "Frater Ludovicus." Ph.D. dissertation, Princeton University, 1962.

———. "Saint Louis' Involvement with the Friars." *Church History,* XXXIII (1964).

Lohrmann, D. "Pierre Lombard, médecin de saint Louis: Un Italien à Paris et ses maisons au quartier latin." In *Septième centenaire.* Paris: 1976.

Loisne, Le Comte de. "Chronologie des baillis de la province d'Artois du XIIIe siècle." *Bulletin philologique et historique,* 1915.

Lombard-Jourdan, A. "Fiefs et justice parisiens au quartier des Halles." *BEC,* CXXXIV (1976).

Longnon, A. *Documents parisiens sur l'iconographie de saint Louis.* Paris: 1882.

Longnon, J. "Les Vues de Charles d'Anjou pour la deuxième croisade de saint Louis: Tunis ou Constantinople." In *Septième centenaire.* Paris: 1976.

Lopez, R. "Back to Gold, 1252." *Economic History Review,* series 2, IX (1956-1957).

Lot, F. and Fawtier, R. *Histoire des institutions francaises au moyen âge,* II. Paris: 1958.

Louat, F. *Histoire de la ville de Senlis.* Senlis: 1944.

The Louvre Museum: General Guide. Paris: n.d.

Lugge, M. *"Gallia" und "Francia" in Mittelalter* (Bonner historischer Forschungen 15, 1960).

Lunt, W. *Papal Revenues in the Middle Ages*, 2 vols. New York: 1934.

Lyon, B. and Verhulst, A. *Medieval Finance: A Comparison of Financial Institutions in Northwestern Europe*. Providence, R.I.: 1967.

McDonnell, E. *The Beguines and Beghards in Medieval Culture*. New Brunswick: 1954.

McGarry, D. *Medieval History and Civilization*. New York and London: 1976.

Mahieu, B. " 'Le Livre des Métiers' d'Étienne Boileau." In *Siècle de saint Louis*. Paris: 1970.

Mahoudeau, F. *Croisade pour Aigues-Mortes*. Montpellier: 1969, privately printed.

Maillard, F. "Mouvements administratifs des baillis et des sénéchaux." *Bulletin philologique et historique*, 1959, 1963, 1966.

Marbot. "Deux bréviaires manuscrits aixois (XIIIe et XIVe siècle)." *Bulletin philologique et historique*, 1895.

Maret, A. "Premier concile général tenu à Lyon en 1245." *Revue du Lyonnais*, VI (1837).

Marquet, J. *La Charte des libertés et coutumes d'Aiguesmortes*. Nîmes: 1893.

Martin, H. *Les Ordres mendiants en Brétagne*. Paris: 1975.

Mauger, G. *Saint-Louis, le chant des béatitudes*. Paris: 1960.

Maurice. *Angerville-la-Martel, son histoire*. Fécamp: 1938.

Melleville, M. *Dictionnaire historique . . . de l'Aisne*, 2 vols. Laon and Paris: 1857.

————. *Histoire de la ville de Chauny*. Laon: 1851.

————. "Notice sur la commune de Laonnois." *SALaon: Bulletin*, III (1854).

Mérimée, P. *Notes de voyages*. Paris: 1971.

Meyer, W. *Ludwig IX. von Frankreich und Innozenz IV. in den Jahren 1244-1247*. Marburg-a.-L.: 1915.

Michaud-Quantin, P. "La Politique monétaire royale en 1265 à la Faculté de théologie de Paris en 1265." *Le Moyen âge*, 1962.

Michel, R. *L'Administration royale dans la sénéchaussée de Beaucaire au temps de saint Louis*. Paris: 1910.

Miel, A. *Histoire locale de Cerny-en-Laonnois*. Laon: 1898.

Miller, E. Review (2 parts) of Count Riant's *Exuviae. Journal des Savants*, 1878.

Millerot, T. *Histoire de la ville de Lunel*. Montpellier: 1880.

Moliner, J. *Espiritualidad medieval: Los Mendicantes*. Burgos: 1974.

Molinier, A. "Enquête sur un meurtre imputé aux juifs de Valréas." *Le Cabinet historique*, XXIX (1883).

Molinier, A. *L'Inquisition dans le Midi de la France*. Paris: 1880.

Mollat, G. "L'Application du droit de régale spirituelle en France du XIIᵉ au XIVᵉ siècle," part 1. *Revue d'histoire ecclésiastique*, XXV (1929).

Morize, J. "Aigues-Mortes au XIIIᵉ siècle." *Annales du Midi*, XXVI (1914).

Morlhon, J. and Lacaze, P. *La Cathédrale et l'île de Maguelone*. Montpellier: 1967?

Mortet, C. "Le Livre des Constitucions demenées el Chastelet de Paris." *MHP*, X (1883).

Munro, D. "The Speech of Pope Urban II. at Clermont, 1095." *American Historical Review*, XI (1905-1906).

Musetti, G. *Fra' Salimbene da Parma*. N.p.: n.d., probably 1953.

Nahon, G. "Les Ordonnances de saint Louis sur les juifs." *Les Nouveaux Cahiers*, no. 23 (1970).

——. "Pour une géographie administrative des juifs dans la France de saint Louis." *Revue historique*, CCLIII (1975).

——. "Les Juifs dans les domaines d'Alfonse de Poitiers, 1241-1271." *Revue des études juives*, CXXV (1966).

Natalis de Wailly, J. "Recherches sur le système monétaire de saint Louis." *Mémoires de l'Académie des Inscriptions et Belles-Lettres*, XXI (1857).

Neale, J. *Queen Elizabeth I*. Garden City: 1957.

Néel, J. *La Tour de Constance*. 2d ed. Valence-sur-Rhône: 1927.

Neveu, B. "Le Nain de Tillemont et la *Vie de saint Louis*." In *Septième centenaire*. Paris: 1976.

New Catholic Encyclopedia, 15 vols. New York: 1967.

"Note sur la monnaie tournois et la monnaie parisis de s. Louis." *HF*, XXI.

"Oaths." *New Catholic Encyclopedia*, X.

O'Connell, D. "The Teachings and Instructions of Saint Louis." Ph.D. dissertation, Princeton University, 1966.

——. *The Teachings of Saint Louis: A Critical Text*. Chapel Hill: 1972.

Olivier-Martin, F. *Les Régences et la majorité des rois*. Paris: 1931.

——. "Le Roi de France et les mauvaises coutumes au moyen âge." *Zeitschrift der Savigny-Stiftung für Rechtgeschichte*, LXXI (1938).

Oman, C. *The Art of War in the Middle Ages, AD 378-1515*. Rev. and ed. J. Beeler. Ithaca: 1953.

Oxford Dictionary of English Etymology. Ed. C. Onions. Oxford: 1966.

Oxford Dictionary of English Proverbs. 3d ed. Ed. F. Wilson. Oxford: 1970.

Ozanne. "L'Hôpital Saint-Nicolas-du-Pont." *Bulletin de la Société historique de Compiègne*, XX (1933).

Pacaut, M. *Louis VII et son royaume*. Paris: 1964.

———. "Louis IX." *Encyclopaedia Britannica*, IX. Chicago: 1960.

Painter, S. "The Crusade of Theobald of Champagne and Richard of Cornwall, 1239-1241." *A History of the Crusades*, II. Ed. K. Setton. Madison and elsewhere: 1969.

———. "Documents on the History of Brittany under Saint Louis." *Speculum*, XI (1936).

———. *The Scourge of the Clergy: Peter of Dreux, Duke of Brittany*. Baltimore: 1937.

Paravicini Bagliani, A. *Cardinali di curia e familiae cardinalzie*. Padua: 1972.

Parkes, J. *The Jew in the Medieval Community*. London: 1938.

"Pentecost Cycle." *New Catholic Encyclopedia*, XI.

Pernoud, R. *Un Chef d'état, saint Louis de France*. Paris: 1960.

———. *Reine Blanche*. Paris: 1972.

Perry, F. *Saint Louis (Louis IX of France): The Most Christian King*. New York and London: 1901.

Petit, É. "Jully-les-Nonnains." *Bulletin philologique et historique*, 1897.

———. "Saint Louis en Bourgogne et principalement dans les contrées de l'Yonne." *Bulletin de la Société des sciences historiques et naturelles de l'Yonne*, XLVII (1893).

Petit-Dutaillis, C. *Les Communes françaises*. Paris: 1947.

———. "L' 'Établissement pour le commun profit' au temps de saint Louis." *Anuario de historia del derecho español*, X (1933).

———. *Étude sur la vie et le règne de Louis VIII (1187-1226)*. Paris: 1894.

———. *Feudal Monarchy in France and England*. Trans. E. Hunt. London: 1936.

———. *"Queremoniae normannorum." Essays in Medieval History Presented to Thomas Frederick Tout*. Manchester: 1925.

P. G. G. "Documents divers relatifs à la croisade de saint Louis contre Tunis (1270)." *Les Cahiers de Tunisie*, XXV (1977).

Phillips, G. *Das Regalienrecht in Frankreich*. Halle: 1873.

Pietro, F. di. *Notice sur la ville d'Aiguesmortes*. Paris: 1821.

Pietro, S. di. *Vita di san Luigi, re di Francia, terziario franciscano*. S. Benigno Canavese: 1899 (or 1900).

Pirenne, H. *Economic and Social History of Medieval Europe*. Trans. I. Clegg. New York: 1937.

Pollock, F. and Maitland, F. *The History of English Law before the time of Edward I*, 2 vols. 2d ed. Cambridge: 1968.

Pompon, O. *Toury*. Gien: 1962.

Pontal, O. "Le Differend entre Louis IX et les évêques de Beauvais et ses incidences sur les conciles (1232-1248)." *BEC*, CXXIII (1965).

Porée, C. "Note sur Pèlerin Latinier, premier sénéchal de Beaucaire (1226-1238)." *Le Moyen âge*, 1921.

Potin de La Mairie, N.-R. *Recherches historiques sur la ville de Gournay (en Bray)*, 2 vols. in 1. Gournay: 1842.

———. *Supplément aux "Recherches, . . ."* Gournay: 1844.

Poulain, A.-G. *Les Séjours du roi saint Louis en Normandie et particulièrement à Vernon-sur-Seine.* Rouen: 1957.

Poux, J. *La Cité de Carcassonne: Histoire et description*, 2 vols. Toulouse and Paris: 1931.

Powicke, F. (later Sir Maurice). *The Loss of Normandy.* Manchester: 1913.

———. *The Thirteenth Century.* 2d ed. London: 1953.

Prévost, A. "Les Champenois aux croisades." *SAAube: Mémoires*, LXXXV (1921).

Purcell, M. *Papal Crusading Policy, 1244-1291.* Leyden: 1975.

Rabinowitz, L. *The Social Life of the Jews of Northern France in the XII-XIV Centuries.* London: 1938.

Reclus, É. *Nouvelle géographie universelle*, II: La France. Paris: 1877.

Ribaucourt, C. "Les Mendiants du Midi d'après la cartographie de l'enquête." *Les Mendiants en pays d'oc au XIIIe siècle* (Cahiers de Fanjeaux 8, 1973).

Richard, J. "La Fondation de l'église de Damiette." *BEC*, CXX (1962).

———. "La Politique orientale de saint Louis: La Croisade de 1248." In *Septième centenaire.* Paris: 1976.

Rigollot, G. "Étude sur le cartulaire inédit de La Trinité de Vendôme." *SAVermandois: Bulletin*, XIX (1880).

Riquet, M. "Saint Louis roi de France et les juifs." In *Septième centenaire.* Paris: 1976.

Rocher, J.-N.-M. *Histoire de l'abbaye de St.-Benoît-sur-Loire.* Orléans: 1865.

Rogozinski, J. "The Counsellors of the Seneschal of Beaucaire and Nimes, 1250-1350." *Speculum*, XLIV (1969).

———. "Ennoblement by the Crown . . . 1285-1322." In Jordan et al. (eds.), *Order and Innovation.* Princeton: 1976.

Röhricht, R. "Die Pastorellen (1251)." *Zeitschrift für Kirchengeschichte*, VI (1884).

Roover, R. de. *L'Evolution de la lettre de change, XIVe-XVIIIe siècles.* Paris: 1953.

Roth, C. "The Jews in the Middle Ages." *Cambridge Medieval History*, VII. Cambridge: 1932.

Rouquette, J. "Saint Louis et le comté de Melgueil." *Revue d'histoire de l'église de France*, V (1914-1919).

Russell, F. *The Just War in the Middle Ages.* Cambridge: 1975.

————. "Varieties of Christian Experience." *One Thousand Years*, ed. R. DeMolen. Boston: 1974.

S., A. de. Review of Callebaut's *Provinciaux . . . de France*. *La France franciscaine*, V (1922).

Sabatier, E. *Histoire de la ville et des évêques de Béziers*. Béziers: 1854.

Sablou, J. "Saint Louis et le problème de la fondation d'Aigues-mortes." *Hommage à Andre Dupont*. Montpellier: 1974.

Saige, G. *Les Juifs du Languedoc antérieurement au XIVᵉ siècle*. Paris: 1881.

Saint-Amans. "Observations sur quelques monnaies anciennes trouvées dans la commune de Castelculier, près d'Agen." *Recueil des travaux de la Société d'agriculture, sciences et arts d'Agen*, I (1804).

St.-M., R. de. Review of Gerin's *Pragmatique sanction de saint Louis*, *Revue des questions historiques*, X (1871).

Sauvage. "Notes sur le monastère des Emmurées de Rouen." *Société de l'histoire de Normandie: Mélanges*, I (1891).

Sayles, G. *The Medieval Foundations of England*. New York: 1961.

Sayous, A. "Les Mandats de saint Louis sur son trésor." *Revue historique*, CLXVII (1931).

Schaube, A. "Die Wechselbriefe König Ludwigs des Heiligen." *Jahrbücher für Nationalökonomie und Statistik*, LXX (1898).

Schneider, J. "Les Villes du royaume de France au temps de saint Louis." *Académie des Inscriptions et Belles-Lettres: Comptes rendus*, 1971.

Schramm, P. *Herrschaftszeichen und Staatssymbolik*, III (Schrifter der MGH). Stuttgart: 1956.

Seay, A. "Le Manuscrit 695 de la Bibliothèque communale d'Assisi," *Revue de musicologie*, XXXIX (1957).

Sède, S. de. *La Sainte-Chapelle et la politique de la fin des temps*. Paris: 1972.

Septième centenaire de la mort de saint Louis. Paris: 1976.

Servois, G. *Emprunts de saint Louis en Palestine et en Afrique*. Paris: 1858.

Shennan, J. *The Parlement of Paris*. London: 1968.

Shepherd, W. *Historical Atlas*. 9th ed. New York: 1964.

Shneidman, J. *The Rise of the Aragonese-Catalan Empire*, 2 vols. New York and London: 1970.

Siècle de saint Louis, ed. P. Labal. Paris: 1970.

Simon, C. *Histoire de Beaumont-sur-Oise*. Beaumont-sur-Oise: 1890.

Sivery, G. "L'Enquête de 1247 et les dommages de guerre." *Revue du Nord*, LIX (1977).

Smyser, H. *The Pseudo-Turpin*. Cambridge, Mass.: 1937.

Soucaille, A. *État monastique de Béziers*. Beziers: 1889.

Southern, R. *The Making of the Middle Ages*. New Haven: 1953.

Spieg, L. "A Review of Contributions to a Psychoanalytic Theory of Adolescence." *Adolescent Development: Readings in Research and Theory.* Ed. M. Gold and E. Douvan. Boston: 1969.

Spiegel, G. "The Cult of Saint Denis and Capetian Kingship." *Journal of Medieval History,* I (1975).

Stead, J. *The Police of Paris.* London: 1957.

Stein, H. "Pierre Lombard, médecin de saint Louis." *BEC,* C (1939).

———. "Recherches sur quelques fonctionnaires royaux des XIIIᵉ et XIVᵉ siècles originaires du Gâtinais." *ASHGâtinais,* xx (1902), xxi (1903), xxxii (1914), xxxiv (1918-1919).

———. "Un Sénéchal du XIIIᵉ siècle, Guillaume de Combreux." *BEC,* xciv (1933).

Stephenson, C. "Les 'Aides' des villes françaises." *Le Moyen âge,* xxiv (1922).

Strayer, J. [N.B.: The articles listed here as being available in Strayer, *Medieval Statecraft* were originally published separately; my references to these articles in the notes give the page numbers only for *Medieval Statecraft.*]

———. *The Administration of Normandy under Saint Louis.* Cambridge, Mass.: 1932.

———. *The Albigensian Crusades.* New York: 1971.

———. "La Conscience du roi." *Mélanges Robert Aubanas.* Montpellier: 1974.

———. "The Crusade against Aragon." *Medieval Statecraft.*

———. "The Crusades of Louis IX." *Medieval Statecraft.*

———. "The Development of Feudal Institutions." *Medieval Statecraft.*

———. "Economic Conditions in the County of Beaumont-le-Roger, 1261-1313." *Medieval Statecraft.*

———. "Exchequer and Parlement under Philip the Fair." *Droit privé et institutions régionales: Études historiques offertes à Jean Yver.* Rouen: 1976.

———. "The Fourth and the Fourteenth Centuries." *American Historical Review,* lxxvii (1972).

———. "France: The Holy Land, the Chosen People, the Most Christian King." *Medieval Statecraft.*

———. *On the Medieval Origins of the Modern State.* Princeton: 1970.

———. *Medieval Statecraft and the Perspectives of History.* Ed. J. Benton and T. Bisson. Princeton: 1971.

———. "Normandy and Languedoc." *Medieval Statecraft.*

———. "Philip the Fair—A 'Constitutional' King." *American Historical Review,* lxii (1956).

———. "The Political Crusades of the Thirteenth Century." *Medieval Statecraft.*

————. Review of Chazan's *Medieval Jewry*. *American Historical Review*, LXXX (1975).

————. Review of Pacaut's *Louis VII*. *American Historical Review*, LXX (1965).

————. "Viscounts and Viguiers under Philip the Fair." *Medieval Statecraft*.

————. "The Writ of Novel Disseisen in Normandy at the End of the Thirteenth Century." *Medieval Statecraft*.

Sulpice, J.-P. "Histoire de l'Hôtel-Dieu Saint Nicolas de Compiègne." *Thèse*, Faculté de médecin, University of Paris, 1968.

Tardif, J. "La Date et le caractère de l'ordonnance de saint Louis sur le duel judiciaire." *Nouvelle revue de droit français et étranger*, XI (1887).

————. "Le Procès d'Enguerran de Coucy," parts 1 and 2. *BEC*, LXXIX (1918).

Tessier, G. *Diplomatique royale française*. Paris: 1962.

Thoison, E. *Les Séjours des rois de France dans le Gâtinais*. Paris: 1888.

Thomson, W. *Friars in the Cathedral: The First Franciscan Bishops, 1226-1261*. Toronto: 1975.

Times Atlas of the World. Boston: 1967.

Treharne, R. *The Baronial Plan of Reform, 1258-1263*. Manchester: 1971.

Turner, R. *The King and His Courts*. Ithaca: 1968.

Ullmann, W. *Law and Politics in the Middle Ages*. Ithaca: 1975.

Vatin, M. *Senlis*. Rev. ed. Ed. E. Dupuis. Senlis: 1876.

Vaughn, E. *Notice historique sur les Quinze-Vingts*. Melun: 1909.

Vaultier, M.-C.-F.-E. *Histoire de la ville de Caen*. Caen: 1843.

Verdier, C. Series of articles, separate titles: "Saint Louis et la monarchie chrétienne," "Saint Louis et l'église de France au XIIIe siècle," "Saint Louis et les papes au XIIIe siècle" (bis). *Études réligieuses, philosophiques, historiques, et littéraires*, 5th series, VII and VIII (1875).

Verdier, F. "Origine et influence des légistes." *Mémoires de l'Académie de Nîmes*, 1895.

Vermeulen, A. *The Semantic Development of Gloria in early-Christian Latin*. Nijmegen: 1956.

Vidal, J. *Monographie de la ville d'Aimargues*. Paris: 1906?

Vidier, A. "Les Marguilliers laïcs de Notre-Dame de Paris (1204-1790)," part 1. *MHP*, XL (1913).

————. "Les Origines de la municipalité parisienne." *MHP*, XLIX (1927).

————. "Le Trésor de la Sainte-Chapelle," part 3. *MHP*, XXXVI (1909).

Viguier, A.-L.-G. *Notice sur la ville d'Anduze*. Paris: 1823.

Villard, P. *Les Justices seigneuriales dans La Marche*. Paris: 1969.

Viollet, P. *Histoire des institutions politiques et administratives de la France*, 3 vols. Paris: 1890-1903.

Wakefield, W. *Heresy, Crusade and Inquisition in Southern France, 1100-1250*. London: 1974.

Wallon, H. *Saint Louis et son temps*, 2 vols. Paris: 1875.

Waquet, H. *Le Bailliage de Vermandois aux XIIIᵉ et XIVᵉ siècles*. Paris: 1919.

Warlop, E. *The Flemish Nobility before 1300*, 2 vols. in 4 parts (to date). Trans. J. Ross and A. Vandermoere. Courtrai: 1975.

Wolff, P. "The Significance of the Feudal Period in the Monetary History of Europe." In Jordan et al. (eds.), *Order and Innovation*. Princeton: 1976.

Wood, C. *The French Apanages and the Capetian Monarchy, 1224-1328*. Cambridge, Mass.: 1966.

————. "The Mise of Amiens and Saint Louis' Theory of Kingship." *French Historical Studies*, VI (1970).

————. "*Regnum Francie*: A Problem in Capetian Administrative Usage." *Traditio*, XXIII (1967).

Wyse, A. "The *Enquêteurs* of Louis IX." *Franciscan Studies*, XXV (1944).

Yver, J. *Égalité entre héritiers et exclusion des enfants dotés*. Paris: 1966.

Zimmer, E. "Medieval Jewry in Northern France." *Jewish Quarterly Review*, LXVI (1976).

INDEX

(N.B. The appendixes of this book have not been indexed in detail.)

INDEX

Etienne de La Porte, 61
Eudes Rigaud, 39, 89, 114-15, 147, 184
Eve (town), 106
Evreux, bp., 117; see, 150
Exchequer, Norman, 38, 85, 172; appellate jurisdiction, 172
excommunication, of debtors, 101; of royal officials, 118, 123
Eydoux, H., views, 194

Falaise, 86; Franciscans, 184
Favier, J., views, 212
Fédou, R., views, 168
Ferdinand III, 30
Ferri du Mesnil, 168
Ferté-Milon, *prévôte*, 162
Fesler, J., views, 49
Fiétier, R., views, 58
Filles-Dieu of Paris, 189
fiscal institutions and procedures, 35, 38, 47, 82, 84, 93, 179; *see also bailliages*; *baillis*; etc.
flagellation, 11-12, 127-29
Flanders, 40, 43-46, 113, 117, 124, 141
Florence, 207
Fontainebleau, Trinitarians, 190
Fontenay-sous-Bois, *leprosarium*, 188
forests and foresters, 46, 51, 57; seigneurial, 169; under Alfonse of Poitiers, 215
Foulbec, 168
Foulques, bp. of Lisieux, 184
Fournier, P., views, 21-23, 205
fourteenth century, crises, 218
France, passim; land of Chosen People, 218; Holy Land, 218
Franchet, C., views, 8
Francia and *Ile de France*, 38, 46, 52, 82-83, 97, 152
Franciscans, 24, 33, 53, 55, 86, 111, 184-85; nuns, 137, 185, 188-89; provincial chapter at Sens, 110
François, M., views, 151
Frederick II, 9, 22, 25-30, 34, 44, 112; consequences of death, 112-13, crusade against, 112; heirs, 205
Fustel de Coulanges, N., views, 158

G., *prévôt* of Beauquesne, 164-65
Galcherus de Vernolio, 169
Galeran d'Escrennes, 160, 181
Gallia, 79-81
gardes, see sergeants
Gascony, *see* Aquitaine
Gâtinais, 53
Gautier Cornut, 108
Gautier Pilate, 169
Gautier de Villers, 160

Genoa, 70; bankers, 103
Geoffroy de Courferaud, 159, 180
Geoffroy de Courlon, 5, 114
Geoffroy de Roncherolles, 159
Gérard d'Abbeville, 209
Gervaise d'Escrennes, 181
Ghent, 144
Giesey, R., views, 217
Gilbert de Tournai, 202
Giry, A., views, 36
Gisors, 105; *bailliage*, 50, 59-60, 83, 94, 97, 120, 146
gîte, 148-52
Goceran de Pinos, 17, 67, 70
Gonesse, 188
Gournay-en-Bray, 105
Grand Chambrier, 35
Grand Sénéchal, 35
Grasse, Notre-Dame de La, 137
Gravier, H., views, 93, 163
Gregory X, 211
Griffiths, Q., views, 120, 140, 143, 184
Guerne de Verberie, 120
guet, 178-81
Guilhiermoz, P., views, 204
Gui, bp. of Auxerre, 118
Gui, bp. of Bayeux, 184
Gui Foucois, 63, 139-40, 204-05
Gui Mauvoisin, 65
Guillaume, abbot of Corona, 16
Guillaume, bp. of Orleans, 118
Guillaume Dampierre, 45, 66-67, 113
Guillaume Le Desréé, 50, 59
Guillaume d'Escrennes, *see* Guillaume de Garennes
Guillaume de Garennes, 180
Guillaume Guiart, 3
Guillaume de Nogaret, 210-11
Guillaume Perceval, 106
Guillaume de Pian, 51
Guillaume Pilate, 169
Guillaume de Puylaurens, 18
Guillaume de Saint-Amour, 201
Guillaume de Saint-Pathus, 62
Guillaume Teularia, 19
Guirard, J., views, 219
Gutnova, E., views, 41

Haakon IV, 32-33
Hainaut, 44, 124, 141, 198
Ham, 147
Hautevillier, *gîte* in, 148
Henneman, J., views, 84
Henry II, 38, 219
Henry III, 15-16, 18, 25-27, 29-30, 34, 37, 40, 43, 86, 123-24, 191, 197-99, 202, 205, 219

LIBRARY OF CONGRESS CATALOGING IN PUBLICATION DATA

Jordan, William C. 1948-
    Louis IX and the Challenge of the Crusade.

    A revision of the author's thesis, Princeton, 1973,
entitled: Saint Louis' influence on French society and
life in the thirteenth century.
    Bibliography: p.
    Includes index.
    1.   France—History—Louis IX, 1226-1270.
2.   Louis IX, Saint, King of France, 1214-1270.
3.   Crusades—Seventh, 1248-1250.   4.   Crusades—Eighth,
1270.   I.   Title.
DC91.J75 1979   944'.023   79-83996
ISBN 0-691-05285-9

CPSIA information can be obtained at www.ICGtesting.com
Printed in the USA
LVOW09s0707190716

496872LV00011B/102/P